LABOURING MEN

Studies in the History of Labour

ERIC HOBSBAWM

WEIDENFELD & NICOLSON

A W&N PAPERBACK

First published in Great Britain in 1964
by Weidenfeld & Nicolson
This paperback edition published in 2015
by Weidenfeld & Nicolson,
an imprint of Orion Books Ltd,
Carmelite House, 50 Victoria Embankment,
London, EC4Y 0DZ

An Hachette UK company

1 3 5 7 9 10 8 6 4 2

A CIP catalogue record for this book
is available from the British Library.

ISBN 978-1-4746-0141-2

Printed and bound by
CPI Group (UK) Ltd, Croydon CR0 4YY

The Orion Publishing Group's policy is to use papers
that are natural, renewable and recyclable products and
made from wood grown in sustainable forests. The logging
and manufacturing processes are expected to conform to
the environmental regulations of the country of origin.

www.orionbooks.co.uk

CONTENTS

PREFACE

THE ESSAYS PRINTED HERE consist partly of articles published in various journals, some of them rather inaccessible, and partly of unpublished studies, the product or by-product of several years' interest in working-class history and affairs. They range, in the main, from the late eighteenth century to the First World War and fall broadly into four groups: up to the middle of the nineteenth century, studies in the 'new trades unionism' of 1889–1914, studies in the late nineteenth-century revival of socialism in Britain, and a group of general papers covering a rather wider chronological span. Most of these have one negative thing in common. They lie outside the borders of the straightforward chronological or narrative history of labour movements. This was ably pioneered by the Webbs and G. D. H. Cole, and in the golden age of British labour history which began about fifteen years ago, a number of excellent scholars have continued, added to, or revised their work. However, there has been comparatively little work about the working classes as such (as distinct from labour organizations and movements), and about the economic and technical conditions which allowed labour movements to be effective, or which prevented them from being effective. In recent years this field has begun to attract greater attention, but it is still fairly thinly cultivated. Most of the essays in this volume belong to the latter category.

Several are expository. The *Aristocracy of Labour, Custom, Wages and Workload*, and the *Tramping Artisan* were first attempts to collect together material about their subjects and to consider some of their implications. This also applies to the studies in the 'new trades unionism'. Others are polemical, or in the nature of historical revisions. Thus *The Machine Breakers* attempts to revise traditional views of Luddism, *Methodism and Revolution* refutes Elie Halévy's well-

vii

known contention that Wesley saved Britain from social upheaval in the early nineteenth century, and the papers on the standard of living are contributions to a controversy among historians which has become rather lively in the past few years. *The Fabians Reconsidered* also sets out to revise traditional views on the subject. Other papers deal with various aspects of radical, labour and socialist ideology. Since some of the essays were written for non-specialist journals or for a non-specialist public, they are less fully loaded with the usual apparatus of scholarship than those aimed primarily at the experts. However, I hope that even the apparently most specialized ones contain something of general interest; for I have tried to make them broader than their titles may sometimes suggest.

Most of the reprinted papers have been left substantially unchanged, except for minor corrections or modifications, and a few references to subsequent literature. The chief exceptions are the main paper on the standard of living, into which I have incorporated material collected since 1957, or embodied in other articles not reprinted here, and *Trends in the British Labour Movement*, first published in 1949, which has a rewritten and much amplified last part. Occasionally I have added a brief postscript on subsequent work which affects my argument. Readers who wish to pursue the matter further should consult the complete bibliography of British work on labour history since 1945, published in earlier issues of the *Bulletin of the Society for the Study of Labour History*.

My thanks are due to the editors of the *Economic History Review*, *History Today*, *Marxism Today*, the *New Left Review*, the defunct *New Reasoner*, the *New Statesman*, *Past & Present*, and Messrs Macmillan and Lawrence and Wishart, for permission to reprint material which first appeared in their pages or under their imprint.

London, December 1963   *E. J. Hobsbawm*

Except for minor corrections and alterations, the British paperback edition is identical with the hardback edition of 1964. This does not imply that the author is unaware of the criticisms which have been made of some of his statements, or would have written the papers reprinted here in exactly the same way, had he set out to do so in 1967.

1

Thomas Paine

A MODERATE REVOLUTION is a contradiction in terms, though a moderate putsch, coup or pronunciamento is not. However limited the ostensible aims of a revolution, the light of the New Jerusalem must shine through the cracks in the masonry of the eternal Establishment which it opens. When the Bastille falls, the normal criteria of what is possible on earth are suspended, and men and women naturally dance in the streets in anticipation of utopia. Revolutionaries, in consequence, are surrounded by a millennial halo, however hard-headed or however modest their actual proposals may be.

Tom Paine reflected this rainbow light of an age 'in which everything may be looked for'. He saw before him 'a scene so new and transcendently unequalled by anything in the European world, that the name of revolution is diminutive of its character, and it rises into a regeneration of man'. 'The present age,' he held, 'will hereafter merit to be called the Age of Reason, and the present generation will appear to the future as the Adam of the new world.' America had become independent, the Bastille had fallen, and he was the voice of both these marvellous events. 'A share in two revolutions,' he wrote to Washington, 'is living to some purpose.'

And yet the actual political proposals of this profoundly and instinctively revolutionary man were almost ridiculously moderate. His goal, 'universal peace, civilization and commerce', was that of most Victorian free traders. He deliberately disclaimed any intention of 'mere theoretical reformation' in economic matters. Private enterprise was good enough for him and 'the most effectual process is that of improving the condition of man by means of his interest'. His analysis of the evils of society, namely that war and high taxes were at the bottom of it all, is still sound doctrine in the Sussex executives' belt, except at times when the profits of armament and the fear of

1

communism outweigh the horror of high government spending. Paine's most radical incursion into the economic process was a proposed ten per cent inheritance tax to finance old-age pensions. When he came to France, he – like other English 'Jacobins' – joined the Gironde, and was a moderate even in that group.

That he should nevertheless have been a revolutionary, is not surprising. There was, after all, a time when the sound industrialists were prepared to raise barricades (or more precisely, to support raising them) against the forces of iniquity which prevented 'the general felicity of which civilization is capable' by preferring kings and dukes to businessmen. What is surprising is Paine's extraordinary, and indeed probably unparalleled, success as a spokesman of revolt. This is what turns him into a historical problem.

Other pamphleteers have sometimes pulled off the coup which justifies the agitator's life and which turns him for a moment into the voice of everyman. Paine did it three times. In 1776 *Common Sense* crystallized the half-formulated aspirations for American independence. In 1791 his defence of the French Revolution, *The Rights of Man*, said all most English Radicals would ever wish to say on its subject. It is said to have sold 200,000 copies in a few months, at a time when the entire population of Britain, including children and other illiterates, was less than that of Greater London today. In 1794 his *Age of Reason* became the first book to say flatly, in language comprehensible to the common people, that the Bible was not the word of God. It has remained the classic statement of working-class rationalism ever since. Clearly such a triple triumph is not due to accident.

It is due in part to the fact that Paine *was* the people for whom he wrote, the self-made, self-educated, self-reliant men as yet not finally divided into employers and hired hands. The man who was successively apprenticed stay-maker, teacher, petty official, tobacconist, journalist and 'an ingenious person, hoping to introduce his mechanical contrivances in England', could speak for all of them. He had, incidentally, the same uncanny rapport with the public as inventor and as journalist. The most popular single structure of the Industrial Revolution, to judge by its innumerable reproductions on jugs, is the iron bridge over the Wear, built to Paine's pioneer design, though – characteristically – not to his profit. The discovery of revolution as a fact gave him, like his readers, the enormous confidence in a future which was theirs.

2

Indeed, the discovery made him. But for the struggle in America, in 1776, he might have become a minor literary figure, or more likely an inventor and failed industrialist, for applied science remained his first and last passion. His friends – but few others – would have admired him as a wit, a charming star of small-town society, a sportsman and a good man at chess or picquet. They would have mildly deplored his fondness for brandy, and might occasionally have commented on the absence of any sex-life in one apparently so sensible to the charms of the fair. Had he not emigrated to America with a recommendation from the astute Franklin, he would be forgotten. Had he not been reborn in the Revolution, he would be remembered only in a rare PhD thesis.

But he is unforgotten; and typically enough, not in the world of orthodox liberalism, but in the partisan universe of political and theological rebellion; and this in spite of his uniform political failure, except as a journalist, and his lack of extremism. (He was the only member of the French Convention who fought openly against the death sentence on Louis XVI, though he had been the first to call for a republic.) Six of the eight lives published before the most recent, Professor Aldridge's, are by left-wingers; a communist has edited his collected works.

Why? Because for most of Paine's readers salvation by private enterprise was not the answer, whatever he or they may have thought. His and their opposition was ostensibly against 'privilege' which stood in the way of 'freedom'; but in fact it was also against unrecognized and new forces which pushed men such as themselves into poverty. They were independent enough – as skilled artisans, small shopkeepers or farmers – to see themselves as the future, not because (like the marxian proletariat) the very degree of their oppression destined them for revolution, but because it was ridiculous and irrational that independent men should not triumph. Not for another 25 years did rationalist artisans of the Painite type seek their salvation through 'general union' and a co-operative commonwealth. But already poverty was for them a collective fact, to be solved and not merely escaped.

For and to these self-reliant poor Paine spoke. His analysis matters less than his unswerving and arrogant devotion to them, expressed with that 'profound reason and energy' which Condorcet so admired in him. When he spoke of human felicity, it was the end of poverty and inequality that he had in mind. The great question of the Revolu-

3

tion, in spite of his devotion to low taxes and free enterprise, was 'whether man shall inherit his rights and universal civilization take place. Whether the fruits of his labour shall be enjoyed by himself ... Whether robbery shall be banished from courts and wretchedness from countries.' It was that 'in countries which we call civilized we see age going to the workhouse and youth to the gallows'. It was that aristocracy ruled over 'that class of poor and wretched people who are so numerously dispersed all over England, who are to be told by a proclamation that they are happy'.

But Paine not only told his readers that poverty was incompatible with felicity and civilization. He told them that the light of reason had dawned in men like themselves to end poverty, and that Revolution showed how reason must triumph. He was the least romantic of rebels. Self-evident, practical, artisan commonsense would transform the world. But the mere discovery that reason can cut like an axe through the undergrowth of custom which kept men enslaved and ignorant, was a revelation.

Throughout the pages of *Age of Reason*, as through generations of working-class discussion groups, there glows the exaltation of the discovery how *easy* it is, once you have decided to see clearly, to discover that what the priests say about the Bible, or the rich about society, is wrong. Throughout the *Rights of Man* there shines the *obviousness* of the great truth. For Burke this revolutionary reason meant that 'all the decent drapery of life is to be rudely torn off' to leave 'our naked, shivering nature' revealed in all its defect. Paine was not afraid of a nakedness which revealed man, self-made, in the glory of his infinite possibilities. His humanity stood naked, like the Greek athletes, because it was poised for struggle and triumph. Even now, as we read those clear, simple sentences in which commonsense rises to heroism and a cast-iron bridge spans the distance between Thetford and the new Jerusalem, we are exhilarated and moved. And if we believe in man, how can we fail, even now, to cheer him?

(1961)

2

The Machine Breakers

IT IS PERHAPS TIME to reconsider the problem of machine-wrecking in the early industrial history of Britain and other countries. About this form of early working-class struggle misconceptions are still widely held, even by specialist historians. Thus, an excellent work, published in 1950, can still describe Luddism simply as a 'pointless, frenzied, industrial *Jacquerie*', and an eminent authority, who has contributed more than most to our knowledge of it, passes over the endemic rioting of the eighteenth century with the suggestion that it was the overflow of excitement and high spirits.[1] Such misconceptions are, I think, due to the persistence of views about the introduction of machinery elaborated in the early nineteenth century, and of views about labour and trade union history formulated in the late nineteenth century, chiefly by the Webbs and their Fabian followers. Perhaps we should distinguish views and assumptions. In much of the discussion of machine-breaking one can still detect the assumption of nineteenth-century middle-class economic apologists, that the workers must be taught not to run their heads against economic truth, however unpalatable; of Fabians and Liberals, that strong-arm methods in labour action are less effective than peaceful negotiation; of both, that the early labour movement did not know what it was doing, but merely reacted, blindly and gropingly, to the pressure of misery, as animals in the laboratory react to electric currents. The conscious views of most students may be summed up as follows: the triumph of mechanization was inevitable. We can understand, and sympathize with the long rear-guard action which all but a minority of favoured workers fought against the new system; but we must accept its pointlessness and its inevitable defeat.

The tacit assumptions are wholly debatable. In the conscious views

5

there is obviously a good deal of truth. Both, however, obscure a good deal of history. Thus they make impossible any real study of the methods of working-class struggle in the pre-industrial period. Yet such a study is badly needed. A very cursory glance at the labour movement of the eighteenth and early nineteenth century shows how dangerous it is to project the picture of desperate revolt and retreat, so familiar from 1815–48, too far into the past. Within their limits, – and they were, intellectually and organizationally very narrow – the movements of the long economic boom which ended with the Napoleonic wars, were neither negligible nor wholly unsuccessful. Much of this success has been obscured by subsequent defeats: the strong organization of the West of England woollen industry lapsed completely, not to revive until the rise of general unions during the first world war; the craft societies of Belgian woollen workers, strong enough to win virtual collective agreements in the 1760s, lapsed after 1790 and until the early 1900s trade unionism was for practical purposes dead.[2]

Yet there is really no excuse for overlooking the power of these early movements, at any rate in Britain; and unless we realize that the basis of power lay in machine-wrecking, rioting and the destruction of property in general (or, in modern terms, sabotage and direct action), we shall not make sense of them.

To most non-specialists, the terms 'machine-wrecker' and Luddite are interchangeable. This is only natural, for the outbreaks of 1811–1813, and of some years after Waterloo in this period, attracted more public attention than any others, and were believed to require more military force for their suppression. Mr Darvall[3] has done well to remind us that the 12,000 troops deployed against the Luddites greatly exceeded in size the army which Wellington took into the Peninsula in 1808. Yet one's natural preoccupation with the Luddites tends to confuse the discussion of machine-breaking in general, which begins, as a serious phenomenon (if it can be properly said to have a beginning) sometime in the seventeenth century and continues until roughly 1830. Indeed, the series of farm-labourers' revolts which the Hammonds baptized the 'last labourers' rising' in 1830 was essentially a major offensive against farm-machinery, though it incidentally destroyed a fair amount of manufacturing equipment too.[4] In the first place, Luddism, treated as a single phenomenon for administrative purposes, covered several distinct types of machine-breaking, which for the most part existed independently of each other, but before and

6

after. In the second place, the rapid defeat of Luddism led to a wide-spread belief that machine-breaking never succeeded.

Let us consider the first point. There are at least two types of machine-breaking, quite apart from the wrecking incidental to ordinary riots against high prices or other causes of discontent – for instance, some of the destruction in Lancashire in 1811, and Wiltshire in 1826.[5] The first sort implies no special hostility to machines as such, but is, under certain conditions, a normal means of putting pressure on employers or putters-out. As has been justly noted, the Nottinghamshire, Leicestershire and Derbyshire Luddites 'were using attacks upon machinery, whether new or old, as a means of coercing their employers into granting them concessions with regard to wages and other matters'.[6] This sort of wrecking was a traditional and established part of industrial conflict in the period of the domestic and manufacturing system, and the early stages of factory and mine. It was not directed only against machines, but also against raw material, finished goods, or even the private property of employers, depending on what sort of damage these were most sensitive to. Thus in three months of agitation in 1802, the Wiltshire shearmen burned hay-ricks, barns and kennels of unpopular clothiers, cut down their trees, destroyed loads of cloth, as well as attacking and destroying their mills.[7]

The prevalence of this 'collective bargaining by riot' is well-attested. Thus – to take merely the West of England textile trades – clothiers complained to Parliament in 1718 and 1724 that weavers 'threatened to pull down their houses and burn their work unless they would agree with their terms'.[8] The disputes of 1726–7 were fought, in Somerset, Wiltshire and Gloucestershire, as well as in Devon by weavers 'breaking into the houses (of masters and black-legs), spoiling of wool, and cutting and destroying the pieces in the looms and the utensils of the trade'.[9] They ended in something like a collective contract. The great textile workers' riot at Melksham in 1738 began with workers 'cut(ting) all the chains in the looms belonging to Mr Coulthurst . . . on account of his lowering of the Prices'[10]; and three years later anxious employers in the same area were writing to London for protection against the men's demands that no outsiders should be employed, on pain of destroying wool.[11] And so on, throughout the century.

Again, where coal-miners had reached the point of aiming their demands against employers of labour, they used the technique of

7

wrecking. (For the most part, of course, miners' riots were still directed against high food-prices, and the profiteers believed to be responsible for them.) Thus in the Northumberland coal-field the burning of pit-head machinery was part of the great riots of the 1740s, which won the men a sizeable wage-rise.[12] Again, machines were smashed, and coal set on fire in the riots of 1765, which won the miners the freedom to choose their employers at the end of the annual contract.[13] Acts of Parliament against the burning of pits were passed at intervals through the later part of the century.[14] As late as 1831 the strikers at Bedlington (Durham) wrecked winding-gear.[15]

The history of the frame-breaking in the East Midlands hosiery trade is too well known to need retelling.[16] Certainly the wrecking of machines was the most important weapon used in the famous riots of 1778 (the ancestors of Luddism), which were essentially part of a movement to resist wage-reductions.

In none of these cases – and others might be mentioned – was there any question of hostility to machines as such. Wrecking was simply a technique of trade unionism in the period before, and during the early phases of, the Industrial Revolution. (The fact that organized unions hardly as yet existed in the trades concerned, does not greatly affect the argument. Nor does the fact that, with the coming of the Industrial Revolution, wrecking acquired new functions.) It was more useful, when intermittent pressure had to be put on masters, than when constant pressure had to be maintained: when wages and conditions changed suddenly, as among textile workers, or when annual contracts came up for simultaneous renewal, as among miners and seamen, rather than where, say, entry into the market had to be steadily restricted. It might be used by all sorts of people, from independent small producers, through the intermediate forms so typical of the domestic system of production, to more or less fully-fledged wage-workers. Yet it was, in the main, concerned with disputes which arose from the typical social relationship of capitalist production, that between employing entrepreneurs and men who depended, directly or indirectly, on the sale of their labour-power to them; though this relationship existed as yet in primitive forms, and was entangled with the relationships of small independent production. It is worth noting that riot and wrecking of this type seem more frequent in eighteenth-century Britain, with its 'bourgeois' Revolution behind it, than in eighteenth-century France.[17] Certainly the movements of our weavers and miners are very different from the superficially trade-union like activities of journeymen's accociations in many more old-fashioned continental areas.[18]

The value of this technique was obvious, both as a means of putting pressure on employers, and of ensuring the essential solidarity of the workers.

The first point is admirably put in a letter from the Town Clerk of Nottingham in 1814.[19] The framework knitters, he reported, were now striking against the firm of J. and George Ray. Since this firm employed mainly men who owned their own looms, they were vulnerable to a simple withdrawal of work. Most of the firms, however, rented out the looms to knitters 'and through them acquire entire control of their workmen. Perhaps the most effectual manner in which the combination could coerce them was their former manner of carrying on war by destroying their frames.' In a domestic system of industry, where small groups of men, or single men, work scattered in numerous villages and cottages, it is, in any case, not easy to conceive of any other method which could guarantee an effective stoppage. Moreover, against comparatively small local employers, destruction of property – or the constant threat of destruction – would be pretty effective. Where, as in the cloth industry, both the raw material and the finished article were expensive, the destruction of wool or cloth might well be preferable to that of looms.[20] But in semi-rural industries even the burning of the employer's ricks, barns and houses might seriously affect his profit-and-loss account.

But the technique had another advantage. The habit of solidarity, which is the foundation of effective trade unionism, takes time to learn – even where, as in coal-mines, it suggests itself naturally. It takes even longer to become part of the unquestioned ethical code of the working-class. The fact that scattered framework knitters in the East Midlands could organize effective strikes against employing firms, for instance, argues a high level of 'trade union morale'; higher than could normally be expected at that period of industrialization. Moreover, among badly-paid men and women without strike-funds, the danger of blacklegging is always acute. Machine-wrecking was one of the methods of counteracting these weaknesses. So long as the winding gear of a Northumbrian pit was broken, or the blast-furnace of a Welsh iron-works out, there was at least a temporary guarantee that the plant would not be operated.[21] This was only one method, and not everywhere applicable. But the whole complex of activities which eighteenth and early nineteenth century administrators called 'Riot' achieved the same purpose. Everyone is familiar with the bands of militants or strikers from one works or locality, touring the whole region, calling out villages, workshops and factories by a mixture of appeals and force (though few workers needed much persuasion in the early stages of the fight).[22] Even much later mass demonstrations and meetings were an essential part of a labour dispute – not only to overawe the employers, but to keep the men together and in good heart. The periodic riots of the North-eastern seamen, at the time when hiring contracts were fixed, are a good example[23]; strikes of modern dockers another.[24] Clearly the Luddite technique was well-adapted to this stage of industrial warfare. If British weavers in the eighteenth century (or American lumber-men in the twentieth) were a proverbially riotous body of men, there were sound technical reasons why they should be so.

On this point too we have some confirmation from a modern trade union leader who, as a child, lived through the transition of a woollen industry from domestic to factory system. 'It is necessary to remember' writes Rinaldo Rigola[25] 'that in those pre-socialist times the working-class was a crowd, not an army. Enlightened, orderly, bureaucratic strikes were impossible. [R. is an extreme conservative among union leaders – E. J. H.] The workers could only fight by means of demonstrations, shouting, cheering and cat-calling, intimidation and violence. Luddism and sabotage, even though not elevated into doctrines, had nevertheless to form part of the methods of struggle.'

We must now turn to the second sort of wrecking, which is generally regarded as the expression of working-class hostility to the new machines of the industrial revolution, especially labour-saving ones. There can, of course, be no doubt of the great feeling of opposition to new machines; a well-founded sentiment, in the opinion of no less an authority than the great Ricardo.[26] Yet three observations ought to be made. First, this hostility was neither so indiscriminate nor so specific as has often been assumed. Second, with local or sectional exceptions, it was surprisingly weak in practice. Lastly, it was by no means confined to workers, but was shared by the great mass of public opinion, including many manufacturers.

(i) The first point will be clear, if we consider the problem as it faced the worker himself. He was concerned, not with technical progress in the abstract, but with the practical twin problems of

10

preventing unemployment and maintaining the customary standard of life, which included non-monetary factors such as freedom and dignity, as well as wages. It was thus not to the machine as such that he objected, but to any threat to these – above all to the whole change in the social relations of production which threatened him. Whether this threat came from the machine, or from elsewhere, depended on circumstances. The Spitalfields weavers rioted against machines by which 'one man can do as much . . . as near twenty without them' in 1675; against wearers of printed calicoes in 1719; against immigrants working below the rate in 1736; and they wrecked looms against rate-cutting in the 1760s[27]: but the strategic objective of these movements was the same. Around 1800 the western weavers and shearmen were simultaneously in action; the former organized against the flooding of the labour market by extra workers, the latter against machines.[28] Yet their object, the control of the labour market, was the same. Conversely, where the change did not disadvantage the workers absolutely, we find no special hostility to machines. Among printers, the adoption of power-presses after 1815 seems to have caused little trouble. It was the later revolution in type-setting which, since it threatened wholesale down-grading, provoked a fight.[29] Between the early eighteenth and the mid-nineteenth century mechanization and new devices greatly increased the productivity of the coal-miner; for instance, the introduction of shot-firing. However, as they left the position of the hewer untouched, we hear of no important movement to resist technical change, though pitmen were proverbially ultra-conservative and riotous. Restriction of output operated by workers under private enterprise is a different matter altogether. It can and does occur in wholly unmechanized industries – for instance, the building trade; nor does it depend on overt movements, organizations or outbreaks.

In some cases, indeed, the resistance to the machine was quite consciously resistance to the machine in the hands of the capitalist. The Lancashire machine-wreckers of 1778–80 distinguished clearly between spinning-jennies of 24 spindles or less, which they spared, and larger ones, suitable only for use in factories, which they destroyed.[30] No doubt in Britain, which was more familiar with social relations of production which anticipated those of industrial capitalism, this kind of behaviour is less unexpected than elsewhere. Nor should we read too much into it. The men of 1760 were still a good way from understanding the nature of the economic system they were about to face. Nevertheless, it is clear that theirs was not a simple fight against technical progress as such.

Nor is there, for the most part, any fundamental difference in the attitude of workers towards machines, taken as an isolated problem, in the earlier and later phases of industrialism. It is true that in most industries the object of preventing the introduction of undesirable machines has given way, with the coming of full mechanization, to the plan to 'capture' them for workers enjoying trade union standards and conditions, while taking all practicable steps to minimize technological unemployment. This policy seems to have been adopted patchily after the 1840s[31] and during the Great Depression, more generally after the middle 1890s.[32] Nevertheless, there are plenty of examples of the straightforward opposition to machines which threaten to create unemployment or to downgrade labour even to-day.[33] In the normal working of a private enterprise economy the reasons which led workers to distrust new machines in the 1810s remain persuasive in the 1960s.

(ii) The argument so far may help to explain why, after all, the resistance to machines was so small. The fact is not widely recognized, for the mythology of the pioneer age of industrialism, which men like Baines and Samuel Smiles reflected, has magnified the riots which actually occurred. The men of Manchester liked to think of themselves not only as monuments of enterprise and economic wisdom, but also – a more difficult task – as heroes. Wadsworth and Mann have reduced the riots of eighteenth-century Lancashire to more modest proportions.[34] In fact we have record of only a few really widespread wrecking movements such as that of the farm-labourers, which probably destroyed most threshing-machines in the areas affected,[35] the specialized campaigns of the small body of shearmen in Britain and elsewhere,[36] and perhaps the riots against power-looms in 1826.[37] The Lancashire wreckings of 1778–80 and 1811 were confined to limited areas and limited numbers of mills. (The great East Midland movements of 1811–12 were not, as we have seen, directed against new machinery at all.) This is not only due to the fact that some mechanization was regarded as harmless. As has been pointed out,[38] most machines tended to be introduced in times of rising prosperity, when employment was improving and opposition, not fully mobilized, could be for a time dissipated. By the time distress recurred, the strategic moment for opposing the new devices was past. New workers serving them had already been recruited, the old hand-operatives stood outside, capable only of random destruction of their competitor, no longer of imposing themselves on the machine. (Unless, of course, they were lucky enough to possess a specialized market which was not affected by machine-production, as hand-bootmakers and tailors did in the 1870s and 80s.) One reason why the wrecking by the shearmen was so much more persistent and serious than that by others was that these highly skilled and organized key-men retained much control over the labour market, even after partial mechanization.[39]

(iii) The mythology of the pioneer industrialists has also obscured the overwhelming sympathy for machine-wreckers in all parts of the population. In Nottinghamshire not a single Luddite was denounced, though plenty of small masters must have known perfectly well who broke their frames.[40] In Wiltshire – where the cloth-finishing middlemen and small masters were known to sympathize with the shearmen[41] – the real terrorists of 1802 could not be discovered.[42] The merchants and woollen manufacturers of Rossendale themselves passed resolutions against power-looms some years before the men smashed them.[43] During the 1830 labourers' rising the Clerk to the Magistrates in Hindon, Wiltshire, reported that 'where the mobs have not destroyed the machinery, the farmers have exposed the same for the purpose of being destroyed',[44] and Lord Melbourne had to send a sharply-worded circular to Magistrates who had 'in many instances recommended the Discontinuance of the Employment of Machines used for thrashing out Corn and for other Purposes'. 'Machines,' he argued 'are as much entitled to the protection of the Law as any other Description of Property'.[45]

Nor is this surprising. The fully developed capitalist entrepreneurs formed a small minority, even among those whose position was technically that of profit-makers. The small shop-keeper or local master did not want an economy of limitless expansion, accumulation and technical revolution, the savage jungle pursuit which doomed the weak to bankruptcy and wage-earning status. His ideal was the secular dream of all 'little men', which has found periodic expression in Leveller, Jeffersonian or Jacobin radicalism, a small-scale society of modest property-owners and comfortably-off wage-earners, without great distinctions of wealth or power; though doubtless, in its quiet way, getting wealthier and more comfortable all the time. It was an unrealizable ideal, never more so than in the most rapidly evolving of societies. Let us remember, however, that those to whom it appealed in early nineteenth-century Europe made up the majority of the population, and outside such industries as cotton, of the employing class.[46] But even the genuine capitalist entrepreneur could be in two minds about machines. The belief that he must inevitably favour technical progress as a matter of self-interest has no foundation, even if the experience of French capitalism, and of later British capitalism were not available. Quite apart from the possibility of making more money without machines than with them (in sheltered markets, etc.), only rarely were new machines immediate and obvious paying propositions.

There is, in the history of any technical device, a 'threshold of profit' which is crossed rather late – the larger the capital that has to be sunk in a machine, the later. Hence, perhaps, the proverbial lack of business success of inventors, who sink their own and other people's money in their projects while they are still inevitably imperfect and by no means clearly superior to their non-mechanized rivals.[47] Of course, the free enterprise economy could overcome these obstacles. What has been described as the 'vast secular boom' of 1775–1875 created situations, here and there, which provided entrepreneurs in some industries – for instance, cotton – with the impetus to leap across the 'threshold'.[48] The very mechanism of capital accumulation in a society undergoing revolution provided others. So long as competition operated, the technical advances of the pioneer section were spread over quite a wide field. Yet we must not forget that the pioneers were minorities. Most capitalists took the new machine in the first instance not as an offensive weapon, to win bigger profits, but as a defensive one, to protect themselves against the bankruptcy which threatened the laggard competitor. We are not surprised to find E. C. Tufnell in 1834 accusing 'many of the masters in the cotton trade . . . of the disgraceful behaviour of instigating workmen to turn out against those manufacturers who were the first to enlarge their mules'.[49] Petty producer and run-of-the-mill entrepreneur were in an ambiguous position, but without the independent power to change it. They might dislike the need for new machines, either because they disrupted their way of life, or because, on any rational accounting, they were not really good business at the moment. In any case they saw them as strengthening the position of the large modernized entrepreneur, the main rival. Working-class revolts against machines gave such men their chance; often they took it. One may reasonably agree with the student of French machine-

14

wrecking who observes that 'sometimes the detailed study of a local incident reveals the Luddite movement less as an agitation of work-men, than as an aspect of competition between the backward and the progressive shop-owner or manufacturer'.[50]

If the innovating entrepreneur had the bulk of public opinion against him, how did he succeed in imposing himself? By means of the State. It has been well remarked that in Britain the Revolution of 1640–60 marks a turning-point in the State's attitude towards machinery. After 1660 the traditional hostility to devices which take the bread out of the mouths of honest men, gave way to the en-couragement of profit-making enterprise, at whatever social cost.[51] This is one of the facts which justifies us in regarding the seventeenth-century Revolution as the real political beginning of modern British capitalism. Throughout the subsequent period the central State apparatus tended to be, if not ahead of public opinion on economic matters, then at least more willing to consider the claims of the fully capitalist entrepreneur – except, of course, where these clashed with older and bigger vested interests. The Squire Westerns in some counties might still toast the shadow of a vanished feudal hierarchy in an unchanging society: there was no significant trace of feudal policy in the Whig governments, at any rate after 1688. London sympathy was to prove of inestimable value to the new industrialists when, in the last third of the century, their meteoric rise began. On issues of agrarian, commercial or financial policy Lancashire might be in conflict with London, but not on the fundamental supremacy of the profit-making employer. It was the unreformed Parliament in its most ferociously conservative period, which introduced full laissez-faire into the relations between employer and worker. Classi-cal free enterprise economics dominated the debates. Nor did London hesitate to rap its more old-fashioned and sentimental local represen-tatives over the knuckles if they failed 'to maintain and uphold the rights of property of every description, against violence and aggres-sion'. [52]

Yet, until the latter part of the eighteenth century the support of the State for the innovating entrepreneur was not unqualified. The political system of Britain from 1660 to 1832 was designed to serve manufacturers only in so far as they bought their way into the ring of vested interests of an older type – commercially-minded landlords, merchants, financiers, nabobs, etc. At best they could only hope for a share of the pork-barrel proportionate to their pressure, and in the early eighteenth century the 'modern' manufacturers were as yet only occasional groups of provincials. Hence, at times, a certain neutrality of the State in labour matters, at any rate until after the middle of the eighteenth century.[53] Western clothiers complained bitterly that the majority of local JPs was biased against them.[54] The attitude of the national government in the weavers' riots of 1726–7 contrasts strikingly with that of the Home Office from the 1790s on. London regretted that the local clothiers needlessly antagonized the men by arresting rioters; pooh-poohed suggestions that these were seditious; suggested that both parties get together amicably, so that a proper petition might be framed and Parliament could take action.[55] When this was done, Parliament sanctioned a collective agreement which gave the men very much what they wanted, at the cost of a perfunctory 'apology for past riots'.[56] Again, the frequency of *ad hoc* legislation in the eighteenth century[57] tends to show that no systematic, consistent and general attempt was made to enforce it. As the century progressed, the voice of the manufacturer increasingly became the voice of government in these matters; but earlier it was still possible for the men occasionally to fight sections of the masters on more or less fair terms.

We now come to the last and most complex problem: how effective was machine-breaking? It is, I think, fair to claim that collective bargaining by riot was at least as effective as any other means of bringing trade union pressure, and probably *more* effective than any other means available before the era of national trade unions to such groups as weavers, seamen and coal-miners. That is not to claim much. Men who did not enjoy the natural protection of small numbers and scarce apprenticed skills, which might be safeguarded by restricted entry to the market and firm hiring monopolies, were in any case bound normally to be on the defensive. Their success therefore should be measured by their ability to keep conditions stable – e.g., stable wage-rates – against the perpetual and well-advertised desire of masters to reduce them to starvation level.[58] This required an unremitting and effective fight. It may be argued that stability on paper was constantly undermined by the slow inflation of the eighteenth century, which steadily rigged the game against wage-earners[59]; but it would be asking too much of eighteenth-century activities to cope with that. Within their limits, one can hardly deny that Spitalfields silk-weavers benefited from their riots.[60] The disputes of keelmen, sailors and miners in the North East, of which we have record, ended, as often as not, with victory or acceptable compromise. Moreover, whatever happened in individual engagements, riot and machine-wrecking provided the workers with valuable reserves at all times. The eighteenth-century master was constantly aware that an intolerable demand would produce, not a temporary loss of profits, but the destruction of capital equipment. In 1829 a leading colliery manager was asked by the Lords' Committee whether a reduction of wages in the Tyne and Wearside coal mines could 'be effected without danger to the tranquillity of the district, or risking the destruction of all the mines, with all the machinery, and the valuable stock vested in them'. He thought not.[61] Inevitably, the employer faced with such hazards paused before he provoked them, for fear that 'his property and perhaps his life (might) be endangered thereby'.[62] 'Far more masters than one might expect,' Sir John Clapham noted with unjustified surprise, supported the retention of the Spitalfields Silkweavers' Acts, for under them, they argued 'the district lived in a state of quietude and repose'.[63]

Could riot and machine-breaking, however, hold up the advance of technical progress? Patently it could not hold up the triumph of industrial capitalism as a whole. On a smaller scale, however, it was by no means the hopelessly ineffective weapon that it has been made out to be. Thus, fear of the Norwich weavers is supposed to have prevented the introduction of machines there.[64] The Luddism of the Wiltshire shearmen in 1802 certainly postponed the spread of mechanization; a petitition of 1816 notes that 'in time of War there was no giggs nor Frames at Trowbridge but sad to relate it is now Increasing Every Day'.[65] Paradoxically enough, the wrecking by the helpless farm-labourers in 1830 seems to have been the most effective of all. Though the wage-concessions were soon lost, the threshing machines did not return on anything like the old scale.[66] How much of such successes was due to the men, how much to the latent or passive Luddism of the employers themselves, we cannot, however, determine. Nevertheless, whatever the truth of the matter, the initiative came from the men, and to that extent they can claim an important share in any such successes.

(1952)

17

NOTES

1 J. H. Plumb, *England in the Eighteenth century* (Harmondsworth 1950), p. 150; T. S. Ashton, *The Industrial Revolution* (London 1948), p. 154.

2 L. Dechesne, *L'Avènement du Régime Syndical à Verviers* (Paris 1908), pp. 51–64 and *passim*.

3 F. O. Darvall, *Popular Disturbance and Public Order in Regency England* (London 1934), p. 1.

4 E.g., woollen- and silk-making machines in Wiltshire, paper-making machines in Buckinghamshire, iron-making machines in Berkshire (Public Record Office, Home Office Papers, HO 13/57, pp. 68–9, 107, 177; Assizes 25/21 *passim*); J. L. and B. Hammond, *The Village Labourer* (various editions) is the most accessible account; see also two unpublished theses: N. Gash, *The Rural Unrest in England in 1830* (Oxford Examination Schools) and Alice Colson, *The Revolt of the Hampshire Agricultural Labourers* (London University Library).

5 For discussion of high-price rioting, T. S. Ashton and J. Sykes, *The Coal Industry of the Eighteenth Century* (Manchester 1929), chap. VIII; A. P. Wadsworth and J. de L. Mann, *The Cotton Trade and Industrial Lancashire* (Manchester 1931), pp. 355 ff.

6 Darvall, op. cit., chap. VIII *passim*.

7 Bonner and Middleton's Bristol Journal, 31-7-1802. Some of these were due to ordinary labour disputes, some to opposition to new machines. See J. L. and B. Hammond, *The Skilled Labourer;* for an account of the movement A. Aspinall (ed), *The Early English Trade Unions* (London 1949), pp. 41–69 for some of the documents.

8 House of Commons Journals, xviii, p. 715 (1718); xx, p. 268 (1724).

9 House of Commons Journals, xx, pp. 598–9 (1726); Salisbury Assize Records qu. in Wiltshire Times 25-1-1919 (Wiltshire Notes & Queries).

10 Gentleman's Magazine (1738), p. 658.

11 Public Record Office, State Papers Domestic Geo. 2 (1741), pp. 56, 82–3.

12 E. Welbourne, *The Miner's Unions of Northumberland and Durham* (Cambridge 1923), p. 21.

13 Ashton and Sykes, op. cit., pp. 89–91.

14 10 Geo. 2, c.32, 17 Geo. 2, c.40, 24 Geo. 2, c.57, 31 Geo. 2, c.42 (E. R. Turner, The English Coal Industry in the seventeenth and eighteenth centuries, *Amer. Hist. Rev.* XXVII p 14). Turner

seems to have neglected 13 Geo. 2, c.21, 9 Geo. 3, c.29, 39 and 40 Geo. 3, c.77, 56 Geo. 3, c.125 which are also directed against wrecking in mines. (*Burn's Justice of the Peace*, ed Chitty, 1837 edn, vol. III, pp. 643 ff.).

15 Welbourne, op. cit., p. 31.

16 W. Felkin, *A History of the Machine-wrought Hosiery and Lace Manufactures* (London 1867) is the main authority.

17 For the French mines cf. M. Rouff, *Les mines de charbon en France au XVIIIe siécle* (Paris 1922).

18 E. M. Saint-Léon, *Le Compagnonnage* (Paris 1901), I, chap. 5.

19 Aspinall, op. cit., p. 175.

20 The men of Bolton were alleged in 1826 to have planned the destruction of all the cotton-yarn ready packed for export, as well as of machines. (Public Record Office, Home Office Papers HO 40/19, Fletcher to Hobhouse 20 April 1826).

21 Cf. the discussion of these problems in E. Pouget, *Le Sabotage* (Paris n.d.), pp. 45 ff.

22 E.g., the Welsh ironworkers in 1816 (*The Times*, 26 Oct. 1816), the general strike of 1842 (F. Peel, *The Risings of the Luddites, Chartists and Plugdrawers*, Heckmondwike 1888, pp. 341–7), and the German miners in 1889 (P. Grebe, Bismarcks Sturz u.d. Bergarbeiterstreik vom Mai 1889, *Hist. Ztschr.* CLVII, p. 91).

23 Aspinall, op. cit., p. 196: 'I cannot help thinking that the morning meetings and roll-callings at present are the *bond* of union.'

24 H. L. Smith and V. Nash, *The Story of the Dockers' Strike* (London 1889), *passim*.

25 R. Rigola, *Rinaldo Rigola e il Movimento Operaio nel Biellese* (Bari 1930), p. 19. R. reports no actual wrecking by weavers, only by hatters.

26 See chapter on 'Machinery' in his *Principles*. On this, inserted only into the 3d edition, see Sraffa and Dobb, *Works and Correspondence of David Ricardo* (Cambridge 1951), I, p. lvii–lx.

27 M. D. George, *London Life in the Eighteenth Century* (London 1925), pp. 187–8, 180.

28 *Parl. Papers* 1802, Report fr. Committee on Woollen Clothiers' Petitition, pp. 247, 249, 254–5. *Rules and Articles of . . . the Woollen-Cloth Weavers' Society . . .* 1802 (British Mus. 906.k.14 (1)).

29 E. Howe and H. Waite: *The London Compositor* (London 1948), pp. 226–33.

30 Wadsworth and Mann, op. cit., pp. 499–500.

31 S. and B. Webb, *Industrial Democracy* (London 1898), chap. VIII: New Processes and Machinery.

32 For policy-change of compositors cf. Howe and Waite; engineers, J. B. Jefferys, *The Story of the Engineers* (London 1945), pp. 142–3, 156–7; tin-plate workers, J. H. Jones, *The Tinplate Industry* (London 1914), pp. 183–4, chap. IX.

33 J. Lofts, *The Printing Trades* (New York 1942) for the long fight of American compositors against the technical revolution in the 1940's.

34 Op. cit., p. 412. See also the detailed analysis of the fate of Hargreaves, pp. 476 ff.

35 *Sel. Ctee. on Agriculture*, 1833, 64 estimates – doubtless with some exaggeration – that only 1 in 100 of the threshing machines existing before 1830 were now in use in Wilts. and Berks.

36 On foreign shearmen's agitation, F. R. Manuel, The Luddite Movement in France, *Journ. Mod. Hist.* 1938, pp. 180 ff.; id., L'Introduction des Machines en France et les Ouvriers, *Rev. d'Hist. Mod.* N.S. XVIII, pp. 212–5. Actual Luddism in France seems to have been virtually confined to shearmen, with less success than in Britain, though Luddite intentions were sometimes expressed by others. See the documents in G. and H. Bourgin, *Le Régime de l'Industrie en France de 1840 à 1830* (Paris 1912–41), 3 vols.

37 Hammond, *Skilled Labourer*, p. 127.

38 Manuel, *J. Mod. H.*, p. 187, Darvall, *passim*. See also the note in Tufnell, *Character, Objects and Effects of Trade Unions* (1834), p. 17, on the reluctance of the men actually working machines to join in the strike against them. But T. admits that they did, threatened or persuaded by their unemployed mates.

39 The shearmen (croppers) raised the nap on the finished cloth and shaved it off with heavy iron shears. They had to be both very strong and very skilful.

40 Darvall, op. cit., p. 207.

41 Aspinall, op. cit., 57–8.

42 Thomas Helliker, executed. as such in 1803 is generally held to have been innocent.

43 G. H. Tupling, *Economic History of Rossendale* (Manchester 1927), p. 214.

44 MS. Correspondence of M. Cobb, clerk to the Justices at Salisbury, in Library of Wiltshire Archaeol. & Nat. Hist. Soc., Devizes: 26 Nov. 1830.

45 Printed Circular 8 Dec. 1830. This is referred to in Hammond, *Village Labourer* (Guild Books edn) II, pp. 71–2.

46 See the brilliant analysis of the 'democratic petty-bourgeois' in

Marx's Address to the Central Council of the Communist League, *Sel. Works of Marx & Engels*, II, pp. 160–1.

47 The phrase 'Threshold of profit' is S. G. Gilfillan's (Invention as a Factor in Economic History, *Supp. to Journ. Econ. Hist.*, Dec. 1945).

48 They were helped by the cheapness of the new machines. A western clothier installed jennies with 70–90 spindles for £9 apiece in 1804. Hence the possibility of piecemeal mechanization.

49 Tufnell, op. cit., p. 18.

50 Manuel, *J. Mod. H.*, p. 186.

51 E. Lipson, *Econ. Hist. of England* (4th edn) II, pp. cxxxv–vi, III, pp. 300, 313, 324–7. Sir John Clapham, *Concise Econ. Hist. of Britain*, p. 301, rightly notes that 'extra streak of hardness that seems to enter public life in the Restoration Age.'

52 See Note 45 above.

53 For the 'revolutionary change' in this period, S. and B. Webb, *Hist. of Trade Unionism* (1894), pp. 44 ff. But parliamentary proceedings may give the wrong impression. The normal course of events was that *laissez-faire* progressed quietly, contrary legislation falling into obsolescence, unless a specially active or effective campaign by the workers occurred. Cf. the repeal of the wage-clauses in the Statute of Artificers in 1813 (W. Smart, *Econ. Annals of the Nineteenth Century*, 1801–20, p. 368).

54 Philalethes, *The Case as it now stands between the Clothiers, Weavers and other Manufacturers with regard to the late Riot, in the County of Wilts*, London, 1739 (Cambridge Univ. Lib., Acton d. 25.1005), p. 7. At any rate as late as 17 Geo. 3, c.55 the hatters secured an Act forbidding any master hatter to sit on the bench in a dispute concerning them—which is more than farmworkers could achieve.

55 Public Record Office: State Papers Domestic Geo. I, 63: pp. 72, 82, 93–4. 64: pp. 1–6, 9–10 (esp. 2–4).

56 Journals of the House of Commons, xx, p. 747.

57 *Burn's Justice of the Peace*, ed. cit., III, pp. 643 ff., V, pp. 485 ff., 552 ff., gives a gruesome picture of this mass of uncoordinated piecemeal legislation.

58 W. Sombart, *Der Moderne Kapitalismus*, I, ii, p. 803 for a bibliography of these; K. Marx, *Capital* I (1938 edn), pp. 259–63. '*The Case as it now stands . . . .*' (Note 54 above), pp. 29, 41, gives typical arguments.

59 E. J. Hamilton, The Profit Inflation and the Industrial Revolution 1751–1800, *Q. Journ. Econ.*, pp. 56 (1942), 256.

60 Hammond, *Skilled Labourer*. M. D. George's observation, op. cit., p. 190 that the rise in weaving prices under the Acts was not comparable with that in other trades during the period, may be true. More significant is the drastic collapse of prices after the repeal of the Acts (ibid., p. 374).

61 Hammond, ibid., p. 26.

62 William Stark on the reasons why machinery was not adopted in the Norwich worsted trade, and wage-reductions were resisted. (Handloom Weavers' Commission, 1838 Ass. Commrs. Report II).

63 J. H. Clapham, The Spitalfields Acts, 1773–1824, *Econ. Journ.* XXVI, pp. 463–4.

64 Hammond, op. cit., p. 142. J. H. Clapham, The Transference of the Worsted Industry from Norfolk to the West Riding, *Econ. Journ.* XX, discusses the question in greater detail.

65 Hammond, ibid., p. 188.

66 Clutterbuck, *The Agriculture of Berkshire* (London & Oxford 1861), pp. 41–2.

3

Methodism and the Threat of Revolution in Britain

DID METHODISM PREVENT REVOLUTION, or the development of a revolutionary movement in Britain? The question has long interested historians. The period 1789–1848 is full of revolutions in all parts of Western Europe, but not in Britain, and it also happens to be the period when Methodism grew most rapidly in this country. That Methodism kept Britain immune from revolution is, indeed, widely believed. The late Elie Halévy's *History of the English People* supports this view very strongly. It may therefore be useful to elucidate the relations between Methodism and the threat of revolution in this period.

We know, of course, that John Wesley and the early leaders of his Connexion, as well as those of Whitefield's Calvinistic Methodists, disapproved violently of revolution. They were extreme conservatives in politics, opposed not merely to social revolution, but also to the liberal and radical reform which later became so closely identified with nineteenth-century British nonconformity, to trade unionism and to other manifestations of labour activity. Hence it is a mistake to argue that the modern labour and trade union movement derives its inspiration from Wesley. He would have been shocked by it. Cornish Wesleyans were proud that their members did not take part in strikes and agitations. Calvinistic Methodists excommunicated supporters of Roman Catholic emancipation and members of trade unions. Wesleyans in radical Leicester were conservative. Government agents were quick to observe that Wesleyans were pillars of the *status quo*. Indeed, the Connexion even fought shy of the militant temperance movement which radical nonconformity held so dear. Neither Wesley nor the early Wesleyans can even be described as democratic in their ideas of church organization and propaganda,

23

and between 1797 and 1849 a number of secessions from the main body occurred, mainly for this reason. After 1850 Wesleyanism was liberalized, and politically speaking it became rather more like the rest of nonconformity. In its youth and 'middle period' (1790 to 1849), however, it was quite certainly not so, and this is the period with which we are mainly concerned.

Though there was no revolution in Britain in the eighteenth or nineteenth centuries, there was, nevertheless, a good deal of revolutionary feeling in large parts of the country, particularly during the bleak half-century from the middle 1790s to the late 1840s. If the actual outbursts of violence were few, limited and rather small, it was not because at certain times – for instance, during the appalling depression of 1841–2 – great masses of British citizens were not angry, desperate, and ready for almost any political action. The strength of Chartism, say, cannot be measured by the feebleness of the actual attempts to translate it into revolt.

As Lenin argued – a specialist on the subject – a deterioration of the conditions of life for the masses, and an increase in their political activity, is not enough to bring about a revolution. There must also be a crisis in the affairs of the ruling order, and a body of revolutionaries capable of directing and leading the movement. Both these were absent. With the possible exception of the years immediately preceding the Reform Act of 1832, the British ruling class never lost control of the political situation. It is conceivable that something like a 'revolutionary situation' might have developed, had the Unreformed Parliament not been wise enough to yield peacefully to the pressure of the middle-class reformers (or to be exact, to the pressure of the masses under the leadership of the middle-class reformers). But the House of Lords was wise enough to yield, and the reforming party quick to make a compromise which gave them perhaps less than their most vocal spokesmen – for instance, Jeremy Bentham's followers – had demanded, but avoided the unpredictable consequences of further mass agitation. As for the revolutionaries, they were throughout the entire period inexperienced, unclear in their minds, badly organized, and divided.

There was thus no revolution and Wesleyan Methodism was hostile to one; but it does not follow that the second fact was the cause of the first. Methodism was not responsible for the moderation and flexibility of the Parliamentary politicians or the Utilitarian radicals. Nor can it be held responsible for the weaknesses of the revolutionary movement among the working classes. In order to demonstrate this, it is necessary to discover – insofar as this is possible – what effect it had on the politics of the British working classes in our period, and especially during the two major periods of unrest within it, the years from the Luddites to Peterloo (1811–19) and the years from 1829 to 1849 which covered the Reform agitation, the great trade union, factory reform and anti-Poor Law movements, Chartism, and the major agricultural unrest. This implies an answer to the more general question: what hold had organized religion, and in particular the various nonconformist sects, upon the working classes in the period of early industrialism?

The first question we must ask is whether the Wesleyans were numerically strong enough to make a decisive difference anyway. For it is quite clear that the other nonconformist sects did not share their political conservatism (with the exception of the Calvinistic Methodists, who were localized in North and Central Wales, which was not a major centre of industry). The 'old dissenters' – Independents (Congregationalists), Baptists of various sorts, Presbyterian-Unitarians (who should not be confused with the Church of Scotland, which had some strength among immigrants on Tyneside) were totally uncommitted to the support of the government, and had no respect whatever for constituted authority as such, which still officially discriminated against them in various ways. The first three groups had indeed long moved towards the 'left', and most active supporters of the French Revolution had come from among them. Unquestionably they became more respectable after the 1790s as they became more numerous. Whether the influence of Methodism, which helped to revivify them, is responsible for this, and if so, to what extent, may be debated. The question cannot be answered conclusively. All one can say is, that there are many other possible reasons why they should have become less Jacobin, chiefly the fact that most Englishmen between 1793 and 1815 had, for obvious reasons, little sympathy for Jacobinism. Hence, that typical seventeenth-century Puritan, Zechariah Coleman in Mark Rutherford's *Revolution in Tanner's Lane* complained bitterly about 'a sad falling off from the days, even in my time, when the Dissenters were the insurrectionary class.' Nevertheless, their sympathies remained throughout with the cause of Radicalism and Reform, and they actively supported both.

The various seceding Methodist groups did not sympathize politically with the Wesleyans. The Kilhamites or *New Connexion* (who left in 1797) proudly claimed in 1848 that they had long anticipated the liberalism which was then all the rage. One of their preachers in Northampton had even been jailed in 1816 for radical propaganda. The *Bible Christians* (1815) went their own quiet way in Devon and other parts of the Southwest, and eventually colonized parts of Kent. Theirs, however, was the fierce old-testamentary way of the elect walking safe from the flames of perdition; and such views do not necessarily make for social passivity. They were to be active in farm-labourers' unions. The same is true, to an even greater extent, of the most serious of the seceders, the *Primitive Methodists* (1811). These, the most purely 'proletarian' of the major sects, broke away because the Wesleyans were insufficiently democratic in the matter of preaching by laymen and women, and opposed to the mass propagandist campaigns of the great revivalist 'camp meetings' which American evangelists had introduced. Their strongholds were to be among the northern miners, the farm-labourers, the Staffordshire operatives. Here Primitive Methodism was so closely identified with trade unions as to become, practically, a labour religion. When Lord Londonderry evicted strikers after the 1844 coal strike, two-thirds of the Durham Primitive Methodist circuit became homeless. (This was at a time when Wesleyans were congratulating themselves because their members did not take part in strikes except under duress.) Whoever was for turning the other cheek, it was not the Primitives. Moreover, though preachers were debarred from politics, several 'probably interpreted this to mean that they were only prohibited from making speeches in the Tory interest'.

Even among the Wesleyans the rank and file were less conservative than their leaders; certainly in Leicester. At least one Yorkshire minister was only just in time to stop the Luddites burying one of their casualties in the Wesleyan cemetery, amid political speeches; from which we may conclude that Methodists were not above machine-breaking. In remote areas, where no more congenial sect penetrated – as in Dorset – Wesleyans might even become trade union leaders, as did the Tolpuddle Martyrs. Before the 1850s, however, this was very much the exception.

How strong, then, were the Wesleyans relatively to the other denominations, and to the total population (which included a very large number of the apathetic and a small minority of the secularist)? The only adequate information we have about these matters is that of the Religious Census of 1851, and it is as well to summarize this, therefore, before groping back into less well-documented periods. Broadly speaking, this gives us the following picture of the industrial areas of England and Wales. The large cities and some, but by no means all, of the backward mining and iron areas were relatively unreligious (that is to say, less than 25 per cent of the *total* population attended divine service on the census Sunday). Bristol, Leicester, Nottingham, Leeds and Liverpool, however – the latter on account of its many Roman Catholics – showed rather high attendance figures. Of the industrial areas *Lancashire*, the most important, was also the least religiously minded. The *North-East* came next in the scale of apathy. *Staffordshire* was divided in the matter. At the other end of the scale there was *South Wales*, where religious attendances amounting to 40 per cent of the *total* population were not uncommon – e.g., in Pontypool, Merthyr, Bridgend – the *West Riding*, and certain parts of *Derby, Leicester and Nottinghamshire*. Rural areas were, of course, on average, much more church-going than urban ones.*

Again with the exception of *Lancashire*, the cities and industrial areas were nonconformist rather than Anglican. The Church of England was not merely a minority group in most of them, but was often completely outclassed. For instance, in eight Poor Law unions of the *West Riding* and in part of the *Potteries* the main nonconformist bodies (Independents, Baptists, Wesleyans) were more than twice as numerous as the Church. In *Wales*, of course, the Church was a negligible force, for national reasons. Among the nonconformists, however, the Methodists as a whole were not equally strong everywhere.

Speaking broadly, they were not a serious force south of a line drawn from the Wash to Dudley in the Black Country and thence west to the Welsh coast; except for certain parts of Norfolk. They were also extremely strong in Cornwall. South of this line the nonconformity that counted was that of the 'old dissenters' – the Independents and Baptists. In South Wales the Methodists were even weaker. Even the Calvinistic Methodists, with their appeal to Welshness, were invariably outnumbered by either Independents or Baptists. The old dissenters also held pockets of Methodist territory, notably in the East Midlands. In fact, within the North and Midland industrial areas Methodism was really strong in only three parts: a

---

* The total population, which includes infants, the sick, etc., is obviously much larger than the potential church-going population. There is no convenient way of estimating how many adult men or women were potential attenders.

region centring on the Southern Pennines – that is, the industrial parts of the West Riding, Derbyshire and parts of Lancashire contiguous to Yorkshire, Durham, and parts of Staffordshire. Of these only the textile districts of the West Riding and, of course, Cornwall and Lincolnshire, can be regarded as the unchallenged fief of the Wesleyans. In Durham they were run close, and often outnumbered by the Primitive Methodists. (In Norfolk, the major centre of farm-labourers' trade unionism later on, they were consistently outnumbered by them.) In Staffordshire they had to contend – sometimes unsuccessfully – with both Primitives and other dissidents. In Derbyshire they were generally outnumbered.

Methodism as a whole, therefore, could be expected to have a major political influence on popular agitations only in the North, Midlands, East Anglia, and the extreme South-west; Wesleyanism as such only in the West Riding. The point is worth making, because a great deal of the radical and revolutionary unrest of the period took place in areas in which both were weak: in London, Bristol and Birmingham, in South Wales, in the East Midlands. Much of it, of course, took place in areas in which organized religion as such was weak – for instance, in Lancashire and the cities.

What was the position in earlier times? Since the days of the Luddites the Methodists had advanced much faster than population as a whole, or even than urban population. Taking all their sects together, they were almost four times as large in 1851 as in 1810; taking only the Wesleyans, rather over two-and-a-half times as large. Though we know practically nothing about the other dissenters, it is likely that, in England as distinct from Wales, the Methodists probably grew faster than they until 1850, with some local exceptions. Hence in 1811–19 or in 1830 they had obviously been relatively and absolutely far weaker than in 1851, when they embraced perhaps half a million members (300,000 Wesleyan) out of a total population of 18 millions. The main pattern of geographical distribution was already – speaking very roughly – established by 1810; the main strongholds of Methodism in Yorkshire and elsewhere had already come into existence. Even within these strongholds they were in general weaker, and their membership more fluctuating. It does not seem likely that a body of, say, 150,000 out of 10 million English and Welsh in 1811 could have exercised decisive importance.

Can we nevertheless detect any major moderating influence of the Wesleyans in any of their strongholds during the first half of the nineteenth century? In *Yorkshire* there is no real sign of it. Huddersfield, Leeds, Birstall, Wakefield were (after Nottingham) the main centres of Luddism; they were the centres of some of the strongest Methodist circuits in the West Riding. (Dissident Methodism was as yet negligible.) The West Riding, again headed by Leeds – which, we recall, had an abnormally high church-attendance for an industrial city – demonstrated and rioted as enthusiastically for the Reform Bill as any other place, French rosettes, cockades and tricolours abounding. During the 1830s and '40s it was perhaps the firmest stronghold of violent Radicalism and Chartism in the North. Huddersfield had the second-strongest Wesleyan congregation in the West Riding in 1851; and certainly the one which had grown most rapidly throughout the whole period since 1814. Yet Huddersfield was the centre of an almost insurrectionary resistance to the New Poor Law, and its Chartists held out for the revolutionary general strike for the Charter in 1839. It had also been a noted centre of Owenism. Bradford had the strongest Wesleyan congregation in the Riding in 1851, and had been a stronghold of the sect for forty years. But Bradford was a centre of Chartism. When Feargus O'Connor planned to tour the North after his release from jail, meetings were arranged for him in seventeen towns in which, presumably, he expected the greatest support – ten of them in the West Riding.* In 1851 the Methodists in these towns formed anything from 5 (Sheffield) to 12 and 15 per cent of the *total* population (Todmorden, Dewsbury, Keighley). Ironically enough, it was in the least Methodist of these towns – Sheffield – that Chartism was, throughout this period, least inclined to extremism.

The truth is that Methodism developed in this area and so did Radicalism. There were perfectly convincing reasons why the woollen and worsted weavers of the West Riding should be desperate and riotous. Worsted weavers' weekly earnings fell from 34*s*. 6*d*. in 1814 to 21*s*. in 1821; from 20*s*. in 1829 to 12*s*. 6*d*. in 1838. While this was so, Methodism had no more chance of preventing large numbers of them from being rebellious than had the Archbishop of Canterbury. Indeed, many Wesleyan operatives must have taken part in the great agitations.

In *Cornwall*, on the other hand, political radicalism and Chartism were weak among the miners who were the main supporters of the

* York, Leeds, Sheffield, Keighley, Halifax, Bradford, Todmorden, Huddersfield, Dewsbury, Barnsley.

Wesleyans. We should not hastily conclude that this was due to the moderating influence of the Wesleyans. Cornish industrial and social structure was, in many respects, archaic. Skilled miners, for instance, could continue to regard themselves not as wage-labourers but as sub-contractors or partners under the so-called 'tribute' agreements. Hence the feeling that workers as a class opposed employers as a class developed slow and late. The first 'labour dispute' occurred in 1831, the first actual strike in 1857. The characteristic form of Cornish social agitation – and the miners were a proverbially riotous group – was the riot against high food prices in times of shortage. As in eighteenth-century France, labour regarded not the employer, but the profiteering middleman as the real enemy. But, Methodism or no Methodism, miners and other workers in Cornwall still marched into the towns to seize food, forcibly to prevent the export of corn, or to force the sale of food at fair prices, in the classical manner of eighteenth-century rioters; for instance, in the hard year 1846-7.

Moreover, miners – whether of coal or metal – were an isolated body of men, often geographically separated from the rest of the working people and concerned less with politics than with their specialized economic struggles. Hence in most parts of the country they took surprisingly little part in the radical and Chartist agitations. In Yorkshire, Lancashire and above all Staffordshire, they struck in the desperate year 1842, together with the rest of the operatives among whom they lived; and as this vast strike movement merged with Chartism they may be regarded as having been in the thick of it. (Hardly any of the leading Chartists, however, appear to have been colliers.) In the main coalfields of the North-east and in South Wales, they did not strike, though they were in the middle of forming a national union which reached the point of explosion a year or so later. Very probably the coalfields which came out in '42 would have waited till then also, had they not been drawn in by the factory workers who surrounded them. In South Wales the Methodists were negligible. In the North-east, the Primitive Methodists, with their championship of unions predominated. The Wesleyans cannot be held responsible for the passivity of these mining communities in 1842. Hence it is probably wisest to put the lack of interest in and feebleness of Cornish Chartism down to factors unconnected with the religion of the Cornish.

Another claim to have prevented revolution has been put forward on behalf of the Primitive Methodists by their official historian H. B.

Kendall, writing in 1906. It rests mainly on the fact that the first great advances of this sect occurred in Nottinghamshire and Leicestershire in 1817–19; that is to say, in two of the chief strongholds of Luddism and radicalism. Examples of villages abandoning 'levelling' doctrines are quoted. This claim cannot be taken very seriously either. In the first place, the twenty-odd villages in Nottinghamshire in which the Primitives established themselves in 1817–18 were overwhelmingly in the least industrialized part of the county; they contained only something like 7 per cent of the county's knitting-frames. (In Leicestershire, however, they were probably more successful among the hosiery workers.) In the second place, the Methodist advances in this area were temporary, and much of the ground was lost again in the 1820s and not regained till much later. In the third place, the East Midlands did not become noticeably less radical after 1818. In fact, Leicestershire is one of the places where more active Methodists than usual appear to have been enthusiastic Chartists. It would have been surprising if the handloom weavers and stockingers, whose weekly income had – according to the Methodist Chartist, Thomas Cooper of Leicester – fallen to 4s. 6d. a week by 1841 – had not been radical when they starved.

We can therefore sum up the relations between Methodism and the threat of revolution somewhat as follows. The official leadership of the Connexion wished to keep it entirely outside any radical, let alone revolutionary agitations. Even had it succeeded in doing so, however, the strength of Wesleyanism was probably not great enough, and not well enough distributed, to affect the political situation decisively. But, in fact, the members did not keep outside radical agitations. It is likely that Wesleyanism lost ground to politically radical sects such as the Primitive Methodists, and there was certainly increasing rank-and-file opposition to the conservatism of the leaders, notably in the 1830s and 1840s; sometimes on political grounds (as in Leicester), more generally on ostensibly moral grounds, such as temperance (as in Cornwall and elsewhere). Many Wesleyans must have taken part in the radical and revolutionary agitations, from Luddism to Chartism, with their non-Wesleyan fellows. The effectiveness of official Wesleyan conservatism has often been exaggerated.

This may be due to a fundamental misconception of the reasons that turned workers in early industrial Britain towards various sects. It is too easily assumed that they did so *as an alternative* to revolutionary or radical politics. To some extent they did. In the early stages of the capitalist transformation of town and countryside we do indeed often meet sects – mystical, apocalyptic, quietist – which preach resignation and complete non-involvement in the affairs of an evil world. Gerhart Hauptmann's magnificent drama, *The Weavers*, which is based on a documentary account of the Silesian weavers' revolt of 1844, contains a wonderful portrait of an old sectarian of this sort. Similar mystical cults of the Virgin spread in the Belgian industrial areas about the same time, while a body called the Nazarenes made headway among the landless Hungarian farm-labourers later in the century. But there is another kind of religion which might seize the miserable mass of the people at such times. Preachers, prophets and sectarians might issue what the labourers would regard as calls to action rather than to resignation. Such sects are equally well documented. In the Northern Rhodesian copper belt, for instance, in our generation, the Jehovah's Witnesses for a time played a similar part to that of the Primitive Methodists in the Durham pits.

We know too little about the life of the common people in Britain during the Industrial Revolution to say with any confidence how they regarded their nonconformity. All we know is that Methodism advanced when Radicalism advanced and not when it grew weaker, and also that the great 'religious revivals' normally did *not* occur when economic conditions were coming to their worst, for instance, at the bottom of trade depressions. The periods when Wesleyanism recruited most rapidly – at an annual average of 9,000–14,000 members – were also, with the one exception of the boom-years 1820–4, periods of mounting popular agitation: 1793–4 (the time of Jacobin agitation), 1813–16 (as unrest increased in the last years of the Napoleonic Wars), 1831–4 (during the great Reform and Owenite agitations, when the most rapid rate of increase was achieved), 1837–41 (Chartism) and 1848–50 (the last wave of Chartism). Conversely, as Chartism declined, so did the sects. The first half of the 1850s saw most nonconformist bodies, Methodist or otherwise, losing members steadily in what was, in effect, the only major recession in their nineteenth-century history. 1850 marks the end of a phase in the development of nonconformism, as in that of the labour movement. When both revived, it was under very different conditions. This peculiar parallelism may be explained either by saying that radical agitations drove other workers into Methodism as a reaction against them, or that they became Methodists and Radicals for the same reasons. Both are probably true. On the whole, the second interpretation is perhaps more likely, since, as we have seen, dissatisfaction among rank-and-file Wesleyans against the anti-radicalism of their leaders grew markedly during the 1830s and 1840s.

The truth is that the times were working against Wesley the politician though they favoured Wesley the evangelist, and this inevitably weakened the political effectiveness of his strongly organized and authoritarian Connexion. But even if it had been fully effective, it is unlikely that Wesleyanism could have prevented a revolution had other conditions favoured one in the first half of the nineteenth century. The world of our own century is full of revolutions made by masses of deeply pious men and women, adhering to religious bodies – whether Hindu, Christian or Buddhist – whose leaders did not favour resistance to constituted authority; and of revolutionary movements composed of such men and women. There is no reason to believe that the conditions of the early nineteenth century made religion as such a stronger safeguard against revolution in Europe than it is in Asia today.

(1957)

NOTE

The classical statement of the view that Methodism prevented revolution in Britain is in E. Halévy's *History of the English People in the Nineteenth Century*, Vol. I, but it is considerably toned down in the last volume of this great work to appear, Vol. IV (1841–52). Since this paper was published (1957) the first really adequate general discussion of Methodism and popular movements has appeared, namely E. P. Thompson's *The Making of the English Working Class* (London 1963). Mr Thompson, whose scope is much wider than mine, shares my scepticism of Halévy, though for slightly different reasons. He gives numerous examples of radical and even revolutionary Methodists. I am inclined to accept his view that *revivalism* sometimes or often 'took over just at the point where "political" or temporal aspirations met with defeat', op. cit., p. 389), but since he agrees that the opposite phenomenon also took place, and since my paper does not set out to discuss revivalism in any detail, I do not wish to modify the present text. The Methodist local preacher who took a leading part in the Pentridge 'rising' (which occurred between two revivalist periods) makes my – and Mr Thompson's – point. On the whole, however, I would regard this later treatment of the subject as more satisfactory than mine on the points where the two are in disagreement.

33

4

The Tramping Artisan

I

THE STORY OF NINETEENTH-CENTURY LABOUR is one of movement and migration. This article deals with one part of it, the so-called 'tramping system' among organized, and generally apprenticed, workers. The system is now so much a thing of the past that few vestiges of it remain in trade-union rules and constitutions, generally so tenacious of the traditions. Yet there was a time when hardly any trade society which provided its members with benefits failed to adopt it; except in occupations localized in single areas.

The general workings of the system are familiar enough – there are good descriptions of it in Henry Broadhurst's autobiography, Kiddier's *The Old Trade Unions*, and elsewhere.[1] The man who wished to leave town to look for work elsewhere, received a 'blank' or 'clearance' or 'document', showing him to be a member in good standing of the society. This he presented to the local secretary or relieving officer in the 'lodge house' or 'club house' or 'house of call' of the strange town – generally a pub – receiving in return supper, lodging, perhaps beer, and a tramp allowance. If there was work to be found, he took it; the 'call-book' (if there was one) was of course kept at the house of call, an unofficial local labour exchange. If there was none, he tramped on. Should he not get permanent enough work to transfer to a new union branch, the traveller would in due course return to his home town, having made the round of all the branches: among the compositors this grand tour was about 2,800-miles long in the 1850s,[2] among the brushmakers over 1,200 miles in the 1820s.[3] The methods of paying tramp relief varied. It could be paid by day or distance, in which case cautious head offices took care to make sure that the tramp went from branch to branch by the shortest route, sometimes

34

furnishing route cards. Relief for the weekend was generally higher than for weekdays.

Payments were either (in the early stages of the system) entirely in the hands of branches, which, from time to time, cleared their expenditure with one another directly, or through head-office;[4] later it became increasingly centralized. Later also a cheque system was sometimes used. The tramp would, on setting out, get a cheque-book valid for so many days – ninety-eight among the masons, less among the bakers[5] – and would cash relief cheques in each branch. Such centralization helped to guard against the bane of the system, its abuse by tramps not entitled to relief at all, or by men who had exhausted their annual maximum of tramping money. The exceptionally full statistics, on which much of this article is based, had the same object. The local secretary had to be able to check the bona fides of claimants – for even the forging of tramp tickets was not unknown, especially among the printers, some of whom travelled with 'documents' issued by entirely mythical branches until apprehended by the watchful brethren. Monthly circulars, therefore, contained lists of men on the road and similar information. Not that tramp relief was on a lavish scale; among the masons it was 6d. a day until late in the century.* Hence relief was fairly regularly supplemented by passing the hat round among fellow-members and their mates on any job the tramp encountered in his travels. Still, the system worked. Indeed, among many unions it was for long the only method of unemployment relief; in some of the building trades as late as the twentieth century.

II

We know extremely little about the early history of the system – it was so called by at least one union† – though its similarity to the continental custom of travel among journeymen has often been noted.[6] In fact, research has not fundamentally altered the picture sketched by the Webbs in 1894, a tribute to those extraordinary scholars. Among the Devon wool-combers, organized tramping existed as early as 1700, spreading to cognate trades between 1700 and 1726.[7] The Taunton weavers appear to have had a rudimentary tramping

---

* Systems of paying relief per mile travelled mitigated the hardship of such flat rates.

arrangement in 1707,[8] though weaving, as distinct from combing, remained organized on a purely local basis.[9] The curriers had a tramping federation by the middle of the century, the hatters in the 1770s.[10] Tramping arrangements among calico-printers, paper-makers and compositors were so well advanced at the turn of the century that they must have flourished for quite a while before then. Certainly by the early nineteenth century the evidence accumulates. 'Blanks' are recorded among cordwainers in 1803, tramp relief among Preston carpenters in 1808.[11] Calico-printers report titanic journeys in search of work of 1,000 and 1,400 miles.[12] By the time of the Select Committee on the Combination Acts, Dublin crafts had tramping arrangements with English ones;[13] Francis Place found houses of call in London among hatters, smiths, carpenters, boot- and shoe-makers, metal-workers, bakers, tailors, plumbers, painters and glaziers, bookbinders and others,[14] and the tramping system among many old-established crafts could be taken for granted.[15]

Though W. J. Ashley did not think so, the problem of the origin of the system is important. Plainly, tramping was a central institution of several old unions, and it is difficult to see how some of the federations of trade clubs which so frightened the authorities after 1792 could have come about without it. Was it the expression of the artisan's new-found mobility, as has been suggested,[16] or did it spring from an old and living tradition of journeyman travel? How did it spread?

At first sight the 'modern' evidence seems the strongest. So far as we know there is no record of customs and institutions like the continental *tour de France* or *Wanderpflicht* here. British tramping systems seem, from the start, not part of the final polish in the craftsman's education, but devices for meeting seasonal or irregular unemployment; this was the case among the wool-combers, West Country weavers and hatters. (No doubt they were also used quite early as a means of giving strike relief, safeguarding against victimization, etc., important later functions.) Moreover, organized tramping in the eighteenth century seems to have been confined to a few trades.[17] The tailors had elaborate houses of call in London and Dublin as early as the 1720s, in Birmingham before the 1770s, in Edinburgh by the 1780s at least;[18] but they did not adopt tramping until sometime before the 1860s, perhaps during or after the collapse of the tight closed shops in the towns in the 1820s and 1830s.[19] There is no doubt that after, say, 1790 the system was adopted by previously non-tramping trades and perfected by tramping ones. Though masons must have tramped, we have no record of the practice among other builders before the nineteenth century. The hatters did not adopt the 'blank' until 1798,[20] though they had houses of call in the 1730s[21] and some sort of tramping federation in the 1770s. Perhaps they used an intermediate form of the system, such as we find among calico-printers, in which tramps were officially authorized to make local collections among their mates.[22]

Nor is it wholly impossible that the system may have been invented in one place – the West Country seems most likely – and was then spread by travelling woollen workers, or perhaps tramping masons from the western quarries. The institutions and rituals of later trade unions are generally held to owe a great deal to those of the woollen workers, and 'blanks' may be part of the debt.[23]

On the other hand, there are archaisms in the old tramp systems which point to the memory, at any rate, of older customs. Thus they were, and remained, entirely adapted to single men. I have come across no case in which provision was made for the wife and family of the tramping journeyman; indeed, one of the earliest complaints against the weavers was that they left their families on the rates while they tramped.[24] Had they been originally designed to meet unemployment they could hardly have failed to bear the married workman in mind. Then again, they were in the strict sense of the word tramping systems. The Boilermakers, who provided for travel by land 'or sailed by water or by means of steam power' as early as the 1830s[25] are, I think, unique. The Steam-Engine Makers did not provide for travel by coasting vessel until the 1840s[26] and the compositors only amended 'tramped' to 'travelled' in 1872.[27] Certainly, as late as the 1850s and 1860s there was a strong prejudice among masons against any mode of travel other than Shanks's pony, the only 'provident' one. It is not clear whether this was old, or merely a rationalization, in the light of Victorian morality, of an older custom.[28] A system designed to send men from slack to busy areas might have considered the most expeditious means of travel, for instance the much-used coasting vessel.[29] How much weight we can attach to the nineteenth-century evidence of a belief that 'no man knows his own ability or what he is worth until he has worked in more towns than one',[30] is uncertain. Our ignorance of the customs and traditions of earlier wage-earners is profound since they were almost unrecorded, so the prevalence of such beliefs is quite possible.[31]

Certainly, in some cases, organized tramping merely systematized older habits. 'It will be nessarey for tramps coming this road to bring their clearances with them. You will likewise demand clearances from any that may come from here [*sic*]' – say the Portsmouth and similarly the Bath cordwainers, announcing the foundation of a local union in 1803.[32] The Birmingham carpenters founded a society in 1808 primarily to appoint a house for 'the reception of workmen travelling for the purpose of getting employment and who are commonly called TRAMPS'.[33] The Bolton ironfounders, in 1809, assume the existence of an unofficial network of such stations, for they are confident, on founding their local union, that the expenses of foreign tramps will be 'reimbursed to this Society by the Society to which the member so relieved [with "supper, one pint of beer, one night's lodging and two shillings in cash to carry him to the next town"] shall belong'.[34] Clearly the practice of tramping was not in itself new. Indeed, the view that the tramping systems were designed to secure mobility begs the question. What the early unions wanted, was not mobility as such, but financially secure mobility, or its control in the interest of a local closed shop. 'None of *their* members,' the cordwainers argued about hatters and curriers, 'are suffered to wander like vagrants out of employment.'[35] That they should wander at all was taken for granted.

There was no reason why they should not. The Settlement Laws hardly incommoded the artisan. The Webbs state categorically that they came across no single case of an eighteenth-century trade unionist removed under them;[36] and a large collection of certificates of settlement from Newark records no single mason, printer or brushmaker (though the latter had a tramp station in the town in the early nineteenth century),[37] and only one hatter and currier over more than a century.[38] The major obstacle to travel would be not the law, but the craft exclusiveness of the towns (though this was weakened by the eighteenth century, and in any case difficult to enforce in times of expansion).[39] Yet the tightly organized Dublin crafts, which excluded even foreign trade unionists, sent and received tramps.[40]

The real question is how the craftsman came to tramp the whole country in the first place. The point is that a national network of 'stations' from Exeter to York such as we see among, say, the early brushmakers, is quite different from the pattern produced by the normal migrations of labour which is primarily regional.[41] Nor is systematic travelling automatically adopted by trades with sharp seasonal fluctuations: if the hatters tramped in the eighteenth century, the tailors did not.[42] Nor did the ordinary operations of trade unionism create national networks at this early stage. In France, where tramping was quite independent of the unions and in the hands of the ancient and rather unadaptable *compagnonnages*, trade unions did not develop national organizations until the 1880s or – like the hatters – the very end of the Second Empire.[43] Where local industrial units were in some sense interdependent, and recognized as forming part of a national whole, as in the woollen industry, tramping is more easily explained; and this may account for its early appearance among the woollen workers. But why should the shoemakers, hatters or curriers, all of whom worked in locally self-contained markets and had little cause to know much about other towns,[44] take to it before the 1790s?[45] Possibly the attraction of the great magnet, London, counts for something.[46] Nevertheless, it seems difficult to explain tramping as a whole without assuming some sort of travelling tradition (at any rate in some crafts) analogous to the continental habits out of which the institutions of the *compagnonnages* had developed.* Among the stonemasons there was certainly such a tradition; perhaps among printers; perhaps among one or two of the others.

It is always unsatisfactory to rest a case on negative evidence; and here we can, at best, leave the verdict open. One thing is clear: both 'ancient' and 'modern' factors contributed to shape the system, even granted that the old customs, which were to be adapted to new trade-unionist needs, were passed on through one or two crafts only. So peculiar and highly organized a system could only be erected on a well-built foundation of custom. On the other hand, its general adoption by the crafts undoubtedly reflected the need to defend local monopolies of apprenticed artisans against novel economic challenges.

III

Among older craft clubs, then, the tramping system became the very backbone of union. The hatters and ironfounders even built their emblems round it, the latter showing a tramping moulder with his pack saying 'Brother craft, can you give me a job' and receiving the

* We need not assume any connexion between British and continental journeymen societies in their developed form; though the parallelism between their institutions – rituals and drinking customs, the *Herberge* and the club-house, the *Geschenk* and the tramp donation, *schmaehen* and the blacklisting of men or masters – is striking.

answer 'If we cannot, we will assist you'. The Nantwich shoemakers were careful to include in their trade procession in 1833 'a shopmate in full tramping order, his kit packed on his back and walking stick in his hand'.[47] By the mid-nineteenth century the system was very widespread. In 1860 it was in use among compositors, lithographers, tailors, coachmakers, bookbinders, smiths, engineers, steam-engine makers, stonemasons, carpenters, ironfounders, coopers, shoemakers, boilermakers, plumbers, bricklayers and various other crafts.[48]

The reasons why it spread are plain. In the first place (though this may not have been its original purpose) it relieved strike funds, and provided a means of countering victimization. Even at the end of the century we know of masons who habitually went on the road as soon as a dispute began, so as not to burden the funds;[49] of course the man who got a temporary job while the fight was on was a great asset. The fight for recognition and a standard rate almost invariably led to victimizations, even if it succeeded. If men were to be 'sacrificed' – the phrase is the compositors' – they must be certain of a livelihood, and the tramping system normally gave them specially favourable treatment, sometimes distinguishing them from ordinary travellers. The masons gave strike tramps a green card, ordinary ones a white one. Tramping thus greatly strengthened the bargaining power of the men, a point already well-established among wool-combers in the mid-eighteenth century.[50] From this to a more sophisticated calculation of political economy was only one step. By removing the unemployed from places of slack trade, and keeping them in circulation, tramping kept the supply in the labour market limited. 'If it had not been in our power,' wrote the General Union of Carpenters in 1846, 'to keep up our tramping transport . . . a general reduction in wages would have taken place.'[51] The printers formulated this most clearly. Tramping, noted the *Typographic Protection Circular* in May 1849, had now become a method of relief rather than of finding work, 'so that the trade is virtually maintaining a local poor law . . . under which pauper aid is dispensed to its casual poor, the rate-payer being the employed, and the Guardians thereof the Society's officers'.

This grim little phrase reflects the radical change in the system when it encountered the massive unemployment of the earlier nineteenth century – whether the technological unemployment which destroyed the calico-printers, wool-combers, etc., or the less permanent, but equally cataclysmic, cyclical unemployment of 1820–50. Once again we observe that the system had not been devised to meet

40

the contingencies of industrial capitalism. It fitted the old wool-combers admirably: a smallish closed group of mobile craftsmen, in a fluctuating trade, operating under fairly stable long-term conditions. In extreme cases of this sort, as the Webbs have shown, it could virtually replace all overt collective bargaining.[52] As the only properly developed form of unemployed relief, it was generally adopted by most trades having need of such payments; but faced with the gigantic stresses of modern capitalism, and above all the trade cycle, it broke down.

It would seem that the system was not strained beyond its powers until the 1830s and 1840s, though the London compositors were already campaigning against it in the 1830s.[53] After that, however, it ran into heavy weather. We can follow the process rather well in the records of the small Journeymen Steam-Engine Makers (founded 1826; since 1921 part of the Amalgamated Engineering Union) as shown in Table I.

Table I. *Tramping among Journeymen Steam-Engine Makers, 1836–41**

Year	Members	Branches	Total number of travellers relieved
1836–7	525	13	44
1837–8	695	15	224
1838–9	794	18	289
1839–40	876	18	893
1840–1	981	22	673
1841–2	994	24	2,226

The Steam-Engine Makers were neither specially migratory, nor specially badly off. Far more striking are the figures from other contemporary unions. The Ironfounders in 1840 paid out the best part of £11,500 on tramping – for a total membership, in and out of jobs, of under 3,500. Seven years earlier they had only spent £800.[54] The four main printing unions, with 3,400 members in 1841–2, relieved no less than 7,200 travellers between them in that year.[55] Of course a great many of these were long-distance tramps, desperately moving through scores of branches in search of work, and registered in each; but that did not lessen the financial burden. As the General Union of Carpenters said, vividly if ungrammatically:

* Annual Reports. The number of travellers relieved is given separately for each branch.

41

Throughout the length and breadth of our native land there has not been a corner or village but what some of our members have perambulated in pursuit of employment; our high roads have resembled that of a mechanical workshop, or a mighty mass of moving human beings; we have various instances where twenty or thirty men in a body, of different mechanical trades, wending their way from town to town, asking leave to toil. . . .[56]

The experience of the 1840s led to a major change: the spread of ordinary unemployment relief. The reasons for this were clearly not financial, for the cost of tramping was not high per person,[57] and was more easily supplemented by local collections and private hospitality than static out-of-work pay. It seems rather that the massive unemployment of those years for the first time impressed the ordinary, non-migratory unionist with the inconvenience of a wholly nomadic method of relief. Once again the Steam-Engine Makers illustrate the point. In 1836 the London branch introduced static out-of-work pay off its own bat, to the grave displeasure of head-office. By 1847, nine other branches, from Leeds to Portsmouth, had followed London's lead. In the 1848 Rules revision branches were formally given the right to institute such payments; in 1851 it was introduced nationally as an alternative to tramping.[58] About the same time the Ironfounders introduced a similar 'donative' payment.[59] The new Amalgamated Society of Engineers started life with it, but then its ancestor the 'Old Mechanics' had never relied purely on tramping – perhaps one reason why it overhauled the somewhat older Steam-Engine Makers.[60] The ambitious National Typographical Association had abolished tramping altogether in the 1840s, but the slump broke it, and its successor, the Provincial Typographical Association (1849), reverted to it, though with misgivings.[61] Not until 1872 was static relief introduced for good, though large local units – Manchester, Leeds, London, Liverpool, and Sheffield – had already taken to it.[62] Even the old-fashioned General Union of Carpenters introduced it in 1863, doubtless as a result of the foundation of the more modern Amalgamated Carpenters in 1860. Of the large tramping trades, few continued to rely exclusively on tramping, like the stonemasons, who kept to it until the present century, filling up to five pages of their rule books with 'tramp laws'.

From this time on tramping declined rapidly.

42

IV

Before we study this decline and the reasons for it, let us recall the very striking mobility of many mid-Victorian artisans, as indicated by tramp statistics of their unions. (Since these unions were far more representative than has often been supposed,[63] it is reasonable to presume that they throw light on the habits of unorganized workers in the trades covered by them, though these may not have been quite so mobile.) Thus in 1872, when tramping was already on the decline, and unemployment was low, 6 per cent of the Ironfounders took out travel cards, and the percentage of men who did so did not regularly fall below 10 until after 1888. The Amalgamated Tailors in 1877 had 5–6 per cent of their members on the road, of whom about one-sixth returned to their home lodges within the year; i.e., 4–5 per cent of the union membership transferred their place of work during this year by means of tramping. The percentage of travel cards taken out between 1869 and 1877 was much the same. Among provincial printers the figures are even more startling. Between February 1873 and December 1876 the union issued travel documents to an annual average of just under 25 per cent of its total membership (though a quarter of all these came from four large and very fluid branches at Manchester, Liverpool, Birmingham and Belfast). Since the average tramp covered several stations, the total number of reliefs was of course much larger – about 100 per cent of the union membership in a prosperous year.[64]

It is not easy to analyse these figures. Some men tramped constantly, like American hobo workers – especially among masons, compositors and ironfounders. Among the latter the permanent nomads only rarely formed more than 10 per cent of those on the road, and after 1870 never formed more than 1·2 per cent of union membership, except in the slump-year 1878–9. Among the printers, whose trade was riddled with casualism, the proportion was probably higher, though how much higher we cannot say, since only the Ironfounders actually tried to calculate the degree of permanent nomadism. A much greater number of men travelled during trade depressions. In the 1860s the percentage of unemployed engineers who went on the road was about 35, and that of plumbers much the same.[65] An unknown number – chiefly of young men – roved for a few years. There are no statistics, but the custom was strong. George Odger, the Cornish shoemaker, came to London after such *Wanderjahre*.[66] The young Robert Knight, subsequently boss of the Boilermakers, went to 'see the world' before returning home to Devon; nor was he the only one in his trade to do so.[67] The engineer, John Burns, took a trip to West Africa and travelled the continent before returning to Battersea and political fame.[68] Even among farm labourers, Joseph Arch roved the south Midlands and Wales before settling down, and the young George Edwards spent a year in foreign parts – some thirty miles from his native Poor Law union.[69] F. W. Galton, himself a member of an old craft, records the liveliness of the tradition as late as the 1890s.[70] Some men again, in that period of rapid industrial growth, were semi-nomadic, leaving a permanent home for varying periods, or shifting their families from time to time, especially among builders, specialist craftsmen and supervisory workers.[71] These movements, again, cannot be accurately measured. In small traditional tramping crafts probably almost everyone reckoned to tramp sometime in his life, apart from depression travel. In all trades, however,

Table II. *Travelling among Ironfounders, 1850–1908**

(1) Period	(2) Annual average number of travel- lers relieved on last Saturday of year	(3) Average number of members per decade, divided by figures in col. (2)
1850–9†	73	71
1860–9	75	126
1870–9	60	190
1880–9	52	232
1890–9	44	361
1900–8	63‡	295

there seems to have been a fairly sharp line between the majority, who no longer reckoned to travel – except in the most unusual circumstances – once they had settled down, and a minority which was more foot-loose.

Whatever the exact kinds of movement – and these are only some of the sorts which inadequate analysis lumps together under the

* Ironfounders Reports. But before 1868 the distribution of travel cards was entirely in the hands of the branches.

† Figures not available for 1850 and 1852.

‡ The rise may reflect the growth of technological unemployment among some craftsmen founders, due to the development of machine-moulding— which the union did not organize – as well as the depressions of 1903–4 and 1908.

general name of 'mobility of labour' – there is no doubt that most of them decreased. By the 1870s George Howell could describe the system as obsolescent.[72] As usual, the Ironfounders' figures are the fullest (Table II).

The number of travellers fell, absolutely and relatively, through the second half of the century, and if we take another index, the percentage of members who annually drew travelling cards, the decline continued even between 1900 and 1908. Not even the major catastrophe of the Great Depression did more than slow it down. Indeed, nothing is more revealing than a comparison of tramping in the 'black years' of, say, 1841–2 and 1879. In the former the Northern Typographical Union relieved about five times as many travellers as it had members; in the latter the Provincial Typographical Association relieved only about double its membership in travellers.*

The decline is especially palpable in depression travel. In the 1860s 35 per cent of unemployed engineers travelled; in the 1890s 10 per cent; in the 1900s, 4 per cent; from 1910 to 1914, 1 per cent.[73] Among the Steam-Engine Makers the proportion of tramp to static unemployed relief ranged between 1 : 2 and 1 : 6 in the 1850s; between 1 : 4 and 1 : 11 in the 1860s; between 1 : 10 and 1 : 60 in the 1870s; 1 : 15 and 1 : 70 in the 1880s. Even more striking is the decline among the traditionally tramping compositors. Between 1880 and 1889 tramp relief amounted to between 20 per cent and 40 per cent of unemployed relief; between 1890 and 1899 between 6 per cent and 20 per cent; between 1900 and 1906 it was never more than 9 per cent and fell as low as 5 per cent. The tramping printer was rapidly becoming extinct.[73a] While tramp relief was the only form of the dole, this tendency was to some extent masked. The speed with which static out-of-work pay overhauled its older rival makes this quite clear. Among the Plumbers, who reintroduced static pay in 1901, evidently because they were beginning to feel the need of some sort of unemployment pay,[74] it was twenty times as important as tramp relief from the start.

Such diminution of tramping did not necessarily mean a decline in mobility. From the 1880s on, for instance, the growth of urban transport made it possible – for the better-off workers at any rate – to look

* 1841–2: 1226 members, 6036 tramp reliefs; 1879: 5200 members, 11,900 tramp reliefs (including payments for weekends, when men did not travel).

for work within a large labour market without automatically changing their lodgings every time they sought, or got, a job beyond
walking distance from their homes. London is a case in point.[75] The
tram replaced the tramp. It need not even mean a decline in long-
distance mobility. The 'new model' unions which introduced static
out-of-work pay also introduced methods of transferring workers
from slack to busy places more efficient than the happy-go-lucky
tramping systems. Engineers, Steam-Engine Makers, Boilermakers,
Ironfounders, Amalgamated Carpenters and others evolved plans for
paying or advancing the rail-fares of their members to distant jobs;[76]
the carpenters even tried to turn themselves into a national labour
exchange for their trade.[77] These devices were not, on the whole,
very successful – indeed, like the emigration benefit, which became
popular in the same period, they are interesting chiefly as signs of the
growing adoption of orthodox economic ideas – but they were not
negligible.

Moreover, the factors causing the decline were, in part at least,
offset by others. This is probably least true of the most important
form of tramping, depression travel, which tended to diminish pretty
constantly, except in catastrophically bad years.* The tramping of
young men, on the other hand, was more than kept alive. In the first
place the stream of apprenticed men from low-wage to high-wage
areas continued unabated, all the more since certain trades – building
for instance – in the cities came to rely for their recruitment of artisans
chiefly on such immigration.[78] Lawrence's 1897 enquiry[79] shows that
several trades in Bristol, the great gateway from the low-paid West
Country, were composed mainly of such travellers, most of them
regarding the town as their first stopping place. Many such young
men would, of course, travel straight from their home town to the
city, especially as there would be a nucleus of fellow-townsmen or
relatives working there, who could find them jobs.[80] Thus the transfer of some Dundee jute workers to Barrow in Furness soon led to
that town becoming 'a sort of vestibule, through which the young
Dundonian passed to the outer world'.[81] On the other hand, the

---

* But short-term tramping within large conurbations may have replaced
much long-distance tramping, even here. Thus the six Tyneside lodges of the
Plumbers in 1892 had an average of perhaps 70 of their 600 members circulating
between them – each visiting two or three towns (United Operative Plumbers,
1892, Quarterly Reports). Since many unions confine the granting of relief
within a small radius of the home branch, such tramping often went unrecorded.

young man was just as likely to make his way to his final place of settlement by stages, for once he was saddled with wife and family, the roving life was no longer easy, and the blank, the lodge-house and the relief gave him the run of the country. There is no doubt that in the later stages of tramping, the system was much used as a means of making the artisan's equivalent of the grand tour; just as the emigration benefit frequently was.

Moreover, with the mechanization of certain crafts, a new incentive to travel appeared, and caused bitter complaints during the Great Depression.[82] Instead of being fully trained as an all-round craftsman, the young man would be set on to man's work as an 'improver' – on less than the full wage. If he wanted to earn a man's wage, he had to take a job in another shop or another town, where only his ability to do the work, rather than his lack of full journeyman status, would count; though of course this sort of movement would be only very faintly reflected in the tramp statistics.

V

Nevertheless, in spite of such offsetting factors, there is little doubt that tramping, in the old sense, grew less. Why?

Let us consider the decline in depression travel first. Sometime between the 1840s and the 1870s a profound change took place in the attitude of the compositors to unemployment. The Typographical Delegate Conference in 1849 heard the argument that tramping was essential since a man with a large family could neither move easily nor emigrate; a contention which assumed that migration was the necessary answer to bad trade.[83] Thirty-eight years later the Manchester compositors, on the contrary, defended the idea of the newly introduced out-of-work dole by the argument that it would 'enable members to stay in various towns awaiting the call for their labour, keep them and their families together, and prevent members from being vagabondized by hawking their labour round the country'; in fact on the opposite assumption.[84] Put crudely, we have here the difference between men who have accepted the trade cycle as the typical form of depression, both national and transitory, and men who have not. But this was a novel point of view. As Labrousse has shown, the cyclical crisis was not, so far as the bulk of workers were concerned, the typical one till well into the nineteenth century.[85] In any case, up to the 1850s its effects appeared to be overlaid by those of other kinds of crisis, generating unemployment which could not be solved by staying put: e.g., the technological changes which broke up older forms of industrial craftsmanship. Moreover, what we may call the non-capitalist sector of the economy long remained large enough, and the capitalist sector localized and diversified enough, to make temporary migration appear a feasible escape from slumps. The mason, hit by depression in Norwich, could reasonably hope to find temporary employment in the small East Anglian towns;[86] the engineer could feel that the next town on his tramp route might not suffer from poor trade.[87] Only in the major depressions did the national character of the slump assert itself, as the traveller found himself launched on the heart-breaking treks which the statistics record.* Hence the capital importance of the hungry 1840s in the break-up of the system; though the conditions which made tramping appear feasible survived, on a smaller scale, long after. Again, an age whose mouthpiece was Cobbett would hardly yet regard depressions as temporary interruptions of triumphant economic expansion, which would pass if only one sat tight for a few months. We may debate how and when the transition took place, but we could hardly expect the optimistic view to be widely popular among workers before the 1850s.

The pendulum was later to swing too far. Both in the Great Depression and the inter-war depression we find trade unions almost exhausting their funds in the belief that these were the usual slumps, which would rapidly pass. The dogged reluctance to migrate of workers in depressed areas between the wars may well reflect the last survivals of this faith in the capacity of the economic system to right itself in all circumstances. It would be wrong, however, to dwell exclusively on this faith in British expansion. In so far as the innovations of the early 1850s – static out-of-work pay, etc. – meant a recognition of the trade cycle, it marked an important stage in the education of the labour movement; the recognition that the capitalist economy was not something to be sidestepped, but had to be dealt with by understanding its specific laws of motion.

* An extreme case from the 1840s: a compositor drew a London card on 1 March 1848, returning just under a year later. He had tramped to Brighton and round the south coast to Bristol, thence via Birmingham, Liverpool and Carlisle to Edinburgh, to Stranraer, Belfast, Dublin and nineteen Irish towns, returning to London via Liverpool, Yorkshire and Cambridge. Relieved in seventy towns, he had worked in three.

This new, and more mature, attitude towards the economic system explains most of the decline in the tramping of the out-of-work. It does not wholly account for the decline in other forms of mobility. Three possible causes of this are perhaps worth mentioning.

The nature of industrial expansion – the increasing size of the labour market on the one hand, the change in tempo on the other – discouraged the tramp. The effect of the former is neatly brought out by the Stonemasons' figures. In 1849 their union considered only four towns worth more than a single day's stay in search of work – London, Manchester, Liverpool and Birmingham. By 1887 there were forty-eight such towns. Table III summarizes the process, as reflected in the various editions of the union's tramp laws. [87a]

Table III. *Towns in which tramping Stonemasons were allowed to stay more than one day*

Year	Number	Remarks
1849	4	2 days
1853	4	3 days in London
1855	6 ⎫	
1862	7 ⎪	
1868	11 ⎬	2, 3 or 4 days
1871	20 ⎪	
1875	29 ⎭	
1887	48	

Evidently one might expect tramping masons to settle locally, for a time at least; to travel shorter distances, or more directly from one main centre to the next; and local ones to feel less often obliged to go on the road. The analogous effect of a slackening tempo of expansion, under certain circumstances, is equally well brought out in Lawrence's 1897 survey.[88] In that year it was estimated that out of eleven trades in Leeds nine had a majority of members recruited locally; out of seven in Bradford, six had. But in Sheffield and Birmingham, which were still in a more effervescent stage of industrial expansion, only three trades out of twelve and three out of ten respectively were mainly composed of native townsmen. The more sluggish the current of expansion, the smaller the number of tramping artisans swept into it.

The second force making for greater immobility was the decline of casualism, the inevitable concomitant of small-scale competitive industry in the *laissez-faire* market.[89] To what extent casualism (or, what is much the same, persistent under-employment for a section of the labour force) decreased, we do not yet know; but a tendency to decrease from the latter part of the century is observable, though the subject still awaits investigation.

The third factor is the growing specialization of the apprenticed artisan. The ideal of the early craftsman, with his all-round training, capable, like the old millwright, of turning his hand to every task in the trade in any part of the country, could be maintained only for a steadily diminishing proportion of the trade. Perhaps there was self-interest in the complaints that Bradford bricklayers could not be admitted to the union, because they were only half-trained, and, if transferred to other towns, could not be expected to earn the full rate;[90] or about the inferior training of engineers from the West Country, or the Yorkshire textile towns. Yet there was some truth in them. Even the men whose specialization did not indicate a decline in skill were affected. In the mid-eighteenth century the skilled woollen workers of Yorkshire and the West Country had been organized in one federation; at the end of the nineteenth, the Yorkshire General Textile Workers Union refused to organize the Stroud Valley, though invited to do so; so little did the two areas now seem to have in common. In the 1850s, shipyard and other boilermakers were in the same union; but had the utmost difficulty in understanding one another's problems.[91] Whether such specialization was one of training or business structure, it probably made the tramping system, on balance, seem less important even to many of its old supporters.

But as the old reasons for tramping lost their force, the opposition to it grew increasingly loud. The tramping section of a given trade included, besides good men with migratory habits, casuals relying on catching the peak demands in various places, also a very large number of the marginal and sub-standard workers; the first to be sacked, the last to be set on. A generation of artisans imbued with prudence and self-help grew steadily less enthusiastic about subsidizing what it felt to be its black sheep. Already in the 1840s and 1850s tension between tramping and non-tramping compositors was marked.[92] If the system survived so long, it was largely because the number of casuals was large enough to establish an important vested interest in it; the Manchester Typographical Society was riven by a major crisis when it tried to abolish it in 1851.[93] As a speaker at the 1856 delegate meeting put it, 'he knew men who had been on the road ever since he was an apprentice. It was impossible to end tramping because of the vast number of incorrigible characters in the profession.'[94] 'It was,' said another speaker, 'admitted on all hands that tramping converted good men into bad ones.'[95] It was equally obvious, as the Plasterers noted in 1879, that tramp relief benefited the foot-loose section of the trade (who were, *ceteris paribus*, not likely to be the best and most desirable workers) proportionately far more than the majority.[96] Thus the hostility to tramping which observers noted in the 1890s and 1900s is easy to understand.[97] Few unions actually abolished it – though the London and Scottish Typographers did so before the century ended; but since it grew steadily less important, this was unnecessary. Few, however, mourned its final disappearance in the decade of the First World War.

VI

One question must still be asked. What effect had a system of such organized mobility on variations in local labour conditions? Certain of the old tramping trades must, in their heyday, have come close to the classical ideal of a perfectly mobile labour force. Ought not therefore tramping to have led to a levelling of conditions in the area it covered? Unfortunately, there is no way of proving this. In the first place, the 'labour conditions' which may be held to determine a worker's choice between jobs include a great many variables, of which only one or two – standard time- or piece-rates, or standard working hours – are readily comparable. These, taken by themselves, may be more misleading than revealing.* In the second place, such wage and hour statistics as we possess before the last quarter of the century – even for well-documented trades like printing – rarely provide full enough comparable time-series to stand much analysis. Lastly, the small levelling effects of tramping (if any) are utterly swamped by other factors; some making for standardization, like the new habit of collective bargaining between employers' associations and trade unions over wide areas;[98] some not necessarily so, like the pace of industrial expansion.*

It may be that closer analysis will bring out some measurable effects

---

* Even figures for actual weekly earnings, virtually non-existent before the end of the century, do not allow us to judge the very important element of regularity of work, of control over working conditions and the general status which goes with it, of promotion prospects and traditional factors, all of which help the worker to choose between alternative jobs, where he is free to do so.

of tramping; thus we do find slightly greater uniformity among the markedly migratory masons in the north of England than among the bricklayers, though this is probably too small to be significant. It may also be that fuller figures about the old-fashioned skilled and closed trades, which had a longish tramping tradition by the middle of the nineteenth century, would reveal a more striking tendency to level conditions.[99] But the difficulty of measuring the tramping craftsman's influence should not lead us to underrate it. We know that he spread trade unionism, founding local branches on his travels;[100] sometimes indeed head offices would deliberately try to bridge exceptionally long stages by founding relief stations or branches. We also know that the traveller acted as a link between different areas, passing on information about local wage-rates, advising on the best times to start a wage-movement, a walking encyclopaedia of comparative trade-union knowledge.[101] To what extent did 'union stereotypes' – standardized forms of demand, the content of which was filled in by local negotiation – travel along the established tramp routes?

We do not know, since the working rules or by-laws of local unions have not been much studied;[101a] yet what we know is suggestive. Those of the Sheffield bricklayers, for instance, fixed a standard working week of $49\frac{1}{2}$ hours in the early twentieth century. Most of the West Riding towns had the same standard week; but it was also in force across the Pennines, in the Ribble valley, along the Lancashire coast north and south of the Ribble estuary, from Merseyside to Blackpool and Fleetwood; and in a ribbon of towns from the Ribble via Darwen to Bolton. The rest of the Lancashire bricklayers worked quite different hours – 53 or 54 per week.[102] Or let us take another Sheffield rule, fixing extra payment for workers on culverts, sewage-work and chimney stacks. Rules of this kind, in a rather standardized form, appear in working agreements only in certain parts of the country – Yorkshire, east Midlands, the north-east (though such payments were not confined to those regions).[102a] We may even observe them on their travels; thus they reached Tyneside somewhere around 1890.†
How far did the flow of tramping artisans, moving along accustomed

---

* Thus, between 1850 and 1870, the weekly time-rates of jobbing compositors in the north-east rose very rapidly; those in the rural south-west, very little. Compared with these major movements, the small effects of tramping mobility are almost impossible to determine.

† In Newcastle they appear in 1893, in Sunderland in 1894, as revised rule editions show.

routes, determine the directions in which such formulae travelled? Again we do not know, for the network of such tracks is difficult to trace through the rise and fall of local union branches. Underneath this flux, however, we can sometimes discover, faintly, the customary ground plan; perhaps in those public houses which long familiarity has named after a trade. In 1849, one-fifth of the stonemasons' lodges or relieving stations were, after all, still held in 'Masons' Arms', 'Bricklayers' Arms' and 'Carpenters' Arms'. Between then and 1859 'Masons' Arms' were used – not necessarily continuously – in at least twenty different towns.[103] We should do well to remember these tool-carrying journeymen, tramping along routes, putting up at lodge-houses which had been fixed by the usage of generations of their predecessors.

Much of this is speculation. What is less speculative is the hard fact that mobility did not, and could not, eliminate very marked local discrepancies, even within small regions. The compositors are a case in point. We need not even consider the variations between district wage-rates, which were extremely large.[104] Let us merely remind ourselves of the proposal made by the Birmingham branch, as late as 1891, that one uniform rate should be established for all branches within six miles' radius of any large printing centre – hardly an excessive distance. The proposal was turned down as impracticable, with very little discussion.[105] Another debate at the same delegate meeting illustrates the difficulties of standardization through mere mobility even more clearly. Should the travelling printer, it was asked, claim his home rate if that of the town in which he found himself was lower? In theory everyone agreed that he should. In practice all sorts of difficulties were raised. How could Sheffield men get their rate in Chesterfield? How could the valley printers in South Wales be expected to find the extra five shillings a week to pay travelling Cardiff men? Was it not better for the Manchester man in Preston to take the lower Preston rate than the even lower Manchester out-of-work benefit?

No doubt a mass exodus from low-wage centres, a mass influx of organized men refusing to work below the rate, might have levelled conditions. But in the nature of things this could rarely happen. Let us take the extreme example of the compositors in 1841–2, when the number of travellers was double the total combined union membership – say, at a guess, two or three times the number of regularly employed members. Let us assume that these 7,000 odd tramps circulated among only forty branches instead of the seventy-two which existed in 1850. Then, on an average, each branch might expect to receive something like three tramps a week, nothing like enough to affect the local labour market in normal circumstances.[106] The very fact that well-organized tramping spread the surplus men thinly over a wide area, a defensive measure, made it difficult to use the system for aggressive purposes. Moreover, the flow of tramps did not spread evenly across a sort of plain, but was forced through a limited number of narrow channels – the local employers. Outside building and contracting, where a multiplicity of small firms and fluctuating jobs, or a smaller number of extremely large undertakings, made conditions more fluid,[107] there was thus little possibility of levelling wages seriously by mere mobility. The willingness of tramping artisans to move from less to more attractive centres was not in doubt. A large enough proportion of them was prepared, at some stage of their career at any rate, to behave like economic men. But their ability to do so depended on the absorptive capacity of the desirable town. Short of a sudden great expansion of general printing in Birmingham, the compositors of Smethwick or Halesowen, however willing, could only move there as and when jobs were vacant. Such levelling as took place must therefore have been a slow, gradual, long-term and not very startling affair.

Even if large expansions took place, it was not easy to use them for a systematic general levelling-up under the conditions of the mid-century. The compositors did consider whether to use the repeal of the paper duties, which was expected to lead to the foundation of numerous provincial papers, to establish a national news-rate. They found themselves unable to do more than suggest a standard percentage increase over whatever rate was already in force locally.[108] The Boilermakers – in their *laissez-faire* period – even had to retreat. Their original plan to establish uniform methods of overtime and night-shift payments all over the country broke down on the hostility of the lodges; and between 1842 and the beginning of district and national negotiation in the 1870s and 1880s each locality was entirely autonomous.[109] It was not the free market mechanism which levelled labour conditions in Britain – except within a very small local labour market.

(1951)

POSTSCRIPT

There has been no systematic treatment of the tramping system since the publication of this paper, but various histories of trade unions and other organizations published since then provide additional details. Cf., in particular A. E. Musson, *The Typographical Association* (Oxford 1954) which discusses the subject fully and ably, as any history of the printing trade must, and P. H. J. Gosden, *The Friendly Societies in England 1815–75* (Manchester 1961) esp. 76–7 and Appendix A, which gives tramp statistics and arrangements for such bodies.

NOTES

1 Henry Broadhurst, *The Story of His Life Told by Himself* (1901), pp. 21–4; W. Kiddier, *The Old Trade Unions* (London 1930), chap. 1; see also S. and B. Webb, *History of Trade Unionism* (1st edn), pp. 438–9; W. Beveridge, *Unemployment* (1930 edn), pp. 241 ff.
  'Typographical Reminiscences' by an old 'Typo', *Typographical Circular*, June 1891, p. 8.
3 W. Kiddier, op. cit., pp. 16–17.
4 E.g., *Bye Laws of Operative Carpenters and Joiners Society of Birmingham* (est. May 1833), IV; probably part of the Operative Builders Union (Birmingham Public Library 239882).
5 Operative Stonemasons, Rules, 1871 and after; Operative Bakers, Rules, 1873.
5a Friendly Society of Operative House Carpenters and Joiners, 1836 Rules. (This is better known as the General Union of Carpenters and Joiners, now part of the Amalgamated Society of Woodworkers.)
6 S. and B. Webb, op. cit., p. 24; W. J. Ashley, *Surveys, Historic and Economic*, pp. 249–62.
7 Hoskins, *Industry, Trade and People in Exeter, 1688–1800* (Exeter 1935), pp. 58–61.
8 Lipson, *Economic History of England*, III, p. 393.
9 *A Short Essay Upon Trade in General by a Lover of his Country and the Constitution* (1741), pp. 40–1 (British Museum).
10 S. and B. Webb, op. cit., pp. 32, 48.
11 Aspinall, *The Early English Trade Unions* (London 1949), pp. 76 ff.; Postgate, *The Builders' History* (London 1923), p. 25.
12 *The Memorial of the Journeymen Calico Printers and others connected with their Trade* (London 1804), pp. 12–13 (Goldsmith's Library).

13 *Select Committee on Artisans and Machinery* (1824), pp. 295–6.
14 Graham Wallas, *Life of Francis Place* (London 1898), p. 211.
15 S. and B. Webb, op. cit., pp. 68–9; J. Dunlop, *Drinking Usages of the United Kingdom* (1844 edn, pp. 128, 132, 168), also reports it among tailors and skinners, and implies it among glass-makers, jewellers, wood-turners and 28 metal crafts of the Birmingham type.
16 Unwin, *Industrial Organization in the Sixteenth and Seventeenth Centuries*, p. 227; Clapham, *Concise Economic History of Britain*, p. 261.
17 *The Book of English Trades* (1808) mentions it only among hatters and wool-combers; but this is obviously unreliable (1823 edn, 441).
18 F. Galton, *Select Documents . . . The Tailoring Trade* (London 1896), p. 3, for London; *A Satyrical Poem on the Society of Journeymen Tailors* (B.M. 1890 e 5 (169)) for Dublin, n.d., but probably 1726; for Edinburgh, D. M. Moir's *Life of Mansie Wauch, Tailor in Dalkeith* (Edinburgh 1828), p. 44.
19 F. Galton, op. cit., LXXXI and *passim*.
20 Place Papers (B.M. Add. MSS. 27799, 77). The Place Papers oddly enough contain very little information about tramping.
21 M. D. George, *London Life in the Eighteenth Century*, p. 293.
22 S. and B. Webb, op. cit., p. 24, n.
23 Ibid., p. 111, n. Certainly the only real sign of antiquity is among the wool-combers, who had 'a spare bench . . . always provided in the shop upon which people on the *tramp* may rest themselves' (*Book of English Trades*, loc. cit.).
24 Lipson, op. cit., p. 393.
25 D. C. Cummings, *History of the United Society of Boilermakers and Iron and Steel Shipbuilders* (Newcastle 1905), p. 31.
26 Steam-Engine Makers, 1846, revised Rules.
27 *Report of Proceedings of the Meeting of Delegates from the Provincial Typographical Association* (Manchester 1873), p. 15. The General Union of Carpenters specifically barred travel by coach or water, except across the Channel, for which 3s. 6d. was allowed (1836 Rules).
28 Henry Broadhurst, op. cit., p. 13.
29 Cf. William Lovett's *Autobiography* (1876), *Life of Sir William Fairbairn* (ed Pole, 1877), and C. Thomson's *Autobiography of an Artisan* (London 1847).
30 F. Galton, in S. and B. Webb, op. cit., p. 438.
31 Knoop and Jones, *The London Mason in the Seventeenth Century*, pp. 58–9, 62, for the smallness of our knowledge even in a well-

studied trade. Hence also the difficulty of using records largely about master-craftsmen to throw light on journeymen wage-earners – e.g., records of operative freemasons' lodges, such as those at Alnwick and Swalwell, described in W. Begemann's *Vorgeschichte u. Anfaenge d. Freimaurerei in England* (Berlin 1907), Knoop and Jones, *The Scottish Mason and the Mason Word* (1939), etc.

32 Aspinall, op. cit., pp. 75, 79.

33 'Rules and Orders to be Observed by a Friendly Society of Journeymen Carpenters and Joiners. . . . Est. July 12th 1808' (Birmingham Public Library), Rules I, XIII, XV. I am grateful to Mr Jack Corbett of Birmingham for supplying me with this reference.

34 *Centenary Souvenir of the Friendly Society of Ironfounders* (Manchester 1909), p. 20.

35 Aspinall, op. cit., p. 83. An example of unorganized tramping among shoemakers is to be found in the amusing *Sixty Years Gleanings from Life's Harvest*, by John Brown (Cambridge and London 1858), pp. 23–5, 44, to which Mr John Saltmarsh of King's College, Cambridge, has drawn my attention. Brown eventually opened a billiards saloon in Cambridge, after a chequered and, if we are to believe him, uniformly brilliant career.

36 S. and B. Webb, *English Poor Law History*, I, p. 336.

37 W. Kiddier, op. cit., pp. 16–17.

38 Some 900 certificates from Newark are printed in Thoroton Society, Record Series, vol. IX, pt. i: *A Miscellany* (1943). They cover the period 1697–1822.

39 Knoop and Jones, op. cit., pp. 9–18.

40 S. and B. Webb, *Industrial Democracy*, p. 75, for Dublin exclusiveness.

41 E.g., out of 105 Newark certificates for artisans and single men only a dozen come from outside Nottinghamshire and the neighbouring counties. See also in general A. Redford's *Labour Migration in England 1800–50*.

42 F. Galton, op. cit., LXXVII.

43 Paul Louis, *Histoire du Mouvement Syndical en France 1789–1910*, pp. 151 ff. But Vial's *Coutume Chapelière* (Paris 1941) suggests that, among hatters, rudimentary tramping arrangements were in being under the Restoration. On the relation between *compagnonnages* and trade unions, see E. Labrousse, *Le Mouvement Ouvrier et les Idées Sociales en France*, fasc. II, pp. 71–82 (Paris, Cent. d. Documentation Universitaire, 1948).

44 Cf. *The Trial of . . . Journeymen Hatters of Macclesfield* (Maccles-field and London 1806), in which much of the argument turned on whether local masters and men (*a*) knew what the rates of wages were in Stockport, or (*b*) ought to be affected by such knowledge (Goldsmith's Library).

45 Wadsworth and Mann, *The Cotton Trade and Industrial Lanca-shire*, p. 377, suggests tramping among shoemakers in the 1750s (S. and B. Webb, *History of Trade Unionism*, pp. 46, 51, 80).

46 *Surrey Apprenticeships 1711–31* (Surrey Record Soc. vol. XXX), XV, where it is estimated that about 40 per cent of apprentices came from outside the masters' town. Lesser towns would naturally also attract outsiders, but London's magnetism was exceptional. Many would return to the provinces after finishing their time, or in bad times (C. E. Howe, *The London Bookbinders 1780–1806* (1950), p. 29).

47 'Thomas Dunning's Reminiscences' (ed Chaloner) in *Trans. Lancs. Ches. Antiq. Soc.* (1947), LIX, p. 98.

48 The *Report on Trade Societies* (Social Science Association, 1860), pp. 141–6, gives an incomplete list.

49 Fred Bower, *Rolling Stonemason* (1936), pp. 45–6, an admirable description of the permanently tramping artisan; Aspinall, op. cit., p. 78, for the Bath shoemakers in 1803: 'Sir, I am ordered to inform you that those men . . . who can leave town are prepar-ing as fast as possible, and some are gone already'; Dunning's 'Reminiscences', op. cit., pp. 101 ff., for the good use made of this technique by the Nantwich shoemakers.

50 S. and B. Webb, *Industrial Democracy*, p. 162.

51 Higenbottam, *Our Society's History* (Manchester, 1939), p. 18.

52 S. and B. Webb, *Industrial Democracy*, pt. II, chap. I, *passim*.

53 Ellic Howe, *The London Compositor* (1947), p. 226. Hostility even in the 1820s is recorded in C. M. Smith's *A Workingman's Way in the World, being the Autobiography of a Journeyman Printer* (London 1853), pp. 13–14.

54 *Centenary Souvenir*.

55 *Typographical Circular* (February 1891), p. 10, quoted from the 1842 delegate meeting of the Northern Typographical Union. If the London compositors are omitted, the tramp-load was proportionately even heavier.

56 Higenbottam, loc. cit.

57 *Typographical Circular* (June 1891), p. 8. The masons paid 6*d*. a day relief until the 1880s, and estimated the cost of a night's lodging at another 6*d*.

58 Annual reports, and various editions of revised Rules.

59 *Centenary Souvenir*, p. 36. Immediately claims for sick pay, which had been inflated as the result of the absence of static out-of-work relief, fell sharply.

60 J. B. Jefferys, *The Story of the Engineers* (1945), pp. 19–21.

61 Provincial printing union documents of the period are available in the full MSS. excerpts of the Webbs and their secretaries, Coll. EA, XXX, in the London School of Economics Library; cf. there the 1844 Rules of the National Typographical Association, and the debate on tramping in the Provincial Typographical Association 1849 delegate meeting.

62 Provincial Typographical Association, 1856, delegate meeting; monthly branch reports.

63 Cf. the calculation of M. and J. Jefferys: 'The Wages, Hours and Trade Customs of the Skilled Engineer in 1861', *Econ. Hist. Rev.* (1947), XVII, 29–30. Less well-organized unions were nevertheless highly representative of the general body of workers in their trade, in such towns as they covered; cf. the calculations of Archibald Neill (British Association, 1875) about the degree of unionization in the Bradford building trade. For the early 1890s we possess the invaluable on-the-spot surveys made by the Webbs for their History, Coll. EA, IV (L.S.E. Library).

64 Reports of Friendly Society of Ironfounders, Amalgamated Society of Tailors, Provincial Typographical Association, esp. P.T. Circular, May 1877. The Tailors' figures for 1869–77 come from the *Daily Chronicle*, 6 February 1879 – obviously communicated by the union, for they are not readily calculable from its reports. Most of these sources are in the Howell Collection, Bishopsgate Institute, London. It should be noted that the membership of the Provincial Typographical Association is not quite the same as that of the Mileage Relief Association set up to look after its tramping in 1861. Some local societies affiliated to one but not the other. This does not substantially affect the nature of the figures.

65 J. B. Jefferys, op. cit., p. 61. I am indebted to the officers of the Plumbing Trades Union for permission to consult their reports for the 1860s, when the union had for a while static out-of-work pay.

66 *The Life and Labours of George Odger* (London 1877).

67 D. C. Cummings, op. cit., pp. 62, 156.

68 W. C. Grubb, *John Burns* (1908).

69 Joseph Arch, *The Story of His Life, Told by Himself* (1898), p. 40; G. Edwards, *From Crowscaring to Westminster* (1922), p. 27.

70 In S. and B. Webb, *History of Trade Unionism*, p. 438.

71 *R.C. on the Housing of the Working Classes* (1884–5), XXX, 3707, 3754, for such builders in London, or George Lansbury, *My Life* (1928), chap. I, for such a semi-nomadic family.

72 *Conflicts of Capital and Labour* (1878, 2nd ed.), p. 141.

73 J. B. Jefferys, op. cit., p. 128.

73a Half-yearly reports of Provincial Typographical Association; annual reports of Steam-Engine Makers.

74 United Operative Plumbers, 2nd Quarterly Report, 1900: 'Formerly when men were employed, there was a general desire to retain their services for a reasonable length of time. Now there is no regard shown, in some cases men are set on one day and discharged the next.' Ibid., 2nd Quarterly Report, 1902.

75 The *R.C. on the Housing of the Working Classes* discusses some of these problems; but with the exception of workmen's trains, we know little about the changes in the journey to work before the twentieth century.

76 The carpenters were prepared to advance fares up to 300 miles; though they halved this during the Great Depression (Rules of Amalgamated Society of Carpenters and Joiners, 1874, 1886).

77 E. Beesly, *The Amalgamated Society of Carpenters and Joiners* (London 1867), pp. 5–6.

78 H. Llewellyn-Smith, 'Influx of Population into East London', in C. Booth, *Life and Labour*, III, pp. 74, 96; N. B. Dearle, *Problems of Unemployment in the London Building Trade* (1907).

79 F. W. Lawrence, *Local Variations in Wages* (1899). The results of his inquiry among trade unions are given very fully, pp. 56–80. They cover: bricklayers, masons, carpenters, plasterers, plumbers, painters, compositors, boilermakers, engineers, bookbinders, lithographers and ironfounders.

80 H. Llewellyn-Smith, op. cit., pp. 129 ff., esp. p. 134. *R.C. on Poor Law*, Appendix IX, p. 729, flatly claims that most countrymen migrating to London come to known jobs. But this does not exclude an element of uncertainty, as Will Thorne's experience shows (*My Life's Battles*, n.d., pp. 49–53).

81 G. Barnes, *From Workshop to War Cabinet* (1923), p. 20.

82 *R.C. on Depression of Trade* (*Parl. Papers* XXII, 1886), p. 8 (Dukinfield Engineers), p. 9 (Glasgow, St Rollox Engineers), p. 12 (Neath Engineers), p. 18 (Bury Ironfounders), etc.

83 Provincial Typographical Association, 1849, delegate meeting.

84 Provincial Typographical Association, 1872, delegate meeting, p. 18.

85 Cf. his *Crise de l'Ancien Régime*; also the valuable chapter of the Sorbonne course already quoted.

86 Broadhurst, op. cit., chap. II.
87 Cf. the great variations in local prosperity indicated even in the 1880s in the trade union answers to the *R.C. on Depression of Trade*; also the great wage variations between neighbouring localities, e.g., Wakefield and Barnsley (Coll. EA, IV: Barnsley Trades Council, L.S.E. Library).
87a Operative Stonemasons' Rules of these dates.
88 Op. cit., pp. 56–79.
89 W. Beveridge, *Unemployment, A Problem of Industry* (1909), chap. V, for a general discussion of it.
90 Coll. EA, X, 255 (L.S.E. Library).
91 Cummings, op. cit., p. 61.
92 Provincial Typographical Association, 1856, delegate meeting *passim*; cf. also: 'You know what the condition of the tramp is. The man's appearance is a discredit to the profession he has spent seven years in acquiring the art of. . . . As a class those who tramp are little short of lost creatures' (1849, delegate meeting). W. E. Adams, *Memoirs of a Social Atom* (London 1903), vol. I, chap. xxxi, sketches some of these characters.
93 Minutes of Manchester Typographical Society, excerpted in Coll. EA, XXX, pp. 58–9 (L.S.E. Library); also *Manchester Typographical Society Centenary Souvenir* (Manchester 1898).
94 Loc. cit., p. 7.
95 Ibid., p. 6.
96 National Association of Operative Plasterers, *Annual Report for 1879* (Birmingham 1880). Out-of-work pay would 'be more beneficial to a greater number of our members who cannot travel than that of travelling is to those who do'.
97 Beveridge, op. cit. (1930 edn), pp. 241–5; Howell, op. cit., pp. 141–2, for a typical trade-union official view.
98 This still awaits study. *Industrial Democracy* has not much about it; J. W. F. Rowe, *Wages in Practice and Theory* (1928), hardly goes back beyond 1906. But in important industries like ship-building significant developments took place in the 1870s and 1880s.
99 E.g., W. Kiddier, op. cit., p. 124. But these were piece-prices, which are always more easily standardized than time-rates, since they have less direct relation to weekly earnings.
100 E.g., of compositors in the Potteries, an important stage between Lancashire and Birmingham (Coll. EA, XXX, 77, L.S.E. Library).
101 F. Bower, op. cit., pp. 45–6.
101a The most accessible collection of these, in printed form, is that

of the bricklayers in the L.S.E. Library, which may be supplemented from the Trade Circular of the Operative Bricklayers Society (London Order).

102 Details in 'Standard Time Rates', 1909. In some towns only 49 hours were worked.

102a Working Rules of the Operative Bricklayers Society (London Order) in Jarrow, Hull, Loughborough, Newcastle and Gateshead, Sheffield, Bridlington, Leicester, Lincoln, Nottingham, Sunderland. Similar rules, but applying primarily to rather specialized local forms of work, pit-shafts, tide-works, work connected with the needle and fish-hook trade, and not as uniform in phrasing as the others, occur in Plymouth, Portsmouth, Redditch and Rotherham. It should be noted that the collection of fifty or so rules I have analysed is poor for southeast Lancashire, but representative enough for other parts of the country.

103 Rules of Operative Stonemasons' Society, 1849, 1852, 1859. The towns are: Bristol, Leeds, Penrhyn, Princetown, Aberdare, Derby, Darwen, Scarborough, Stapleton, York, Bradford-on-Avon, Grantham, Liverpool, Retford, Warrington, Neath, Southport, Old Swan (Birmingham?), Leamington, Fishponds (possibly the same as the Bristol 'Arms'). Other 'Builders' Arms' used were in Brighton, Birmingham, Cardiff, Chester-le-Street and London.

104 E. Edwards, 'The Disease and the Remedy' (Prize Essay of the London Society of Compositors, London, 1850), quoted in Howe, op. cit., pp. 305–7, gives very full wage figures. He estimates Scottish rates at 12–19s. a week, north of England 18–22s., south-east 18–24s., south-west 18s., and London 25s.

105 Typographical Association, *Proceedings of Delegate Meeting* (Manchester 1891), pp. 67–8, 75–6. The Birmingham problem, typically enough, arose out of an arbitration award making a rise conditional on a similar one in the surrounding and lower-paid towns. Birmingham immediately started a local unionizing campaign (Coll. EA, XXX, pp. 73–5; Coll. EA, IV, p. 118 (Dudley), pp. 294–8 (West Bromwich, Oldbury, Smethwick)).

106 But the strain could be much worse. An informant of J. Dunlop, *Drinking Usages of the United Kingdom* (7th edn, London 1844), p. 132, reports a branch of Skinners, twenty-five strong, who received up to thirty tramps a month; doubtless in 1841–2.

107 Rowe, op. cit., pp. 65–7.

108 Slatter and Hackett, *The Typographical Association, A Fifty Years Record* (1899), p. 39. Not much greater was the progress in

standardizing piece-rates undertaken in 1891 (delegate meeting, pp. 8, 52–3). Only a local correlation with time-earnings was recommended.

109 Cummings, op. cit., p. 33. Compare the highly standardized Port Rules for ship repairing and maintenance work in the 1890s.

5

The British Standard of Living 1790-1850*

THE DEBATE ABOUT THE STANDARD OF LIVING under early industrialism has now continued for some thirty years. Among academic historians, in Britain at any rate, the pendulum has swung away from the classical view, held by enquirers and historians of all political views[1] until the appearance of Clapham's *Economic History of Modern Britain*. It is today heterodox to believe that early industrialization was a catastrophe for the labouring poor of this or other countries, let alone that their standard of living declined. This article proposes to show that the currently accepted view is based on insufficient evidence, and that there is some weighty evidence in favour of the old view. So far as possible, I proposed to refrain from using the type of evidence (Royal Commissions, observers' accounts) which has been criticized as biased and unrepresentative. I do not in fact believe it to be unreliable. It is dangerous to reject the consensus of informed and intelligent contemporaries, a majority of whom, as even critics admit,[2] took the dark view. It is illegitimate to assume that even reformers who mobilize public support by drawing attention to dramatic examples of a general evil, are not in fact attacking a general evil. But the classical case can be based, to some extent, on quantitative evidence, and, in order to avoid irrelevant argument, I shall rely mainly on it. For the sake of convenience the classical (Ricardo-Malthus-Marx-Toynbee-Hammond) view will be called the *pessimistic*, the modern (Clapham-Ashton-Hayek) view the *optimistic* school.

* I am obliged to the staff of the Customs House, Goldsmith's and School of Hygiene and Tropical Medicine libraries for help, and to Prof. T. S. Ashton and Mr. John Savile for comments and criticisms.

I

An initial observation is perhaps worth making. There is no *a priori* reason why the standard of living should rise markedly under early industrialism. An initial rise must almost certainly take place, on demographic grounds,[3] but it may be very slight indeed and need not be lasting once the new rhythm of population increase has been set up. It should be remembered that the decrease in mortality which is probably primarily responsible for the sharp rise in population need be due not to an *increase* in per capita consumption per year, but to a *greater regularity of supply*; i.e., to the abolition of the periodic shortages and famines which plagued pre-industrial economies and decimated their populations. It is quite possible for the industrial citizen to be worse fed in a normal year than his predecessor, so long as he is more regularly fed.

This is not to deny that the increase in production, which greatly exceeded that of population, in the long run brought about an absolute improvement in material living standards. Whatever we may think of the relative position of labourers compared to other classes, and whatever our theory, no serious student denies that the bulk of people in North-western Europe were materially better off in 1900 than in 1800. But there is no reason why living standards should improve at all times. Whether they do, depends on the distribution of the additional resources produced among the population. But we know that under early industrialism (a) there was no effective mechanism for making the distribution of the national income more equal and several for making it less so, and (b) that industrialization under then prevailing conditions almost certainly required a more burdensome diversion of resources from consumption than is theoretically necessary, because the investment mechanism was inefficient. A large proportion of accumulated savings were not directly invested in industrialization at all, thus throwing a much greater burden of savings on the rest of the community. In countries with an acute shortage of capital a depression of popular living standards was almost inevitable. In countries such as Britain, where plenty of capital was theoretically available, it was likely, simply because much of what was available was not in fact pressed into the most useful investment. At best, therefore, we should expect improvements in the standard of living to be much slower than they might have been, at worst we should not be surprised to find deterioration.

There is no reason to assume that in countries with a rapidly rising population and a large reserve of rural or immigrant labour, shortage as such is likely to push up real wages for more than limited groups of workers. It may be argued that industrialization and urbanization automatically improve living-standards in any case, because industrial wages normally tend to be higher than non-industrial or rural ones, and urban consumption standards than village ones. But (a) we are not merely concerned with the incomes of one section of the labouring poor, but of all. We must not isolate any group of the labouring poor, whether better or worse off, unless it forms a majority of the population. Moreover (b) the argument is not always correct. Thus while in many continental countries social indices, like mortality and literacy, improve faster in town than country, in Britain this was not always so. Lastly (c) we must beware of interpreting the qualitative differences between urban and rural, industrial and pre-industrial life *automatically* as differences between 'better' and 'worse'. Unless we bring imponderables into the argument, townsmen are not necessarily better off than countrymen; and as the Hammonds showed, imponderables can also be thrown on the pessimistic side of the scale.

One final point must be made. Optimists often tend to exonerate capitalism from blame for such bad conditions as they admit to have existed. They argue that these were due to insufficient private enterprise, to hangovers from the pre-industrial past or to similar factors. I do not propose to enter into such metaphysical arguments. This chapter is concerned primarily with fact, and not with accusation, exculpation or justification. What would have happened if all citizens in Europe in 1800 had behaved as textbooks of economics told them to, and if there had been no obstacles or frictions, is not a question for historians. They are, in the first instance, concerned with what did happen. Whether it might have happened differently, is a question which belongs to another argument.

II

We may now consider the views of the 'optimistic' school. Its founder, Clapham, relied primarily on calculations of real wages which showed them to rise in the period 1790 to 1850 at times when contemporaries, and the historians who followed them, assumed that the poor were getting poorer. On the money side these calculations depended mainly on the well-known collections of wage-data by

Bowley and Wood. On the cost-of-living side they depended almost wholly on Silberling's index.[4] It is not too much to say that Clapham's version of the optimistic view stood or fell by Silberling.*

It is now generally realized that the statistical basis of Clapham's conclusions is too weak to bear its weight; especially as the argument for the period 1815–40 odd turns largely on the question whether the curve of the cost-of-living sloped downwards more steeply than that of money-wages, it being admitted that both tended to fall. Clearly in extreme cases, e.g., when prices fall and wages rise or the other way round, even a thin index may be reliable. In this case, however, the possibilities of error are much greater.

Now our figures for money-wages are chiefly time-rates for skilled artisans (Tucker, Bowley). About piece-workers we know very little. Since we also know little about the incidence of unemployment, short-time, etc., our figures cannot be regarded as a reliable reflection of actual earnings. (Clapham, by the way, makes no attempt to discover the extent of unemployment, though mentioning the absence of data about it. His index to vol. I does not even contain the word.) For large sections of the 'labouring poor' – the unskilled, those whose income cannot be clearly expressed in terms of regular money-wages, we are almost completely in the dark. We therefore possess nothing which would be regarded as an adequate index of money-wages today. The weakness of the cost-of-living figures is equally great. Silberling has been criticized by Cole, by Judges, and most recently by Ashton, the most eminent of the 'optimists'.[5] For practical purposes it is no longer safe to generalize about the working-class cost-of-living on this basis. Indeed, practical, as distinct from methodological, doubt has been thrown on such attempts to construct real wage indices for the first half of the nineteenth century. Thus Ashton's figures for retail prices in some Lancashire towns, 1790–1830, show nothing like the post-war fall which Silberling would lead one to

---

* To a slight extent it also depended on the choice of period. Today, when most economic historians would place the turning-point between the post-Napoleonic period of difficulties and the 'golden age' of the Victorians rather earlier than was once fashionable – in 1842–3 rather than in 1848 or thereabouts – few would deny that things improved rapidly in Britain (though not in Ireland) from the earlier forties on, the crisis of 1847 interrupting a period of progress rather than initiating it. But the admission that the middle and later forties were a time of improvement does not imply that the whole of the period 1790–1842 or 1815–42 was, though this is sometimes assumed in careless discussion, as by Chaloner and Henderson, *History Today*, July 1956.

expect.[6] Tucker's index of London artisan real wages shows the major improvement in their position in the period 1810–43 to have occurred in 1813–22.[7] But, as we shall see, these were years of stagnant or falling per capita consumption of meat in London, and of sugar and tobacco nationally; facts which hardly support the assumption of rising real wages.

In defence of Clapham it ought to be said that he was more cautious in his conclusion than some of the optimistic vulgarizers have been. Thus Silberling's index itself shows living-costs to have remained fairly steady for about twenty years after 1822, rising and falling about a level trend. Not until after 1843 did they drop below the 1822 level. Tucker's, a later index, shows that between 1822 and 1842 the real wages of London artisans rose above the 1822 level in only four years, the average improvement for the whole period, even for them, being only about 5 or 6 per cent. The two decades of, at best, relative stagnation of real wages – which R. C. O. Matthews confirms for the 1830s[8] – are significant, though often omitted from the argument. In fact, one is bound to conclude that Clapham has had a surprisingly easy passage, thanks largely to the extreme feebleness of the reply of his chief opponent, J. L. Hammond,[9] who virtually accepted Clapham's statistics and shifted the argument entirely on to moral and other non-material territories.

However, today, the deficiencies of Clapham's argument have been admitted and the most serious of the optimists, Professor Ashton, has in fact abandoned it, though this fact has not always been realized.[10] Instead, he relies on arguments or assumption of three types. First, on various theoretical arguments designed to prove that a rise in real wages must have taken place. Second, on factual evidence of rising material prosperity – such as improvements in housing, food, clothing, etc. Third, on the – so far as one can judge – unsupported assumption that the part of the labouring population whose real wages improved must have been larger than the part whose real wages did not. It is admitted that conditions for part of the working population did not improve. I do not propose to discuss the first lot of arguments, since, if there is evidence that the standard of living did not improve significantly or at all at the relevant periods, they automatically fall to the ground.

It is perhaps worth observing how scanty the hard evidence for the optimistic view is today, when it can no longer rely on Clapham's type of support. It rests essentially on the sort of evidence adduced by

McCulloch, an early optimist, in 1839, though today it is often less detailed.[11] Now McCulloch's case[12] is built on the following foundations. The substitution of white bread for brown is shown by the known, but not measured, decline in the consumption of brown cereals since 1760, in Cornwall of barley-eating since 1800. But McCulloch's estimate that only 20,000 rye-eaters were left by 1839 is patently wild. (Incidentally, his source for Cornwall[13] seems to talk only of the St Austell area, not the whole county.) The increase in meat consumption rests on the assumed increase in the weight of livestock sold at Smithfield, the actual numbers of animals having only kept pace with the growth of London population since 1740–50. But (a), as we shall see, the number of beasts sold at Smithfield had *not* kept pace with London population growth, as McCulloch must have known quite well, and at least one contemporary did know.[14] Moreover, (b) the view that weight increased dramatically has been virtually put out of court by Fussell.[15] Lastly, (c) McCulloch's estimate of 800 lb as the contemporary carcass weight of beef was grossly inflated. Other estimates give it as 668 lb (1821), 630 lb (1836), 640 lb (Smithfield 1842),[16] while both Braithwaite Poole (1852) and the Smithfield butchers consulted on McCulloch's estimate in 1856 were also less sanguine.[17] For clothing, McCulloch relied on the fall of prices of cotton goods and not on direct evidence. For Scotland he gave a confident, but statistically undocumented, comparison between past and present. He did not mention potatoes, dairy produce, groceries, etc.

His statistical basis was thus slight, and his bias verged on the disingenuous. (The critics of industrialism were not the only ones to choose evidence to suit themselves.) Subsequent optimistic scholars have not investigated the evidence much further. Thus the data on meat consumption appear to have been almost totally neglected. Even Professor Ashton's paper on the standard of living, 1790–1830, perhaps the fullest recent discussion, and vastly more scholarly than McCulloch, rests on few and scattered data.[18]

The evidence is certainly too sketchy to sustain the assumption, which today appears to be fundamental to the optimistic view, that the proportion of the labouring population whose conditions improved must have been larger than the rest. There is, as we have seen, no theoretical reason for making this assumption about the period 1790–1840 odd. It is, of course, impossible to verify owing to the absence of adequate data on the British income structure at the time, but what we know about this structure in later periods (and in admittedly better-off periods at that) does not support it. As I have attempted to show at greater length elsewhere,[19] about 40 per cent of the industrial working class in later periods lived at or below the poverty-line, i.e., at or below subsistence level on the prevailing definitions of this concept. Perhaps 15 per cent belonged to a favoured stratum which was in a clear position to improve its real wages at almost all times. That is, the first group lived in what amounted to a permanently glutted labour market, the second in one of permanent relative labour scarcity, except during bad slumps. The rest of the labouring population was distributed between the two groups. Only if we assume *either* that in 1790–1850 the favoured stratum was markedly larger, the poor stratum markedly smaller than later *or* that at least five-sevenths of the intermediate stratum were more like than unlike the labour aristocracy, does the optimistic view, insofar as it is based on assumptions about income structure, hold good. This is not very plausible, and until there is more evidence for the optimistic assumption, there is no reason for making it. For the sake of brevity, I do not propose to enter further into the complex discussion of social stratification among the 'labouring poor' here.

It thus seems clear that the optimistic view is not based on as strong evidence as is often thought. Nor are there overwhelming theoretical reasons in its favour. It may, of course, turn out to be correct, but until it has been much more adequately supported or argued, there seems to be no major reason for abandoning the traditional view. In view of the fact that there is also statistical evidence tending to support that view, the case for its retention becomes stronger.

III

We may consider three types of evidence in favour of the pessimistic view: those bearing on (a) mortality and health, (b) unemployment and (c) consumption. In view of the weaknesses of wage and price data, discussed above, it is best not to consider them here; in any case actual consumption figures shed a more reliable light on real wages. However, we know too little about the actual structure of the population to isolate the movements of working-class indices from the rest of the 'labouring poor' and of other classes. But this would be troublesome only if the indices showed a fairly marked rise, which they do not. Since the 'labouring poor' clearly formed the majority of the population, a general index showing stability or deterioration is hardly compatible with a significant improvement of their situation, though it does not exclude improvement among a minority of them.

A. *Social indices*

Our best indices are mortality rates (average expectation of life, infantile, TB mortality, etc.), morbidity rates and anthropometric data. Unfortunately in Britain we lack any reliable anthropometric data such as the French, and any index of health such as the percentage of rejected recruits.* Nor have we any useful morbidity figures. The Friendly Societies, whose actuarial advisers made some useful calculations about sickness rates,[20] cannot be regarded as representative samples, since it is agreed that they included mainly the more prosperous or stably-employed workers; and in any case, as Farr (1839) demonstrates,[21] there is little enough evidence from them before that date. It is possible that work on hospital records may allow us to find out more about sickness trends, but too little is available at present for judgment.[22]

We must therefore rely on mortality rates. These have their limitatations,† though it has been plausibly argued that even the crudest of them – general mortality below the age of 50[23] – is a sensitive indicator of living standards. Still, a high or rising mortality rate, a low expectation of life, are not to be neglected. We need not be too much troubled by the known imperfections of the figures, at any rate where trends emerge over periods of time. In any case, the worst imperfection, the fact that births are less completely registered than deaths – thus swelling earlier figures for infant mortality – helps to correct a pessimistic bias. For as registration improves, recorded mortality rates also drop automatically on paper, though in fact they may change much less in reality.

The general movement of mortality rates is fairly well known. On

* We cannot assume that British service-men in this period, or prisoners, are a representative sample of the population.

† Since 1957 the traditional view of population change in this period has been very seriously criticised, especially by J. T. Krause, 'Changes in English Fertility and Mortality 1781-1850' (*Econ. Hist. Rev.* XI, 1958). However, for the time being one may still agree, with P. Deane and W. A. Cole (*British Economic Growth* 1688-1959, p. 125), that 'at present the evidence does not seem so overwhelming that we are justified in completely reversing the picture suggested by the crude statistics, defective as these undoubtedly are.'

71

theoretical grounds, such as those discussed by McKeown and Brown,[24] it is almost inconceivable that there was not a real fall in mortality rates due to improvements in living standards at the beginning of industrialization, at least for a while. General mortality rates fell markedly from the 1780s to the 1810s and thereafter rose until the 1840s. This 'coincided with a change in the age-distribution favourable to a low death-rate, namely an increase in the proportion of those in healthy middle life'.[25] The figures therefore understate the real rise in mortality rates, assuming the same age-composition throughout the period. The rise is said to have been due chiefly to higher infantile and youth mortality, especially in the towns, but figures for Glasgow 1821-35 suggest that there it was due primarily to a marked increase in the mortality of men of working age, greatest in the age-groups from 30 to 60.[26] Social conditions are the accepted explanation for this. Edmonds, who discusses the Glasgow figures, observed (1835) that 'this is just what might be expected to occur, on the supposition of the rising adult population possessing a lower degree of vitality than their immediate predecessors'.[27] On the other hand we must not forget that mortality rates did not improve drastically until very much later – say, until the 1870s or 1880s – and may therefore be less relevant to the movement of living standards than is sometimes supposed. (Alternatively, that living standards improved much more slowly after the 1840s than is often supposed.) Nevertheless, the rise in mortality rates in the period 1811-41 is clearly of *some* weight for the pessimistic case, all the more as modern work, especially the studies of Holland during and after World War II, tend to link such rates much more directly to the amount of income and food consumption than to other social conditions.*

B. *Unemployment*

There is room for much further work on this subject, whose neglect is rather inexplicable. Here I merely wish to draw attention to some scattered pieces of information which support a pessimistic rather than a rosy view.

Little as we know about the period before the middle 1840s, most

---

* Prof. McKeown of Birmingham has drawn my attention to these. The rise of Dutch death and sickness rates during and their fall after the war must have been due exclusively to variations in food consumption, since other social conditions – e.g., housing – did not improve seriously during the period when the rates declined.

students would agree that the real sense of improvement among the labouring classes thereafter was due less to a rise in wage-rates, which often remained surprisingly stable for years, or to an improvement in social conditions, but to the up-grading of labourers from very poorly to less poorly paid jobs, and above all to a decline in unemployment or a greater regularity of employment. In fact, unemployment in the earlier period had been heavy. Let us consider certain components and aspects of it.

We may first consider *pauperism*, the permanent core of poverty, fluctuating relatively little with cyclical changes – even in 1840–2.[28] The trends of pauperism are difficult to determine, owing to the fundamental changes brought about by the New Poor Law, but its extent is sufficiently indicated by the fact that in the early 'forties something like 10 per cent of the total population were probably paupers. For the sake of comparison, between 1850 and 1880 the ratio of paupers to total population was never higher than 5·7 per cent (1850). It averaged 4·9 in the 1850s and 4·6 in the 1860s. The paupers of the period with which we are concerned were not necessarily worse off than the rest, for Tufnell, in the Second Annual Report of the Poor Law Commissioners, estimated that farm-labourers ate perhaps 30 per cent less in crude weight of foodstuffs than paupers. This was also the case in depressed towns like Bradford-on-Avon, where in 1842 the average working-class consumption of meat was not two-thirds of the workhouse minimum.[29]

The impact of *structural* unemployment cannot be measured. Those who were most affected by it were often precisely those independent small craftsmen, out-workers or part-time workers whose sufferings, short of absolute catastrophe, were reflected in falling piece-prices, in under-employment, rather than in cessation of work. The sufferings of the largest group among them, those working the half-million or so handlooms[30] (which may have represented perhaps one and a quarter million or more citizens[31]) have been amply documented. If, taking the more modest figures of Gayer, Rostow and Schwartz, we bear in mind that in the course of the 1830s well over half these weavers abandoned their looms, we have some measure of the possible impact of structural unemployment in this occupation, though this is, of course, no guide to any other.

As to the impact of cyclical slumps or other periods of acute depression, we have a good deal of evidence for two of these (1826 and 1841–2) and scattered evidence for other dates.[32] The figures we possess naturally tend to some extent to overstate the distress, for particularly bad areas were more likely to attract attention than less hard-hit ones; especially in 1826, when our source is a relief committee. Nevertheless, the figures are so startling that they can bear a good deal of deflation. They suggest that in the hard-hit areas of Lancashire between 30 and 75 per cent of the total population might have been destitute in the course of this slump; in the woollen areas of Yorkshire, between 25 per cent and 100 per cent; in the textile areas of Scotland, between 25 per cent and 75 per cent. In Salford, for instance, half the population was wholly or partly out of work, in Bolton about one third, in Burnley at least 40 per cent.[33]

For the slump of 1841–2, which was almost certainly the worst of the century, our figures are more representative, for a great deal of information was collected at this time, not only for purposes of relief, but for purposes of political argument (notably by the Anti-Corn Law League). Moreover, several of these enquiries command confidence, being evidently based on serious and detailed surveys by hard-headed, statistically-minded local businessmen.

Ashworth's survey of Bolton may be summarized in the following Table I:

Table I. *Unemployment in Bolton 1842**

Source: H. Ashworth, 'Statistics of the present depression of trade in Bolton', *Journ. Stat. Soc.* V (1842), p. 74.

Trade	Total employed in 1836	Total employed whole or part-time in 1842	Percentage Unemployed
Mills	8124	3063 (full time)	60
Ironworkers	2110	1325 (short time)	36
Carpenters	150	24	84
Bricklayers	120	16	87
Stonemasons	150	50	66
Tailors	500	250	50
Shoemakers	80	40	50

It will be seen that unemployment of ironworkers in this industrial centre was higher than the national average for the Ironfounders' Union, which was then about 15 per cent.

* The percentages do not allow for the possible increases in the labour force since 1836, and thus overstate unemployment. But they may serve as an order of magnitude.

Again, in the Vauxhall Ward of Liverpool[34] a little over 25 per cent of smiths and engineers were unemployed, in Dundee[35] somewhat over 50 per cent of the mechanics and the shipbuilders. Slightly under 50 per cent of the Liverpool shoemakers, over half the Liverpool tailors, two-thirds of the London tailors[36] were unemployed, only 5 out of 160 Dundee tailors were in full work. Three-quarters of the plasterers, well over half the bricklayers in Liverpool, almost five-sixths of the masons, three-quarters of the carpenters, slaters, plumbers, etc., in Dundee had no work. Neither had half the 'labourers' and almost three-quarters of the women workers in the Liverpool ward. The following Table II summarizes various contemporary enquiries:

Table II. *Unemployment in some towns, 1841–2*

Town	Fit for work	Fully Employed	Partly	Unemployed
Liverpool, Vauxhall	4,814	1,841	595	2,378
Stockport	8,215	1,204	2,866	4,145
Colne	4,923	964	1,604	2,355
Bury	3,982	1,107	–	–
Oldham	19,500	9,500	5,000 (half-time)	5,000
Accrington (textiles)	3,738	1,389	1,622	727
Wigan	4,109	981	2,572	1,563

The list could be prolonged. (For some indices of skilled unemployment at this period see the preceding essay, *The Tramping Artisan*, pp. 41–9.)[37]

Such figures mean little, unless we remember what they implied for the standard of living. Clitheroe (normal population, 6,700, normal employment in the five main factories, 2,500) had 2,300 paupers in 1842; the Brontes' Haworth (population 2,400), 308.[38] 20 per cent of the population of Nottingham was on the Poor Law, 33 per cent of that of Paisley on charity.[39] 15–20 per cent of the population of Leeds had an income of less than *one shilling* per head per week;[40] over one-third of the families in the Vauxhall Ward of Liverpool had an income of less than five shillings a week, indeed most of them had no visible income at all.[41] 3,196 of the 25,000 inhabitants of Huddersfield had an average income of 8*d* per person per week. In Bradford, even in January 1843, 'many of the most respectable have long since pawned their watches and other valuables, and they have been unable to redeem them; and the clothes pawned are now seldom redeemed'.[42] In Stockport (where, as we have seen, unemployment ran at 50 per cent) the average weekly income of those *fully* employed was 7*s*. 6¼*d*., the average of those partly employed 4*s*. 7½*d*.[43]

The effect of such depressions on consumption can fortunately be measured. It was profound. In the Vauxhall ward of Liverpool total earnings had halved since 1835, meat consumption had halved, bread consumption had remained stable, oatmeal consumption had doubled, potato consumption had risen by more than a third.[44] In Manchester the decline can be measured even more precisely. Between 1839 (not an outstanding year by any means) and 1841 the receipts of 50 Salford shopkeepers went down as follows:[45]

	1839	1841	(in £s)
13 provision dealers	70,700	47,300	
14 butchers	27,800	17,200	
10 grocers	63,800	43,300	
13 drapers, etc.	35,400	22,300	

Other figures for declines in meat consumption during slumps are quoted on p. 84. However, one particularly gruesome, though admittedly exceptional case may be quoted, combining the effects of secular decline and cyclical depression: Bradford on Avon, in the dying West of England woollen area (whose support of the extremes of physical-force Chartism is thus explained only too convincingly). In this tragic town, in the 13 weeks from October 1st to December 1st 1841, the 8,309 inhabitants consumed 9,497 lb of meat and 9,437 quartern loaves. But of this amount, 6,000 lb was eaten by 2,400 of the more prosperous citizens and the 409 inmates of the workhouse, leaving 3,088 lb of meat (or 8⅜ ozs per week) for the other 5,909. The consumption of bread and meat since 1820 had fallen by 75 per cent.[46]

Since all but a minority of workers possessed no reserves whatever to meet such contingencies, unemployment was likely to plunge them into destitution. They could and did pawn their property. But this might be negligible. Thus in Ancoats and Newtown (Manchester), 2,000 families (8,866 persons) in 1842 held between them 22,417 pawn-tickets; but the average value of these per family amounted to a mere £1 8*s*. A larger sample of 10,000 families, which is less biased towards the very poorest, held an estimated average of £2 16*s*. in pawn-tickets each. (12,000 destitute families then represented a third of the population.) What this represented in domestic equipment can be guessed: at the prevailing rates, a mattress, bed-quilt, blankets and two sheets could be pawned for a total of 11s. 11½d.[47] However, if we assume a family income of 10s., even £3 in pawnable property would hardly maintain an unemployed family for more than six weeks.

But how long did unemployment last? In 1841–2 it could last for more than a year, as is shown by various counts made in 1843.[48] But even if we suppose a man to have been unemployed for 6 months, and to be capable of surviving on his domestic possessions for 6 weeks, he would either have to go on relief, or into debt, or both. And supposing his credit with local shopkeepers to be good for two months, he would still have to repay, say, £8 in debts when back in full work, which (at a weekly rate of repayment or redemption of 2s.) would prolong the effects of unemployment on his standard of living for another 18 months. Such calculations are, of course, speculative, but they may serve to suggest the effect of the periodic cataclysms which were likely to hit the early nineteenth-century worker.

Except in years like 1839–42 it is, of course, likely that the effects of unemployment or short-time were unevenly spread, being always worst among the unskilled and the workers in declining trades, least among the skilled in non-cyclical occupations. Thus in Burnley 83 per cent of the destitute on charity in 1842–3 were composed of weavers' and labourers' families.[49] While in London (October 1841) almost two-thirds of the capital's 26,000 tailors were said to be out of work, normally rarely more than one-third were unemployed even in the bad season, though this figure is high enough for a trade which had been 100 per cent unionized in 1830 and had been capable of resisting all wage reductions since 1815.[50] Among the unemployed working on the Manchester roads in 1826, 356 were labourers, mostly Irish, and only 89 in the textile trade, though this doubtless indicates the greater reluctance of 'respectable' men to declass themselves. On the other hand, in a sample of the 'poorest class of operatives' analysed by relief workers in Glasgow during the 1837 slump there was rather more than one 'trade unionist' for every two 'weavers'.[51]

Unfortunately the scattered statistics of trade unions (among whom the unemployment figures of the Ironfounders go back to our period; some material can be derived from the 'tramping' accounts) do not help us, partly because the unions with the best statistics were too small to be representative, partly because such unions would normally contain an abnormally prosperous sector of their trades. Thus, the average of unemployment for the Ironfounders for 1837 to 1842 inclusive was just over 13 per cent (1841: 18·5 per cent). Bad as this is for a skilled trade in a normally extremely prosperous occupation, and over a period of no less than six years, it pretty certainly understates the severity of unemployment in 1841–2; and perhaps also the minimum of permanent unemployment in such a trade at the peak of a boom (as in 1836), which stood at 5 per cent. Moreover, even such as they are, these figures are misleading, for they take no account of the average *length* of unemployment per member. Fortunately the union's expenditure on tramp relief (which reflects this length, because payments represent unemployed days and not merely unemployed men) indicates the degree of such error. Thus, while the relationship between unemployment in 1835 and 1842 is roughly as between 1 and 2, the relationship between tramp relief in 1835 and 1842 is as between 1 and 14. No discussion which overlooks the massive waves of destitution which swamped large sections of the labouring poor in every depression, can claim to be realistic.

Vagrancy provides another little-used index of unemployment, since out-of-work labourers tended to tramp in search of jobs. The actual amount of vagrancy was large enough to have appalled the Tudor administrators who were troubled with sturdy beggars. The only full 'census' of vagrants, that undertaken in 1847–51 by the police of the Derwent division of Cumberland, recorded 42,386 in 1847 (*excluding* Poor Law vagrants), 42,000 in 1848 (*including* them) and – as proof of the cyclical nature of this aspect of unemployment – rapidly declining numbers in subsequent years: 33,500, 24,000, 18,000.[52] Allowing for those who used neither common lodging houses nor the Poor Law, but probably not allowing for the 'tramping artisans' who were catered for by their unions, we may well have had something like 1,000 tramps a week passing up and down this highway during a slump. Whether the estimate that 13,000 vagrants of all kinds passed through Preston in 1832[53] indicates incomplete information or a rise in unemployment between 1832 and 1847–51, is an open question.

It is, however, clear that vagrancy tended to increase from the Napoleonic wars until the early 1830s, largely because of 'commercial fluctuation[54], partly because of the increase in Irish vagrants – that is to say, Irish-born unemployed rather than seasonal harvesters.[55] The following Table III illustrates this trend:

Table III. *Vagrancy trends 1803–34*

	Great North Road Vagrants with passes		Irish vagrants passed out of		
	all*	Irish‡	Middlesex‡	Berks†	Wilts‡
1803	569 (Royston)				
1807–28	540				
1811–12	1,014	1811 7	1811 1,464	301	80
1815–16	2,894	1816 58	1816 1,974	690	121
1820	7,000		1821 4,583	1,850	1,148
		1826 331	1826 3,307	2,044	1,811
		1831 1,751	1831 9,281	5,428	4,510

Unemployment indices such as these may bear directly on the argument between optimists and pessimists, as in the case of the building trade, where the optimistic view (Clapham) based on 'real wages' clashes particularly sharply with the pessimistic view (Postgate), based also on literary evidence.[56] There is no debate about the relatively good wages of building artisans. However, Shannon's brick index[57] shows that output, and hence also employment, in the industry fluctuated in the following manner: periods of rapid expansion (e.g., 1800–4) are followed by periods of slower expansion (e.g., 1805–14) and these in turn by slumps (e.g., 1815–19). Both the latter phases create unemployment, for in an industry geared to expansion – and which, haphazardly recruited under private enterprise, tends to produce an excess labour force anyway – even a slowing of expansion will throw marginal workers out of jobs. In an era of pioneer industrialization under private enterprise this effect will be all the greater, because workers are not yet accustomed to a fluctuating and blind economy. Thus builders in pre-industrial places are accustomed to a labour force whose size is fairly well adjusted to the 'normal' amount of repair and replacement, and perhaps to a gradual expansion of demand by known consumers.§

Now we know for a fact that builders, including artisans, tended to become exceptionally militant in the early 1830s. There is also some literary evidence about poverty and destitution among them. Clapham's argument cannot explain the first or admit the second, but Shannon's index explains both, for it suggests a short, sharp, building

* V.C.H. Cambridgeshire, II, 103–4.
† *Report of R.C. on Poor Law*, App. E. *Parl. Papers* 1834, XXXVIII, pp. 249–50.
‡ Same source. Includes Scots paupers.
§ The case of large capital cities and public works is somewhat different.

boom in 1820–4, followed by a slowing expansion in 1825–9 and a marked slump in 1830–4.

Again, our information from Scotland confirms the existence of heavy unemployment. In Edinburgh the building boom of the early 'twenties was followed by disaster – the number of masons working in the town fell from about 3,000 at the end of 1825 to little more than 100 at the end of 1827 – and the years 1826–32 were the worst ever experienced by this trade in Edinburgh. One man's average weekly earnings in these seven years are given as 11s. 3d. Other building trades record equally bad times then, though the revival of trade unionism in the early 1830s appears to mark their end.[58] Nothing is more plausible than that, by the early 'thirties, there should be both poverty and discontent. This example shows very clearly how dangerous it is to rely on what purports to be statistical evidence, while neglecting equally relevant quantitative factors, which happen not always to be as easily traced as in the building trade.

Nor is the force of such arguments confined to builders. They apply to all manner of other crafts (including their attached labourers and dependents) which made the transition from the pre-industrial to the industrial rhythm of economic movement. The London furniture-makers whose plight Mayhew describes, and whose decline is shown by the collapse of their unions and collective agreements in our period, are a case in point.[59] Local studies would no doubt reveal similar cases elsewhere, perhaps among the Sheffield metal operatives, after the collapse of their 'golden age' in the 1810s and 1820s. It is too often forgotten that something like 'technological' unemployment was not confined purely to those workers who were actually replaced by new machines. It could affect almost all pre-industrial industries and trades surviving into the industrial age; that is, as Clapham has shown, a great many. Doubtless the general expansion of the early industrial period (say, 1780–1811) tended to diminish unemployment except during crises; doubtless the decades of difficulty and adjustment after the wars tended to make the problem more acute. From the later 1840s, as I have tried to show elsewhere,[60] the working classes began to adjust themselves to life under a new set of economic rules, recognized and – insofar as 'political economy' and union policy could do so – counteracted. But it is highly probable that the period 1811–42 saw abnormal problems and abnormal unemployment, such as is not revealed by the general 'real wage' indices.

Whether further study can give us more adequate figures about unemployment in the first half of the century is a matter for debate. It will certainly be unable to measure adequately the occasional, seasonal or intermittent unemployment and the permanent bulk of under-employment, though no estimate of real wages is worth much which neglects this. An estimate for Leeds is given in the following Table IV:

Table IV. *Average unemployment per year, and weekly wages corrected for this, Leeds, 1838*[61]

Trades working 12 months	Weekly wages	Corrected weekly wages	Trades working 11 months	Weekly wages	Corrected weekly wages
Clothdrawers	24/6	24/6	Tailors	16/–	14/8
Smiths	19/–	19/–	Joiners	19/6	17/11
Millwrights	26/–	26/–	Saddlers	21/–	19/3
Plane Makers	21/–	21/–	Curriers	20/–	19/1
Gunsmiths	25/–	25/–	Brassfounders	25/–	24/1
Mechanics	24/–	24/–	Coopers	20/–	19/1
Ironmoulders	25/–	25/–	Printers	21/–	19/3
Turners	22/–	22/–			
Worsted Piecers	4/6	4/6			
Preparers	6/6	6/6			

Trades working 10 months			Trades working 9 months		
Shoemakers	14/–	11/8	Painters	20/–	15/–
Plumbers	23/–	19/2	Clothpressers	20/–	15/–
Woolsorters	21/–	17/6	Slubbers	24/–	18/–
Woodturners	17/–	14/2	Plasterers	18/–	13/6
Masons	22/–	18/4	Bricklayers	23/–	17/3
Weavers	13/–	10/10	Woollen Piecers	5/–	3/9
Hatters	24/–	20/–	Woollen Fillers	6/–	4/6
Woolcombers	14/–	11/8	Dyers	22/–	16/6
Wheelwrights	18/–	15/–	Woodsawyers	20/–	15/–

It almost certainly underestimates the case, for earlier estimates show the London builders to have worked a season of 6–7 months,[62] and contemporary ones show, e.g., two-thirds of the Edinburgh painters to have been idle for 4 months a year.[63] However, it does indicate the sort of deductions which would have to be made from theoretical wage-rates to allow for real average earnings even in times of relative prosperity. The mass of unskilled and, by definition, casual trades are not comprised in this or any other practicable list. However, it is perhaps worth quoting the general estimate of a contemporary observer of proved acuteness and a good sense of statistical information.

Henry Mayhew is not a negligible informant. And if, as E. P. Thompson has lately reminded us again, in his valuable discussion of the standard-of-living problem, the 'controversy really depends on a "guess" as to which group was increasing most – those "who were able to share in the benefits of economic progress" and "those who were shut out" – then Mayhew's guess is worth our attention':[64]

> Estimating the working classes as being between four and five million in number, I think we may safely assert ... that ... there is barely sufficient work for the *regular* employment of half our labourers, so that only 1,500,000 are fully and constantly employed, while 1,500,000 more are employed only half their time, and the remaining 1,500,000 wholly unemployed, obtaining a day's work *occasionally* by the displacement of some of the others.[65]

I would not place too much weight on this or any other guess, until it can be verified by reliable figures. Unfortunately this is not yet – and may never be – possible, for our data are too scattered to allow us to deflate any real wage index which we choose to construct. All we can say is that cyclical unemployment was plainly much higher before the mid-forties than after, for the trade union figures which become available after 1850 (and which are reasonably representative for at least part of the skilled engineering, metal and shipbuilding workers) can show nothing like the catastrophes recorded above. Between 1850 and 1914, the worst year for any group of unions was 1879, when 15·3 per cent of the engineering group were out of work; the worst period of consecutive heavy unemployment was 1884–7, when 11·9 per cent of the same group were without work. The average annual unemployment for the six most booming years between 1850 and 1873 was 1·8 per cent for the same trades, which is very much better than even the Ironfounders' figures for the pre-1850 period, and incomparably better than 1841–2. We can certainly claim that unemployment figures throw doubt on any optimistic calculations which neglect them. But by themselves our data are insufficient to establish an alternative view.

IV

C. Consumption figures

The discussion of these neglected sources is necessarily rather long, and the technical aspects of it have been relegated to a special Appendix. As Britain was not a bureaucratic state, we lack official national data, except for wholly imported articles. Nevertheless, we can get a good deal more information than has hitherto been brought into the discussion. This shows that, from the later 1790s until the early 1840s, there is no evidence of any major rise in the per capita consumption of several foodstuffs, and in some instances evidence of a temporary fall which had not yet been completely made good by the middle 1840s. If the case for deterioration in this period can be established firmly, I suggest that it will be done on the basis of consumption data.

Tea, sugar and tobacco, being wholly imported, furnish national consumption figures which may be divided by the estimated population to give a crude index of per capita consumption.[66] However, we note that Clapham, though an optimist and aware of the figures, wisely refused to use them as an argument in his favour since absolute per capita consumption in this period was low, and such increases as occurred were disappointingly small. Indeed, the contrast between the curve before and after the middle 1840s when it begins to rise sharply, is one of the strongest arguments on the pessimistic side.[67] All three series show a slowly rising trend and after the 1840s a much sharper rise, though tobacco consumption fell (probably owing to increased duties) in the 1810s. The tobacco series includes Irish consumption after the middle 1820s and is thus difficult to use. The tea series is also hard to interpret, since it reflects not merely the capacity to buy, but also the secular trend to abandon older beverages for a new one. The significance of tea-drinking was much debated by contemporaries, who were far from considering it an automatic sign of improving living standards. At all events it only shows four periods of decline – 1815–16, 1818–19, a dramatically sharp fall in 1836–7 after a sharp rise, and a slighter fall in 1839–40. Tea seems to have been immune to the slumps of 1826 and, more surprisingly, 1841–2, which makes it suspect as an index of living-standards. Tobacco does not reflect the slump of 1836–7, but does reflect the others, though not much. Anyway, this article shows virtually stable consumption. Sugar is the most sensitive indicator though – owing to various outside factors – it does not always reflect trade-cycle movements. It shows the slumps of 1839–40 and 1841–2 well. Broadly speaking, there is no tendency for sugar consumption to rise above the Napoleonic peak until well into the 1840s. There is a sharp post-war decline, a sharp rise to rather lower levels after 1818, a slow rise – almost a plateau – until 1831, and then an equally slow decline or stagnation until 1843 or 1844. Tea, sugar and tobacco indicate no marked rise in the standards of living, but beyond this little can be deduced from the crude series.

The case of *meat* is different. Here we possess at least two indices, the Smithfield figures for London for the entire period, and the yield of the excise on hides and skins for the period up to 1825. The Smithfield figures[68] show that, while London's population index rose from 100 in 1801 to 202 in 1841, the number of beef cattle slaughtered rose only to 146, of sheep to 176 in the same period. The following Table V gives the figures by decades:

Table V. *Decennial percentage increase in London population, Beef and Sheep at Smithfield, 1801–51*

Census date	Animals ave. of	Index figure			Decennial increase		
		Popu- lation	Beef	Sheep	Popu- lation	Beef	Sheep
1801	1800–4	100	100	100			
1811	1810–12	119	105	119	+19	+ 5	+19
1821	1819–22	144	113	135	+25	+ 8	+16
1831	1830–4	173	127	152	+29	+14	+17
1841	1840–3	202	146	176	+30	+19	+24
1851	1850–2*	246	198	193	+43	+42	+17†

It will be seen that the increase in beef lagged behind that in population in all decades until the 1840s. Mutton also lagged – though less – except in the first decade. On the whole a per capita decline in London meat consumption up to the 1840s is thus almost certain.

The excise on hides and leather yields somewhat cruder figures. (The sources are discussed in the Appendix.) The following Table VI summarizes what little we can get from them:

* The choice of base-dates for the animals cannot be rigid. Thus 1800–4 is chosen, because, say, 1800–2 would give abnormally high figures, thus under-stating the rise in the following decade. For sheep 1840–2 has been taken as a base-date, because the exceptionally high figure for 1843 would overstate the decennial rise. The choice of different dates would change the results slightly, but not substantially.

† A possible explanation for this low figure is found in the Appendix.

Table VI. *Yield of Excise on Hides and Skins in London and Rest of Country 1801 (1800–1 for Excise)* = *100*

Date	Population	Country yield	London yield
1801	100	100	100
1811	114·5	122	107
1821	136	106*	113*
1825	150	135	150

Without going further into the somewhat complex discussion of the sources, it seems clear that the figures do not indicate a major rise in per capita meat consumption.

About *cereals* and *potatoes*, the staple of the poor man's diet, we can also find out some things. The fundamental fact is that, as contemporaries already knew,[69] wheat production and imports did not keep pace with the growing population, so that the amount of wheat available per capita appears to have fallen steadily from the late eighteenth century until the 1840s or 1850s, the amount of potatoes available rising about the same rate.[70] The best figures for the rise in wheat productivity[71] show fairly stable yields up to 1830, a modest rise of about 10 per cent in the 1830s and a startlingly large one of 40 per cent after 1840, which fits in with the picture of very rapid improvement in living standards after the effects of the 1842 depression had worn off. It follows that, whatever the literary evidence, some people *must* have shifted away from wheat, presumably to potatoes. The simplest view would be that the major change from brown to white bread had already taken place by, say, the 1790s, and that the drift from wheat took place thereafter; but this would not explain the almost certain later drift from brown to white bread in the North and West. But this may have been 'paid for' by a decline of per capita consumption elsewhere. This is technically possible. The mean consumption of bread-stuffs among farm-labourers in 1862 was about 14½ lb per week. Twelve counties[72] consumed less than this – from 10¼ to 11¾ lb, six more than 13 lb, fourteen about the average.[73] Where capital consumption varied so widely – between 10¼ and 15¼, not to mention the 18¾ of Anglesey, there is scope for both an earlier decline in per capita consumption in some places and for considerable 'compensation' between counties. However it is not my purpose to suggest explanations. All we can say is, that a rise in the per capita consumption of white bread in this period *at nobody's*

* For reasons discussed below, this is probably understated.

expense is out of the question. Wheat consumption may have fallen with or without additional potato consumption, or some areas may have seen it rise at the expense of others (with or without a rise in potatoes).

We have no general statistics about the consumption of other common foodstuffs. It is difficult to see anything but a decline of *milk*, because cow-keeping must have declined with urbanization (though it probably continued in towns on a larger scale than is sometimes admitted) and because of the decline in the traditional rural diet which relied heavily on 'white meats'. The estimates of London cow-keeping are unreliable. As against one of 20,000 metropolitan and suburban cows in 1854, we have another of 10,000 in 1837; one or both are likely to be wrong.[74] However, even in 1862 some fortunate groups of poor workers stuck to the old diet; the Macclesfield silk weavers consumed 41·5 fluid oz per head per week, as against the 11 oz of the Coventry weavers, the 7·6 oz of the Spitalfields weavers and the 1·6 oz of Bethnal Green.[75] But all the evidence points to a decline in milk consumption. Not so with *butter*, which was evidently – and naturally, since bread formed so large a part of the labourer's diet – considered a greater necessity than meat.[76] In Dukinfield and Manchester (1836) outlays on it were comparable to those on meat, and conparison with 1841 shows that they were rather inelastic.[77] The few comparable budgets from Eden.[78] show a similar pattern of expenditure, though perhaps a rather smaller outlay on butter than on meat. The poor man thus ate butter; only the destitute man might be unable to. It is not impossible that butter consumption rose during urbanization, for other things to spread on bread – e.g., lard or dripping – must have been harder to come by when people kept fewer pigs and meat-consumption was low and erratic. *Cheese* consumption seems to have declined, for many urban workers seem not to have had or to have developed the fashion of substituting it for meat. In Dukinfield and Manchester they spent much less on cheese than butter, and the 1862 farm labourers ate much more of it, even allowing for their slightly better position, than the 'urban poor'. *Eggs* seem to have been of small importance. Per capita consumption can hardly have risen. The view that the consumption of perishable commodities either declined, or can hardly have risen much before the railway age, has also been taken by other scholars, though it has been challenged on no very obvious grounds.[79]

A notable increase in consumption is, however, recorded for *fish*.[80]

In Birmingham per capita consumption – negligible in 1829 – had more than doubled by 1835 and continued to grow at a rapid rate until 1840.[81] Undoubtedly this improved the nutritive value of the poor man's diet, though it may not indicate that they *felt* themselves to be eating better; for the poor had always had a marked prejudice against this cheap and abundant food, and 'the lower class of people entertain a notion that fish is not substantial enough food for them, and they prefer meat'.[82] They may well have moved to fish because they could not afford enough meat.

The evidence is thus not at all favourable to the 'optimistic' view. Though it does not necessarily or firmly establish the pessimistic one, consumption study rather points towards it. The growth of *adulteration* slightly strengthens the pessimistic case. The increase of adulteration has been doubted, but on quite inadequate grounds. It grew rapidly.[83] The *Lancet* enquiry in the 1850s[84] brings the following points out very clearly: (i) *all* bread tested in two separate samples was adulterated; (ii) over half of oatmeal was adulterated; (iii) *all* but the highest-quality teas were invariably adulterated; (iv) a little under half the milk and (v) *all* butter was watered. Over half the jam and preserves included deleterious matter, but this may have been due simply to bad production. The only commodity of common use not largely adulterated was sugar, almost 90 per cent of which seems to have been straight, though often filthy.

The discussion of food consumption thus throws considerable doubt on the optimistic view. However, it should be pointed out that this does *not* mean that early nineteenth-century Britons had an 'Asiatic' standard of living. This is nonsense, and such loose statements have caused much confusion. Britain was almost certainly better fed than all but the most prosperous peasant areas, or the more comfortable classes, in continental countries; but then it had been so, as Drummond and Wilbraham pointed out[85] long before the Industrial Revolution. The point at issue is not whether we fell as low as other countries, but whether, by our own standards, we improved or deteriorated, and in either case, how much.

V

There is thus no strong basis for the optimistic view, at any rate for the period from c. 1790 or 1800 on until the middle 1840s. The plausibility of, and the evidence for deterioration are not to be lightly dismissed. It is not the purpose of this chapter to discuss the evolution of living standards in the eighteenth century, since the major discussion on living standards has been about the period between the end of the Napoleonic Wars and 'some unspecified date between the end of Chartism and the Great Exhibition'. It is altogether likely that living standards improved over much of the eighteenth century. It is not improbable that, sometime soon after the onset of the Industrial Revolution – which is perhaps better placed in the 1780s than in the 1760s[86] – they ceased to improve and declined. Perhaps the middle 1790s, the period of Speenhamland and shortage, mark the turning-point. At the other end, the middle 1840s certainly mark a turning-point.

We may therefore sum up as follows. The classical view has been put in Sidney Webb's words: 'If the Chartists in 1837 had called for a comparison of their time with 1787, and had obtained a fair account of the actual social life of the working-man at the two periods, it is almost certain that they would have recorded a positive decline in the standard of life of large classes of the population.'[87] This view has not been so far made untenable. It may be that further evidence will discredit it; but it will have to be vastly stronger evidence than has so far been adduced.

(1957–63)

NOTES

1 Cf. J. L. Hammond's list in 'The Industrial Revolution and Discontent', *Econ. Hist. Rev.* II (1930), pp. 215–28.

2 T. S. Ashton, 'The standard of life of the workers in England, 1790–1850' (*J. Econ. Hist.* Supplement IX (1949)), pp. 19–38.

3 T. McKeown and R. G. Brown, 'Medical Evidence relating to English population changes', *Population Studies*, IX (1955), p. 119. I find it difficult to escape from the conclusion on p. 141.

4 Clapham, *Economic History of Modern Britain* I, p. 601. It may be noted that the value of the Bowley-Wood collections of money-wage data is not in question. What it is legitimate to doubt, even in the light of a recent attempt to rehabilitate the Clapham approach (Deane and Cole, *British Economic Growth 1688–1959*, Cambridge 1962), is how far it represents the movements of real *earnings* as distinct from rates, and how far a realistic real wage index can be constructed on this basis, whether by the use of Silberling or Gayer-Schwartz-Rostow.

Deane and Cole, of course, admit that unemployment would affect such an index.

5 Cole & Postgate, *The Common People*; G. D. H. Cole, *Short History of the British Working Class Movement* (1947 edn); A. V. Judges in *Riv. Stor. Italiana*, 1951, pp. 162–79; T. S. Ashton, loc. cit.

6 T. S. Ashton, loc. cit.

7 R. S. Tucker, 'Real Wages of Artisans in London 1729–1935' (*J. Amer. Stat. Assn. XXXI* (1936, no. 193).

8 R. C. O. Matthews, *A Study in Trade Cycle History: Economic Fluctuations in Great Britain, 1833–42* (Cambridge 1954).

9 J. L. Hammond, loc. cit., and J. H. Clapham, I, ix–x.

10 T. S. Ashton, loc. cit., and *Economic History of England: The Eighteenth Century* (1955), pp. 233–5.

11 T. S. Ashton in *J. Econ. Hist.*, and *The Industrial Revolution* (1948).

12 *Statistical Account of the British Empire* (1839), II, pp. 494 ff.

13 *Select Committee on Agriculture, Parl. Papers*, 1833, V, Q.3431 ff.

14 *London* ed. C. Knight (1842), II, p. 318 (chapter: 'Smithfield') estimates the rise in population from 1740–50 to 1831 at 218 per cent, in beef at 110, in sheep at 117 per cent. As the author is also aware that Davenant's estimate of 370 lb for the carcass weight of beef in the early eighteenth century is probably much too low, it is difficult to see how he arrives at his optimistic conclusions about the per capita rise in London meat consumption.

15 G. E. Fussell, 'The size of English cattle in the eighteenth century', *Agricultural History*, III (1929) pp. 160 ff.; also *Agric. Hist.* IV (1930). McCulloch accepts Sinclair's estimate of Smithfield weights in 1785 uncritically.

16 *Select Committee on the Depressed State of Agriculture, Parl. Papers*, 1821, IX, p. 267; *General Statistics of the British Empire* (1836); Knight, op. cit. II, p. 325.

17 Braithwaite Poole, *Statistics of British Commerce* (1852); G. Dodd, *The Food of London* (1856), p. 213.

18 In addition to the usual wage-sources (Bowley and Wood, Gilboy, Tucker) this paper, in fact, contains only factual material about Lancashire prices drawn from Rowbottom, the *Manchester Mercury* and A. Redford's *Manchester Merchants and Foreign Trade 1794–1858* (1934), and an opinion of Thomas Holmes. This last is the only new source definitely supporting the optimistic view. Of course, Prof. Ashton's purpose in the paper was to provide new arguments rather than new evidence.

19 See below, chapter 15.

20 E.g., F. G. P. Neison, 'Contributions to Vital Statistics', *J. Stat. Soc.* VIII (1845), pp. 290 ff.; IX (1846), pp. 50 ff.

21 In J. McCulloch, *Statistical Account*, II.

22 However, two long series for Doncaster and Carlisle (1850) in the *Reports to the General Board of Health* point in the same direction.

23 S. Swaroop and K. Uemura 'An attempt to evolve a comprehensive indicator to quantify the component "health, including demographic conditions"', *World Health Working Paper No 8*, WHO/PHA/25 (22 Nov. 1955), duplicated. I owe this reference to Mrs M. Jefferys, School of Hygiene and Tropical Medicine, London.

24 loc. cit.

25 T. H. Marshall, 'The Population Problem during the Industrial Revolution', *Economic History* (1929), p. 453.

26 T. R. Edmonds, 'On the Mortality of Glasgow and on the increasing Mortality in England', *Lancet*, II (1835–6), p. 353. Summarized by Farr in McCulloch, op. cit., II.

27 T. R. Edmonds, 'On the law of mortality', *Lancet*, I (1835–6), p. 416.

28 Thus in 581 unions the number of able-bodied paupers only rose by one-eighth from the Lady-Day quarter of 1841 to that of 1842: *J. Stat. Soc.* VI (1843), p. 256.

29 *Devizes and Wiltshire Gazette*, 13 Jan. 1842.

30 Clapham, *Economic History of Modern Britain* I, p. 179. Gayer, Rostow and Schwartz, quoted by Neil Smelser, *Social Change in the Industrial Revolution* (1959) give a smaller figure of 240,000 in 1830, but as Clapham points out, no census of them was ever taken.

31 Following Smelser op. cit., p. 138, I assume that between 30 and 50 per cent of the looms were operated by other members of the weaver's family; also – as a rough guess – three children per family.

32 As C. Chisholm, 'On the statistical pathology of Bristol and of Clifton' (*Edinburgh Medical and Surgical Journal*, 1 July 1817, p. 274) who quotes a census (or estimate) made by the mayor in January 1817, a time of improving trade after a bad slump, but of high prices. Then 3,045 persons were wholly or partly unemployed out of a total population of perhaps 78,500. This might, of course, represent 15 per cent or more of the population, if the average size of the family is taken as four.

33 The main source is the *Report of the Committee appointed*

at a public meeting on the second of May 1826 for . . . relief to the 'WORKING MANUFACTURERS'. (London 1829). The Home Office Papers (e.g., HO 40/19 for 1826, letter from J. W. Paget, Preston on Darwen) also contain relevant material.

34 J. Finch, *Statistics of the Vauxhall Ward, Liverpool* (Liverpool 1842); a first-rate piece of work, which gives unemployment figures for each working-class stratum, and part-time figures broken down into 5, 4, 3, 2, 1 days' work. The last two groups he reckons among the unemployed, the first two among the employed.

35 *Report of the Statistical Committee appointed by the Anti-Corn Law Conference held in London 8–12th March 1842* (London, n.d.). All data in this paragraph, except where otherwise stated, are from this valuable compendium.

36 *Facts and Figures. A periodical record of statistics applied to current questions* (London, Oct. 1841), p. 29.

37 See above, chapter 4.

38 *Report to the General Board of Health: Clitheroe* (1850), ibid., *Haworth* (1853).

39 *Statistical Committee of Anti-Corn-Law League*, p. 45.

40 *Facts and Figures*, loc. cit.

41 Finch, op. cit., p. 34.

42 *Report of the Committee . . . for the relief of the Distressed Manufacturers* (London 1844), pp. 19, 41.

43 Quoted in W. Cooke-Taylor, *Notes on a Tour in the Manufacturing Districts of Lancashire* (London 1842), pp. 216–17.

44 Finch, op. cit., p. 34.

45 J. Adshead, *Distress in Manchester. Evidence . . . of the state of the Labouring Classes in 1840–2* (London 1842), p. 55.

46 *Devizes and Wiltshire Gazette*, 13 Jan. 1842.

47 J. Adshead, op. cit., pp. 18–24.

48 *Parl. Papers* 1843, XXVII, Factory Inspectors, pp. 313–15. *Report of Committee . . . for the relief of the Distressed Manufacturers*, pp. 27–8, 41, 62.

49 *Report of Committee . . . p. 62.*

50 *Facts and Figures*, pp. 29 ff. *Sel. Ctee. on Manufacturers' Employment (Parl. Papers* 1830, X, p. 226).

51 C. R. Baird, Observations upon the poorest class of operatives in Glasgow in 1837, *Journ. Stat. Soc.* I, p. 167.

52 *Report to the General Board of Health: Keswick* (1852), p. 45. Part of the diminution was due to a Poor Law ruling to bar long-distance vagrants.

53 *Report of Royal Commission on the Poor Law*, Appendix E, Parl. Papers, 1834, XXXVIII, p. 318.

54 *R.C. on Poor Law*, loc. cit., pp. 305–6: 'It cannot be denied that our annual reports tend to prove that the gross number of pauper travellers has been doubled between the years ending 1 January 1822 and 1 January 1833. It has been a period of great commercial fluctuation and much political excitement.' (S.S. Duncan of Bristol).

55 *Select Committee on Irish Vagrants, Parl. Papers*, XVI (1833), p. 362 (40) specifically points out that they were not seasonal harvesters.

56 Clapham, *Economic History of Modern Britain*, I, p. 548, esp. the superior-sounding footnote; R. W. Postgate, *The Builders' History* (1923), p. 33.

57 H. A. Shannon, 'Bricks, a trade index', *Economica*, 1934.

58 File of newspaper clippings on the condition of the working classes in Edinburgh and Leith in and before 1853, in *Goldsmiths' Collection* B.853 (London University Library).

59 H. Mayhew, *London Labour and the London Poor*, III, pp. 232 ff. For a similar crisis among tailors 1825–34, *The Red Republican*, I, 23 (1850), pp. 177–9.

60 'The Tramping Artisan', loc. cit.

61 'Condition of the Town of Leeds and Its Inhabitants', *J. Stat. Soc.* II (1839), p. 422.

62 R. Campbell, *The London Tradesman* (1747).

63 *Goldsmith Collection*, B. 853.

64 E. P. Thompson, *The Making of the English Working Class* (1963), p. 250, to which I am indebted for a reminder of the Mayhew quotation.

65 *London Labour and the London Poor* II, pp. 364–5.

66 The most accessible source for them is Gayer, Rostow and Schwartz, *Growth and Fluctuations of the British Economy 1790–1850*.

67 Henderson and Chaloner, loc. cit., blur this distinction by using the sugar consumption figures for 1844–7 to indicate an improvement which, e.g., the consumption figures for 1837–43 do not show.

68 There are numerous printed sources for these: For the eighteenth century, Ashton, *Economic History of England, The Eighteenth Century*. Thereafter, *H. of Lords Sessional Papers 56 of 1822*: Meat cattle and sheep sold in Smithfield 1790–1821; *Parl. Papers*, 1837–8, XLVII, p. 164; *Statistical Illustrations of the British Empire* (1827), p. 105; J. Fletcher, 'Statistical Account of the

markets of London' *J. Stat. Soc.* X (1847), p. 345; Dodd, op. cit., p. 241. The sources give weekly figures. For the population figures see R. Price-Williams, 'The Population of London 1801–81', *J.R. Stat. S.* XLVIII (1885), p. 349.

69 W. Jacob in *Select Committee on the State of Agriculture*, Parl. Papers, 1836, VIII, i, Q. 26–32.

70 I have followed the calculations of R. N. Salaman, *History and Social Influence of the Potato* (Cambridge 1949), Appendix IV, which discusses sources. Other estimates, such as Drescher's ('The Development of Agricultural Production in Great Britain and Ireland from the early Nineteenth Century', *Manchester School*, May 1955) agreed that wheat production just failed to keep pace with population. The view that the bulk of the transfer from brown to white bread had already taken place by 1790, is strengthened by the discussion in P. Deane and W. A. Cole, *British Economic Growth 1688–1959*, pp. 62–7.

71 M. J. R. Healy and E. L. Jones, 'What Yields in England 1815–59' *J.R. Stat. S.* Series A, vol 125, pt 4, 1962.

72 The first, quoted in R. M. Hartwell, 'The Rising Standard of Living in England 1800–50' *Ec. Hist. Rev.* XIII, 1961, p. 412; the second from John Hogg, *London as it is . . .* (London 1837), p. 226.

73 Six in the Southeast and South, the rest industrial ones. No figures are given for six other southern and southwestern counties.

74 *6th Report of the Medical Officer to the Privy Council* (1863), pp. 216–330: The Food of the Poorer Labouring Classes. A pioneer investigation.

75 Ibid.

76 The (non-quantitative) survey of town workers' diets in *Royal Commission on the Poor Laws*, App. B., *Parl. Papers*, 1834, XXXVI, Q. 40 of questionnaires seems to mention butter mainly as part of rather poor diets.

77 W. Neild, 'Expenditure of the Working Classes in Dukinfield and Manchester in 1836 and 1841', *J. Stat. Soc.* IV (1841), p. 320.

78 *The State of the Poor*: 6 cases. In three the quantities are given: 1/6 lb, 2/7 lb, 1/2 lb (woolcomber).

79 A. J. Taylor, 'Progress and Poverty in Britain 1780–1850' (*History* XLV, 1960), p. 22; for criticism, R. M. Hartwell 1961, loc. cit., pp. 409, 412.

80 I had neglected this in the original version, but it is briefly discussed in R. M. Hartwell, op. cit.

81 *Facts and Figures principally relating to Railways and Commerce*, by Samuel Salt (London and Manchester 1848), p. 3.
82 Hartwell, op. cit., p. 411.
83 Cf. John Burnett, *The History of Food Adulteration in Great Britain in the Nineteenth Century* (London Ph.D. 1958).
84 A. H. Hassall, *Food and its adulteration* (1855).
85 J. Drummond and A. Wilbraham, *The Englishman's Food* (1939).
86 J. U. Nef, 'The Industrial Revolution Reconsidered', *J. Econ. Hist* III (1943).
87 S. Webb, *Labour in the Longest Reign*, Fabian Tract 75 (1897), p. 2.

APPENDIX
Problems of food consumption

Four problems must be considered: (i) the theoretical problem of the change from old to new types of diet, (ii) the technical problem of measurement and the use of sources, (iii) the problem of trends and (iv) the problem of the actual quantities consumed. The last three will be discussed in terms of *meat-consumption*.

(i) The adoption of a new type of diet does not *a priori* mark either an improvement or a deterioration in living standards. The first view seems to be held by some optimists about *white bread, tea*, etc., the second by pessimists like J. Kuczynski (*History of Labour Conditions*). A new food can be regarded as evidence of a rising standard of living only if it is adopted because believed to be superior (nutritionally or socially) to the old, and if bought without sacrificing what people believe to be necessities. Thus the mere fact that a new diet is nutritionally inferior to an old one is irrelevant, except to the nutritionist. If white bread is adopted because it is *believed* to be a sign of a higher standard, then its adoption must be regarded as a sign of improvement. Conversely, if – as was widely held in the early nineteenth century (Hammond, *Village Labourer*, pp. 124 and 125 for opinions) – labourers take to tea in order to make an increasingly grim diet tolerable, an increase in tea-drinking cannot prove a rising standard of living. Nobody would claim that the labourers of Sunbury who in 1834 lived on 'bread, potatoes, a little tea and sugar' (*R.C. on Poor Laws, Parl. Papers*, 1834, XXXVI) were better off just because sixty years earlier – I am assuming they ate white bread – they had probably consumed less of all these new foodstuffs.

The general problem has long since been well formulated by

Grotjahn in *Ueber Wandlungen in der Volksernaehrung* (Leipzig 1902). Industrialization leads to a change in the traditional and – except in famines – nutritionally adequate if dull diet. If enough is spent on the new diet, it can be equally good and more varied. However, often only the well-paid worker can spend enough on it, and few workers know enough initially to choose an adequate new diet. (See the complaints of bad domestic management in *R.C. on Poor Laws*, 1834, XXXVI, *passim*). Hence, for equal incomes, the old diet is normally nutritionally better than the new. Until either the workers earn enough, or governments take adequate action, industrialization tends to produce a worse-fed population for a time. However, if we blame the diet of the early nineteenth century, it is not only because the dietician prefers the magnificent dietaries of the old North Country (see e.g., Marshall, *Review of the Reports to the Board of Agriculture for the Northern Department* (York 1808), to white bread, potatoes, tea and sugar, but because the new diet contained less of the foods which Englishmen regarded as desirable, than did earlier ones.

(ii) It is reasonable, especially in England with its mystique of meat-eating, to take meat consumption as a criterion of the standard of living. However, all our sources have considerable weaknesses.

There are the general estimates of which Gregory King's (quoted in Trevelyan's *English Social History* (1946 edn), p. 276) is the first to interest us. It claims that half the poor households at the end of the seventeenth century ate meat daily, most of the rest ate it twice weekly, and only paupers once weekly. How much we rely on this depends on our estimate of the accuracy and judgment of that able man. Later general estimates, such as Mulhall's guess (*Dictionary of Statistics*) of 80 lb per year in 1811–30, 87 in 1831–50 are based on no known facts, since there were no censuses of livestock during this period. As we shall see, they are almost certainly too high.

Our largest single body of information about meat consumption comes from descriptions, budgets, and a few investigations which may perhaps just deserve the name of social surveys. For the *eighteenth* century the most impressive evidence comes from the 70-odd workhouse dietaries recorded in Eden's *State of the Poor*, since pauper diets are obviously constructed for the least prosperous and exigent type of labourer. Sixty of these dietaries served meat three times a week or more, fifteen from five to seven times a week. Where quantities are given, they are sometimes surprisingly high—$\frac{1}{2}$ lb per meal per person. What men thought desirable for full-grown hard-working labourers can be seen from the harvest diets (Batchelor, *Agriculture of Bedfordshire* (1813), p. 584, *Agriculture of Hertfordshire* (1813), p. 219): meat three times a day including one-quarter or one-third butcher's meat, beef or mutton daily. We do not know where the average consumption lay between these two conventional extremes. It is not unreasonable to assume that it rose during the eighteenth century, and was quite high by the 1790s, when the food situation turned worse: 'Now they dine off butcher's meat, potatoes and pudding' (Westmorland, 1793, in Marshall, *Review of the Reports to the Board of Agriculture for the Northern Department* (York 1808), p. 214). It is also reasonable to assume that in England, unlike the continent, the worker who ate 'John Bull's food: bread, beef, beer' (*R.C. on Poor Law*, 1834, XXXVI, answers from Warsop) would not regard himself as wildly rich, but as decently paid, while one who could not afford meat regularly would regard himself as near-destitute. (One recalls the phrase of 'A Lady' – *Domestic Cookery* (1819), p. 290 – advising on cooking for the poor: 'Cut a very thick upper crust of bread, and put it into the pot where salt beef is boiling and near ready; it will attract some of the fat, and when swelled out, will not be an unpalatable dish for those who rarely taste meat'.)

It seems clear that after the 1790s the meat consumption of farm-labourers declined, as probably did cottage pig-keeping. For Shropshire both declines seem established (J. P. Dodd, 'The State of Agriculture in Shropshire, 1775–1825', *Trans. Shropshire Archaeological Society*, LV (1954), p. 2; Marshall, *Review of Reports . . . for the Western District* (1810), p. 242). In the 1830s local parsons and similar people believed that, out of 899 parishes, labourers in 491 could live on existing wage-rates with meat; but the detailed returns show (a) that meat rarely meant butchers' meat and (b) that it was not normally eaten regularly or in quantity. (These returns are discussed in R. Giffen, 'Further Notes on the Progress of the Working Classes', *J.R. Stat. Soc.* XLIX (1886), pp. 55–61, 81–9.) In fact, the picture of the Hampshire labourers in 1813 eating bacon and pickled pork only, the Berkshire ones bacon, seems to be fairly typical. (Vancouver, *Agriculture of Hampshire*, p. 338; Mavor, *Agriculture of Berkshire*, p. 419; *R.C. on Poor Laws*, 1834, XXXI, question 14, *passim*). The first estimate of quantities, made in 1862, shows farm labourers to have eaten on average 16 oz per week per adult (*6th Report of Medical Officer to Privy Council*, 1863.) It is difficult to believe that this diet, even though probably an improvement on the earlier nineteenth century, was more plentiful in meat than that of the later eighteenth century, or that men fed on it would have developed the myth of the bluff, beef-fed John Bull.

As to the towns, we must forget the optimistic estimates of middle-class observers who saw labourers eating 6 lb of meat or thereabouts per week (W. Lethaby, *Lectures on the Economy of Food*, 1857; *The Family Oracle of Health*, 1824). Even Le Play's Sheffield cutler in 1855 seems to have had an annual adult consumption of only 81 lb, which is considerably less (Le Play, *Les Ouvriers Européens* (1855), p. 197). An estimate for a London artisan family in 1841, earning the good wage of 30 shillings, allows for a weekly per capita consumption of 2·8 lb, say an adult ration of 4 lb. At the 20 shilling level this declines to 1·4 lb, at the 15 shilling level to 1 lb, estimates which incidentally show the high income elasticity of demand and the wide range of consumption (S. R. Bosanquet, *The Rights of the Poor* (1841), pp. 97–8). The town questionnaires of 1834 (*Parl. Papers*, 1834, XXXVI) give results not unlike the rural ones. Out of something like 57 towns about whose working-class diets adequate details are given, meat is not mentioned in 10, consumption is described as 'ample', 'decent' or 'four or more times a week' in 6, in some such terms as 'occasionally', 'a little', 'once a month' in 24, and no quantities are mentioned for the rest, except for 7 cases where consumption is described as 'fair' or 'one or two days a week'. The meat eaten was normally pork rather than butcher's meat (i.e., bacon, pickled pork), though pork at ordinary times, butcher's meat on high-days and holidays is sometimes mentioned. The answer from Limehouse (London) may provide a link with the cost of living: 'A family might subsist upon £100 with meat twice a week; the general fare consisting of soup, gruel, bread, potatoes, herrings, and other fish when cheap'. But an income of almost £2 a week was high.

Neild's figures for Manchester and Dukinfield, 1836 and 1841 (*J. Stat. Soc.* IV, p. 320) are the most detailed for the industrial areas. In 1836 the average per capita expenditure there ranged from 2½d. to 11½d. per week, the mode being nearer 3d. than 4d. At prevailing prices this would hardly have bought 1 lb. Some other estimates: the best of the depressed class of Keighley wool-combers (1855) ate 1¼ lb (one family), two families ate about ½ lb a head, 15 not more than 5 oz but generally much less, while half did not buy meat or calculate meat consumption by the week at all (*Report to the General Board of Health: Keighley*, 1855). Of the urban poor investigated by the Privy Council in 1862 (loc. cit.) 96 per cent ate meat, the average consumption being 13·6 oz per adult, ranging from the 18¼ oz of the glove-stitchers to the 3·25 oz of the Macclesfield silk-weavers.

For comparison we may note that in 1936–7 the poorest class, those earning less than £2.10s.0d. a week, ate on average 30·4 oz of meat a week (W. Crawford and H. Broadley, *The People's Food* (1938), pp. 177–88), while the poor law dietaries recommended by Chadwick in the 1830s ranged from 8 to 16 oz. (W. Guy, 'Sufficient

97

and insufficient dietaries', *J.R. Stat. Soc.* XXVI (1863), p. 253). It is thus not unreasonable to assume that the average urban meat consumption per head in the first part of the nineteenth century was at least one-third below that of the poorest class in 1936–7, and probably not much more than 1 lb, if that. That of butcher's meat was obviously much less.

There remain the statistical sources. These consist primarily of the Smithfield and Excise series, but also of a few other scattered data. Further research would doubtless add to them.

The chief weakness of the Smithfield series is that it does not comprise all the meat sold in London, since it neglects pork, and both home- and country-killed meat, which was sold mainly at Newgate. About pork we know little, except that urban pig-keeping was almost certainly negligible: in the Birmingham urban area in 1843 only 3,375 pigs were kept. (Appendix to *Second Report of the Inquiry into the State of Large Towns, Parl. Papers* 1845, XVIII, p. 134). Home-killing of other kinds of meat almost certainly declined. Indeed, some of the meat consumption indicated by the market figures may be due to a transfer from home- to butcher-killed meat such as, Dr Pollard tells me, took place in Sheffield. Our ignorance about home-killing thus gives our figures, if anything, an upward bias.

We have no quantitative estimates for country-killed meat before the later 1840s (*Report of the Commissioners . . . relating to Smithfield Market, Parl. Papers* 1850, XXXI; G. Dodd, *The Food of London* (1856), p. 273). But, for the following reasons, I do not believe that it invalidates the Smithfield figures, which were certainly regarded as representative in the middle 1830s. (*On the condition of the agricultural classes of Great Britain and Ireland.* With extracts from the parliamentary papers and evidence from 1833 to 1840, and remarks by the French editor, published at Vienna. With a preface by Henry Drummond, Esq., 1842, vol II, p. 259).

Supplies of Scottish-killed meat by steamer to London are already noted in the middle 1830s, the time of transport being about two days (John Hogg, *London as it is,* London 1837, p. 273; Drummond and Wilbraham, *The Englishman's Food,* 1939, pp. 262–3). We may perhaps take the middle 1820s as the date when this form of transport became economically significant. But while this source of supply was clearly no longer negligible, except in summer, I know of no suggestion in the contemporary sources that it was anything like large enough to fill the gap between population and meat which existed in this decade. Railways, of course, made an even bigger difference both to the supply of country-killed and of live meat, especially from the Home Counties, which had previously sent carcass meat to town, the main increase of dead meat now coming from further afield (*Smithfield Commission*, Q. 795, 892–3). But in 1842 these had clearly not yet affected supplies very much (C. Knight ed, *London* (1842) II, p. 322; see also the evidence of R. Moseley for the Eastern Counties Railway in *Smithfield Commission*, Q. 1,871). The really drastic increase in meat or cattle transport by railway seems to have come in the middle forties, as the following table for live-stock traffic on the Grand Junction Railway from Liverpool (an important port for Irish traffic) illustrates. (Source: *Facts and Figures, principally relating to railways and commerce*, by Samuel Salt, London and Manchester 1848, p. 57):

Year	Cattle	Number of Pigs (nearest '000)	Sheep
1839	43	57,000	–
1840	–	66,000	–
1841	322	66,000	–
1842	4,086	98,000	–
1843	7,197	142,000	–
1844	6,789	132,000	–
1845	23,682	234,000	55,000
1846	53,586	327,000	104,162

We may therefore take it that railways do not seriously disturb the picture until after the 1842 depression. This view is strengthened by the movement of meat market prices in London for the 1840s (*Parl. Papers* 1850, LII, pp. 310 ff.). These show that the cheapest beasts sold (per stone) at 3s 1d. to 3s. 4½d. in 1840–2, and thereafter fell markedly, averaging about 2s. 8d. for the rest of the 1840s, except for the bad years of 1847–8. (The price of sheep, however, shows no such fall, though the price of calves does, from 1842 inclusive.)

On the other hand, at earlier periods there had been a marked *decline* in dead meat. It had almost halved from 1818 to 1830 (*Smithfield Commission*, Q. 892). We may take it that this offsets the possible new supplies of dead meat by steamer in this period, even if it does not include these supplies.

It is doubtful whether even in 1850 Smithfield had lost much ground to the other markets. At all events, in spite of considerable pressing, the witnesses before the Smithfield Commission were unwilling to say that it had (Q. 250 ff., 1,105.) At most we may therefore hold that the Smithfield figures increasingly understate the numbers of *sheep* available in London, as the sale of dead mutton passed to Newgate (*Report*, p. 17), a view which is supported by the tendency of Smithfield sheep sales to lag in the three months in which the sales of dead meat were briskest – December to February (Q. 1,866). For obvious reasons dead meat could hardly be brought to market in summer.

We can thus conclude – in the present state of our knowledge – (a) that the sheep series may be affected somewhat; (b) that the beef series is not really affected; (c) that conversely the neglect of dead meat introduces an optimistic bias between 1818 and 1830 and (d) that the distorting effect of new methods of transport or sources of supply is not likely to be very great until the early forties, when per capita consumption was beginning to rise in any case. On the whole, therefore, the Smithfield series can be used for London without too much hesitation. Since the original publication of this paper it has increasingly been so used (B. R. Mitchell and Phyllis Deane, *Abstact of British Historical Statistics* (1962), p. 341).

It has been argued that these figures are affected by a supposed increase in the average size of beasts sold at Smithfield. There is no evidence of this. The estimates for the contemporary carcass weight of beef we have are 668 lb for 1821, 630 lb for 1836 (another estimate for that date is 656 lb) and 640 lb for 1842. This is roughly of the order of the 6–7 cwt which the Navy fixed as the size of beasts to be bought for salting at the end of the eighteenth century. (*Select Committee on the Depressed State of Agriculture, Parl. Papers* 1821, IX, p. 267; *General Statistics of the British Empire* (1836); H. Drummond, *On the condition of the agricultural classes* . . . (1842), II, p. 261, quoting Youatt; C. Knight op. cit., II, p. 325; Phyllis Deane and W. A. Cole, *British Economic Growth* 1688–1959 (1962), pp. 69–70, quoting Beveridge.) The general picture therefore would seem to be one of some improvement in the size of beasts in the eighteenth century, which Deane and Cole estimate at about 25 per cent, but no significant increase in our period. From the early 1840s on it may well be that the increase is more important.

We are left with the large and unanswerable question, how far the Smithfield series is representative of general trends. We cannot assume that it is, but unfortunately after 1825 we have no figures which can be used nationally, and no series which can even be used regionally. Our most important national source is the Excise on hides and skins, which has been accepted as a potential indicator of meat supplies by Deane and Cole, following its use for this purpose in the original version of this chapter.

The chief question about the Excise series – which stops short in 1825 – is how far they can be used as indices of meat consumption at all. All one can say is that they were so used as far back as 1821 (*S. C. on the Depressed State of Agriculture, Parl. Papers*, 1821, IX). Unfortunately only national series are available for longer periods, except for a single one which distinguished between the yield of London and the Country Collections (*Customs House Library*.) Some of the national series are also available in *S.C. on Agriculture, Parl. Papers*, 1833, V. p. 628; *Parl. Papers*, 1830, XXV, p. 61; 1851–2, XXXIV, p. 503 and in *Statistical Illustrations of the British Empire* (1825), pp. 68–9. For the problems of these series, see Gayer, Rostow and Schwartz, *Growth and Fluctuations of the British Economy*, II, p. 720). Figures for the individual Country Collections must have once existed, for they are used in the *S.C. on the Depressed State of Agriculture*, 1821, but the only ones which appear to survive in the Customs Library are one Abstract of Country Collectors Accounts for Consolidated Duties of Excise 5 Jan. 1826 to 5 Jan. 1827, which provides only a static comparison of orders of magnitude. These excises have the advantage that the rate for all but vellum and parchment and a few rare skins (elk, buck, deer) remained quite unchanged for the whole period, except for the period 1812–22 when they were doubled. They were normally charged by the lb, so that they – at least to some extent – allow for changes in the size of animals. Hence the actual yields can be used as an index of production, though if we divide the yield in 1812–22 by two, the result is rather lower than the rest of the curve justifies, presumably due to a greater amount of evasion. In order to avoid the complications which arise when one seeks to put together series representing, say, sheep or beef-cattle from among the skins tanned, tawed or dressed in oil, in their various sub-varieties, I have relied on the gross produce of collections, though this also includes skins of other animals, and is thus rather cruder than is desirable.*

The annual gross produce figures for London and the Country are printed in Table A overleaf as percentages of 1801, the accounting year running from 5 July to 5 July.

It will be seen that the London yield showed no sign of absolute increase until 1810. It seems improbable that meat consumption as measured on this basis had recovered to anything like the 1800 level by 1820, even allowing for the underestimate of the series, but the boom of the early 1820s was marked. The series is not incompatible with the Smithfield figures. The provinces were clearly better off – or at least they lagged less – except for the rather bad years of 1815–21.

The actual local figures, as given in the 1821 Committee, demon-

---

* Gross produce is what the collectors actually collected. The accounts are made up in the old-fashioned way, the 'Charge' facing the 'Discharge'.

Table A. *Gross produce of Excise on Skins and Hides 1796–1826 as percentages of 1801*

Year	London	Country	Year	London	Country
1796–7	87	96	1811–2	126	128
1797–8	89	96	1812–3*	97	117
1798–9	94	92	1813–4	106	119
1799–1800	103	96	1814–5	110	120
1800–1	100	100	1815–6	100	106
1801–2	94	100	1816–7	97	106
1802–3	89	99	1817–8	108	111
1803–4	87	100	1818–9	116	111
1804–5	90	106	1819–20	110	106
1805–6	87	111	1820–1	113	106
1806–7	84	113	1821–2	108	101
1807–8	84	114	1822–3†	142	123
1808–9	94	119	1823–4	142	129
1809–10	90	122	1824–5	150	135
1810–11	107	122	1825–6‡	137	133

strate, above all, the remarkable income elasticity of demand for meat. Thus, between 1818 and 1820, Birmingham slaughterings fell by 29 per cent, Walsall ones by 38 per cent, Dudley ones by 29 per cent, Leeds ones by 19 per cent, Liverpool ones by 18 per cent, but Manchester only by 13 per cent and Sheffield by 12 per cent. Conversely the slaughter of calves in Liverpool rose by about 25 per cent in 1803–5, that of beef by 37 per cent (1814–17), by 26 per cent in Manchester in the same period. The 1842 depression shows equally sharp drops. In the Yorkshire woollen trade it was estimated that meat and groceries consumption had halved since 1835–6, in Kendal that it had fallen by one third, in Rochdale that it stood at half of 1837 (*Report of Statistical Committee of the Anti-Corn Law League*, pp. 18, 28, 33). This last estimate seems modest, since C. Knight (op. cit., II, p. 325) gives the figures of Rochdale slaughterings as 180 oxen a week in 1836, 65–70 in 1841. The turnover of 14 Manchester butchers fell from £27,800 in 1839 to £17,200 in 1841. (J. Adshead, *Distress in Manchester* . . . London 1842, p. 55).

Comparisons by decades are only possible for Liverpool and Manchester in the period 1801–20, and show a decline in per capita consumption in Liverpool, a probable rise in Manchester. See Table B:

* New duties: figures represent half their yield. Allow for greater evasion!
† Return to old duties.
‡ Annual figures represent yield on half-year multiplied by two.

Table B.

	Liverpool	Manchester
Percentage rise in population 1811–20 over 1801–11	22	25
Percentage rise in annual average slaughter of *beef*, same periods	18	29
Percentage rise for *veal*	0	20
Percentage rise for *mutton*	12	25

All the data given in the *S.C. on the Depressed State of Agriculture* (1828) (pp. 243–4, 265–7) are tabulated overleaf in Table C.

For Birmingham the figures for 1818 are 127, 91 and 582; for 1819, 104, 93 and 470; for 1820, 91, 90 and 388. It will be observed that the depression 1815–16 appears not to affect beef slaughtering in any of the four towns, and veal only in one. Only mutton is consistently affected. This is surprising, since we should normally expect the cheapest meat to be less sensitive to such fluctuations.

A few individual estimates are also available for Dundee and Glasgow, 1833 (in M'Queen, op. cit.), Wolverhampton, Liverpool, Manchester, Glasgow, Newcastle for 1848–50 (in Braithwaite Poole, op. cit.). For Glasgow, these show an increase of 25 per cent in beef, a decrease of 60 per cent in veal and of 10 per cent in mutton. There are also figures for comparative weekly slaughter in Leeds, 1835–6 – 2,450 animals and in 1841 – 1,800 animals, and in Richdale – 180 oxen a week in 1836, 65–70 in 1841 (C. Knight, op. cit., p. 325). I do not know what are the sources for these figures.

The question of changes in the size of animals has not yet been discussed. All one can say is that in London beef consumption must have declined unless the average carcass weight of beef cattle increased by at least 40 per cent between 1801 and 1841, that of sheep by at least 15 per cent. Even if the average weight of both had gone up by 25 per cent or so, a decline is still likely.

All these figures are global; that is, they do not distinguish working-class consumption from the rest, or the consumption of different strata of the labouring poor. This means they are subject to misinterpretation on the optimistic side, for the changes in meat consumption by the relatively small section of the population which ate a good deal of meat, carry a disproportionately heavy weight. The possibilities of error inherent in such figures may be gauged by the following example. The *Report of the Statistical Committee appointed by the Anti-Corn Law Conference*, held in London 8–12 March 1842 (London, n.d.), p. 18, estimates that in Leeds consumption had declined by 25 per cent since 1835–6; but since the consumption of

103

the better-off classes had not declined, it estimated the reduction in working-class consumption at 50 per cent.

Table C. Number of Hides inspected (in '00s) in various centres, 1801–20

Date	Liverpool			Manchester			Sheffield			Leeds		
	Beasts	Calves	Sheep	Beasts	Calves	Sheep	Beasts	Calves	Sheep	Beasts	Calves	Sheep
1801	105	133	681	105	124	569						
1802	95	158	670	114	145	571						
1803	85	128	593	100	132	481						
1804	86	150	584	93	127	589						
1805	94	169	606	124	98	576						
1806	95	170	670	109	120	696						
1807	96	188	582	102	130	770						
1808	103	187	598	116	107	503						
1809	112	192	687	117	109	512						
1810	109	180	679	121	132	602						
1811	100	180	633	111	130	604						
1812	100	168	588	106	122	414	35	45	310			
1813	104	168	614	126	128	717	35	40	390			
1814	105	147	698	132	124	760	39	40	300			
1815	118	170	788	151	143	827	45	50	324	39	56	526
1816	120	148	736	163	164	730	53	58	320	45	68	521
1817	144	179	817	166	167	822	50	51	311	45	62	550
1818	133	171	766	165	162	845	54	39	301	50	54	560
1819	122	170	706	161	160	837	55	43	318	50	50	530
1820	110	166	700	145	170	835	44	43	274	44	56	490

6

History and 'The Dark Satanic Mills'

FOR MOST OF THE PAST hundred and fifty years the debate on what social conditions were like under early industrial capitalism has been pretty one-sided. The majority of the British people in the first half of the nineteenth century was convinced that the coming of industrial capitalism had brought them appalling hardships, that they had entered a bleak and iron age. So was the majority of the skilled and educated observers. The economists assumed that the condition of the labouring poor must be rather miserable: much of their theory was designed to show why this was inevitable. (After all, consider the notorious population theory of Robert Malthus, to the effect that population must grow faster than the means of subsistence, so that the poor must in practice be on the verge of subsistence or famine. Nobody applies this theory to Britain today, for the simple reason that the British working class is obviously not on the verge of famine. On the other hand such theories *are* applied, even today, to countries like India, where the bulk of the population is desperately poor. Theories explaining, rightly or wrongly, why semi-starvation is inevitable only look plausible, even to those who construct them, when there is semi-starvation to be explained away.) Statisticians and social investigators had no difficulty in showing that Britain's productive power and trade were increasing by leaps and bounds; but though some of the more wildly enthusiastic of them tried to prove that the condition of the people had also improved, they found this very much harder, at any rate up to the middle 1840s. Indeed, majority opinion was against them. A whole boatload of blue-books, pamphlets, journals and other literature was published on social problems. Few who have read much of this writing come away with any impression but one of considerable gloom. So little argument was there about the general awfulness of the situation among the labouring masses at this period, that subsequent historians of all shades of political opinion were in general agreement on it. Conservatives, Liberals and Fabians rejected Marx and Engels in other respects, but Engels' account of Britain in 1844 and Marx's descriptions of nineteenth-century social conditions were substantially accepted as standard. Most people accepted Marx's and Engels' evidence, even if they disagreed with their analysis and conclusions. Up to the end of the first world war there was really no argument on the subject, except about minor details. As can be seen in chapter 13 below, few serious scholars could do more than discover a few silver linings to a very large and very black cloud.

The historians who want to take a different view – and in the past thirty or forty years they have been very influential – have a very difficult job on their hands. This article proposes to discuss some of the ways in which they have attempted to tackle it. It happens that a particularly flagrant example of such whitewashing of early industrial Britain has just been published: the new edition of Engels' *Condition of the Working Class in England* by two Manchester University researchers, W. H. Chaloner and W. O. Henderson. However, they are not alone in their methods, though fortunately historians of their opinions are now losing influence. Furthermore, readers who are not historians may also find it useful to study some of the ways in which people try to argue that black is white, or at least that it isn't black, or possibly that if it is, it is nobody's fault.

The cheerful school of historians about early industrial Britain has to explain away a mass of very inconvenient facts: the majority opinion of contemporary observers and students, the huge weight of documentation about the awful social and economic conditions of the working population in the first half of the nineteenth century, and, of course, the massive discontent of the labouring poor, which broke out, time and again, in vast movements of radicalism, revolutionary trade unionism, Chartism, in riots and attempted armed risings.

The simplest way to do so is to argue that all the contemporaries were mistaken, because statistics show that things were better than before, and improving all the time, or almost all the time. 'I was reading a work the other day,' said a character in Disraeli's gloomy novel *Sybil* (1845), 'that statistics proved that the general condition of the people was much better at this moment than it had been at any known period of history': the statistical argument has long been

106

the sheet-anchor of the optimists in this field of studies. However, it was not until some thirty-five years ago that an American scholar, Professor Silberling, thought he had found a firm statistical basis for the view that the standard of living was rising at this period, and for a generation the cheerful school pinned their faith primarily to him. He constructed an index of money wages and of the cost of living for the first half of the nineteenth century, and, combining both, arrived at the conclusion that the real wages of the working-class had risen. Obviously, if he was right, all the other evidence was at least partly irrelevant. If it said that things were black, or even getting blacker, it *must* be unrepresentative or mistaken. All that remained was to explain why so widespread an illusion got about. Unfortunately, for the last ten years the Silberling index has been discredited. In the first place it has been shown that we simply do not know enough to construct such series realistically. We know the money-wage rates of a good many (generally skilled) workers on time rates, and a lot of piece rates, which are, of course, not very helpful by themselves. We know next to nothing of what people actually earned. How much overtime or short time did they work? How often were they unemployed and for how long? Who knows? As for the cost-of-living index, it is equally shaky, being largely based on guesswork. Anyway, we know from modern experience how full of pitfalls cost-of-living indices can be even in our own time, when considerable efforts are made to collect statistics specifically for their compilation. What is more, we can actually catch the statisticians out. For instance, they argued that the cost of living fell very steeply after the Napoleonic wars, so that people were better off. But by chance the actual retail prices paid in shops in some Lancashire towns in 1830 were discovered, and these show that Lancashire shoppers paid about as much in 1830 as they had in 1790. Again, the statistical series argues that London artisans improved their position most rapidly between 1810 and 1820. That may be so, but we happen to know from other sources, that the consumption of meat per head of the population in London went down quite notably in this period, i.e., that Londoners in general were able to afford less meat. A third example is even more revealing. The late Sir John Clapham the founder of the 'cheerful' school, rebuked R. W. Postgate in very schoolmasterly terms, because he had argued, on the basis of other evidence, that the builders in the 1830s were suffering very badly. Did not statistics show that their money-wages were rising, and that they were (as is quite true) rather well paid? So they do. But it so happens that for the building trade we actually have some idea of unemployment also; and the (indirect) statistics for that show that the early 1830s were a period of profound depression for the building trade. Clearly a mass of builders was out of work. (There was, of course, no dole then.) Nothing is more natural than that many of them were ragged and starving, and that, as we know, this normally skilled and well-paid trade became extremely discontented and radical.

The attempt to prove statistically that early capitalism made people better off has failed, for the time being. Professor Silberling has been quietly dropped. The cheerful historians are left with the mass of evidence, which remains gloomy. What can they do? They can attempt to discredit it, and the new edition of Engels is a particularly fine example of how they set about this. Now there is a well known and venerable academic technique for proving that, let us say, a desert is not dry and infertile. The critic points out that it is not actually waterless and lifeless. There are wells in it, and occasional temporary torrents, and sometimes it rains. Camels and bedouin, and various animals, down to fleas and mosquitoes, live in many parts of it, and so do plants, sometimes in profusion. Nor is it all composed of sand. It is therefore wild and unscholarly exaggeration to say a desert is dry and infertile, and though the true scholar will not question the motives of other people ('It is far from easy to prove the motive which has inspired the action taken by any man', as Drs Chaloner and Henderson say when attacking Engels for throwing doubt on those of the capitalists) it is pretty clear that those who say so are unscholarly or probably actuated by a prejudice against deserts. Admittedly there is a lot of evidence that many people regard deserts in this light, but they should know better. This method is extraordinarily useful: it has been used, for instance, to prove that there have never been such things as revolutions (including the Industrial Revolution). A realistic historian has once said that it is possible so to define subsistence agriculture as to prove that it never existed anywhere, and the same goes for deserts, revolutions, poverty – increasing or diminishing, capitalism, or whatever we choose. The only trouble is that, if the scholar were actually to find himself in a desert, he would not be helped by the proof that it did not, strictly speaking, exist, or if it existed, was not as dry and infertile as was often said. Fortunately for themselves the historians of Britain's early industrial age, having proved by these means, e.g., that the 'Hungry Forties' are misnamed (as Dr Chaloner tried to do in a Historical Association pamphlet), will not find themselves in the situation of an English or Irish labourer of that period.

The cheerful historians have systematically tried to discredit the contemporary evidence in this manner. That Drs Chaloner and Henderson have concentrated on Engels is due to the fact that his book on the condition of the working class was the *only* important contemporary work which tried to deal with the working class as a whole, that it has been consistently in print, and is widely (and rightly) regarded by non-Marxist historians as 'a reliable account which they can safely recommend to their students' (p. xix). But it is worth remembering that similar attempts have been made to discredit other contemporary observers and the Parliamentary Reports, for instance by Professor W. Hutt in the volume *Capitalism and the Historians* (1954) edited by Prof. F. A. Hayek, the author of the *Road to Serfdom*, a book which frankly sets out to defend the good name of capitalism against the historians.

The first and simplest way of doing so is to point out Engels' slips and minor errors, which are very numerous. It is surprising how shady a book can be made to look by systematically listing all errors in transcription and the like: until we look at the nature of these errors. To be shown on page after page that Engels did not quote his blue-books textually, that he wrote '16 years' when the source says '17', that he said a sample of children was drawn from one Sunday school, whereas it was two, and so on, naturally saps the confidence of the reader. But it proves only that anyone wishing to quote blue-books textually should go to the original sources and not lift the quotes from Engels; *not* that Engels' account is unreliable. In actual fact, the concrete cases where Engels' slips or bias are alleged to have led him to give a wrong or misleading impression of the facts, can be counted on the fingers of two hands, and some of the accusations are wrong. This is not the place to go through them in detail, but it may be worth mentioning the two which a reviewer in the *Sunday Times* has picked out as particularly bad examples of his 'cheating'. The first is 'a sensational account of the illegitimate birth-rate among female operatives in a particular factory (which) turns out to refer not to 1840 but to 1801'; the second 'a gloomy account of the sanitary condition of Edinburgh (which rests) upon an article written in 1818'.

As to the first case, Engels does not say that it took place in 1840.

In the course of analysing the social effects of overwork and night-work, he instances the case (reported in the Factory Enquiries Commission of 1833) of a factory which in the past introduced nightshifts of twelve hours, which demoralized the workers so much – the illegitimacy rate doubled during the two years the system was in force – that it had to be given up. It so happens, as Drs Chaloner and Henderson point out, that this case occurred in 1801; also that the witness who reported it claimed that the nightwork had been introduced only because a mill had been burned down and the owners operated double shifts in another mill to keep the workers employed. (No doubt they didn't think of their own profits at all.) But this is neither here nor there. If a man says: 'when soldiers are kept on parade too long, some of them faint; I can give you a concrete instance where this happened once', the validity of the statement is not affected by claiming that it happened much longer ago than one might think, or that they were kept on parade for the best of motives. Engels might be attacked if he said 'Immorality is going up by leaps and bounds today; as witness this case' which then turned out to refer to forty years ago. But he does not say this.

The second example is even more illuminating, because Engels does not base his justifiably gloomy account of the housing conditions in Edinburgh on an article published in 1818 at all. He bases it on accounts dated respectively 1836, undated (1818), 1842, 1843, which is contemporary enough for 1844. (Why should he *not* use an article of 1818 if it confirms, as Engels claims, the evidence of 1836, 1842 and 1843? Drs Chaloner and Henderson don't pretend that the 1818 article gives a misleading impression of later housing conditions.) There is, indeed, as the editors point it, one mistake in this account. Two sentences, presumably taken from the report of 1842, refer not to Edinburgh but to Tranent, though this report also contains a description of the Edinburgh slums. Drs Chaloner and Henderson do not suggest that the bits about Edinburgh which Engels did not quote – presumably by a slip – give a better impression of that city than the sources he did quote. In other words: there is no evidence here that Engels 'cheated', and no evidence that his account gives a wrong impression of what his sources say, or of reality.

The second way of discrediting Engels is to argue that the sources he uses are unrepresentative or selective. This is a well-known method of throwing doubt on the contemporary evidence of bad social conditions. It runs roughly as follows: 'These blue-books (or books, or pamphlets, or articles) were not disinterested searches for truth. They were compiled by reformers, passionately anxious to abolish certain abuses (or by revolutionaries, passionately anxious to discredit capitalism). Therefore they picked out the worst cases, because these would cause most public indignation. It does not follow that things were as bad as all that generally.' A good instance of this is Drs Chaloner and Henderson's treatment of the famous (or rather infamous) women in the mines: 'Engel's account of coal-mining in Britain in the 1840s may give readers the impression that women and children worked underground in all the colliery districts. Actually at this time the employment of women was virtually confined to mines in the West Riding, Lancashire, Cheshire, Scotland and South Wales' and they add 'The number of workers involved was quite small. In 1841 some 6,000 women and girls were employed underground and at the pithead in *all kinds* of mines in Great Britain. In the *coal mines* 1,185 females over the age of 20 and 1,165 females under that age were employed underground and at the pithead' (p. xxv). They also add that Engels said the 1842 Act forbidding the employment of women and children underground was virtually a dead letter, since no inspectors had been appointed under it: but he was wrong. One inspector had been appointed.

The nature of this procedure may be illustrated by applying it to some other topic. The argument would then run as follows: '(a) people have said there is a problem of drug-addiction, but really there are only 6,000 addicts of whom no more than 2,400 are actually on morphine. (b) It has been suggested that this is a general problem, but really it occurs only in all major cities except Newcastle and Birmingham. After all, let us not lose our heads and start making wild accusations against drug-peddlers.' As for whether the single inspector under the 1842 Acts was likely to have made much difference by 1844, we need only quote a later inspector for only one mining district, to the effect that it would take him 4 to 5 years to inspect all the collieries in his district *once*. It merely remains to add that Engels, so far from suggesting that the number of women in the mines was greater than it was, actually reprinted the detailed table containing the statistics quoted above (p. 274).

In a word, this method of attempting to discredit contemporary evidence is based on two kinds of blindness. It is blindness not to see that good men can be legitimately outraged even by 6,000 miserable wretches (as Blake wrote: 'A dog starv'd at his Master's gate, Predicts the ruin of the State'). It is even greater blindness not to see the general abuse behind the exceptional examples which reformers and revolutionaries often (but by no means always) use to arouse public opinion against it. The historian of the twenty-first century who will throw doubt on the hardships of old-age pensioners, because he finds out that a lot of them are not quite as miserable as some of the cases quoted by campaigners for better pensions, will be a fool. The historian who does the same for the sufferings which provoked a ruling class not noted for its soft heart towards the poor to produce a mountain of evidence about their hardships and to recognize the need for reforming them, is no wiser. If, in addition, he uses the same procedures to defend the capitalists which he accuses their critics for using against them, he is trebly blind.

But this is exactly what Drs Chaloner and Henderson, and other writers of the same school, do. For instance, they blame Engels, who gives a well-known account of the sufferings of seamstresses, for not mentioning that 'the wretched condition of these unfortunate girls had received a good deal of newspaper publicity, and their plight had evoked public sympathy', and for failing to quote a case (reported in the *Northern Star*) where a magistrate had taken pity on one of these girls (p. xxiv). 'This hardly looks,' they say, 'as if the middle classes were utterly indifferent to the sufferings of the seamstresses.' As a matter of fact, it looks like nothing at all, except a single magistrate who was sorry for a girl. Even if typical, which Drs Chaloner and Henderson do not suggest it was, it does not argue that anything effective was done for the girls. It only remains to add (a) that the editors do not challenge Engels' description of that situation at all, and (b) that Engels did *not* fail to mention the public outcry, since he observes that early in 1844 'the press was full of accounts of the distress among the needlewomen' and devotes a long footnote to Thomas Hood's 'Song of the Shirt', which, as he notes, appeared in *Punch* (pp. 239–40). I think we need not spend much time on further illustrations of the editors' attempts to apply whitewash.

The third method of discrediting contemporary evidence is to argue that it is biased against the capitalists, and therefore (presumably) reflects the writer's bias rather than the facts. The present edition of Engels is a good example of this, for the authors argue essentially that 'Engels in 1842 was an angry young man with a very large chip on his shoulder' who took it out on his father, a pious Rhineland businessman, by attacking the British bourgeoisie. We need not waste our time psychoanalysing the young Engels, because the motives which may or may not have urged him to become a Communist are totally irrelevant. The Congo outrages which Roger Casement and E. D. Morel exposed fifty-odd years ago are no less real because at least one of the investigators had very marked psychological peculiarities. (There is, by the way, no evidence whatever that Engels did not feel perfectly genuine, and understandable, fury against the British bourgeoisie simply because of what he saw around him in Manchester.) The question can be answered quite simply by quoting the editors. 'It is understandable,' they say (in between suggestions that it is not), 'that Engels should have taken a gloomy view of the English scene when he arrived towards the end of 1842 . . . Little wonder that Engels thought that he had come to a country that was on the whole very overworked, underfed and underpaid' (xxviii–ix). We may add (though the editors shy away from saying so directly) that it is understandable, because he had in fact come to a country which *was* 'on the whole very overworked, underfed and underpaid'. If we follow Engels as he walks through the Manchester cotton-mills and slums in this book, we shall have no difficulty in generating horror and fury even at 114 years' distance. Why then bring in Engels' family rows? There is a story told of the late Emperor Francis Joseph who visited a Bohemian town, where, shockingly enough, the royal salute was not fired. The emperor summoned the mayor for an explanation. 'Your majesty,' said the mayor, trembling, 'there are three reasons why we didn't fire the salute. The first is, that we had no gunpowder . . .' 'Thank you,' said the monarch (showing unusual perspicacity for an emperor) and dismissed him. Drs Chaloner and Henderson might ponder this.

The fourth method of discrediting contemporary evidence is to argue that it isn't good enough. This is naturally easiest when the abuses in question are such as not to lend themselves to accurate statistics. A useful example is that of the morals of factory owners. 'One charge which he repeatedly made was that an English factory was little better than a harem and that manufacturers had immoral relations with their female employees.' But 'there is little (in the Report of the Factories' Enquiry Commission) to support Engels' statement' (p. xxvi, 168 n.). Now Engels does *not* say that factories were little better than harems. He says (p. 168) that the girls were at the mercy of their masters; that some masters did not seduce their girls while others did, and in extreme cases there was nothing to stop

113

them doing it wholesale. Such cases were known. Nor should we expect too high a standard in the past, considering the kind of people who became masters in the early days of the factory system.* All this sounds reasonable enough, at least to an age brought up on cartoons of bosses chasing their typists round desks, so long as we do not expect to have it proved by accurate, or even approximate, statistics of the number of masters actually seducing factory girls. In the nature of things, however well known the practice, such statistics are not likely to be available or reliable. I really do not know how widespread such seduction was, and neither, of course, do Drs Chaloner and Henderson. However, I do know that if we asked the nineteenth-century novelists who tell us, time and again, of the sons of bourgeois families who got their first sexual experience with their parents' housemaid, for statistical proof of the relative frequency of such episodes, they would not be able to supply it. I am prepared to believe the novelists without statistics, partly because they are good observers, partly because the thing is far from unlikely. Why should we not believe Engels on similar grounds, until there is strong evidence to the contrary? It remains to add that the editors counter-attack Engels by suggesting that he is the last one to throw stones because 'his own mistress (Mary Burns) had been a cotton operative' (p. xxvi). It is evident that some people find it difficult to distinguish between a boss who seduces his staff by threatening the sack, and a man who lives as man and wife with a former factory girl for 18 years until her death, the girl being recognized as his effective wife even among 'my philistine acquaintances'. (A refusal to be officially married was long common among continental Socialists on grounds of principle.) As is well known, Engels had his only major row with Marx, when Marx failed to express sufficient sympathy for Engels' loss at the death of Mary Burns. We need not pursue this accusation against Engels further.

The last and undoubtedly the most effective method of discrediting the gloomy evidence of Engels and other contemporaries would be to produce an equal amount of evidence on the other side. However, the

---

* In passing I note one of the frequent slips and errors of the new translation. The translator, whose respect for factory girls is evidently less than Engels', says 'inclination to chastity' instead of 'occasion' or 'inducement' (no doubt confusing the German *Veranlassung* with *Veranlagung*). The old translation, e.g., in *Marx and Engels on Britain*, though as usual more clumsy, is also as usual more accurate.

cheerful school have rarely done this, confining most of their energies to negative criticisms and speculation.

It follows from all this that considerable efforts have been made to shake the gloomy (and traditional) view of the condition of the British labouring people in the first half of the nineteenth century, but so far with little result. In the case of Engels' book these efforts have been quite heroic. The two editors have clearly worked for years checking every reference of Engels, discovering every slip and error, not to mention some which are not there. Rarely has a book been subjected to such systematic and painstaking hostile cross-examination. It can be said quite categorically that he comes out of it with flying colours; much better, in fact, than one might have expected. (I wish the same could be said of all subsequent attempts by Marxists to write accounts of working class conditions under capitalism.)

Having failed to shake the contemporary evidence seriously, the cheerful historians are left with three resources. The first, on which we need not waste any time, is to admit that things were awful, but to claim that this was not the fault of capitalism: the cup was broken, but it 'came apart in my hands'. For instance, it was the fault of the workers themselves: 'in the 1840s much hardship among the workers was due to "secondary" or "self-induced" poverty – the result of excessive and feckless expenditure on drink, gambling and tobacco' (Chaloner and Henderson, *History Today*, 1956, p. 855). The second, which need not detain us either, is that the horrors of this period were not due to cruelty or ill-will: many people, including capitalists, were good and full of the best intentions. No doubt, but as we know, the way to hell is paved with good intentions. The indictment against early nineteenth-century capitalism becomes no less black if we assume that every capitalist was like Dickens' Brothers Cheeryble, and that there were no Gradgrinds at all. It would make the indictment even blacker, for it would show that the horrors of the period were not due to 'abuses' by bad men, but to something in the nature of the society.

The third resource is to claim that, bad as things were, they were still an improvement on the previous period.

This line is also quite venerable, and consists in blackening the eighteenth century to make the nineteenth look less black. To some extent this is easy, because so much less is known about the standards of living in the eighteenth century, that nobody can say for certain that black is the wrong colour. As it happens, the view that eighteenth-century conditions were superior in some respects to early nineteenth-century ones is not as outrageous as Drs Chaloner and Henderson suggest: what little is known about the movements of the popular standard of living suggests some improvement in the earlier part of the eighteenth century, and no improvement, or deterioration from the 1790s on. In the present state of knowledge I would not even like to guess at what happened in between. However, the anti-eighteenth-century argument is interesting not so much as an example of mis-placed confidence, but as a text-book illustration of the lack of historical, or human imagination and realism which afflicts so many of the 'cheerful' scholars. This may be shown by the well-known example of the 'domestic workers' *v*. 'factory workers'.

The almost universal argument of the optimists is that cottage-workers and outworkers before the industrial revolution were ex-ploited as harshly as the factory proletariat, while their pay and material conditions were worse. But this is an artificial contrast. The early industrial period was not one which *replaced* domestic workers by factory workers, except in a very few trades (outside textiles, and especially cotton, hardly at all until 1850). On the contrary: it multi-plied them. That it later starved them to death, like the handloom weavers, or drove them elsewhere, is another matter, in itself relevant to the problem of social conditions under early capitalism; but the point is, that the handloom weavers and others who were starved out were not simply 'survivals from the middle ages', but a class multi-plied, and largely created *as part of capitalist industrialization in its early phases* just as the factory workers were. The armies of seam-stresses sewing cotton shirts in their garrets for 2*s*. 6*d*. or 3*s*. 6*d*. a week belong to the history of the rise of the cotton industry just as much as the mule-spinners in the mills, or for that matter the Negro slaves who increased by leaps and bounds in the Southern States of America in response to the insatiable demand of Lancashire for raw cotton. It is as unrealistic to leave the non-factory workers of the early industrial period out of the picture, as it would be to confine the discussion of the social effects of the introduction of the typewriter to the wages and grading of workers in the mass-production engineering factories which make them, and leave out the typists.

Now, whatever the social conditions of cottage industry and outwork had been before industrialization, they were almost bound to become worse during it. (That is why the practice of documenting the bad conditions of eighteenth-century domestic workers from the reports of the 1840s – as Drs Chaloner and Henderson do (p. xiv) – is so footling. Incidentally, they blame Engels bitterly for not using contemporary evidence.) As G. D. H. Cole once said:

> 'Twelve insanitary houses on a hillside may be a picturesque village, but twelve hundred are a grave nuisance, and twelve thousand a pest and a horror.'

But this is precisely what was happening at this period: villages were turning into towns, towns into cities, while improvements in housing and sanitation, if they got beyond the village level at all, did not keep pace with the growth. Hence, by the way, the rise of new epidemic diseases after 1830, such as cholera. The same is true of working conditions. 'Grinders' disease' (roughly, *silicosis*) was worse in Sheffield in the early nineteenth than in the eighteenth century, because more grinders were crowding into the small workshops in a bigger, filthier, smokier town, where the improvement of working and housing conditions had simply not kept pace with the increase in the demand for cutlery.

To this extent the argument about the (correctly observed) poor conditions of domestic workers is an argument *against* the cheerful view of the first half of the nineteenth century; not, as its proponents think, for it. The fact that, amid all this gloom, factories generally were rather less awful than cottage or garret or cellar workshops, is true, but as pointless as the advice of the soft-hearted magistrate (whom Drs Chaloner and Henderson quote against Engels) to the seamstress who was up before him. He told the girl to take a job in a workshop, rather than to work for middlemen sweaters. But (leaving aside the fact that a sewing workshop in the 1840s was, as Engels shows, far from a bed of roses) the essence of the needlewoman's trade at this time was that it was a trade with *few* factories. No doubt if the magistrate had been a prophet, he could have told the girl that in a century's time it would all be very different, and girls like her would earn their living as shop-assistants, factory workers, waitresses or in offices. But would that have cheered her up, or us, as we look at the miserable scene of those times?

However, the argument about the superiority of factory work to domestic work is not only that in fact it was better, but that it *ought to have been* better. And this shows up extremely vividly those who make it. Take this extract from an older history-book:*

* L. Knowles, *Industrial and Commercial Revolutions*, p. 86. (1933 edn.)

Although the sentimentalists were shocked by the break-up of family life, yet the Commissioner (enquiring into the condition of handloom weavers) considered that 'domestic happiness is not promoted but impaired by all members of the family muddling together and jostling each other constantly in the same room'.* In the opinion of the Commissioner the man was improved morally by working regular hours, which were said to engender regular habits.

Now, as Engels himself points out, the workers of that period were undoubtedly often ignorant, brutalized, and shortsighted, and no wonder. It would be romanticism to say that they must be right, because – as we know – they didn't like to go into factories unless compelled to, or that their ideas of domestic happiness were ideal ones. At the same time the middle-class observers who said things like this, and the historians who echo them, clearly had no clue to what industrial capitalism actually did to people's feelings as well as to their bodies. I daresay the Commissioner honestly believed that families would be happier if men, women and children were separated, each working in an early nineteenth-century mill instead of at home. I daresay the Poor Law reformers honestly believed that paupers were morally improved by the separation of wives and husbands in the workhouse; for all I know they may have thought it improved domestic happiness also. So far as the victims of these views were concerned, the results were as bad as – perhaps worse than – if they had been achieved by deliberate cruelty: inhuman, impersonal, callous degradation of the spirit of men and women and destruction of their dignity. Perhaps this was historically inevitable and even necessary. But the victim suffered – suffering is not a privilege of well-informed persons. And any historian who cannot appreciate this is not worth reading.

Let us sum up. In Thomas Peacock's novel *Crotchet Castle* (published 1831) there is a moment when the discussions of the upper-class characters assembled in Chainmail Hall are interrupted by a crowd at the door: 'Captain Swing' has come, and the miserable farm-labourers have risen. The Rev Dr Folliott, an intelligent Tory, says here is proof of the 'march of mind' – the progress about which the capitalists are always bragging: the peasant war. Mr McQuedy, the Scots economist, who stands for the pure ideology of capitalism,

* The solution of giving them several rooms did not strike the Commissioner, it appears.

says this is impossible. How can the peasant war and the 'march of mind' be brought together? Mr Chainmail, the romantic reactionary, says the cause is the same in the dark ages as in the present: 'poverty in despair'. And Dr Folliott sums up: 'It is the natural result, Mr McQuedy, of that system of state seamanship, which your science (of bourgeois political economy) upholds. Putting the crew on short allowances, and doubling the rations of the officers, is the sure way to make a mutiny on board a ship in distress, Mr McQuedy.' That is how England looked to intelligent members of the ruling classes in the period which is now ineffectually being whitewashed. The description is correct, though we may quarrel with the analysis. Nothing the cheerful school have done has invalidated it. But in case we are tempted by these quotations from ruling-class sources to get mistaken ideas about those who made them, it is just worth quoting the continuation of the dialogue. 'We have not time to discuss cause and effect now,' said Dr Folliott. 'Let us get rid of the enemy.' And the assembled members of the ruling class drop their analyses, take up arms, and rush out of Chainmail Hall to scatter the miserable labourers into the night.

(1958)

The Standard of Living Debate: A Postscript

THE PRECEDING TWO ESSAYS were, in their original form, an attack on those who believed that the Industrial Revolution had led to a substantial improvement in the standard of living of the British people. During the years when comparatively little historical thinking about industrial revolutions took place, this view established itself widely and by the middle 1950s it had become something like an academic orthodoxy. Though Chapter 5 was by no means the only one to criticize the 'optimists', it was probably the most elaborate statement of the case against them and was therefore not only widely referred to in the very lively discussion on the subject which has since developed,[1] but also – and perhaps naturally – regarded as an attempt to argue that the standard of living had deteriorated in this period. Since controversy dims the eyesight, it may be worth repeating what is, I should hope, expressed with sufficient clarity in all my writings, namely that that this is *not* what I set out to prove.

The purpose of the paper was to demolish the 'optimistic' view, that a substantial improvement in the real incomes of most labouring Britons in the first period of industrialization could be statistically demonstrated. This did not imply that the opposite view, 'that there was substantial, or any, deterioration' in real incomes had been established, or could be established on the evidence at present available. My argument amounted 'to the assertion that no certainty in this field is as yet possible, but that the hypothesis of a marked or substantial rise in the standard of living of most Britons between the early 1790s and the early 1840s is, as things stand, an extremely improbable one'.[2] Even the consumption data which, together with the discussion of unemployment, form the main contribution of the paper to the discussion, were not claimed as conclusive, but merely as evidence which could not lightly be dismissed, but which had hitherto been lightly dismissed.

This negative case is now pretty generally accepted, though the debate continues between those who hold that on balance there was some improvement in real incomes, those who still think there is a case for some deterioration, and the agnostics, who include those who suggest that 'the inconclusive nature of the current debate . . . is perhaps a warrant for supposing that a substantial and general and demonstrable rise in the real wages of industrial workers did not occur until the 1850s and 1860s'.[3] However, this is a rather marginal debate. Its limits are now very narrow, and for most of us it does not greatly matter whether it turns out that there was a small rise, a small decline or no change at all in the real incomes of most labourers. For most purposes the statement that real incomes did not change much, on average, one way or another over the period under discussion, will probably suffice.

However, it may be as well to be clear about the sort of evidence which *could* give us a conclusive answer, if it were available. *If* we had meat consumption figures for a representative sample of the population, and not merely for London, they would go far to settle the question. *If* we could devise an index of unemployment (or part-time employment) which could be used to deflate the calculations of real wages, it would also go a good way to settle the question, unless flatly contradicted by consumption data. And if we could discover some way of establishing the social and income structure of the British labouring population with any degree of accuracy, it would help a lot. Conversely, the question can not be settled merely on the basis of global calculations of the movements of the national income, of unrepresentative statistics (e.g., those which give the incomes or consumption of the comfortable and rich classes, or individual localities or occupations), and still less on *a priori* grounds of theory. This is because hypothesis must yield to fact, if the two are in conflict and the fact is right, and also because there is no *a priori* hypothesis which would allow us to argue with any degree of conviction that in the early stages of industrialization the standard of living of the labouring poor must rise or fall at a certain rate, or indeed at all. On theoretical grounds a *substantial* rise in the standard of living at this historical period is probably the least likely hypothesis, but neither a modest rise nor a modest decline are excluded.

The discussion so far has not, therefore, been inconclusive. It has for the time being eliminated the hypothesis of a substantial rise in average real incomes, though leaving the choice between others open. It has thus eliminated, at least in its simpler versions, the argument by means of which the optimistic scholars attempted to by-pass the traditional and predominantly gloomy interpretation of the social effects of the Industrial Revolution and the evidence and arguments on which it was based. It has once again put the burden of invalidating this traditional view on the optimists. Yet this has been achieved at the cost of confining the debate largely to the ground originally chosen by the 'optimists', namely the quantitative calculations of such things as real incomes. And in doing so it has risked diverting us from the real historical problem which the original observers of the Industrial Revolution and the classical historians saw, but the 'optimists' have failed to see. The effects of the Industrial Revolution on the labouring poor are both economic (in the narrowly quantitative and material sense) and social. The two cannot be isolated from each other. And now that the attempt to prove that economic benefits were so great that there was really no material reason for discontent, has been rejected, it is time that we returned to the wider and more sensible perspective of the pre-Claphamite historians.

Their case has been reformulated in modern terms as follows. The Industrial Revolution was a bad thing for the labouring poor – at least for several decades – because it produced 'pressure on consumption and material standards of living of the mass of the population at a time when it is forced to adapt itself to major social changes'.[4] (It is worth repeating that this does *not* imply an absolute tendency of standards to deteriorate, though most traditionalists probably believed that they did up to the 1840s.)

The debate so far has concentrated almost entirely on the first half of this statement, and obviously it had to. If the optimists were right, and the poor, though subjectively disturbed and unhappy, merely wept all the way to their increasingly ample Sunday dinners, then the analysis of the social effects of industrialization clearly required a good deal of revision. Moreover, much of British history in the early nineteenth century became extremely hard to understand, notably the uniquely deep and widespread and desperate popular discontent of the period. But the second half of the classical case was always of equal or even greater importance. For instance, Engels' pioneer work of 1844 probably pays more attention to the sociology of industrialization than to the material standards of living, and certainly pays more attention to it than to the actual movement of real wages.[5] J. L. and B. Hammond, the classical exponents of 'pessimism', laid equal stress on sociological factors.[6]

This is realistic. Even if we leave out of account the element of deliberate exploitation, the hardness of heart of the rich in the face of the poor, the failure of economic liberalism to provide any answers to their social needs, and other characteristics of capitalist industrialization in the early nineteenth century, it is a sociological commonplace that 'it is typical, especially of the first impact of new economic patterns, that they threaten or disrupt the previous social relationships, while not immediately supplying new security devices in their place'.[7] Moreover, it is a matter of observation that the Industrial Revolution produced a 'catastrophic dislocation of the lives of the common people'.[8] It is perhaps significant that the pioneers of the 'optimistic' view tended not only to maximize the material gains of the poor, but also to minimize the impact of the Industrial Revolution. Both Clapham and Ashton stressed the gradual and continuous nature of economic change, and Ashton, who was frankly suspicious of the very term 'industrial revolution', succeeded in writing an entire economic history of England in the eighteenth century without actually mentioning it. Fortunately, just as the Industrial Revolution itself has, after some decades in the wilderness, once again come into the centre of historical and economic discussion, so the sociological aspects of industrialization are once again attracting serious attention.[9] Henceforth it will be impossible to conduct the debate on its social and economic effects simply as an argument about real incomes.

A return to tradition should once again reveal the full weight of the pessimistic view. It cannot at present be established purely in terms of real wages, and perhaps the evidence will never allow us any certainty, though the question is not closed. All we can say for certain is, that 'the "average" working man remained very close to subsistence level at a time when he was surrounded by the evidence of the increase of his national wealth, much of it transparently the product of his own labour and passing, by equally transparent means, into the hands of his employers'.[10] It probably could be established in nonmaterial terms, at least for anyone capable of appreciating the full depth of the dislocation in the lives of the common people, as the thinkers of T. L. Peacock's *Steam Intellect Society* were not, and their modern successors still are not. When the economic pressure which kept standards no more than just about level in a period of

123

headlong economic expansion, is combined with the effects of social dislocation, the 'pessimistic' case becomes very difficult to answer. What is more, it also fits the facts of British history. On a gloomy interpretation, the popular discontent of the early nineteenth century makes sense; on an optimistic interpretation it is almost inexplicable. However, a view that on balance the condition of the common people took a turn for the worse between the 1790s and the 1840s does not imply an equally pessimistic view of the preceding and subsequent periods in their history, still less a predetermined view about long-term tendencies towards absolute pauperization.

NOTES

1 The chief British contributions to this discussion so far have been: D. Woodruff, 'Capitalism and the Historians' (*Journ. Econ. Hist.* XVI, 1956, p. 1); W. H. Chaloner. *The Hungry Forties* (Historical Association, Aids to Teachers Series, I, 1957); E. J. Hobsbawm, 'The British Standard of Living 1790–1850' *Econ. Hist. Rev.* X, p. 1, 1957); W. H. Chaloner and W. O. Henderson, edition of F. Engels, *Condition of the Working Class in England* (London 1958); S. Pollard, 'Investment, Consumption and the Industrial Revolution' (*Econ. Hist. Rev.* XI, p. 2, 1958); R. M. Hartwell, 'Interpretations of the Industrial Revolution in England' (*Journ. Econ. Hist.* XIX, 1959); A. J. Taylor, 'Progress and Poverty in Britain 1780–1850' (*History* XLV, Feb. 1960); R. M. Hartwell, 'The Rising Standard of Living in England 1800–50' (*Econ. Hist. Rev.* XIII, p. 3, 1961); E. J. Hobsbawm, En Angleterre: Révolution industrielle et vie matérielle des classes populaires (*Annales* XVII, p. 6, 1962); 'The Standard of Living during the Industrial Revolution: A Discussion' by E. J. Hobsbawm and R. M. Hartwell (*Econ. Hist. Rev.* XVI, p. 1, 1963); E. P. Thompson, *The Making of the English Working-Class* (London 1963), pt. II. The question has been incidentally discussed in a number of other works.

2 Hobsbawm and Hartwell, op. cit., pp. 120, 123.
Since the original publication of this book the debate has continued. Mention may be made of the articles of J. E. Williams and R. S. Neale in *Econ. Hist. Rev.* XIX, 3, 1966. One aspect of the question has been significantly advanced; the study of diet (see J. Burnett, *Plenty and Want*, 1966; T. C. Barker, J. C. Mackenzie and J. Yudkin ed. *Our Changing Fare*, 1966).

3 H. J. Habbakuk, *American and British Technology in the Nineteenth Century* (Cambridge 1962), pp. 138–9.

4 Pollard, op. cit.

5 It is often overlooked that Engels did not believe that proletarian revolution would break out in Britain because of a tendency to absolute pauperization, but because of a long-term tendency towards social polarization, and the periodic and disastrous slumps. Intolerable periodic unemployment would, if anything, be the spur. (Chaloner & Henderson edition, p. 334). His opinions about wages were marked by caution. He supposed that 'average' wages would be above the 'minimum' – which itself would allow 'a household in which there were a number of wage-earners (to be) fairly well off', and might be considerably above it, if 'the level of culture of the workers' made it impossible to lower the wage-level; e.g., 'if the workers are accustomed to eat meat several times a week' (pp. 90–2).

6 E.g., *The Bleak Age* (Penguin edn), p. 15.

7 Wilbert E. Moore, *Industrialization and Labor* (Ithaca 1951), p. 21.

8 Karl Polanyi, *Origins of Our Time* (London 1945), p. 41.

9 Cf. Neil Smelser, *Social Change in the Industrial Revolution* (London 1959), and E. P. Thompson's *The Making of the English Working-Class* (London 1963).

10 E. P. Thompson, op. cit., p. 318.

8

Economic Fluctuations and
Some Social Movements since 1800

I

THIS CHAPTER* DEALS with the periodic and sudden expansions
in the size, strength and activity of social movements, mainly in
nineteenth- and early twentieth-century Europe.† The period is,
roughly speaking, that in which the economic fluctuations of an industrial and capitalist economy are of decisive importance; the area
one in which the structures of society in general, and the labour market in particular, are fairly similar. For this reason such countries as
Australasia and the United States have been omitted. The article will
deal primarily with the questions why such movements are 'jumpy'
and discontinuous, why they occur when they do; and, to a lesser
extent, with problems of international co-ordination. Since continuous measurement, however crude, is almost impossible except for
such phenomena as strikes and trade-union movements, these will be
mainly considered. Similarly, since the material, poor as it is, is much
better for Britain – at any rate before the 1890s – than for other
countries, British data are mainly used. Even so, a good deal of the
discussion must remain speculative.

The most dramatic of sudden expansions of social movements are
the great social revolutions of 1789–1917; but the pattern of discontinuity is quite general even in less disturbed times and in narrower
fields. The graph of the membership of virtually every trade-union
movement, for example, looks like a series of sloping steps, or of
broad valleys broken by sharp peaks, or a combination of both; very

* Based on a paper read before the annual meeting of the Economic History
Society in April 1951.
† For the sake of brevity I shall call these phenomena '*explosions*' or '*leaps*'.

rarely is it a mere rising slope. In Britain the 'jumps' about which we are best informed are those of 1871-3, 1889-91 and 1911-13. Each about doubled the basic strength of the trade-union movement, though even higher peaks were temporarily reached during the explosive periods.[1] We know too little to measure the size of the earlier explosions – e.g., those of 1833-5, 1838-42, and others,[2] or those of most continental countries before the 1890s. After that their size varies. The Norwegian unions increased about two and a half times in 1904-6, the Austrian ones about three times, the Hungarian ones rather less than doubled; the Swedish ones rather more than doubled in 1905-7 and so on. The best-known 'explosions', which happen also to be among the most recent, in France and the U.S.A. in 1936-7, show something like a quadrupling and a doubling respectively within the year. Sometimes the discontinuity is seen not in an absolute increase in numbers, but in a sudden change of direction in the membership curve, e.g., in Germany after 1899.[3] The sudden and sharp variations in the amount of labour activity – e.g., strikes – as distinct from the membership of organizations are, of course, so well known as to need no proof.

Curves, of course, cannot reveal the whole truth. The characteristic thing about our 'explosions' is that they mark qualitative as well as quantitative changes. They are, in fact, generally expansions of the movement into new industries, new regions, new classes of the population; they coincide with a clustering of new organizations, and the adoption of new ideas and policies by both new and existing units. Thus the 'explosion' of the early 1830s in Britain saw old local craft societies adopt quite new techniques of national co-ordination, and the fusion of socialist-cooperative and trade-unionist ideas. That of the 1870s saw the extension of trade unionism to agriculture, the beginning of the labour conquest of formerly weaker areas, like the north-east coast and South Wales, and the first serious experiments in independent labour representation. That of 1889-90 saw not merely regional extensions and the conquest of new industries and types of labour, but changes in the techniques of old craft societies, and the impact of socialist ideas on the practical tactics of the movement. If we confine ourselves mainly to studying quantitative variations, it is merely for convenience, because these seem to provide a reasonably useful index of the more complex qualitative ones.

The 'leaps' have attracted remarkably little attention among stu-

127

dents. Scholars have recently done some work on the period before 1850,[4] sometimes without observing clearly that the explanations they offer do not apply to subsequent periods. There is also a fairly ample literature on the correlation of labour movements with the trade cycle, showing that the size and activity of the movements increase at times favourable to bargaining, and slacken at others.[5] These, too, are not always aware that their conclusions are not universally, or simply, applicable. With rare exceptions[6] they fail to get to grips with the problem, for the size of the 'leaps' bears no apparent relation to the size of the cyclical up- or down-swing in which it occurs, at any rate after 1850. 1868–73 was admittedly an outsize in booms, but one would hardly claim that the up-swings of 1887–90 or 1909–12 in Britain were so much bigger than 1880–2, 1896–1901 or 1904–7 as to explain the absence of comparable 'explosions' in those years. It has indeed been argued[7] that the great 'leaps' occur after exceptionally severe slumps, which impress workers with the value of organization. However, while this may be a contributory factor in Britain in 1889 as in the U.S.A. in 1933–7, it obviously does not apply to the turn of the 1860s, a time of almost universal 'leaps' throughout Europe; to many of the Continental expansions of social movements of 1899–1908 or to Britain in 1911–13. No adequate explanation of the phenomenon therefore exists—at any rate after 1850. All we know is that they are related in some way to short-term cyclical fluctuations, and probably also to the longer periods of economic change with which most students now operate: the economic expansions of the period up to 1815, from the 1840s to the early 1870s, and from the late 1890s to the First World War, and the periods of difficulty and crisis which alternate with them.

II

Our first task must be to see what light changes in the livelihood and working conditions of the labouring classes throw on the problem. The most usual indices used by statisticians, those of wages, cost of living, and unemployment, are extremely defective; first, because of our abysmal ignorance of the way in which various classes of the population got their living and how economic fluctuations affected them; second, because of technical drawbacks in the indices themselves which, in any case, were rarely designed for our purpose. The fact that most of them are averages of components whose movement varies greatly, and may even simultaneously go in opposite directions[8] is not, perhaps, fatal; for the great 'leaps' normally affect widely differing groups at the same time. Yet it is important to remember that they often obscure such vital distinctions as that between the section of workers who normally lived – in Britain at least – under conditions of full employment, and those who normally lived in a glutted labour market.[9] A more serious drawback is this. If a wage or unemployment index is to be used, one must assume that it applies to a regular wage-earning class, employed in a fairly permanent form, and supplying most of its need by cash purchases in a market. The further we recede from 1880–1913, or the further we go from highly proletarianized countries like Britain or Saxony, the less representative do they become. They cannot be applied without the greatest caution to domestic workers, sub-contractors, or other forms of small commodity producers on the way to joining the working-class; or to the large body of casual, floating and irregular labour; or to semi-agricultural labour. Thus for the casual man in the nineteenth century a depression would mean, not an absolute frontier between work and idleness, but merely an increase in the length of the always present spells between work, a shortening of working spells – a difference in degree rather than kind. For the independent producer or outworker it might not mean unemployment at all, but merely harder work for longer hours in order to make ends meet less adequately. Moreover, we cannot even assume that the general state of the labour market was much the same among those to whom trade-union indices did not apply as among those to whom it did. At the very least we must assume a much greater volume of constant, if concealed unemployment than the indices show.[10] Their use is thus dangerous, though it becomes less risky as more workers come to fit into a standard pattern of full-time wage-earners, though on different levels of income and status.

Lastly, we do not possess any usable indices for certain important factors which affect working-class behaviour – for instance, intensity and discomfort of work – and can, at best, improvise a few scattered and partial series.

III

Armed with such fragile tools, what can we discover about our 'explosions'? Very much less after 1850 than before, in spite of the increasing abundance of our material. Sometime around the 1840s there is an economic watershed, whose nature is only now beginning to attract attention.[11] Before 1850, and in some backward countries after that date also, social movements were greatly affected by catastrophic and simultaneous increases in misery for most of the working population, which even the sketchiest evidence reveals. Expansions occurred at or near the bottom of slumps. So much may this be taken for granted that Prof. Rostow can construct a legitimate, though somewhat arbitrary[12] 'index of social tension' for 1792–1850 on the assumption that the trough of the slump and a rise in food prices (the two being normally combined) inevitably indicate maximum unrest. Professors Labrousse and Ashton have shown why this should be so.[13] Depressions then began in the main in the agrarian sector – most often with bad harvests – and affected the industrial sector through raw material shortages, but chiefly through contracting the main body of home demand, which was rural. Consequently, high unemployment tended to occur at times of famine prices* a situation which almost compelled rioting. We may add that in the absence of unions, and of employment policies which were adopted, if at all, only much later, depressions normally meant extremely drastic wage-cuts for the less skilled factory workers, and very sharp falls in earnings for the vast penumbra of semi-dependent artisans and outworkers.[14]

This analysis can only be applied to Britain with some reserve. The primacy of the genuine trade cycle here is not in much doubt after 1815, or perhaps even from the 1780s, though the 'Labroussian' nature of our export markets no doubt influenced it, and the policy of the agricultural interest up to 1846 probably kept food prices fluctuating more sharply than they need have done. Thus we do not find the clear seasonal pattern of the 'pure' unrest of the old type: mounting to a minor peak towards the end of the year, after the immediate effects of the harvest have worn off, and towards a major one in the months just preceding the new one. (See Table I.) Still, slump 'explosion' remains the rule before 1850, maintained doubtless by contemporary wage-policies, by the narrow zone which separated workers from destitution, even at good times, by rigidities in the system of food distribution and similar factors.

After 1850 matters changed. The trade cycle won its general victory – 1857 was perhaps the first world-wide crisis. The bottom of the

* Local prices tending to fluctuate quickly and wildly.

Table I. *Seasonality of riots in England and Wales, 1740–1800*[15]*

Percentage of disturbed years in which riots occurred

January	8	May	33	September	22
February	5·5	June	35·5	October	25
March	11	July	25	November	11
April	22	August	14	December	3

Table II. *Seasonality of unrest in Britain, 1800–50*†

Year	Description	Part of Year (peak months in heavy type)
1802–3	Trade Unions. Luddism of shear-men, etc.	April to **July**
1808	Lancashire weavers' strike	June
1811–12	Nottingham Luddites	**March; November**
1812	Nottingham Luddites	November–December
	Lancashire Luddites	March–**April**
	Yorkshire Luddites	February–June (**April**)
1816	Luddism and Farm-labourers	May–June
1817	Blanketeers, Derby and Huddersfield 'risings'	**Early June**
1818	Lancashire strikes	July–August
1819	Peterloo (Reform agitation)	Early summer–**August**
1826	Luddism	April–May
1830	Farm-labourers rising	October–November
1830	‡Ten Hour Campaigns (North Country)	January–**March**
1831	‡Reform Riots	November
1832	‡Reform Riots	May
1833	‡Ten Hour Campaign	January–March
1834	Grand National Consolidated Trades Union: most rapid expansion	January–April (**March**?)
1837	Anti-Poor Law campaigns	January–**early June**; **November**
1838–9	Chartism	December–June (**May–June**)
	Chartism: Newport Rising	December
1842	Chartism: general strike	**August**
1843	Wales: Rebecca Riots	**May–June**
1848	Chartism	**April–June**

* Riots are recorded in 36 years of the period.
† This table includes only the main episodes, and is thus not strictly comparable with Table I. Sources are too numerous to list conveniently.
‡ Affected by parliamentary time-table.

depression and the peak of the cost of living no longer tended to coincide. Indeed, if anything the opposite was true: the scarcity of 1853–5 was the first which did not produce major unrest in most countries,[16] being offset by the exceptionally full employment of that monumental boom.[17] In any case the disappearance of famines and the smoothing of cost-of-living fluctuations in Western Europe in the succeeding two generations, caused the old pattern to lose some of its distinctness.

No equally distinct pattern replaced it. For one thing, a wide variety of countries, each at a different stage of economic development, now came into the orbit of the capitalist economy, and in many of these the old rhythm was still dominant, and it remained important in others with an exceptionally low general level of earnings. The Belgian miners' *Jacquerie* of 1886, the great political strikes of the depression years 1893 and 1902 are at least as prominent in the social history of that country as the trade-union expansion of the 1904–7 up-swing.[18] (1902, indeed, was a great year for general strikes all over Europe.)[19] The Italian movements present an almost classic 'depression pattern' until well into the twentieth century; notably in the nation-wide riots of January to May 1898, which were set off by an old-fashioned leap in the cost of living.[20] Even the main trade-union expansion in 1901 may have coincided with a dip rather than a rise in the economic curve,[21] and the old cost-of-living pattern was still very much alive in 1906.[22] In the genesis of the Russian Revolution of 1905 the depression periods – the middle 1880s and the early 1900s – are more immediately important than the boom expansions of industrial agitation in the later 1890s. Nor, of course, did the depression pattern disappear entirely in countries like Britain, after it had lost its primacy. It has been observed that franchise campaigns, even after 1850, tended to revive in times of slump, when industrial forms of activity were inadvisable,* just as even before 1850 trade-union expansions had, sometimes without attracting more than local attention, tended to occur in the up-swing of booms, e.g., in 1792, 1818, 1824–5 and 1844–6.[23] Nevertheless, it remains true that striking 'leaps' increasingly tended to occur, less at the bottom of slumps, and more at times of cyclical up-swing, of rising employment or, a special case of great importance in the twentieth century, of war.

* The sharp distinction between industrial and political action is, however, artificial, especially on the Continent where permanently weak trade unions habitually relied on political campaigning.

Much might be said about the political implications of these changes, which led to a sort of dispersal of unrest, both between different classes in one country, and between different countries. The history of 1848, for instance, might well have been different if the deepest trough of the countries dominated by an industrial rhythm had not occurred some years previously – in 1839–42;[24] if the old and new rhythms had more nearly coincided over the whole Continent. British history in the 1880s was much affected by the fact that the peaks of the Irish movement – an affair of small sellers and tenants – occurred in the cyclical troughs of 1879–81 and 1886–7 and not, like those of the British Labour Movement, on the up-swing of 1888–91.[25] Again, the observer cannot help noticing the oddly syncopated rhythm of the European trade-union 'leaps' between 1889 and 1914, notably the habit of the main British stresses (1889–90 and 1911–13) of falling on comparatively less accentuated Continental beats.* Similar phenomena may be observed in the world-wide trade-union expansions of the second half of the 1930s, which were rather less marked in Britain than in most other countries, including notably, in many British colonies and dependencies.[26] Such changes are reflected in the evolution of the ideas and tactics of those who believed in European or world revolution, from the traditional assumptions of the men of 1848 to the complexities of Lenin's 'law of uneven development'. We should, however, add that the increasing political interdependence of countries, and the unifying force of such things as wars have to some extent counteracted this 'dispersal'.

IV

The new model of 'explosion' is thus not so easy to analyse. Certainly the analysis of the available indices of labour conditions is more complicated, though it does help in settling the problem of the exact timing of the 'leaps'. The most measurable of these, in Britain, occur on the up-swing of trade cycles, but appear to have been hatched in periods when important groups of workers became less well-off.

Real wage figures are too artificial and unreliable to measure this. Fortunately we have some rough, but more realistic, indications in consumption figures for certain staple goods and the pauper returns. This evidence is by no means conclusive, though it does show that,

* The Russian labour revival from 1912 and the Belgian general strike of 1913 are the main Continental exceptions.

between 1867 and 1911, our pattern fits the three up-swings in which expansions took place, does not fit the two in which they were absent, and may or may not fit that of 1903–7 in which there was no major trade-union activity, but – to judge by the general election of 1906 – a marked political 'leap'. Table III[27] sets out the data for the three expansions of 1871–2, 1889–90 and 1911–12. It shows that the rate of adult and able-bodied pauperism failed to fall between the trough of the slump and the period just before the 'explosion', and might even show a tendency to rise. *Per contra*, in the periods 1880–4 and 1893–8 there was a fairly steady decline, though not in 1902–7.* Similarly a stronger tendency to buy less of certain staple goods appears before the 'explosions', than in the up-swings which do not contain any.

Table III. *Changes in Working-Class Standards before Trade-Union Expansions, 1871–2, 1889–90 and 1911–12*

Year	Consumption Changes (a)	Paupers per 1,000 of population (b)	'Ordinarily able-bodied paupers' per 1,000 population (c)
		I. 1867–72	
1867	1	45·0	6·9
1868	3	48·0	7·7
1869	4	47·7	7·8
1870	3	48·8	7·9
1871	4	48·2	7·7
1872	0	43·0	6·6
		II. 1886–9	
1886	6	29·9	3·7
1887	2	29·9	3·7
1888	4	29·0	3·7
1889	3	27·9	3·5
		III. 1908–11	
1908	5	25·7	3·2
1909	1	26·1	3·5
1910	3	25·9	3·6
1911	1	24·8 (d)	3·5

* This whole period, however, sees a generally rising trend of able-bodied pauperism, which may be due to the abnormal depression in London, at its peak in 1905–6. Hence able-bodied pauperism in 1903–7 does not show a mere failure to decline from depression levels – in fact, the slump made hardly any impact on it – but a sharp jump in 1905–6.

(a) This series expresses the number of the following eight commodities whose consumption per head fell in the year: Tea, Sugar, Tobacco, Beer, Currants and Raisins, Cocoa, Coffee, Rice. *Sources*, as used by G. H. Wood, 'Some Statistics Relating to Working Class Progress', *J.R. Stat. Soc.* vol. 62 (1889). For 1900–11 the commodities used by F. Wood, 'The Course of Real Wages in London 1900–12', *J.R. Stat. Soc.* vol. 77 (1913–14) have been used. Since her table includes Meat and Flour, but excludes Rice and Coffee, the series are not comparable. The inclusion of other commodities in the earlier series does not change their shape.

(b) R.C. on Poor Law (*Parl. Papers*, 1909, XXXIX, App. p. 117), Local Govt. Board Report (*Parl. Papers*, 1912–13, XXXV, p. 152). This rate includes all paupers, and thus differs for that excluding the insane and casual which is sometimes given (*Parl. Papers*, 1910, LIII, p. 29).

(c) Local Government Board Reports.

(d) From 1 Jan. 1911 persons who had received poor relief since 1 Jan. 1908 became eligible for Old Age Pensions; hence some or all of the decline in the rate (*Parl. Papers*, 1912–13, XXXV, pp. viii, 105, 117).

Thus it is fairly clear that money was getting tighter for the working-class household in the later 1860s. This is borne out by the statistics of the Oddfellows; resignation from that Society rose steadily from 1864 to 1869 and did not really begin to fall until 1871.[28] The increase in pauperism was striking enough to cause a marked tightening of Poor Law administration in 1869 and 1871,[29] for it was ascribed, on no very obvious evidence, to laxity. The tightest period seems to have been in 1870. The evidence for 1886–9 is somewhat less strong, though suggestive enough. The decline in real wages in the years before 1911 is a matter of common knowledge.[30] About the 1833–5 outbreak we know hardly anything, since we lack both general consumption and poor law figures. It would be unwise to read much into the few figures we possess. Though wholesale wheat prices were falling, we know that retail prices did not decline in proportion, if they declined at all. The results of an investigation into their change since 1814 by the Chartist Convention in 1839[31] may be summed up in the words of one of the questionnaires: 'While wages have been steadily falling provisions have not. My memory can serve me for 1830. The difference if any is trifling on either side.'[32] The general picture is thus one of wages lagging behind prices in the early stages of these booms, while the decline in unemployment and the expansion of overtime or other elastic forms of earning had not yet offset the rise.

The unemployment situation is more complex. We know hardly anything about the early 1830s, except that unemployment among the favoured Ironfounders rose until 1833.[33] Still, in general it must have declined from the 1832 peak, though this may not have affected the men hit by technological changes. In 1871 unemployment had been improving for two years or so in the metal industries, and was just beginning to improve in building, printing and other less cyclical and more sluggish occupations, which may, however, give a better idea of what happened to unorganized workers.[34] In 1889 unemployment in the main cyclical industries showed a sharp decline from the great peak of 1886, flattening out somewhat in 1888–9 and rising a little in 1889–90. The figures of unemployment among builders, printers, cabinet-makers, showed the expected lag in 1887–8, declined more steeply in 1888–9 and flattened out in 1889–90. Some industries, however, which we know to have been greatly affected by the subsequent 'explosion', were heterodox. The boot- and shoemakers had their unemployment peak in 1888 and had only just begun their decline.[35] The railwaymen and locomotive engineers also had delayed unemployment peaks in 1887 and 1888. In 1911 the rise in employment is more uniform. Even the builders whose figures of unemployment had been sluggish for a decade, were coming out of their depression, though there was an odd, and quite untypical, lay-off of 5 per cent of them in June, which may be interesting.[36]

Unfortunately, it is difficult to compare this with other countries' experience. The data are scantier[37] and in view of the less industrialized state of other areas, less representative of the classes which join labour movements. Such as they are, they fit fairly well. Thus, consumption figures and general evidence suggest a temporary increase in labour's difficulties at the end of the 1860s and in the early 1870s, at any rate in Prussia.[38] For Saxony, we get the same impression for the late 1880s and 1890s from some figures of meat consumption per head;[39] for all Germany and for some widely separated towns the same seems to apply in 1904–6.[40] How much value is to be put on these and other isolated and tricky indices[41] is another question. It is perhaps worth noting that the first steps in labour organization in Asian countries are widely ascribed to the lag of wages behind prices in the abnormal booms of war-time, which may be regarded as an extreme instance of what we have been describing.[42] There is room for much more research in this difficult field.

Nor is it possible without laborious, and probably vain, researches and calculations, to make any general estimates of the annual changes in intensity and discomfort of work in any European country of our period. That these have an important connexion with 'explosions' is highly probable. There is some general evidence on this matter[43] and it is interesting that the periods of 'explosion' are normally among the few in which demands for shorter hours, which, in this period, may generally be taken at their face value,* play a significant part in labour struggles: the Short Time Committees of the early 1830s, the Nine Hour Campaign of 1871–2, the Eight Hour Campaign of the late 1880s and early 1890s spring to mind in this country. We may also gauge the importance of this factor by comparing the behaviour of groups whose labour had been intensified with those where it had not. Thus Simiand's excellent figures show five major periods of labour activity in the two northern French coalfields between 1850 and 1902. Table IV shows that the fields in which intensification of labour took place were those in which labour activity was greatest, up to 1893. (The last expansion, 1900–2, took place at a time of rapid mechanization and falling output per head, and does not fit.) A similar correlation emerges if we compare the effects of the trade-union expansion of 1889–91 in different British railway companies. If

Table IV. *Intensity of Effort and Strikes in Nord and Pas de Calais Coalfields, 1850–90*[44]

Years	Net increase (decrease) in effort per head†		Remarks
	Nord	Pas de Calais	
1864–6	+ 8·5	− 9·5	Outbreak in N. 1866
1870–2	+27	+26·5	,, both 1872
1882–4	+ 3·5	− 0·5	,, N. 1884
1886–9	+ 0·5	+17	,, P.d.C. 1889–93

we take the rate of non-fatal injuries to railway-men as a rough guide to changes in the intensity of work, we shall find that it rises sharply in three major companies between 1886 and 1891, and falls, some-

---

* These may sometimes be disguised demands for wage-rises through over-time pay. But during the Great Depression in Britain they were often disguised demands for spreading unemployment evenly.

† The percentage rise or fall in production per man-day and in machine H.P. per 100 workers has been calculated, the first year of each series = 100. Decreases in the H.P. ratio have been added, increases subtracted, from the first figure to make a crude allowance for that part of increased output which is not attributable to extra physical effort.

times steeply, in three others.[45] Table V compares the fortune of the main railwaymen's union in the companies concerned:[46]

Table V. *Expansion of membership and branches of Amalgamated Society of Railway Servants in two groups of Companies, 1888-91*

	Companies whose accident rate	
	(I) Rose*	(II) Fell†
1. Number of branches in 1888	91	55
2. Number of branches with little membership change, as per cent of 1888	14	33
3. Number of new branches 1888-91, as per cent of 1888	61·5	29
4. Number of new and rising branches 1888-91, as per cent of 1888	144	96

However, the difficulties of using partial, often unsuitable and tricky data of this kind are very great. In any case, more work is needed before we can tell how far such changes in effort are functions of cyclical movements – e.g., in depressions, as Simiand suggests,[47] functions of the inelasticity of wages, in booms of that of the labour supply – and how far they express long-term factors.[48] Nor do we know exactly what importance they have in the minds of workers compared to other causes of discontent. Meanwhile we can only be uneasily aware of their possible importance in our problem.

V

All this, however, only tells us at what moment in the short term an 'explosion' is most likely to occur. But the crux of the matter is whether the whole labour situation is sufficiently inflammable to ignite. (It is not, of course, necessary that all sections of labour should be at the point of spontaneous ignition, for 'explosions' have great power to propagate themselves, once they begin in one area of industry.)[49] Not every trade cycle produces such general inflammability. In Britain, after 1850, it seems to occur roughly every other decade.[50] Longer trends in our indices throw little light on this

---

* London and N.W., G. Northern, North Eastern.
† G. Western, London and S.W., Great Eastern.

problem. The 'explosions' of the early 1870s and 1900s appear in secular boom periods, those of the 1830s and 1880s–90s in secular depression phases. That of 1872 occurs at the end of a period of probably falling unemployment, rising money and real wages; that of 1889 during one of heavier unemployment, stable money and rising real wages; that of 1911 while unemployment falls, money wages remain stable and real wages fall. The troubles of the 1830s – if one is to hazard a guess about the period – may have coincided with rising unemployment, falling real and money wages. Continental 'explosions' occur against movements which are hardly more uniform.

Clearly the study of isolated series of statistics will carry us no farther. We must consider the 'explosion' as a whole, in relation to the structure of the economy, and the particular phase of economic change in which it occurs. Perhaps the most useful assumption is that, under nineteenth- and early twentieth-century conditions, the normal process of industrial development tends to produce explosive situations, i.e., accumulations of inflammable material which only ignite periodically, as it were under compression. This would appear to be so in all the three main phases of the economy, that of the transition to industrialism, of classical 'free competition', and of the modern forms of state and corporation capitalism,* though each has its own forms of inelasticity, as well as its specific counteracting factors. In countries which start late on the road to industrialization we may – as in Italy – find curious combinations of all these. For most of the nineteenth century analysis is simplified since we have, speaking broadly, to consider only growing economies, and can neglect the major modifications introduced by the latter phases of economic development. Thus active government intervention before 1914 is mainly confined to providing a legal framework for industrial bargaining, to police actions, to relations with their own employees, who are not normally (apart from railwaymen) an important section of the working class, and to occasional interference in large disputes, and occasional encouraging gestures by administrations of the left like Waldeck Rousseau in France, Zanardelli and Giolitti in Italy, tending to boost incipient expansions of social movements. The formation of huge business combinations in our period does not as yet

---

* Or, for those who prefer Schumpeterian terms, the three 'Kondratiev waves' which more than cover our period.

lead to important joint-monopolies with labour* but, tilting the bargaining balance sharply in favour of employers, usually intensifies the old-fashioned attitude of management to unions. Serious recognition, institutionalized collective bargaining, etc., are only beginning to develop.[51]

This does not mean that our analysis could not be applied, *mutatis mutandis*, to the later phases. While we should expect each phase of economic development to have its own patterns of accumulation and ignition, there is a certain family resemblance between all of them.[52] It is uncertain whether we should regard the whole process on the – necessarily crude – analogy of the ordinary internal combustion engine, whose explosion is ignited by an outside spark, or the more elegant Diesel engine, in which the compression itself produces the explosion. We can find examples of both. In any case, a spark plug is readily available in the trade cycle, or in political events.

Even when all simplifications have been made, the phenomenon remains rather complex. Perhaps the most convenient way to approach it is therefore to take a particular 'explosion' as a starting-point: that of 1889–90 in Britain. Though this is traditionally associated with the London Dock Strike, the organization of the unskilled, and the 'revival of Socialism', in fact it touched almost all industrial parts of the country, and a wide variety of industries and grades of labour with very varying political affiliations.[53]

We may range the various groups affected by this phenomenon into a sort of spectrum. At one end of it we find those whose 'explosion' was dominated by the trade cycle (in the specific wider setting of the Great Depression), e.g. coal-miners and traditional heavy industries; at the other end, groups like the gas-workers, almost unaffected by cyclical movements. In fact, most groups were somewhere between these extremes, though the cyclical factors which affected them were not so much sharp periodic jabs of unemployment or wage-cuts in slumps, as more indirect and piecemeal forms of pressure which bore on them, as employers attempted to escape the general tendency of profit-margins to fall. The movements dominated by the cycle began well before the main outbreak – among the miners, in the trough of the selling-price of coal, in the shipyards, just after their most disastrous year, in cotton even earlier.[54] They had surprisingly little immediate effect on the rest of the country, which waited for the

* It would take us off the track of the present argument to discuss the interesting exceptions to this statement.

spark to come from sailors, dockers and gas-workers two years later.[55] Moreover, they continued semi-independently of the main movement, though sometimes, like the miners in the TUC, allying with it in pursuit of common demands (1889–93). Of the wider unions among the unskilled, that which had its headquarters in the north-eastern shipyards was the only one not to be under socialist leadership.[56]

We may note in passing that 'explosiveness' was less, where regular institutions existed which were believed capable of safeguarding the general bargaining position of the men, and their basic minimum of life. Cotton did not explode in the 1880s, but adjusted gradually; wool, which lacked any such machinery – like cotton in the 1820s and 1830s – and coal-mining, which suffered under sliding-scales, did 'explode'.*

We may thus conclude that long-term depression factors (as expressed in cycles within such periods) helped to accumulate inflammable material rather than to set it alight. However, it should be remembered that the direct pressure of the Great Depression on labour in Britain was rather milder than in the 1815–47 period, or between the wars. Such pressure was not, of course, confined to secular depression periods. In secular periods of expansion there might be less cause for employers to attack labour conditions directly, but the indirect effects of business policies might be equally serious, e.g., changes in the direction of investment. In so far as such factors – which we need analyse no further here – affect labour conditions and wages, they have already been briefly considered in section IV above.

We may next group our industries differently. At one end of the scale we shall place those which increased their output or activities without any significant technical or organizational change, e.g., the gas-workers; at the other those undergoing rapid technical revolution of the sort most likely to affect workers, e.g., mass-production clothing-manufacture. Since Britain (unlike contemporary Germany or the U.S.A.) was not, on the whole, undergoing any very startling change in technique or business organization, most groups at this

---

* The main achievements in cotton – the formation of the Card-Room Amalgamation (1886), its admission of ring-spinners (1887), the formation of the Northern Counties Amal. Assoc. of Weavers (1884), and the negotiation of the final Bolton spinning list (1887), all antedate the expansion. There are only faint signs of 'explosiveness' here in 1889–90, compared with the 1830s and 1911–12.

period are clustered near the former end of the scale, though some, quite prominent in the explosion – boot-and-shoe workers, tramway-men, electricians, workers in chemicals, flour- and oil-mills, clothing-workers, etc. – are nearer the other. This enables us to distinguish the two main forms in which technical change accumulated tensions.

The first of these is best illustrated by the classically pure case of the gas-workers between their two 'explosions' of 1872 and 1889.* Their industry expanded output at an even rate, almost unaffected by techni-cal innovations, and, except for the secondary by-products market, un-affected by the trade cycle.† Moreover, it worked without substantial unused capacity to complicate the picture.[57] For 16 years it had been virtually free from unions or labour troubles – until the almost uni-versal demand in 1889, not for wage-increases, but for a shorter shift – i.e., for a decreased intensity of work. The increase in this intensity may be roughly measured: from 1874 to 1888 the amount of coal carbonized in London gas-works rose by 76 per cent, the number of manshifts worked by only 48 per cent;[58] though this greatly underrated the 'felt' as distinct from the 'real' intensification of work.‡ But the same process which caused the workers discontent, also made management temporarily much more vulnerable to their pressure. This may also be measured. The industry conceded the demand for an 8-hour instead of a 12-hour shift virtually without a fight (doubtless with a side-glance at the up-and-coming electrical industry), though this was then believed to involve a 33 per cent increase in the wage-bill without any offsetting factors.[59] We thus have a very elegant mechanism, which produces its increasing tensions; a spark-plug in the form of a disproportionately great temporary increase in the vulnerability of management, and also, a delaying mechanism. For after each spurt of technical and organizational change both employ-ers and labour adapt themselves to specific forms of relationships which, like all institutions, are fairly inelastic, dams which both help to collect the rising water and prevent it from overflowing until it has reached a certain height.

The explosive mechanism is less simple in the ensuing phases of

* See below, p. 158.
† But since many seasonal gas-workers worked in cyclically sensitive occupa-tions—e.g., brickmaking—they must have been affected by it. Hence perhaps the timing of the 'explosion' in 1889.
‡ Since almost any changes in heavy labour, which establishes its conven-tional rhythm, is likely to be regarded as causing discomfort.

technical change. Perhaps the most important factor making for discontinuous social movements is the tendency of the innovations themselves to cluster; a phenomenon we need not investigate further here.* Thus round the turn of the 1880s several groups of workers were simultaneously affected by them – printers, engineers, clothing and boot-and-shoe workers, as well as wholly new groups like electricians. But technical changes normally displace groups both within the industry and outside it, or at any rate shift their bargaining positions, creating discontent by down-grading, the possibility of rapid organization by opening new tactics to others. The 'explosion' of 1889 is not perhaps the best for the study of this phenomenon. We do not here find – what was obviously a major factor behind the outbreaks of the 1830s – the down-grading of domestic workers and hand-working artisans after their 'golden age' in the revolutionary and Napoleonic period; the collapse of the earnings of handloom weavers, of the local closed shops of craftsmen turning out consumer goods – tailors, furniture makers, perhaps builders; the threat to key industrial craftsmen faced with machines – wool-combers and spinners.[60] We do, however, find minor, but not negligible, shifts to the left among several crafts groups,[61] and less easily definable unrest among that sensitive group, the semi-independent home-workers and subcontractors on the fringe of consumer-goods industries.[62] In any case a change in the productive apparatus involves a change in the superstructure of institutions and policies which rest on it; since these are to some extent rigid, the adjustment† is not likely to be smooth or immediate. We shall almost certainly find a period of experimenting, both by employers and workers – and hence of latent or open unrest – before a new pattern of industrial relationships succeeds the old one. The history of industrial relations in the boot-and-shoe industry before the 'settlement' of 1895[63] may illustrate what happens during a period of technical innovation; the history of relations between the Shipping Federation and the seamen's and waterside unions may show what happens during the transition to an oligopolist structure.[64] Both industries were much affected by the 'explosion' of 1889. Mining and textile unionism in most countries follow similar

---

* There has been some discussion of it in connexion with the Schumpeterian system of economic development.

† 'Adjustment' is a general and relative term. Some adjustments are more easily made than others, some may not be made at all in the lifetime of a profit-making economy.

patterns. Yet these by-products of technical change produce explosive material, rather than explosions, though very likely somewhere in the restless mass a spark may be generated.

Yet there are factors, inherent in the rate of industrial growth, and the social structure of the country, which prevent any gradual dissipation of such unrest. Some of these *time-lags* are familiar to the sociologist and historian. For convenience, we shall here consider only one sort. Industrial expansions in the nineteenth century normally found their labour-force (with some exceptions) outside the industrial working-class, e.g., from the villages, or outside regular industrial labour.[65] These new recruits were often attracted by the prospect of better earnings, and other incentives, and consequently, for a time, better contented. (They might not be more docile: ex-peasants have their own rhythm of discontent, which is sometimes fiercer than that of established workers.) In any case they were not conditioned to play the industrial game according to its own rules. The process of conditioning them to do so has been studied from the employer's point of view, but less often from that of the labour leader, whom it also serves. The habit of industrial solidarity must be learned, like that of working a regular week; so must the common sense of demanding concessions when conditions are favourable, not when hunger suggests. There is thus a natural time-lag, before new workers become an 'effective' labour movement. Where industries grow up round a sufficiently strong nucleus of 'mature' labour, as during the Second World War in Britain, or where conditions are under direct attack, as in secular depression periods, this will be shorter than when secular boom conditions postpone the urgency of organized demands, or where new centres grow up in the isolation of Le Creusot, or the Silesian mines, or the Quebec backwoods. Helplessness or ignorance may artificially prolong it – for new workers in new industries (or old workers for that matter), disposing only of inadequate old techniques, may simply not know what to do next. Thus in the years before the 1834 outbreak we may see them casting round for new techniques of national or industrial organization with which to cope with problems which baffle the methods of local craft societies.[66] The early 1900s are full of similar strategic and tactical discussions in several European countries.* Various factors may precipitate such artificially retarded entrances of workers into organized labour activity. The news of labour unrest elsewhere, once it

* Mainly on industrial versus craft unionism.

144

penetrates the new area, may set it off. So may political events and stresses, e.g., the French general election of 1936 or the setting up of Congress provincial governments in India in 1937.[67] In most European countries one may suspect that the political and military events of the middle 1860s, followed by the great boom of the early 1870s, are largely responsible for the remarkable simultaneous 'explosions' in so many places.

The mechanism of this may be illustrated by the British railwaymen, prominent in all three expansions between 1850 and 1914; and differing from most foreign railwaymen not prevented from organizing by law, in being among the last rather than the earliest industrial groups to do so.[68] Outside the skilled footplate and workshop grades most of them were drawn from the villages, or other unorganized groups.[69] In addition to the factors already mentioned, the structure of the industry virtually forced an explosive pattern on to them: either they had to organize on an all-grades basis and over a whole network – in itself a difficult task requiring novel techniques – or not at all.[70] Yet as soon as they had established themselves, they immediately became centres of labour activity, especially in the country-side, thus helping to propagate the 'explosion' of which they formed part.[71] They leaped, with one bound, from extreme backwardness to one of the leading and most effective positions in the labour movement.

In practice these various sorts of patterns are combined in every 'explosion': static and expanding industries, technically inert and dynamic ones, short- and long-term cyclical factors, time-lags, etc. Thus the miners' movement was not only an orthodox cyclical wage campaign but, under the slogans of a Minimum Wage and an Eight Hour Day, an attempt to meet long-term pressure on colliers' standards. It was also very concerned about the displacement of established groups, for (as among the seamen) the late 1880s saw an abnormally rapid recruitment of raw labour.[72] The railways showed a pattern similar to the gas-workers,[73] though sharpened by the much less favourable situation of the industry, and its greater vulnerability to fluctuations. The London Docks, as Beatrice Potter[74] described them, present an almost classic picture of competitition for diminishing profits by an expanding, but technically stagnant industry – and hence of increased pressure on the workers. The shipping industry, the other great pioneer of the expansion, had similar problems. Again one notes the increased vulnerability to Labour pressure, which turned the Dock Strike of 1889 into so portentous a success:

between 1878 and 1888 the tonnage entered and cleared at the London Docks increased by over 35 per cent[75] (the average increase in other ports affected by the expansion was much greater)[76] while the number of some skilled key-men – lightermen, for instance – actually declined.[77] Piles of explosive material were stacked all over the country, ready for the spark.

One final factor must be briefly mentioned: the part played by bodies of agitators, propagandists and organizers, armed with new ideas and new methods, and ready to carry them into hitherto inert and unorganized areas. Doubtless widespread 'explosions' are possible without them: the periodic simultaneous price-rioting over many parts of eighteenth-century England are examples, though they lack precisely the qualitative innovations in the movement which are so characteristic of the most typical 'explosion'. These have normally been associated with new types of leadership, organization or demands, themselves doubtless the product of the period of economic change with which the 'explosions' attempted to come to terms: Owenite and Chartist in the 1830s, the International Workingmen's Association and its companion movements in the late 1860s and early 1870s, the revived socialism – Marxism or otherwise – in the late 1880s, 1890s and early 1900s, or else its revolutionary or syndicalist left wing. If we prefer, we may regard this as another example of that institutional rigidity which helps to make the movements discontinuous. Established leaders and organizers – for instance the Trade Union Congress leadership in the 1880s – might quite well have done much of the organizing that was left to Marxist and quasi-Marxist agitators; but it was to the latter that the unorganized had to turn for help and advice. The new leadership helped to give the 'explosions', as it were, a historic individuality; so much so that the layman automatically thinks of Owen and the Grand National, of Burns, Mann and the Dockers, of the Syndicalists, when the explosions of the 1830s, 1880s and 1910s are mentioned, and remains less aware of the ideologically not so striking 'explosion' of 1871–2. Apart from the public relations side of the matter, however, they helped to weld a mass of discrete local, regional or sectional movements into a larger whole. The great all-embracing national unions of the unorganized after 1889 were those dominated by the left wing – Dockers and Gasworkers; those which were not, tended to remain purely sectional or regional.[78] Beyond this, they provided the larger unifying force of common aims and slogans. Without the Owenites in 1834, or the Six

Points of the Charter after 1838, the very heterogeneous (and often contradictory) forces of discontent would almost certainly not have become a single, however fragile, national force. Historians might merely have noticed their co-existence. The same is true, to a lesser extent, of such slogans as that of the Eight Hour Day in the 1880s and early 1890s. At certain moments such bodies as working-class Internationals even succeeded in impressing a common stamp on simultaneous 'explosions' in different countries, though perhaps they attached too sanguine hopes to such activities.* Yet where the ideological impetus is greater than that provided by conference resolutions and the like, its power to make sparks leap from one country to others should not be underrated. It did so in 1830 and 1848; and the 'explosion' in Central Europe in 1905-7 owed more than a little to the news of the greater one in Russia.[79]

We may sum up briefly and tentatively. Only individual analysis can reveal the specific combination of tensions which make up any given 'explosion', and attempts to discover exactly the same combination (as distinct from a general family resemblance in the patterns) are likely to be unsuccessful. Thus in Britain the main factors in the 1830s were perhaps the secular displacement of previously well-established groups, and direct pressure on labour standards. In the 1860s and 1870s time-lags and discontinuities of technical growth may have been the most important. In 1889 the situation seems to have been dominated by the peculiar Great Depression pattern of technical stagnation, expanding business activity and falling profits. In 1911 all major factors may be traced, though technical discontinuities and falling real wages stand out.[80] No doubt fuller analysis would attempt to distinguish smaller 'families' of 'explosions' within the larger one which has been considered here: those of countries engaged in the transition from pre-industrial society to industrial capitalism, those of classical nineteenth-century 'free market' and competitive capitalism,† and those of the modern capitalist economies, dominated by government, imperfect competitition, and the 'second Industrial Revolution', and the various ways in which the

* The First International merely by common organization, the Second by the device of simultaneous mass demonstrations for standard demands, to which we owe May Day.

† Probably the only 'pure' case of this type, not significantly distorted by transition from pre-industry, by the monopolist phase, or by both, is that of Britain in the second half of the century.

uneven development of economies combines and telescopes these. It is neither possible nor desirable to do this here. However, we may suggest that further study will not be much concerned with cyclical factors (unless, with Kondratiev, we choose to call qualitatively different phases of economic evolution 'cycles'). Purely short-term cyclical factors would seem to explain the timing of 'explosions' within individual cycles, but not much else.

(1952)

NOTES

1 G. D. H. Cole, *Short History of the British Working-Class Movement* (1948), is the most convenient source for British figures, available from the 1860s. Individual continuous series for certain crafts go back further, but need careful use. For other countries see reference 3 below.

This is the shape of a growing movement. Once it is well established, especially once it has won the majority of the people it set out to organize, or a high degree of public recognition, the 'jumpiness' is less evident in membership, though not in activity.

2 For the former, S. and B. Webb, *History of Trade Unionism* (1894 and subseq. edns), cap. 3; R. W. Postgate, *The Builders' History* (1923), caps. 3–4; W. Warburton, *History of the Trade Union Organization in the Potteries* (1931), caps. 3–5; S. Chapman, *The Lancashire Cotton Industry* (1904), cap. 9; Trades Union Congress, *The Martyrs of Tolpuddle* (1934); G. D. H. Cole, 'Attempts at General Union 1829–34', *Int. Rev. Social History*, IV (1939); for the latter, the numerous histories of Chartism.

3 The most accessible sources: *Abstract of Foreign Labour Statistics* (from 1899); *Labour Gazette* (from 1894); 'The Growth of Trade Unions since 1913', *Int. Lab. Rev.* (1922), III, p. 78 and (1922), IV, p. 53; W. Kulemann, *Die Gewerkschaftsbewegung* (Jena, 1900 and later edns) and the uneven *Int. Handbuch d. Gewerkschaftswesens*. Useful statistics are available in several secondary works, e.g., for France, G. Lefranc, *Hist. d. Mouv. Syndical Français* (Paris 1937); for Italy, R. Rigola, *Storia del Mov. Operaio Ital.* (Milan 1947); for Germany, K. Zwing, *Gesch. d. deutschen freien Gewerkschaften* (Jena 1922); for Belgium, E. Vandervelde, *Le Parti Ouvrier Belge* (Brussels 1925); for Sweden, Svenilsson, *Wages in Sweden 1860–1932* (London 1935), II; for Austria, J. Deutsch, *Gesch. d. oesterr. Gewerk-*

schaften (Vienna 1908 and later edns); for Russia, W. Grine-witsch, *Gewerkschaftsbewegung in Russland 1905–14* (Berlin 1927).

4 C. E. Labrousse, *Le Mouv. Ouvrier et les Idées Sociales en France* (Paris, n.d.); W. W. Rostow, *British Economy of the Nineteenth Century* (Oxford 1948), Pt. II.

5 E.g., A. H. Hansen, 'Cycles of Strikes', *Amer. Econ. Rev.* XI (1921), p. 616; N. Barou, *British Trade Unions* (London 1947), pp. 86–7, App. VI.

6 E.g., Horace B. Davis, 'The Theory of Union Growth', *Q. Journ. Econ.* LV (1940–1), pp. 621 ff., 632–3.

7 Davis, loc. cit., p. 623.

8 See, for example, D. Chadwick, 'On the Rate of Wages in Manchester and Salford and the Manufacturing Districts of Lancashire 1839–59', *J.R. Stat. Soc.* XXIII (1860), p. 1, which shows that the rates of 6 out of 6 skilled metal craftsmen rose, those of 2 out of 7 semi-skilled grades rose, 3 remained stable and 2 fell; while of 3 unskilled rates 1 remained stable and 2 fell.

9 Cf. the opposition of skilled artisans in favoured trades to the radicalism of the 1830s and 1840s (S. and B. Webb, op. cit. (1894 ed.), pp. 180–1).

10 It is misleading to deduce from them a baker's dozen of periods of 'virtual full employment' between 1800 and 1914 (Rostow, op. cit., p. 33) or to assume that that term has the same connotation in the nineteenth century as to-day.

11 Mainly in France, by Labrousse and others. See J. Fourastié in *IXe Congrès International des Sciences Historiques* (Paris 1950), I, p. 223. Professor Ashton has also observed that such phenomena as Keynes's 'Gibson Paradox' (*A Treatise on Money*, II) seem not to be valid before the 1840s.

12 Op. cit., pp. 124–5. The choice of weights for wheat prices seems arbitrary at first sight.

13 C. E. Labrousse, *La Crise de l'Economie Française à la Fin de l'Ancien Régime* (Paris 1944), Introduction; C. E. Labrousse, *La Politique Financière et Econ. de l'Assemblée Constituante* (Paris, n.d.), cap. II, pp. 16–24.

14 But see E. Phelps Brown and S. Hopkins, 'The Course of Wage Rates in Five Countries', *Oxford Econ. Papers*, N.S. II (June 1950), pp. 234–5, for opposition to the widely accepted view that the wage structure has tended to become less flexible.

15 *Source*: the full, though not exhaustive, chronicle of riots in R. Wearmouth, *Methodism and the Common People of the Eighteenth Century* (London 1945).

16 For exceptions – Piedmont – see A. Frilli, *I Partiti Popolari* (Florence 1900), p. 22.

17 Conversely, depressions have tended to become periods of falling living costs, thus partly counteracting the effect of heavy unemployment. Cf., M. H. Dobb, *Studies in the Development of Capitalism* (London 1946), p. 334.

18 J. Destrée and E. Vandervelde, *Le Socialisme en Belgique* (Paris 1903), Pt. II, caps. 1, 4, 10. Vandervelde, op. cit.

19 E. Georgi, *Theorie u. Praxis d. Generalstreiks* (Jena 1908), pp. 52, 57, 89 – for Belgium, Sweden, Trieste, Barcelona; A. J. C. Rueter, *De Spoorwegstakingen van 1903* (Leiden 1935). See also W. H. Crook, *The General Strike* (Chapel Hill 1931). For the Russian general strikes of 1902–3, J. Mavor, *An Econ. Hist. of Russia* (London 1914), II, Bk. 7, cap. 1.

20 N. Colajanni, *L'Italia nel 1898, Tumulti e Reazione* (Milan 1951 edn), caps. 3, 11. For a detailed list of riots, *Almanacco Socialista* for 1899.

21 There is evidence both ways in E. Lemonon, *L'Italie Econ. et Sociale 1861–1812* (Paris 1913), pp. 159–78. On the trade-union 'explosions' of 1901, M. Bettinotti, *Vent'Anni di Movimento Operaio Genovese* (Milan 1932), pp. 54–5, 63, and the admirably full figures in *Origini, Vicende e Conquisti delle Organizzazione Operaie aderenti alla Camera del Lavoro in Milano* (Milan, Società Umanitaria, 1909).

22 See the review of A. Boscolo, 'I Moti del 1906 in Sardegna', *Movimento Operaio*, II (June–July 1950), pp. 9–10.

23 We have only fragmentary and roundabout evidence for those before 1824–5, e.g., in A. Aspinall, *The Early English Trade Unions* (London 1948), pp. 7, 246–313; Cole and Filson, *British Working-Class Movements 1789–1875* (London 1951), pp. 149–58. For 1824–5 see ibid., p. 241; S. and B. Webb, op. cit., pp. 98–100. For 1844–6, Cole and Postgate, *The Common People* (London 1946), pp. 316–17.

24 The other industrialized country, Belgium, seems actually to have been in part untouched by the crisis of early 1848. See J. Dhondt, 'La Belgique en 1848', *Actes du Congrès Historique de la Rev. de 1848* (Paris 1948), p. 120.

25 An earlier, and striking, example of this is to be found in Southern England. In 1830 the farm-labourers' unrest stopped within a few miles of the traditionally riotous textile centres, which were booming. (See the MS. Cobb correspondence, Wilts Arch. and Nat. Hist. Soc. Library, Devizes.) In 1839, when physical-force Chartism dominated the latter (P.R.O. *Home*

Office Papers, H.O. 40/40, 40/48), agrarian unrest in the country, as measured by rick-burning and similar offences, was at its lowest point for the decade (see the annual parliamentary return 'Numbers of Criminal Offenders' from 1834). Between them the areas of unrest in 1830 and 1839 cover most of the country, but they hardly overlap.

26 H. A. Marquand (ed), *Organized Labour in Four Continents* (London 1939); V. Thompson, *Labor Problems in South-east Asia* (Yale 1947); K. Kurihara, *Labor in the Philippine Economy* (Stanford 1945); S. D. Punekar, *Trade Unionism in India* (Bombay 1948), bring this out.

27 Consumption indices are preferable to real-wage ones, in view of the absence or the known weaknesses of cost-of-living figures. The table gives both the general pauper rates (which are over-weighted by the old and infirm), and those for normally adult and able-bodied, which may be taken as a rough check on the trade-union unemployment rate, from which they diverge quite interestingly. Care should be taken not to use these figures as more than general pointers, or outside their scope. Thus they are not intended to contribute to the discussion on the movement of real and money wages in cycles (see Dunlop, Keynes, Tarshis and Richardson in *Econ. J.* XLVIII (1938), p. 412; XLIX (1939), pp. 34, 150, 425; Ruggles, Dunlop, Tarshis in *Q. J. Econ.* LV (1940–1941), pp. 130, 683, 691, 697), and they do not in fact clearly support either side in that controversy.

28 *J.R. Stat. Soc.* XL (1877), pp. 42 ff., 'Some statistics of the Affiliated Orders of Friendly Societies'; also F. G. P. Neison, *The Manchester Unity of Oddfellows* (London 1869).

29 Cf. Goschen's Minute of 1869 and the Local Government Board's Circular of 2 Dec. 1871.

30 It has been argued (*Labour Gazette* (1912), p. 2) that the drought of the summer of 1911 accentuated the rise in the cost of living; but one cannot be sure how far this would affect a movement which was at its height in August–September.

31 B.M. Add. MSS 34, 245 A and B. The returns represent only a few areas well, notably Scots and West of England textile towns.

32 Loc. cit., B, p. 284. See also T. S. Ashton, 'The Standard of Living of the English Working-Class, 1790–1830', *Journ. Econ. Hist.* Supp. IX (1949).

33 Woytinsky, *Three Sources of Unemployment* (Geneva 1935).

34 *J.R. Stat. Soc.* LXII (1899), pp. 640–2.

35 *J.R. Stat. Soc.* LXVII (1904), p. 58.

36 W. H. Beveridge, *Unemployment* (1930 edn), p. 429.

37 Unemployment figures are scanty before the 1890s, and not much use before the twentieth century. The material for consumption figures is well surveyed in K. Apelt, *Die Konsumtion d. wichtigsten Kulturlaender* (Berlin 1899). Wage and price figures are more abundant, but the dangers of manipulating real wage indices should be evident from the discussions of British working-class standards in the first half of the century.

38 Apelt, op. cit., p. 22 (bread), p. 95 (coffee); F. Mehring, *Gesch. d. deutschen Sozialdemokratie* (Stuttgart 1898), II, pp. 320–1. But an improvement in living conditions is suggested, without evidence, in J. Schmoele, *Die sozialdemokr. Gewerkschaften in Deutschland seit d. Erlass d. Sozialistengesetzes* (Jena 1896), p. 39.

39 R. Martin, 'Fleischverbrauch im Kgr. Sachsen', *Ztschr. d. Kgl. Saechs. Statist. Bureaus* (1895), pp. 119 ff., 150; 'Stoerungen im deutschen Wirtschaftsleben', *Schriften d. Vereins f. Sozialpolitik*, vol. 109 (1903), pp. 5, 238).

40 'Kosten d. Lebenshaltung in deutschen Grossstaedten', *Schriften d. V. f. Soz. Pol.* vol. 145 (1914), I, 93 (Halle), 211 (Leipzig), 145, II, 58 (Barmen), 145, IV, 49 (Chemnitz), 384 (all Germany). The marked agreement between the movement of these series is notable.

41 Important rises in the cost of living in Paris for the end of the 1880s and early 1890s are suggested by G. Moreau, *Le Syndicalisme* (Paris 1925), pp. 312 ff., and C. Tyszka, *Loehne u. Lebenskosten in Westeuropa im 19. Jh.* (Leipzig 1914), p. 21. No useful consumption data for French industrial or urban centres are, however, readily available, the Octroi statistics for certain towns (*Bulletin de Statistique et Legislation Comparée*, annual) being very difficult to use. The serious study of these sources has recently begun: cf., R. Laurent, *L'Octroi de Dijon au XIX siècle* (Paris 1955).

42 B. Shiva Rao, *The Industrial Worker in India* (London 1939), p. 181; Sen Katayama, *The Labor Movement in Japan* (Chicago 1918), p. 36, for the period of the China–Japan war, 1896–7.

43 L. Dechesne, *L'Avènement du Régime Syndical à Verviers* (Paris 1908), pp. 102 ff., on the importance of the struggle against the 'two-loom system' in the genesis of the 1906 outbreak. This is one of the few monographs of a trade-union 'explosion'.

44 *Source*: F. Simiand, *Le Salaire des Ouvriers des Mines de Charbon en France* (Paris 1907), Tableau B (p. 112), pp. 351–5.

45 *Parl. Papers*, 1893–4, LXXIX, 'Return of Injuries to Railway Servants'. These figures exclude injuries *not* caused by the move-

ment of trains, which are not conveniently available until after 1896. Nor do they give the proportion of injured to those 'exposed to risk', the number of which changes at a different rate from that of all railwaymen. (See the annual *Railway Accident Reports.*) Similar calculations for later periods are more difficult owing to changes in the methods of reporting accidents in 1906, and of both methods of reporting and the classification of workers concerned, in 1896. For earlier periods we possess no useful data. Cf., F. G. P. Neison, *The Rate of Fatal and Non-Fatal Accidents in and about Mines and on Railways* (London 1880); available in the Library of the Royal Statistical Society. Also by the same, 'Analytical View of Railway Accidents II', *J.R. Stat. Soc.* XVII (1854), p. 219. The rate of fatal accidents is not useful for our purpose.

46 Union figures compiled from the *Annual Reports* of the Amalgamated Society of Railway Servants, 1888–91.

47 Op. cit., pp. 242–3.

48 See the discussion in H. Verney, 'On the recent considerable increase in the numbers of reported accidents in factories', *J.R. Stat. Soc.* LXXIII (1910), p. 95. For similar German and Austrian figures showing a secular increase in the industrial accident rate from the 1880s and 1890s, see art. 'Unfallstatistik' in early editions of the *Hwb. d. Staatswissenschaften.*

49 The exact methods by which they do so, deserve further study. The general shape of a curve plotting their propagation would, however, seem to resemble that of the spread of epidemics, panics and similar social phenomena (L. S. Penrose, *The Objective Study of Crowd Behaviour*, 1952). Organizational and political factors would normally prevent the curve from declining in the expected manner.

50 Attempts to discover more precise periodicities—e.g., a 17-year one in the USA (Davis, op. cit., pp. 621–2) are better avoided at present. Nor can any regular relationship between 'explosions' and the phases of economic periods be discerned, though it is tempting to seek them towards the end of each. However, while this would fit quite well – 1847–8 for the 1817–48 period, 1868–73 for the 1848–73 one, 1889–93 for the 'Great Depression' and the war-time expansions for 1896–1920 – it does not account for mid-term 'explosions' like those of the early 1830s in Britain and 1898–1907 on the continent. (Chartism would fit, since it is arguable that in Britain the real secular turning-point came in the early rather than the late 1840s.) Since we have only six phases in our period, statistical manipulation cannot help us here.

51 The *Webb MSS.* (Coll EA. VI, L.S.E. Library) contains an interesting list of British unions in the early 1890s having national, local, shop or no agreements with employers. For the prevalence of local and shop agreements (where any existed), see H. Koeppe, 'Fortschritte d. Arbeitstarifvertrages in Deutschland, Oesterreich, etc.', *Jrb. f. Nationaloek. u. Statistik*, XLIV (1912), p. 362; D. Saposs, *The Labor Movement in Postwar France* (N.Y. 1931), pp. 190 ff.

52 It may be argued that most social processes follow such a pattern, which may be called 'the transformation of quantity into quality' by some, change 'which so displaces its equilibrium point that the new cannot be reached from the old by infinitesimal steps' by others. (J. A. Schumpeter, *Theory of Econ. Development*, p. 64 n.)

53 No adequate history of the 'New Union' explosion of 1889–90 as yet exists. The Webbs are notably weak on it, and recent attempts to reappraise the problem, like A. E. P. Duffy, 'New Unionism in Britain 1889–90' (*Econ. Hist. Rev.* 2d ser. XIV (1961), pp. 306–20) add nothing of real interest and serve rather to fudge the problem of discontinuity. Some aspects of this explosion are dealt with in other chapters of the present volume. Among the trade union histories of special interest, one may note R. P. Arnot, *The Miners* (London 1948); J. W. Jefferys, *The Story of the Engineers* (London 1945); R. W. Postgate, op. cit.; A. Fox, *History of the National Union of Boot and Shoe Operatives 1874–1957* (Oxford 1958); P. Bagwell, *The Railwaymen* (London 1963); B. Turner, *Short History of the General Union of Textile Workers* (Heckmondwike 1920); R. B. Suthers, *The Story of Natsopa* (London 1929).

54 R. P. Arnot, op. cit., cap. III; H. Pelling, 'The Knights of Labour in Britain 1880–1901' (*Econ. Hist. Rev.* 2d ser. IX (1956), pp. 313–31); K. D. Buckley, *Trade Unionism in Aberdeen 1878–1900* (Aberdeen 1955); H. R. Turner, *Trade Union Growth, Structure and Policy* (London 1962) for cotton unions; E. R. Pease, 'Labour Federation', *Today* (June 1887). A. E. P. Duffy, loc. cit., discusses these early starts at length.

55 For the London impetus, W. Thorne, *My Life's Battles* (n.d.); Ben Tillett, *Memories and Reflexions* (1931); Tom Mann, *Memoirs* (1923); Smith and Nash, op. cit.; for the northern one, *The Life of Sir James Sexton, Agitator, by Himself* (1936); J. Havelock Wilson, *My Stormy Voyage Through Life* (1925), pp. 134–6, caps. XVI, XVIII; *The Times*, 28 Jan.–19 Feb., 1889.

56 See below, p. 182.

57 *Journ. Gas L.* LIV (1889), p. 683.

58 Calculated from the annual returns of balance sheets for the Metropolitan Gas Companies (*Parl. Pap.* 1870–1906) and John Field's annual *Analysis of Metropolitan and Suburban Gas Company Accounts* (from 1869). Since stokers were overwhelmingly paid on a straight time basis, rates did not change, and overtime existed only in the form of extra shifts (cf., Wage Census 1906, *Parl. Pap.*, 1910, LXXXIV), the amount of carbonizing wages can be used as an index of man-shifts.

59 *Journ. Gas L.* LIV (1889), pp. 458, 838, 885. Indeed, it turned out to be greater up to 47 and 53 per cent in London and the suburbs, 35 and 36 per cent in the provinces (Field's *Analysis*, 1888–91). For the failure to consider the economies of eight-hour shifts before 1889, *Journ. Gas L.* LIII (1888), p. 894.

60 On the 'golden age', Cole and Filson, op. cit., p. 20, and the consensus of opinion as to the ineffectiveness of Combination Acts against the 'artisans', M. D. George, 'The Combination Laws', *Econ. Hist. Rev.* VI (1936), p. 172. On the collapse of strong local bargaining combinations, F. Galton, *The Tailoring Trade* (1896), p. lxxxi and *passim*; H. Mayhew, *London Labour and the London Poor* (1861–2), III, pp. 232–41 – furniture makers. For wool-combers and spinners, E. C. Tufnell, *Character, Objects and Effects of Trades' Unions* (1834), pp. 49–62; W. Marcroft, *The Marcroft Family* (Rochdale 1889); H. Ashworth, *An inquiry into the origin, procedure and results of the strike of the operative cotton spinners . . . 1836–7* (1838).

61 Jefferys, op. cit., p. III, cap. 6; D. M. Good, 'Economic and Political Origins of the Labour Party' (M.S. thesis, L.S.E. Library). The small group of skilled crafts which joined in the socialist-led Labour Representation Committee before Taff Vale consists largely of those affected by such changes.

62 E.g., the domestic outworkers in the Bristol and Norwich boot-and-shoe trade. L. Dechesne, op. cit., pp. 131 ff. for similar unrest among the *façonniers* in the Belgian woollen trade in the 1890s.

63 S. and B. Webb, *Industrial Democracy* (1902 ed.), pp. 185–92, cap. VIII; E. Brunner, 'The Origins of Industrial Peace', *Oxf. Econ. Papers*, N.S. 1 (June 1949), pp. 247–60; Alan Fox, op. cit.

64 L. H. Powell, *The Shipping Federation 1890–1950* (London 1950), caps. 2–3.

65 German studies are the most systematic: R. Ehrenberg, Krupp-studien III, 'Fruehzeit d. Kruppschen Arbeiterschaft', *Thuenen-Archiv.* III (1908), pp. 1–165, and the 'Auslese und Anpassung'

volumes in the *Schriften d. V. f. Soz. Pol.* vols. 133-5, I–IV (1910–12). The skilled tended to come more from artisan backgrounds.

66 G. D. H. Cole, *Attempts at General Unions*, loc. cit.

67 These, of course, are not necessarily independent of the economic roots of labour discontent. Grinewitsch, op. cit., p. 145, gives figures which well bring out this stimulating effect of individual political events on union membership in Russia, 1905–6.

68 For the locomotive engineers, J. R. Raynes, *Engines and Men* (Leeds 1921) and N. McKillop, *The Lighted Flame* (London 1950); for the rest, P. Bagwell, op. cit. The general body of railwaymen, though active in 1871–2 and 1889–91 were not in effective action until after 1907; Cole and Arnot, *Trade Unionism on the Railways* (London 1917). For the relatively early start of railwaymen in other countries, Rigola, op. cit., p. 228; V. Thompson, op. cit., p. 53; W. Kulemann, op. cit., p. 333; G. Chaumel, *Histoires des Cheminots et de leur Syndicats* (Paris 1948); H. A. Millis (ed), *How Collective Bargaining Works* (N.Y. 1942), p. 323.

69 E.g., H. Llewellyn-Smith, 'The Influx of Population into East London', in C. Booth, *Life and Labour*, III, 58–166; *R.C. on Housing of the Working Classes*, 1885, Q 10, 615; Alfred Williams, *Life in a Railway Factory* (London 1916).

70 Hence the general interest of railway unions in industrial unionism, general strikes and other novel labour techniques. See the works quoted in ref. 68 above, and A. J. C. Rueter, op. cit.

71 I am grateful to Dame Florence Hancock for information about this in Wiltshire. See also F. E. Green, *A History of the English Agricultural Labourer 1870–1920* (London 1920), pp. 118, 253.

72 Arnot, op. cit., p. 112. Statistical Abstract 1875–90, *Parl. Pap.*, 1890, LXXVIII, p. 156 for seamen.

73 J. Mavor, *The Scottish Railway Strike* (Edinburgh 1891); J. Mavor in *Econ. Journ.* I (1891), p. 204.

74 In Booth, *Life and Labour in London*, vol. IV.

75 *Parl. Pap.*, 1902, XLIV: R.C. on the Port of London, p. 232.

76 A calculation based on Mulhall, *Dictionary of Statistics* (1898 edn), shows an average increase in tonnage entered and cleared in London, Liverpool, Cardiff, Newcastle, Shields, Bristol, Hull and Glasgow of between 45 and 50 per cent.

77 Census 1881, 1891. Again, the vulnerability was proportionately greater than thus measured, for the increased complexity of a port which expanded without rationalizing its lay-out and

methods put an increased premium on experienced workers, who knew the steadily more tangled ropes. See, for example, R. Williams, *The Liverpool Docks Problem* (Liverpool 1912), pp. 21–2, and below pp. 211–13.

78 E. J. Hobsbawm, loc. cit.

79 *Jrb. f. Nationaloekonomie*, 1905, p. 580, on the Czech Railway strike; Otto Bauer, *The Austrian Revolution* (London 1924), cap. IV, on the January 1918 strikes.

80 The most comprehensive account of this 'explosion' is E. H. Phelps Brown, *The Growth of British Industrial Relations* (London 1959) VI, but Askwith, *Industrial Problems and Disputes* (London 1920), Watney and Little, op. cit., and other contemporary works should still be consulted.

9

British Gas-workers 1873–1914[1]

THE STUDENT of the history of collective bargaining is generally at a great disadvantage, as soon as he stops recording the exiguous facts, and tries to analyse them. It is not often possible to disentangle the influence of, say, the trade union, from the many others which shape industrial policy and organization; and even if it is, few industries are sufficiently documented to allow him to get much further in any case. Yet there is at least one industry in which a fair amount of quantitative analysis is possible: the British gas industry at the end of the nineteenth and in the early twentieth century. Though, as a public utility, and one largely under municipal and monopolist ownership, it is not necessarily typical of British industry at this period, it is well worth investigating, and this chapter attempts to do so.

Let us first look at the problem. The British gas industry presents a remarkable and extreme example of the rise of trade unionism. Gas-workers were – in common with others who were conventionally thought of as 'unskilled' – believed to be incapable of strong and stable trade unionism; and indeed, with shortlived and local exceptions,[2] they had never formed important and lasting organizations before 1889. For 17 years before that date they possessed no traceable unions at all. Yet when in 1889 they demanded concessions which, it was generally held, would raise the industry's wage-bill by one-third,[3] their demands were conceded virtually without a struggle. Moreover, the new unions maintained themselves against subsequent counter-attack. Over a large part of the country, therefore, the industry changed overnight from a wholly unorganized into an exceptionally unionized one; with important effects on its structure and policy. Why did it change? Why did it remained changed? What effects had the rise of the union?

The question should interest others besides students of trade unionism. The general picture in the established British industries after the end of the Great Depression is one of technical stagnation, and a tendency for productivity per man to fall.[4] Among the few exceptions to this is the gas industry; and 1889 marks a turning-point in its technical history as well as in that of its industrial relations.

I

The gas industry, in the thirty years after 1860, was an exceptionally sheltered one. Since 1860 cut-throat local competitition had been replaced, under various Acts of Parliament, by a jig-saw puzzle of local monopolies, an increasing number municipally owned. It was immune from competitition, for electricity was not as yet seriously in the field. It was immune from cyclical fluctuations, for its main outlets, public and private lighting, were most inelastic, though subject to violent regular seasonal fluctuations. The use of gas in industry was small, even gas-stoves were in their infancy[5] and only the relatively unimportant by-products market really reflected depressions. Thus gasworks grew with the growth of the city population, without any need for exertion except what was necessary to produce enough gas of statutory quality.

There was thus no important competitive incentive to technical change. Nor was the industry troubled by high labour costs, for it was that relatively unusual thing in mid-nineteenth century Britain, a heavily capitalized continuous-process industry propelled almost entirely by specialized semi-skilled men (the retort-house stokers, firemen, etc.), and by labourers. In 1889 carbonizing wages – the only reliable guide[6] – amounted to between 9·2 and 14·1 per cent of total expenditure in nine London and provincial works; a mean of 13·4 in London, and under 11·1 in Manchester, Birmingham, Leicester, Stafford and Warrington.[7] The actual labour cost per 1,000 cubic feet of gas produced varied between 2·26d. and 5·29d. in 20 towns in 1883, between 1·84 and 4·80 in 1888 (see Table I).

Hence it is not surprising to find that technical progress was extremely sluggish. Gas-making in the 1880s was still recognizably what it had been at the beginning of the century.[8] Coal was brought to the works in carts or barges, and moved from wharf or yard to the retort-house in wheelbarrows or small trucks. Carbonization itself – the work of making and stoking fires, filling the retorts with coal,

Table I. *Labour Cost (carbonizing) per '000 cu. feet of gas sold in 1883 and 1888.* (*Pennies*) (Source: *Field's* Analysis of Gas Company Accounts, *1883, 1888*)*

Town	1883	1888	Town	1883	1888
London†	3·49	3·34	Brighton	3·53	3·13
Suburbs‡	4·03	3·53	Bristol	5·29	4·80
Birmingham	3·02	2·45	Liverpool	3·59	3·56
Bolton	3·31	3·47	Newcastle	3·01	2·92
Leeds	4·47	4·24	Plymouth	2·95	3·06
Leicester	2·59	2·52	Portsea	2·26	1·84
Manchester	2·99	2·78	Preston	4·84	3·95
Oldham	3·49	3·36	Sheffield	2·77	2·71
Salford	4·39	3·38			
Bath	2·38	2·45			

spreading it and drawing the coke – was still essentially unmechanized. The retort, 'a small horizontal tube into which a few hundredweight of coal are put every four or five hours, and rather more than half the weight of coke is drawn out at the same intervals',[9] was perhaps tending to become somewhat larger. The primitive method of filling it by one-man shovel only persisted in small local works. In large ones great scoops were lifted and propelled into it by three-man teams: an exceptionally taxing process in the heat and glow of the house, requiring muscular men. Teams of stokers and firemen worked twelve-hour shifts (eighteen hours at the weekend changeover), for production was necessarily continuous.[10]

The primitive nature of the basic operation had begun to tempt inventors, and from the early 1870s (after the first stokers' strikes, in fact) attempts to mechanize stoking were seriously made, but came to little, owing to the cheapness of labour.[11] In any case the really novel idea of making the retorts inclined or vertical, thus using the force of gravity to fill them, was not widely adopted until after 1889, when (as we shall see) the incentive to large re-equipment was much greater.[12] The work of the fireman had been affected more seriously with the increasing adoption of generator and regenerator firing in the early 1880s (after an abortive start in the 1860s). Generator firing

* Provincial figures are not available before 1883, though London figures go back to 1869.

† The three metropolitan companies, Gas, Light and Coke, South Metropolitan and Commercial.

‡ 14 (by 1888 merged into 12) suburban companies.

burned not the coal, but carbon monoxide, which could be conveyed to where it was needed and then fired, with less heat and draught, by feeding more air into it; regenerator firing added the principle of the recovery of waste heat. The general effect of these improvements was to make the maintenance of regular heat slightly less dependent on the steadiness, experience and skill of the fireman. No serious attempt was made to rationalize works' organization. Here and there an undertaking introduced three eight-hour shifts instead of two 12-hour ones, but so little impact had these experiments made on technical opinion, before the men began for their own reasons to demand an eight-hour day, that the leading trade journal professed to be unaware of their existence.[13]

On paper, therefore, the bargaining position of the stokers and firemen, the key-men in the whole process, as they were to be the core of the union, was exceptionally strong. They could put a strangle-hold on the works whenever they wanted. A relatively slight reduction in their efforts, and the lighting power of the gas would fall below the statutory requirement; or even, lights might go out. Almost everything depended on their exceptional strength and judgment as individuals and teams. Why, then did they not succeed in organizing permanently before 1889? It is true that they were well-paid. Five shillings a shift or thereabouts was by no means bad money in the 1880s,[14] even though they laboured much harder for it than recognized skilled men in similar wage-brackets, and had little chance of extra earnings. It is also true that no significant attack on their wages and hiring conditions seems to have been made during the Depression. Nevertheless, since there are few signs of a deliberate 'high-wage' policy,[15] the wage-rates of stokers are a reflection of their potential bargaining strength, rather than a proof of their satisfaction. They do not explain why they remained unorganized.

Two factors, one real, the other conventional, do help us to explain it. The work was extremely casual. Seasonal fluctuations were immense: the winter load was three times – according to an American observer five times – the summer load,[16] and the winter labour force might be double that of the summer months.[17] Even the company whose labour policy was as advanced as its hostility to unions was implacable, the South Metropolitan, employed 20–25 per cent more in winter than in summer.[18] Casual hiring led as usual to persistent under-employment, so that even at the peak period of winter a pool of unemployed stokers would persist.[19] Strikers could therefore

161

easily be replaced; especially as managements organized the import of strike-breakers from all over the country: a Bristol strike was blacklegged from all over the West, and from Liverpool; a Halifax strike from London, Burnley and York.[20]

It is true that in practice hiring was much less casual than in theory. For one thing, gasworks had long appreciated the advantages of a low labour-turnover, and even to some extent of 'welfare capitalism';[21] for another, the same seasonal men came back year after year, so much so that men even claimed a 'vested right to the job' with which it was thought dangerous to interfere.[22] Again, many stokers had evolved a regular seasonal alternation of jobs – gasworks in winter and brickyards in summer was the most usual, though not the only one,[23] and thus enjoyed a good deal of security. Yet seasonality did weaken the chance of effective bargaining. A firm always had six slack months in which to revoke concessions granted at the Christmas peak, replace and retrain its men. Men could always be tempted with really permanent jobs. After all, stokers were necessarily adult men,[24] and therefore married and might well think twice before they turned seasonal migrants.

Moreover, stokers had a dead weight of tradition and convention against them. They were not apprenticed, and their skill could be quickly acquired by any likely yard-labourer. They were themselves regarded as temporarily seconded labourers, who could and would be put to work in the yard if business were slack or if it suited the firm.[25] Management did not feel that they needed special incentives – they continued to be paid a flat shift rate, though a rather higher one than elsewhere.[26] It is significant that when they organized, they did so in a single industrial union with most other grades in the industry, even though, from a bargaining point of view, they virtually carried the rest, and could quite easily have formed a craft union. The modern continuous-process industry operated by semi-skilled men was rare. The 'craftsman-labourer' pattern was still regarded as the normal one in industry; and unless the stokers (like the coal-hewers) made demands which clearly placed them in the upper stratum, they would go on being treated as part of the lower. A considerable impetus was therefore needed to overcome this deadweight of tradition and irregular labour.

II

What was the nature of this impetus? There is no doubt at all that the stokers complained of the intensification of labour. The very fact that the demand of the men in 1889, however different their local circumstances, was almost universally for an 8-hour shift, bears this out.[27] On the other hand, the argument of the union's pioneers, that mechanization was the cause of their trouble, cannot be accepted;[28] as we have seen, there is no sign of any major mechanization, though groups of key-men in some large works may have been affected by the experimental introduction of some devices.

Intensification of work is, of course, what we should expect to find in an industry which continues to expand production for 17 years, without making any major changes in technique or works organization. Thus, taking 1874 as 100, the amount of coal carbonized in the London gasworks making returns had, by 1888, risen to 176; the amount of gas produced to 187 – while the amount of carbonizing wages (rates remaining unchanged) had only risen to 148.[29] Thus in 14 years each stoker had, on average, increased his output considerably – most of it, though by no means all, by extra muscular exertion. Yet the exertion which he felt himself to be making was much greater than this.

It is a great mistake to make overall statistical figures the measure of such subjective exertion. Demand expanded; but there must inevitably be a time-lag between this expansion and the hiring of new men, during which the old staff had to work that much harder. If new men were hired, they could not get going until new houses had been built and new retorts installed – and in the interval, once again, the old staff, working inadequate old equipment, had to work like the devil to keep the gas pressure up. For the industry, as we know from the bitter complaints of managements in 1889–90, operated without any significant reserve capacity or equipment. Moreover 'speed-up' might take place at some times of the working shift and not at others. The stoker's 12 hours consisted of alternating packets of short and hard effort, and complete rest.[30] If this balance of work and rest were altered slightly – even if the total work were not increased, even if it were conceivably decreased – the stoker might still feel himself to be working harder or less comfortably: for instance, if a rather larger retort were introduced which needed fewer but longer charges. But even if there were no real change in effort, the very fact of change might cause legitimate discontent. Semi-skilled routine labour is a very conventional thing, working to rhythms, and in patterns, which have been unconsciously tested and evolved over long periods: the swing of the peasant's scythe, the navvy's or the stoker's shovel, or the housewife's scrubbing-brush. The very absence of mechanization forced the stoker to turn himself into a specialized machine.

> 'So far does (this) adaptation go that the men working beside him, whose business is to wheel barrow-loads . . . to the furnace door, can wheel barrows all day, but could not carry on the furnace operations; while the furnace man, if put into the yard, where he has general labouring to do, will be found at first very unfit for such toil . . .'[31]

The more specialized and strenuous the conditions of work, the greater the need to adapt oneself to them completely for the time being, and the greater the discomfort of any change, even one for the better – at any rate in the short run.

We may therefore legitimately assume that the 17 years of unbroken expansion accumulated tensions and discontents which were quite enough to break out at the first opportunity: the boom of 1888–1890. (It should be remembered that, if gas managements were insensitive to trade fluctuations, stokers were not: thus numerous seasonal ones worked in summer in so sensitive an industry as brickmaking.) By the second half of 1888 signs of unrest are faintly discernible in the trade press.[32] In the first half of 1889 separate unions were formed in Birmingham, London and Bristol (the latter soon to merge with London), and there was trouble in the West Riding.[33] By August the Londoners had won the Eight-Hour Day, and unrest had gained Lancashire, the North-east, Nottingham, Sheffield and Rotherham, Derby, Bath, Swansea, Northampton, Norwich, Glasgow and Edinburgh (which formed a separate union).[34] The only important areas in which nothing seems to have happened were the Potteries and Monmouth – East Glamorgan. Most of the men went into three unions: the Birmingham Gas-workers and Brickmakers, the Tyneside and National Labour Union (later National Amalgamated Union of Labour), but mainly into the London 'Gas-workers and General Labourers Union' of Will Thorne and Eleanor Marx; though independent local bodies existed also.[35] This exceptional co-ordination in a widely scattered industry of many self-contained units is no doubt due to the universal adoption of certain standard demands: eight-hour shifts with a fixed number of retorts and charges for stokers, wage-rises for workers not on shift. There were a few other demands – Sunday, and 'good-time' pay in the North-east, holidays with pay and the abolition of subcontracting, but they hardly alter the picture. Even the towns which had long been on eight-hour shifts[36] joined wholeheartedly in the demand for fewer retorts and charges. Another reason is probably the influence of the socialists, who dominated the London gas-workers, and whose local groups naturally linked up with them – for instance in Lancashire, Yorkshire and Bristol. It is thus not surprising that the gas-workers came nearer to building a really national union than any other group of newly-organized workers in 1889, with the short-lived exception of the seamen.

III

The men's demands were ambitious. The Gas Light and Coke Company estimated their annual cost at £50,000,[37] the Birmingham Corporation thought they would add some £8,000–£10,000 to a wage-bill of £35,000,[38] Bradford saw an extra £5,000,[39] Glasgow £20,000.[40] To grant such demands,[41] put forward by an *ad hoc* body of unskilled men who had hitherto never succeeded in forming a stable union, seemed grotesque. Yet between June and December 1889 most of the important gasworks in the country yielded, hardly even testing the men's strength.[42] This remarkable fact requires explanation.

The fact was, the industry discovered itself to be at the temporary mercy of its stokers. Its position was bitterly summed up by the authoritative *Journal of Gas Lighting*:[43]

'A pleasant prospect opens before these gentlemen' it wrote of the conservative committee-men and directors, 'with the advance of winter. There may be just enough retorts or just enough storage room to carry on with, if matters go comfortably in the works, and the afternoon gang are content to wait about with the lids slacked off until the putting on of the night pressure calls upon every retort to be charged in order to keep the (gas) holders off the ground. Suppose, however, the old gangs are broken up, and scratch ones have to be put in their places. Then the possession of a few extra retorts to help the less regular and efficient working of the new hands may make all the difference between keeping up the supply and plunging the town into darkness. . . . Whatever lessons these labour troubles teach gas administrators, they prove the necessity

165

of keeping plant well up to the mark, so that there will be time to turn round in case of a sweeping change of working staff.'

The industry had fallen into a rut, and worked without a margin. Nothing stood between it and breakdown, except the personal efforts of experienced men. When these threatened to strike, it was as though Jeeves had suddenly threatened to leave Bertie Wooster.

But breakdown was something the industry could not afford. Quite apart from its electoral repercussions in municipally-owned works, Gas was just then anxiously watching the advances of a potential rival, Electricity. In London, at least, power stations had just begun to be constructed seriously.[44] Any sign that gas was unreliable might encourage thoughtless public authorities to introduce electricity. Had not this very thing happened in Halifax?[45] Moreover, monopolies are always unpopular, and the local labour vote had to be reckoned with, after the Acts of 1884–5 and 1888. Though the Fabians were wrong in assuming that municipal ownership guaranteed a progressive labour policy – in Manchester it patently did not[46] – certain authorities (Edinburgh, Bradford, Leeds, Birmingham)[47] played politics and recognized the union.

IV

The effect of the union on the industry was striking, and wholly beneficial. At a time when most established British industries were content to stagnate, Gas embarked on a programme of major technical reorganization, and re-equipment – and this before its sheltered markets had been seriously invaded by rivals. In any case, the figures speak for themselves. The adoption of the three times eight-hour shift in the major works was general, and lasting (see Table II).[48]

In the five years 1880–4 the metropolitan gas companies spent an annual average of roughly £127,000 on 'extension of buildings and machinery' (exclusive of land-purchase). In the three years immediately following the rise of the union, 1890–2, they spent an annual average of £320,000 – and prices had dropped considerably since 1884.[49] The adoption of new machinery advanced more rapidly in Britain than anywhere else.[50]

The consequent increase in efficiency and productivity can be very roughly indicated by a few figures. Thus between 1874 and 1888 carbonizing wages (per 1,000 cubic feet of gas sold) fell at an annual average rate of about 1·8 per cent. Between 1893 and 1911 (when the

Table II. *Retort-House Grades on 8-Hour shifts in 1906 in towns of 100,000 inhabitants and over.* (Source: *Earnings and Hours Enquiry, Parl. Pap. L X X XIV of 1910*)

Region	Stokers		Percentage	All Retort Grades		Percentage
	8 hrs.	12 hrs.		8 hrs.	12 hrs.	
London	2,127	481*	82	4,862	1,612	75
Northern Counties	243	0	100	539	0	100
Yorks., Lancs., Cheshire	1,623	82	95	3,809	153	96
N. & W. Midlands	742	0	100	1,702	5	100
Rest England and Wales	168	46	79	355	175	67
Total U.K.†	5,505	609	90	13,457	2,097	86

unbroken decline ended) they fell at an annual average rate of 3·2 per cent; between 1900 and 1911, indeed, by an average of 4·5 per cent per year.[51] This fall was not due to a decline in wage-rates. These, in fact, advanced in most major works by between 2 and 10 per cent in the boom years of 1897–1901.[52] As the absolute decrease of the carbonizing wage-bills demonstrates (see Table III), it was largely due to the saving of manpower in the retort-houses. A student in 1914 could observe that

'the number of retort-house men employed per million cubic feet of gas made per week has been successively reduced from something over 12 to something between 2 and 3.'[53]

Moreover, coal was used more efficiently. From the middle nineties the quantity carbonized, which had hitherto increased at a slightly smaller rate than the output of gas in the London gasworks, tended to remain stable, and even to fall slightly. The output of gas continued to expand at much the same rate as before 1888, though a little less evenly.

There is no doubt that the desire to eliminate skilled labour was the major incentive in the early stages of this re-equipment, when the economies of the new methods were still a matter of debate, and the

* One company, on defeating the union in 1890, re-introduced the 12-hour day and kept it, largely out of *amour propre*.

† In the small towns and works, the 12-hour day still maintained itself with some success.

Table III. *Carbonizing Wages in the main Gasworks in England.**
(Source: *Field's Analysis*) *In £000*

Year	Total	Year	Total
1891†	1,020	1905	905
1892–9‡	957	1906	798
1900§	1,049	1907	893¶
1901	1,044	1908	867
1902	966	1909	817
1903	939	1910	787
1904	942		

wage-bill had shot up high enough to wipe out, for the time being, declared profits. Mechanization did not seriously begin to pay for itself until the new century,[54] and even then gas technicians – especially in medium and small works – could debate the matter without reaching any real conclusions.[55] (Still, in 1901 it was the merits of different mechanical methods that were debated, as often as those of manual against mechanized processes.) Nor can it fairly be claimed that the fear of trade unionism remained the only, or even the main incentive. The advance of electricity, and rival forms of gas production, the increasing importance of heating, cooking and industrial gas-consumption (which made the industry more sensitive to industrial fluctuations, while tending to equalize the gas-load between different seasons and different times of day), the growth of the by-products market, the fluctuations and rise in raw material prices: all these preoccupied the gas-manager or engineer of the early twentieth century more than the problem of the skilled worker.

Yet there can be no doubt that the initial impetus was due to the union.[56] For the first time, after 1889, the discussions of the experts have a note of urgency, inventors point out that their devices are designed deliberately with a view to being operated by the average man, and not the exceptionally big or little, strong or quick, who could still be picked up on the labour market, but who would no

* London, suburban, provincial municipalities, provincial companies as in Note 40. With the following modifications: *Leeds* drops out between 1893 and 1907: *Bradford* enters from 1900; *Preston* drops out from 1894, *Liverpool* from 1898; *Derby* between 1898 and 1906. *Rochester and Chatham* enter from 1895.
† Peak wage-bill after 1889–90 increases.
‡ Annual mean.
§ Includes wage rises of 1897–1900.
¶ Rise is due to re-entry of *Leeds* into the table.

longer, alas, forego the bargaining advantage of their relative indispensability.[57] For the first time it was discovered that what the industry needed was 'something that will do for gas-making what the self-binder reaper does in the harvest field'.[58]

Yet in spite of these efforts, the union remained in partial control of the situation, while all round it the 'new unions' of 1889 fell like ninepins. At any rate it kept its hold on some 30 to 50 towns, many of them important ones,[59] and even in 1908, the worst period for 'new unions', its organization could be described as 'considerable'.[60] Again we must ask, why? The great concessions of 1889 had been followed by determined counter-attacks from management. Up to a point these had been successful, for once firms were, like the South Metropolitan in 1889–90, prepared to fight to a finish at whatever cost – and the firm itself estimated it at £100,000 for three months[61] – it could obviously overcome the union. Moreover, managements had the summer of 1890 to put their house in order, attempt to force long-term contracts on their men, sack troublemakers, etc.[62] The attack was, it is true, halted that summer by the men's victory in a bitterly-fought strike at Leeds, which for reasons of municipal politics was disinclined for total war. Such a victory, coming at the worst season of the year, heartened the union branches everywhere.[63] But even without it, it was doubtful whether the union could have been immediately wiped out.

> 'Have they plenty of gas-holder room?' asked the *Journal* plaintively after Leeds.[64] 'Are the retort-houses ample, easily worked, and sufficiently stocked with machinery and labour-saving appliances of the most approved descriptions?'

They were not. And what if they were? 'The gas-stoker,' admitted the president of the North British Society of Gas Managers, 'is a skilled labourer – it may be a very elementary kind of skill, but it is such that it cannot be acquired at any moment, as some imagine'[65] and 'Dissatisfied stokers have unfortunately ample means of making the works suffer . . . (by) wasting coals or continuing to do their work in an insubordinate manner.' It was a major admission: the industry had to treat its labour as 'artisans', who required incentives, and not as mere 'labourers', who 'possessed nothing but the mere value of labour'.[66]

Why, however, did the mechanization of the subsequent 15 years not achieve what the immediate counter-attack could not? Clearly,

169

the absolute bargaining position of the stoker was somewhat weak-ened. Gas-making no longer depended quite so much on manual skill, strength and reliability, and seasonal fluctuations with their consequent casualism did not decline so rapidly as the use of manual stoking, for they depended less on the way the work was organized, than on the nature of the demand for gas. The winter peak was still double the summer demand, and while the gap between the number of winter and summer workers had been halved between 1885 and 1906, there were still some 10,000 seasonal labourers out of a total of 72,000.[67] Moreover, the mechanization and the decreasing season-ality of brickmaking, and the depression of the building trade after 1900 cannot have been without effect on the stokers, for they had provided the regular summer occupations for many.[68] In the new and more casual summer jobs the seasonal gas-worker might expect lower and less regular money than in the well-paid if strenuous days of hand-brickmaking. He would consequently feel less independent-minded in winter. Admittedly, all this was to some extent offset by other factors. The continued expansion of the industry more than absorbed the men displaced by machines; between 1885 and 1906 the average number of workers in the gas-undertakings which made returns to the government had more than doubled.[69] Hence no ex-ceptionally large 'reserve army of labour' came into being. More-over, the smaller proportion of retort-house men still kept control of the vital production bottleneck, and the decreasing percentage of their wages to the firms' total outlay made employers more ready to bargain with them.[70] Nevertheless, on balance stokers were certainly weaker, firms less vulnerable in 1910 than they had been in 1888.

Labour-saving and labour-simplifying devices do not, however, automatically dislodge key groups of workers from their strongholds. They do so only when such groups are unable to maintain their rela-tive indispensability (i.e., their bargaining strength) during the crucial transition period, and cannot therefore 'capture' the new devices for recognized unionism, the standard rate, and standard working con-ditions. Thus in the last decades of the nineteenth century printers almost everywhere, and to a lesser extent skilled engineers in Britain 'captured' mechanized type-setting and automatic machine-tools, assimilating the new semi-skilled work to the old artisan status; American engineers failed to do so, and remained virtually without unions for some 30 years. Whether a key group can succeed in doing this will, of course, depend on a combination of many variable factors, but the gas-stokers were favourably placed. The dream of the perfect machine worked by any man picked up in the street was pursued, but not with much immediate success.[71] Thus the labour force for the new machines could not be drawn, as in opencast coal-mining from a completely different body of men, but came from among the old stokers.[72] Moreover, if there was technical advance, there was no technical revolution. The nineteenth-century British gas industry had long been hamstrung by the natural, but dangerous, reluctance to scrap the heavy capital investment represented by old and inefficient gasworks. Since it was largely a monopoly, it could pass its high costs on easily to the consumer.[73] So long, however, as the industry relied to some extent on its older plant (in which, as we have seen, the bargaining position of the stokers tended to be rather strong), it provided a certain degree of shelter not only for the stokers there, but also in the more modern works. Lastly, the pace of its expansion was comparatively leisurely;[74] far slower, for instance, than the great inrush of workers into multiple trading or certain sorts of mass production between the wars, which created large pools of unorganized labour even in quite strongly organized industries like engineering. In addition to all this the workers continued to enjoy the dual protection of the law, which imposed certain standards of service, and the public, both as users and – increasingly important – as municipal voters; or, to put it another way, of the industry's technical inability to keep really large enough stocks with which to maintain services during major interruptions. The industry had therefore to resign itself to unions, and if that was too much, to outbidding the unions – for this is what the increasingly popular co-partnership schemes really amounted to.[75] The unions, meanwhile, succeeded, even in a period of depression, in safeguarding their status against the machines.[76]

V

The history of the unionization of the British gas-workers is therefore instructive in three respects.

First, it provides a neat and elegant model of a trade union explosion. A body of workers technically quite capable of strong collective bargaining have, for reasons of custom or convention, failed to develop unions. Over a period of time there is a growing discrepancy between the fairly static technical and organizational structure of the industry and the expansion of its output. This produces, on the one hand a gradual accumulation of discontent, and on the other an increasing sensitiveness and vulnerability of management to the workers' pressure. A relatively slight outside stimulus then suffices to produce explosion. Unions, previously almost unknown, become universal overnight. However, though elegant, this model is not universal. It may serve to explain trade union explosions in certain industries, or certain aspects of general explosions, but probably no more.

Second, gas provides a striking example of an industry which enters upon a period of modernization almost entirely because of the pressure of labour, and therefore of the technologically beneficial effects of labour militancy. No doubt this example is also somewhat untypical, but it has considerable general interest. Technological conservatism is widespread, especially in countries of archaic industrialism like Britain, and the folklore of businessmen, which is reflected in much of even informed public opinion, has consistently tended to present militant labour demands as a mere obstacle to change. They are not. Where business is sufficiently sluggish, they may be an essential stimulus.

Third, gas illustrates the considerable strength of groups of skilled or otherwise indispensable workers in a situation of technological innovation, especially when this takes place within an already old, well-established and heavily capitalized industry.[77] Unlike so many other unions of the 1889 vintage, the gas-workers were never effectively dislodged from the positions they had occupied then. It is, of course, possible to imagine situations in which they could have been, and in which it would have been more worth the employers' while to dislodge them. But the fact that they did not collapse under the employers' counter-attack of the 1890s as so many other unions effectively did, remains.

A fourth reflection is suggested by the gas-workers' experience. Of all the industries of the late nineteenth century, gas, being a public utility, was the most closely involved with public ownership, public control, and public opinion.[78] Their bargaining strength undoubtedly derived in great part from this, and perhaps part of their fondness for political affiliations does also. At the time of their foundation the combination of public control with a labour force of potentially strong bargainers was exceptional. It has since become very much less so. Probably the exceptional nature of this industry explains why historians of trade unionism have paid so little attention to the

172

extraordinary episode of the gas-workers' sudden emergence, triumph, and the transformation of the industry which they achieved.

NOTES

1 The main sources for this article are: (1) the annual returns of most private and municipal gas undertakings (*Parliamentary Papers*, 1881–2 onward); (2) the annual returns of balance sheets for the Metropolitan Gas Companies (*Parliamentary Papers* 1870–1906); (3) Field's *Analysis of Gas Companies' Accounts* (1869 to date) which covers London from 1869, the London suburbs from 1880, and a selection of provincial undertakings from 1883; (4) the invaluable and voluminous *Journal of Gas Lighting* (weekly), which contains comprehensive information and discussion on all aspects of the industry. It is here quoted as *G.J.* (5) the *Transactions* of various associations of gas managers, technicians and others connected with the industry. The trade union sources – though quite copious from 1890 – are less useful.

2 For earlier agitations see S. Everard: *History of the Gaslight and Coke Company* (London 1948), pp. 122–3 (1825), p. 201 (1859), p. 244 (1867–72). Also *The London Gas Stokers. A Report by the Committee of their Trial etc.* (London 1873), and the contemporary files of the *Beehive*.

3 See below Sect. III.

4 Clapham, *Economic History of Modern Britain III*; G. T. Jones: *Increasing Returns*; D. L. Burn: *The Economic History of Steel-Making 1867–1939*.

5 F. Popplewell: 'The Gas Industry' in S. Webb and A. Freeman: *Seasonal Trades* (London 1912), pp. 181–3.

6 Since (a) the retort-house was the key to gas trade unionism and (b) carbonizing wages are the nearest approximation to the labour-cost of actual gas production.

7 *Report to the Board of Trade on the Relation of Wages in certain Industries to the Cost of Production* (BPP 1890–1: LXXVIII). These data are not strictly comparable. In some cases they clearly refer only to carbonizing wages, in others they include purification – a small matter; or even all 'wages and salaries at works'. They thus exaggerate the carbonizing percentage slightly.

8 Most of the technical details from *G.J.*, esp. vol. 49 (1887), p. 299: Presidential address to the Midland Association of Gas Managers. For a general bibliography, see W. R. Chester:

Bibliography of Coal Gas (1892). See also S. Hughes and O'Connor: *Gasworks* (1904 edn), p. 81.

9 *G.J.* vol. 54 (1889), p. 594.

10 W. Thorne: *My Life's Battles* (London n.d.), pp. 36–9, describes a 24-hour change-over shift.

11 'The Problem of the Day' (*G.J.* vol. 54 (1889), p. 594). Also ibid., vol. 55 (1890), p. 1,182.

12 But patent difficulties held up its introduction between 1889 and 1899 (see the 'Early History of Inclined Retorts' in *G.J.* vol. 79 (1902), esp. p. 541.

13 *G.J.* vol. 53 (1889), p. 894.

14 *Royal Commission on Labour* 1891–3, Group C: Evidence of W. A. Valon for the Gas Institute on wages, hours and changes since 1887 (pp. 25, 696 ff.); also the series of wage-rates 1838–91 in Livesey's evidence, pp. 26, 709.

15 However, there seems to have been a practice of paying a shade more than the current district rate for unskilled labour. ('The Management of Workmen', *G.J.* vol. 52 (1888), p. 286. Also discussion of a paper on the same subject by R. Fish at the Gas Institute meeting, Glasgow, July 1887 (ibid., vol. 49 (1887), p. 109).

16 Popplewell, op. cit., pp. 161–2; *G.J.* vol. 55 (1890), p. 1,182.

17 *R.C. on Labour*, Group C, pp. 26,022–26,430.

18 Ibid., p. 26,695.

19 Thus *G.J.* vol. 54 (1889), p. 65, regrets that the introduction of eight-hour shifts will leave winter work open 'only to a shifting labouring population', since the better men will all be regularly employed.

20 *G.J.* vol. 54 (1889), pp. 538, 712, 739, 862. The Liverpool directors wrote for blacklegs to 26 towns.

21 'The Management of Workmen' – 3 articles, loc. cit. – recommended accident and sickness funds, paid by the men, and superannuation, for 'once a man has remained for a few years in the employment of the company, there is the prospect of "losing his pension" by bad behaviour or dereliction'. . . (p. 331).

22 Ibid., p. 244.

23 *R.C. on Labour*, Group C, pp. 24,919, 25,748. Both London and Birmingham unions automatically organized brickmakers as well as gas-workers. For other seasonal alternatives see *G.J.* vol. 52 (1888), p. 286 (Harvesting); *J.R. Stat. Soc.* (1911), pp. 693 ff. (docking, coal-portering); Thorne, op. cit. (navvying); *Gasworkers and General Labourers' Union*: 1904 Conference Sou-

venir (miscell. factory work); *Trans. Inc. Gas Institute* (1890) (Yacht crews in Southampton).

24 Youths were rarely strong enough. See also *Econ. Journ.*, June 1911: Heath, 'Underemployment and the Mobility of Labour'.

25 Popplewell, op. cit., p. 165. The training of teams of men who had to work together, took much longer, though, than the lack of skill of single men would indicate. Hence much of the industry's vulnerability to strikes (*R.C. on Labour*, Group C, p. 26,702).

26 Even the 1906 *Earnings and Hours Enquiry* (*Parl. Papers* 1910 LXXXIV) gives only 144 stokers on piece-work out of a total of 11,655. However, abroad, payment by results was much more widespread (cf., M. Henry Laming, 'Nouvelles Methodes de Salaires' in *Société Technique de l'Industrie du Gaz, Compte-Rendu du 32e Congrès* 1905).

27 There is little to bear out the view of *G.J.* vol. 55 (1890), p. 583, that this was merely a disguised wage-movement; though, naturally, a change from twelve to eight hours implied the raising of weekly rates, if earnings were not to fall.

28 Thorne, op. cit., p. 64. But he also mentions regenerator firing, and simple speed-up (pp. 65–6), which is more likely.

29 These figures are calculated from the annual returns of the Metropolitan Companies balance-sheets.

30 *G.J.* vol. 50 (1887), pp. 109–10. For a full analysis of very similar work, see *R.C. on Labour*, Group C (Chemical Industry) *Parl. Pap.* 1893–4, XXIV, pp. 656 ff. Also Thorne, op. cit., pp. 39, 65–6.

31 T. Oliver (ed), *Dangerous Trades* (London 1902), p. 572.

32 In Leith, Salford, Bolton, Birmingham.

33 *G.J.* vol. 53 (1889), pp. 32, 170, 355, 778, 915 ff.

34 Ibid., vol. 54 *passim*. Agitations are recorded from the following areas:

Lancashire & Cheshire	27	South & S.W. England	3
Yorkshire	15	E. Midlands	2
North East Coast	8	Scotland	2
West Midlands	4	East Anglia	1
London	4	South Wales	1

35 E.g., Leith, Bolton.

36 E.g., Dundee, Liverpool, Nottingham, Southampton, Darlington, Bolton, Birkenhead, Burnley, Bristol.

37 *R.C. on Labour*, Group C, pp. 29,470–82.

38 *G.J.* vol. 54 (1889, p. 458.

39 Ibid., p. 838.

40 Ibid., p. 885.

41 Indeed, the rise in the industry's wage-bill burned out to be even greater:

Amount of Carbonizing Wages in various English Gasworks 1888 and 1890–1. In £s. (*Source*: Field's Analysis)

Town	1888	Mean 1890–1	Percentage increase
London	343,846	506,965	47
Suburbs	54,746	84,062	53
8 Municipalities*	159,682	216,188	35
10 Companies†	139,091	189,398	36

42 *G.J.* vol. 54 (1889), p. 781, where an editorial holds that the single defeat of the Bristol Gas Company after a short strike must seal the fate of all companies. Also its reports, *passim*.

43 Ibid., p. 683 (8 October 1889).

44 The slow progress of electric lighting in England during the 1880s is no guide to the anxiety caused by world progress at this time.

45 *G.J.* vol. 53 (1889), p. 707; also *passim* for these preoccupations.

46 Cf., Redford, *History of Local Government in Manchester*, III, cap. 23.

47 *G.J.* vol. 54 (1889), pp. 798, 1,072; vol. 56 (1890), p. 39.

48 The annual Reports on *Changes in Wages and Hours* (*Parl. Papers*, Trade), available from 1893, show that with few exceptions (Blackburn, 100 stokers in 1897, West Hartlepool, 60 stokers in 1899) no important works changed from twelve- to eight-hour shifts between 1893 and 1906.

49 From the annual returns of Balance Sheets (Capital Account).

50 To take the case of Inclined Retorts: 'undoubtedly the most important method of saving labour in gasworks'. In 1900 Britain had installed some 20 per cent more of them than all other European countries and the USA put together, and had well over double as much capacity as her nearest rival, Germany. (C. E. Brackenbury: *Modern Methods of Saving Labour in Gas Works* (London 1901), p. 16). 'A Comprehensive list of Inclined Retort installations in 1902', *G.J.* vol. 79, p. 542, gives a total British capacity of over 38,000,000,000 cubic feet per year. London possessed Inclined Retort capacity equal to about 20 per cent of its output, Field's sample of provincial municipalities, capacity equal to 25 per cent.

As for stoking machinery, Brackenbury claims this to have been

* Birmingham, Bolton, Leeds, Leicester, Manchester, Nottingham, Oldham, Salford.

† Bath, Brighton, Bristol, Derby, Liverpool, Newcastle, Plymouth, Portsea, Preston, Sheffield.

virtually a British monopoly (op. cit., p. 25; *Gasworks Plant & Machinery* (1905), pp. 13–14).

51 Field's *Analysis* for the London works.

52 Annual Reports on *Changes in Wages*, etc. The next round of increases occurred in 1911–13. The London increases in 1897 amounted to about 7·5 per cent on the average rate.

53 Popplewell, op. cit., p. 178.

54 See Table III.

55 E.g., *Reports of Proceedings of Associations of Gas Engineers and Gas Managers* (1902), pp. 24 ff., 213 ff.; (1903), p. 87.

56 Cf., *G.J.* vols. 55–7 *passim*; esp. vol. 54, p. 589, 'The Problem of the Day'.

57 *G.J.* vol. 57 (1891), p. 943: 'But the author's desire was to have the whole of the work arranged so that any ordinary labourer would be able to perform it'. (A scoop and carriage for inclined retorts.)

58 Ibid., vol. 54 (1889), p. 594.

59 This is a very rough guess, derived from the records of the Gas-workers Union, the N. Amal. Union of Labour, and the reports of labour matters in the *G.J.* They included many big northern towns, Birmingham, Bristol; several Welsh towns, etc.

60 Popplewell, op. cit., p. 159.

61 *R.C. on Labour*, Group C, p. 26,913. Manchester also launched an early counter-attack with success.

62 *G.J.* vol. 55 (1890), *passim*: p. 925 implies that this was a co-ordinated campaign. See also ibid., vol. 56 (1890), editorial of July 1. Still, the attempt to impose long-term contracts is itself an admission of defeat, in an industry overrun with casual labour in the past.

63 *Fifty Years of the National Union of General and Municipal Workers* (1939), p. 71. For an account of this strike, which played a major part in the formation of independent labour sentiment in Leeds, cf., E. P. Thompson, 'Homage to Tom Maguire', in A. Briggs and J. Saville, *Essays in Labour History* (London 1960), pp. 299 ff.

64 Vol. 56 (1890), p. 72.

65 Ibid., p. 288. This may explain the apparent decline in the management's preoccupation with labour problems later: henceforth it was taken for granted that stokers, etc., had to be 'humoured' to a much greater degree, as a matter of course.

66 For a brief discussion of this problem, see my 'General Labour Unions in Britain, 1889–1913' (*Econ. Hist. Rev. Sec. Series* vol. I, pp. 2 & 3 (1949) pp. 123 ff., esp. pp. 125–9.

67 Popplewell, op. cit., p. 208.
68 Ibid., pp. 168–71, and refs. as in note 23.
69 Ibid., p. 208.
70 Thus in 1889 carbonizing wages formed about 38 per cent of the total wage-bill in London works; in 1906 only about 25 per cent (calculated from *Parl. Papers* 1890–1, LXXVIII, pp. 61 ff. and *Parl. Papers* 1910, LXXXIV: Gas-workers). The fall was, of course, largely due to the great expansion in the distributive costs of the industry.
71 *G.J.*, vol. 58 (1891), p. 658.
72 A fact reflected in the rates for the new operations, which were clearly fixed in relation to skilled stokers' wages, and not (as for instance in the building trade) by adding a few pennies to the unskilled rate. See the annual *Standard Time Rates of Wages in the United Kingdom*.
73 S. Everard, *History of the Gaslight and Coke Company*, p. 254.
74 Cf., for example, E. W. Smith's paper on 'Improvements in Carbonization in Recent Years' (*Rep. of Proc. of Assocs. of Gas Engineers and Gas Managers* (1901), pp. 291 ff.). It is also worth noting that, while, as we have seen (n. 50) Inclined Retorts progressed in some places, others were slow to adopt them. Out of the eight provincial companies in Field's sample, with a total make of 12,463 mill. cu. ft. in 1902, only one had by then introduced Inclined Retorts, with an annual capacity of 419 mill. cu. ft. (This does not mean that they had not moved technically, of course.)
75 Popplewell, op. cit., pp. 194–6 gives particulars of the twenty companies (eight of them, including the Big Three, in the London area) which possessed co-partnership schemes. Two of these were adopted between 1890 and 1899, three between 1900 and 1905, fourteen in 1908–9. Payments amounted to an average bonus on wages of 4·85 per cent. *These payments are not included in the wage-figures used in this article.*
76 Cf., Gas-workers' Union Reports, e.g., *Quarterly Report* July–Sept. 1903, pp. 74–5, for full details of terms negotiated on working Inclined Retorts in S. Shields.
77 Cf., H. J. Habbakuk, *American and British Technology in the nineteenth century* (Cambridge 1962) for a full discussion of these problems.
78 The railways, the nearest comparable case, had no publicly-owned sector at this time. Muncipal transport based on advanced technology was still in its infancy.

10

General Labour Unions in Britain, 1889-1914*

I

'GENERAL LABOUR UNIONS' which enrol all classes of labour, irrespective of skill or occupation, have existed, at some time or other, in most industrial countries. In Britain, where they play a greater part in modern trade unionism than elsewhere,† they have been permanently established in strength since the late 1880s. While 'general unions' have used many of the bargaining techniques of 'craft' unionism in the past, and have increasingly tended to adopt those of 'industrial unionism',[1] they cannot wholly be analysed in terms of either of these classical divisions of trade union organisation. They have, in fact, fulfilled three quite distinct functions – often simultaneously. As '*class*' unions they have attempted to unite all workers against all employers, generally under socialist or revolutionary inspiration. As '*labourers*'' unions, they have attempted to provide effective organization for workers incapable of, or excluded from, orthodox craft unionism. As '*residual*' unions, lastly, they have organized any body of workers not effectively covered by other unions (and some that were). Neither the first nor the third functions call for any special form of organization. Indeed, the modern 'class' union – the Industrial Workers of the World in the USA and elsewhere, the One Big Union in Canada, the various communist unions between the wars – have been among the chief propagandists of rigorous 'industrial' unionism. But the problem of organizing the 'unskilled' and 'labourers', where the 'skilled' and 'artisans' were already in strong and exclusive unions of their own, did demand

---

* My thanks are due to the officers of the National Union of General and Municipal Workers for giving me access to the sources at their disposal.

† Though powerful foreign examples exist; e.g., the Australian Workers Union.

tactics and policies peculiar to 'general' unions. It is with these, and with their changes, that this article will be mainly concerned, though an inquiry into them will also involve some analysis of the actual composition of these unions. The subject is, on the whole, a neglected one.

The unions formed in the expansion of the late 1880s recruited workers of all grades of skill, and adopted numerous forms of organization. Yet it is no accident that the 'New Unionism' is normally associated with the great 'general' societies, the largest and most prominent bodies produced by the movement – Dockers, Gasworkers, Tyneside Labour Union and a number of others.* Most of these have since merged to form the two giant unions of Transport and General Workers and General and Municipal Workers which to-day include something like a quarter of the total British trade union membership. Yet their history has been by no means one of unbroken success. The absence of reliable statistics makes it impossible to measure the relative and absolute strength of 'general' unions in the 'New Unionism' of 1889–92; but their proportionate strength

Table I.† *Membership of certain unions 1892–1912 (in thousands); average annual members over 3- and 2-year periods*

	1892–4	1895–7	1898–1900	1901–3	1904–6	1907–9	1911–12
All Unions	1,555	1,614	1,895	2,010	2,058	2,492	3,277
'General' (a)	76	69	88	81	67	74	186
'All-grade' (b)	19	22	29	34	45	60	109
'Local crafts' (c)	12	12	12	12	11	12	24

(a) London Dockers, London Gas-workers, Birmingham Gasworkers, NAUL, National Amalgamated Labourers Union.

(b) London Carmen, Amalgamated Carters, Amalgamated Tram and Vehicle Workers, Municipal Employees, Liverpool Dockers.

(c) London Stevedores, Thames Watermen, Cardiff Trimmers, Mersey Quay and Rail Carters, Winsford Saltmakers.

* The main ones are: Gas-workers and General Labourers (1889; later: N.U. Gas-workers and Gen. Lab.; N.U. Gen. Lab.; here called: *London Gasworkers*); Dock, Wharf, Riverside and General Lab. U. (1889; here called: *London Dockers* or *Dockers*); Tyneside and General L.U. (1889), later National Amalgamated Union of Labour; here called: *NAUL*; Amal. Soc. Gas-workers, Brickmakers (1889); here called *Birmingham Gas-workers*; Nat. Amal. Union of Labourers (1889); Workers Union (1898); National Federation of Women Workers (1906).

† Source: Reports on Trade Unions.

was undoubtedly very great.[2] Like most other 'new' unions, they collapsed badly in the depression of the early 1890s; but unlike some others, the 'general' societies did not fully recover until after the renewed expansion of 1911–14. Between the two expansions they appeared to have shot their bolt, and very definitely lost ground. Table I gives a brief comparative picture of the fortunes of various types of 'new' unions (all composed of conventionally 'unskilled' men) between 1892 and 1912.

It is clear that we have here three patterns: the 'craft' societies with their stable (and restricted) membership; the General Unions, fluctuating, but without any marked upward tendency, yet climbing almost vertically after 1911; and the 'industrial' or compound unions, growing steadily from 1900, though rather faster after 1911. In, say, 1910 it might have seemed that the second group was destined, if not to replace, then increasingly to overshadow the third. But in fact, the opposite has happened. Both groups (a) and (b) have merged to form the two vast general unions of to-day. We can thus distinguish three phases in the development of the general unions: the expansion of 1889–92, the relative decline in their importance between 1892 and 1910, and their renewed, and as it turned out, permanent, expansion after 1911. Each of these phases developed its peculiar forms of organization and policy.

II

The theory in the mind of the founders of the general unions of 1889 (and of their predecessors) was fairly simple. The 'labourer', mobile, helpless, shifting from one trade to another, was incapable of using the orthodox tactics of craft unionism. Possessing 'merely the general value of labour'[3] he could not, like the 'skilled man', buttress a certain scarcity value by various restrictive methods, thus 'keeping up his price'.[4] His only chance therefore was to recruit into one gigantic union all those who could possibly blackleg on him – in the last analysis every 'unskilled' man, woman or juvenile in the country; and thus to create a vast closed shop.

'If we should confine ourselves,' said Will Thorne, 'to one particular industry, such as gasworks, alone, and if those other people in various parts of the country are let go unorganized, then, if we had a dispute with any of the gas companies, these men would be brought up to be put in our places.'[5] Theoretically, therefore, there was no limit to the union and its leaders recognized it. The Tyneside Labour Union soon became the National Amalgamated Union of Labour. A purely regional body in South Wales called itself the National Amalgamated Union of Labourers of Great Britain and Ireland; the Lancashire Labour Amalgamation became the British Labour Amalgamation, even as its effective radius contracted to some twenty miles from Piccadilly, Manchester. This was not grandiloquence, but – so it was thought – the bare recognition of facts.

Similarly, the acknowledged weakness of 'labourers' led them to rely much more than the 'artisans' on political pressure and legislative action.[6] Thus a natural alliance sprang up between politically quite immature men seeking to organize certain 'weak' groups of workers – dockers, gas-workers, woollen workers, etc. – and the revolutionary socialists of the 1880s, who supplied, or converted, the leaders of most, but not of all, general unions.[7] It would be artificial to draw an exact frontier between those which began as ordinary 'trade unions' (like Tillett's Tea Operatives—the ancestor of the Dockers' Union), coming under socialist leadership later, and those formed, like the Owenite unions (and perhaps the National Labour Federation on Tyneside, 1886–93),[8] as much with trade union ideas as with some wider social or moral transformation in mind. Both unions of 'weak' workers, and politico-industrial bodies tended to grow at much the same times of social tension and unrest; and by the late 1880s a body of socialist organizers and propagandists was once again available in Britain. One may, however, guess that the large national and regional 'general' unions of 1889 were the offspring of a marriage between the class unionism of the socialists and the more modest plans of the unskilled themselves.* The expansion of the early 1870s, in other respects an important – and neglected – forerunner of the 'New Unionism', produced unions of a far more sectional type.[9]

This, then, was the theory. One cannot fully understand its weaknesses without reminding oneself of contemporary beliefs about the structure of the working class, above all about that sharp frontier which divided the 'skilled' from the 'unskilled', the 'artisan' from the 'labourer'. At first sight the sharpness of this division is surprising, for both middle-class and artisan economists believed the rewards of labour (with or without assistance) to be broadly propor-

* The only general union with a really national network, the Gas-workers, secured this largely through the help of local socialist groups.

tional to merit, and to physical, intellectual and moral superiority.[10] A gradually ascending scale, such as that suggested by our division into 'unskilled', 'semi-skilled' and 'skilled'* might have appeared more suitable for such views. But, in fact, labour was divided into two groups: the one 'differentiated by training and experience, to such an extent that its transference to other occupations would involve, *ceteris paribus*, an appreciable industrial loss', the other 'the general mass of rude or unskilled labour',[11] undifferentiated, and not tied to any special occupation.

In the minds of many, this distinction camouflaged a much more old-fashioned one – the pre-industrial line between the skilled all-round 'craftsman', the genuine maker of things, and the 'labourer' who merely fetched and carried for him.[12] Nor was this distinction purely traditional. We have increasingly come to remember how much of nineteenth-century British industrial organization, at any rate before the age of mass-production and 'dilution', was really cast in a pre-industrial mould. Builders and engineers, boilermakers and tailors might still reasonably imagine that they were capable of making houses, machines, ships and clothes without the convenient, but not indispensable, help of the labourer; as a hotel chef could, at a pinch, produce a dinner without the help of the potato-peeler and bottle-washer. Alternatively, their position as sub-contractors or co-employers of the labourers[13] would also lead them to regard the difference between 'artisan' and 'labourer' as one of kind, not merely, like that between craftsman, improver and apprentice, as one of degree.[14] The higher wages, the greater respect, the other ponderable and imponderable perquisites of the 'aristocrat of labour' would thus be interpreted as a tribute to his peculiar excellence; and those groups of semi-skilled who, for one reason or another, succeeded in obtaining them – cotton-spinners, locomotive drivers, some coal-hewers – would readily assimilate their position to that of the 'craftsman'.

But such groups formed a minority of the organized trades, and before the introduction of the block-vote in the Trade Union Congress of the 1890s, their full numerical weight was in any case not appreciated.[15]

The 'artisan-labourer' pattern was thus conventional as much as real; and every industrial and technical change tended, on the whole, to increase its unreality. The 'artisans' were all members of groups

---

* But this classification did not become familiar until the present century.

which exercised effective bargaining strength (though not necessarily because they were skilled or craft-trained). But the 'labourers', defined by exclusion, did not necessarily contain only men without such strength; though it was easy to conclude that this was so.[16] On the contrary. The Great Depression saw labour on the defensive, and the leaders of the movement more inclined to reinforce restrictive barriers against blacklegs than to spread trade unionism. Hence, in spite of certain advances of semi-skilled groups towards 'artisan' status,* by the late 1880s the ranks of the 'labourers' contained an increasing number of men immediately capable of orthodox unionism, and often of great bargaining strength. All they required was the impetus to organize, and this the explosion of 1889 gave them.[17] But even the ideal 'general labourer' of the Victorian convention – fluid, shifting from trade to trade, doing his undifferentiated fetching and carrying as well or as badly wherever he was put – was probably rather less common than was supposed. Moreover, as mechanization and modern factory methods spread, employers came to doubt whether even he lacked all 'special value'.[18] The general unions thus found themselves recruiting a great many men who, for one reason or another, commanded that power to make themselves scarce; to cause appreciable loss upon transference, or to be worth inducements for greater efficiency, which were the basis of orthodox bargaining strength; an unexpectedly well-armed force.

This was fortunate for them, for the genuinely floating, or mobile worker, however skilled, was devilishly hard to organize under *laissez-faire* conditions. Unions composed of such men – the Navvies in Britain, the IWW in America[19] – were content if they could keep a few hundred regular members, and a few regular offices or centres, whence they could recruit a temporary mass membership and exercise temporary job control as and where the fight flared up. The vast national, regional or even local closed shops in which the old General Union saw its salvation were difficult to maintain generally, beyond the first flush of expansion. It is thus not surprising that the leaders of the general unions should have modified their policy. What appears surprising is that they should have been unaware of its inadequacies from the start, and have clung to it for so long.

* London Stevedores, Tyne and Thames Watermen, Northern Trimmers all emerged as official trade unions between 1870 and 1873. Boot and Shoe Operatives, Cotton Weavers, Card and Blowing Room Operatives, Locomotive drivers are among those who grew during the Depression.

III

The official foundation of the unions was the 'local branch' comprising all kinds of workers.[20] A more realistic division was based on trades, places of employment and the like. The Gas-workers,[21] pioneer and largest of general unions, provide examples of both. Organization in the fluctuating London area was general, forty-four out of the sixty-one branches in 1897, thirty-seven out of fifty-five in 1906 being so described, or unspecified. It seems clear that these branches grew out of the original nuclei of stokers organized round their local gasworks; but the leader of the union strongly resisted attempts to break up these agglomerations, sometimes thousands strong, into trade branches on the provincial pattern.[22] This had the advantage of allowing them to change character rather than to dissolve if, as gradually happened, the original stokers faded away. Nevertheless, it must have been extremely clumsy, for we constantly find it supplemented by 'place of employment' organization of one kind or another. Alone of district secretaries, the London man spent much of his time going round building jobs, coal wharves and factories, checking cards and the like. Some of the clumsiness is indicated by the fact that members claiming compensation against one large contracting firm came from no less than seven branches as far apart as West Ham and Battersea.[23] Shop-stewards, such as the northern Amalgamated Union of Labour allowed its branches, existed, but attempts which were made from time to time – by northern delegates and London builders – to give them official functions other than the simple collection of contributions, were resisted.[24]

Outside London, however, the number of occupational or employment branches outnumbered – outside ports and small towns greatly outnumbered – the general ones, as Table II, overleaf, shows.

It is thus clear that, from the start, the membership of general unions did not fit easily into an organization designed for the mobile and fluid, and those not tied to individual industries.

How far indeed were the union organizations for the 'general' labourer? Since the term is vague, and its meaning varies with region and industry, we cannot say. Moreover, most of our figures refer to branches, and a 'general' branch may have consisted not of general labourers, but merely of an assortment of miscellaneous trades, each too small for a separate branch. Broadly, it is clear that the proportion of general labourers went up in time of expansion, or during

G 185

great strikes, when they flocked into unions. In normal times it might be small. The best figures available, from an occupational list of the NAUL in 1895,[25] give 1,088 out of 11,000 members as 'general labour'; two years earlier a similar proportion had belonged to general branches in the same union: 2,700 out of 22,000 in thirteen branches out of 103 on the north-east coast, three out of thirteen in Sheffield.[26] One cannot really conclude much from such occasional figures.

Table II. *Gas-workers' Union. Number of 'General' branches in districts at various periods, 1890–1911**

| | | | 'General' | |
District	Year	Total number of branches	Wholly	Partly or unspecified
Birmingham	1896 (*a*)	25	0	0
	1899 (*a*)	33	0	0
	1909	30	1	1
Bristol	1891 (*b*)	10	0	0
	1893	11	0	0
	1896	11	1	0
	1904	8	0	0
Lancs.	1903	41	10	10 (*b*)
Leeds	1890–1	28	2	0
	1891–2	23	9 (*c*)	0
	1896	30	7 (*c*)	0
Mersey	1891	21	9	2
	1896	14	4	0
East coast	1909	33	8–9	0
North-east	1896	16	1	0
	1899	36	4	0
	1904	37	1–2	0

(*a*) 'Birmingham Metal Trade Alliances' in force.

(*b*) 'General' here includes a number of municipal branches; also perhaps some engineering labour. Lancs. described itself as 'occupationally organized' until 1911 (NUGMW (1929) Souvenir, p. 26).

(*c*) Misleading. E.g., in 1896 'general' includes up to six municipal branches and one of steelworks labourers.

* Leeds and Mersey figures 1890–2 from locally published balance sheets (Brit. Lib. Pol. Sci.; Coll. E.B., cvi); the others from Quarterly Statements. Since branches are not described uniformly from district to district, or year to year, the data can only be presented in a fragmentary way.

One thing, however, is clear. The General Unions, at any rate between 1892 and 1911, depended far more on their foothold in certain industries and large works than on their ability to recruit indiscriminately, hence (one may suppose) on the whole on a stabler and more regular type of worker than they had originally envisaged.[27] Local recognition by employers, of course, reinforced this tendency. Thus in the Leeds district of the Gas-workers the two 'recognized' groups of Dyers and Gas-workers made up twelve out of twenty-eight branches in 1891, ten out of twenty-three in 1891–2, sixteen out of thirty in 1896. On the north-east coast the strength of the NAUL in the shipyards – where it was recognized – is well brought out in Table III. Thus while something like half the 1893 strength of branches in general labour dissolved, fifteen-sixteenths of the shipyard strength remained stable. While we have no comparable figures for other unions, it is clear that things were much the same there. The Labour Protection League relied largely on its foothold in Woolwich Arsenal (in addition to its control over specialized grain and timber porters on the docks), the Birmingham gas-workers on their ties with the Corporation, even the small Machine and General Labourers of Bolton noted that 'we have gained a substantial foothold with a few employers'.[28]

Table III. *National Amalgamated Union of Labour. Branches closed 1896–1900, through loss of members**

Occupation	Total closed, 1896–1900	Total of branches in occupation, 1893	
		Wholly	Partly
Shipyard workers	3	43	5
Iron and steel	2	8	3
River, waterside	5	13	2
Chemical, lead, copper	4	14	0
Engineering labour	5	10	6
Navvies, builders	3	8	1
General	10	17	4
Others	4	18	4

* Annual Reports, (1893 and 1896–1900). Ten more branches closed because of secession to other unions, bankruptcy of employers, etc. 1893 is a fair base-year, though by 1896 the Lincolnshire district (Docks, engineering labour, general) had gone and the Sheffield district (mainly iron, steel and coal) had risen from thirteen to thirty-four branches and from 704 to 1,955 members. The table is thus likely to underrate the stability of iron and steel, and to overrate that of dock and riverwork in the union.

187

And these were, of course, mainly the large ones. Thus we know that, at a time when the entire 300-odd branches of the Gas-workers had only some 29,000 members, five branches alone of engineering, rubber, bridge-yard, cotton and iron-workers, each of men in a single firm, made up some 3,000 of the total;[29] and district reports make it clear how the entire union could be 'carried', especially during a depression, by a few large works branches.[30] It is doubtful whether we can estimate the extent to which general union branches were composed of employees of large works, or of single works. However, the following attempt may just give an order of magnitude, though the after-effects of the slump of 1902-4 may exaggerate the importance of the large works somewhat. Assuming an equal degree of 'concentration' in Barnsley (for which we have no details) as in Nottingham, we find that about half of the unions branches outside London were in 'large firms'. Membership, of course, is likely to have been far more concentrated. The estimate below in Table IV, is probably on the conservative side.

Having established such footholds, possibly – though we cannot measure the extent – in what J. R. Clynes called 'classes of work in which the evil effects of competition could not be felt',[31] the union could ride out bad times. It is quite remarkable, and wholly unlike American unionism, that the general unions were evidently quite as

Table IV. *Gas-workers' Union, Second Quarter, 1905. Branches in 'large firms'*[*]

District	Number of branches	Dec. 1905 Members	Branches with members mainly in 'large firms'
Barnsley	22	2,018	?
Birmingham	33	2,346	6–8
Bristol, south-west	20	1,472	5–6
East coast	15	1,644	6
Lancs.	37	4,665	15–20
Leeds	34	4,012	24
London	–	5,758	–
North-east	35	3,801	26–8
Nottingham	10	Incl. in London	7
South Wales	28	2,234	13–14
Total (without London)	234		102–13

[*] The London area comprises all branches not in separate districts, and the Nottingham branches.

capable of hanging on in industries subject to the trade cycle as elsewhere. True, among the Gas-workers, Bristol, Leeds and Lancashire districts had strong cores of gas and municipal labour; but Birmingham was built round the metal trades, South Wales on tinplate and tubes, the north-east (like the bigger NAUL) on ships and engineering, Barnsley and Nottingham on iron, steel and pit-top men, Hull on docks and shipyards. The Dockers' Union rested largely on tinplate. The point illustrates the importance of 'recognition' by the employers. Once a firm tolerated or accepted the union, as the shipbuilders did the NAUL,[32] a slump would not bring the otherwise inevitable expulsion and destruction. Clearly, the class-conscious militancy of the early leaders was less likely to commend itself in such a state of affairs than a more cautious and conciliatory policy.

IV

Insensibly, then, policy was modified. The classical 'labourers'' union knew perfectly well that it could win little without a strike; at any rate an occasional one.* But the NAUL, well dug in on Tyneside, boasted about its freedom from strikes just like the boilermakers.† The Marxist Londoners in the Gas-workers' Union continued to demand the abolition of piecework, instead of which they wanted a high-standard living wage; but the men from Birmingham, Lancashire and Llanelly objected. Piecework was becoming increasingly popular,[33] and in any case the tinplate trade had just decided to 'follow the machines', i.e., to abandon restriction of output.[34] In the same way, the Workers' Union, whose main strength lay in semi-skilled engineering, was later to support the mechanization against which so many older unions fought.[35]

But there was a more striking change. Like most general unions the Gas-workers had originally dreamed of the eventual unification of all labourers' societies into One Big Union;[36] or, as a second-best, of the universal interchangeability of union cards: 'one man, one ticket'.[37] From the point of view of shifting or nomadic labourers, moving from job to job and trade to trade, nothing could be more logical. Wherever they went, whatever their union, any *ad hoc* collec-

* In 1892, 1899 and 1902, for example, more than half the Gas-workers' income went in dispute benefit.

† Its Annual Reports give detailed tables. Generally about 90 per cent of disputes were settled peacefully; which argues a high degree of recognition.

tion of organized labourers could act as a single society for the purpose of exercising temporary job control. On building sites, for
instance, this frequently happened. But since the floating labourer
was not really the core of the general union, 'one man, one ticket'
found an increasingly lukewarm reception from the champions of the
alternative tactic, which we may call 'one ticket, one job': the local
job monopoly. Each union, having perhaps just scraped local recognition, came to regard immigrants, not as reinforcements which
enabled it to hold strongpoints in an ever-shifting labour market, but
as potential blacklegs. 'Take any dock in the country,' argued Ernest
Bevin in 1914. 'What is the serious problem we have to face? It is that
where the men have been organized longest, and have been able to
build up certain conditions, the employer is always doing his best to
attract a big surplus of labour around him so as to intimidate the
men.'[38] If indiscriminate mobility were to be encouraged, unionists
might be quite as much of a menace as non-unionists.

The original leaders, sceptical of a job monopoly held by 'labourers', had not troubled much about this. Mobile men, like the builders,
and perhaps the expanding and far from crystallized Midland semi-
skilled engineering workers, might maintain the old view. (Hence the
support of the London district of the Gas-workers, and perhaps the
spokesmen of the Workers' Union for the old slogan in 1911-14.[39])
Revolutionaries who thought in terms of class militancy would
detect the 'reformist' danger in restrictionism and champion the one
big union, as Larkin and Connolly did. Yet, in fact, it was clear by
1910-14 that the union of all 'unskilled' workers, however desirable,
would not be one of a mass of individual floating labourers, but one
of a great many local job monopolies and closed shops, whose special
interests had to be safeguarded, if they were to give up their independence. The extremely significant unity discussions between the
General Labourers' National Council and the Transport Workers'
Federation in 1911-14 reached deadlock on this very point.[40] It was
only some ten years later, when the Dockers' Union (largely on the
model of Bevin's Bristol organization) had evolved a scheme of
autonomy for trade groups, that the vast mergers which gave birth
to the Transport and General and General and Municipal Workers
became possible.[41] (However, the adoption of a more flexible organization was merely a condition of their success; the power which
propelled separate unions towards amalgamation was largely political
and revolutionary unrest.)

We can thus distinguish three stages in general union tactics: the old-fashioned general unionism of 1889–92; the cautious, limited and conservative 'sectional' unionism of 1892–1910; and the revolutionary urge for amalgamation, the industrial unionism or the articulated 'general' organization of the modern Transport Workers, which arose out of the expansions of 1911–20. Both the first and the third aimed at the organization of all 'unskilled' workers. The second – chiefly under the pressure of circumstance – renounced it in practice, confining itself to the organization of those groups capable of old-fashioned bargaining. It is significant, for example, that it utterly failed to organize the genuinely weak – e.g., the women. In spite of its early enthusiasm for women's organization, the 32,000 members of Gas-workers in 1908 contained only some 800 women.[42] General unionism in this period between the expansions had indeed become something like the sectional unionism of certain 'unskilled' groups in the American Federation of Labour between 1896 and 1935; the Teamsters, the Hod-Carriers, etc. Had there been no second expansion within twenty years of the first, it might well have been assimilated to the craft-pattern, as in the USA.[43]

The 'new unionism' of 1889 thus became uncomfortably like the 'old unionism' it had once fought; and the politics of its leaders changed accordingly. The revolutionary Marxists who led the Dockers and Gas-workers then, were increasingly replaced by much milder socialists (though for auld lang syne some of them continued to call themselves Marxian Social Democrats). Ernest Bevin, not Tom Mann, was to dominate the Dockers after their second expansion. The Gas-workers, a very markedly 'party-dominated' organization, whose leader was a protégé of Engels, whose *éminences grises* in the early 1890s were the Marx-Avelings, and most of whose key positions were held by social democrats, became the union of the Rt. Hon. J. R. Clynes, and a distinctly moderate body.

V

Yet after 1906 the fall in real wages and the rank-and-file unrest forced unions once again on to the offensive. The problems of massive recruitment and aggressive bargaining obliged leaders to reconsider their tactics. Hitherto this had not been really necessary. The impetus of the expansion of 1889 had given them all the offensive strength they originally needed. When slump and employers' attacks

had weeded out all but the strongest, the general unions had discovered powerful defensive resources which enabled them to survive.
They spread their risks between industries and areas not all of which
were liable to attack at the same time. They acted, in fact, as a
convenient 'banker' for a multiplicity of local and sectional bargaining units.[44] Such spreading of risks was quite essential, for the
'labourers'' union faced actuarially quite unpredictable risks: at any
moment its funds might be drained by disputes between masters and
'artisans', or between skilled unions. Hence nothing would have been
gained, had the NAUL turned itself into a pure shipyard union, or
the Dockers split up into separate waterside and tinplate trade
societies. On the contrary; the incentive to recruit widely remained.
Thus the Gas-workers took in the pit-top men they had originally
refused,[45] and the three main general unions used the boom of 1898–
1900 to make important conquests – their only really solid advances
between the two expansions – into coal, iron, steel and tinplate in
South Wales, and the Nottingham-Derby-South Yorkshire area. If
much of the membership fluctuated, that need not weaken the union
provided it had a nucleus of regular branches. On the contrary, a
steady influx of entrance fees and temporary subscriptions merely
added to the funds of societies which could not charge the high dues
of the craft unions.[46]

The more acute left-wingers, however, had long recognized the
need for a more adequate aggressive tactic. Even in the 1889 days all
manner of federations and centralized 'general staffs' had been suggested.[47] Tom Mann, incomparably the ablest of the radicals, had
even used the small expansion of 1898–1900 to found a body halfway
between 'general' and 'industrial' unions, the 'Workers' Union',
which was to embrace all industries and grades of skill, including the
highest.[48] This union was not very successful until after 1911, when it
became one of the major general unions, and one which long retained
certain oecumenical ambitions.[49] Mann's theories did, however,
enable it to make exceptional headway among farm-labourers, and in
the mass-production engineering of the Midlands, where the co-
ordinating of various degrees of skill was urgent, and the national
craft unions relatively weak. From 1906, however, other unions –
again largely under the impulse of the left – awoke to the importance
of 'strategic' recruiting, and systematic all-grades bargaining. Certainly by 1911 the Bristol dockers were systematically recruiting
strategically important grades,[50] and the Dockers' Union as a whole

192

took up the cause of 'industrial unionism' and the new Transport Workers' Federation with enthusiasm.

For most general unions, however, the problem of 'industrial' bargaining resolved itself not so much into one of forming bodies covering an entire industry, but into one of recruitment, of demarcation, and of unscrambling their eggs. Recruitment was easy, at any rate in times of expansion. Demarcation was more difficult, for they naturally cut across whatever industrial boundaries could be drawn. It was indeed on this rock that systematic unionism eventually foundered in the 1920s.[51] However, certain local arrangements had long been made – the Bristol dockers promised not to poach galvanizers, the Gas-workers refraining from coal-porters[52] – and wide federations like the Transport Workers' were some help.* But within each union the trades formed a jumbled mass; unless, as happened sometimes, a particular district was predominantly composed of men in one industry, and could thus form a *de facto* 'trade section'. NAUL thus had its geographically distinct waterside and ship-repairing groups, the Dockers their tinplate district, the Gas-workers their dyers, etc. Yet that was not enough. As early as 1893 the gas-workers in the Gas-workers' Union had wanted to federate with the miners, with whom their strategic interests lay; as the Coal-porters' union had done. But the dyers and chemical workers in the union objected strongly to paying out affiliation fees for what was quite irrelevant to them, and the matter was shelved.[53] So long as the old indiscriminate organization existed, trades would inevitably get in each other's way.

As the unions grew after 1906, and above all as they took in non-localized industries, they thus had to develop greater flexibility. The Dockers took the lead in this, no doubt because the two strongly marked and contrasting units of Bristol waterside and Welsh tinplate workers, which dominated the union, forced them to grant each considerable autonomy. In 1911–14 we can see the seeds of the new model sprouting in the west: the 'Tinplate District' was converted into a trade section, to be a pattern for others, and, an even greater break, a 'galvanizing section' was set up on a mainly non-geographical basis.[54] The Transport and General Workers' Union was later to be built on systematic trade autonomy. It had its reward. In 1910 the Dockers were, speaking nationally, one of the least successful, and by

* The fact that outside unions (like Gas-workers and NAUL) affiliated on behalf of their transport members was a sign of welcome flexibility.

no means the largest of the general unions. In the course of the next twenty years they were to overhaul the less systematically organized Gas-workers, to become the largest union in the country. But, whether the adoption of trade autonomy was systematic or not, all general unions moved in the same direction. By the time of the great amalgamations after World War I, they were on their way to becoming alliances of trade and industrial sections, rather than, in the past, of local bargaining units. It is as such that they function to-day.

VI

We have traced the slow progress of General Unions from the policy of 1889 to the modern federation of industrial sections. It remains to account for this slowness, and to sketch some of its results.

A number of reasons may be suggested why alliances of local closed shops, composed of regular employees, perhaps restricting entry to their job, continued to think of themselves as something like unions of floating casuals; or why semi-skilled engineers, organizing modern mass-production shops, failed to realize that their bargaining position differed essentially from that of bricklayers' labourers.[55] In the first place, the gap between 'labourer' and 'artisan', though not quite as real as in the convention, was real enough. One was apprenticed, the other picked up the job anyhow. Even the experienced gas-stoker or seaman could see himself changing industries much more easily than he could conceive a boilermaker becoming a carpenter. Hence the advance of mechanization would appear, to begin with, simply as something that added to the number of 'labourers' as against 'artisans'; and thus to raise no fundamentally new problem.[56] Moreover, what little we know of the actual process of 'picking up' new skills – sometimes of quite a high order – shows us the young worker drifting from one works to another, perhaps from one trade to another, certainly from one machine or department to another before finally settling down.[57] In the second place, the great irregularity, seasonality and fluctuation of many non-apprenticed jobs suggested greater fluidity than actually existed. Thus a large proportion of gas-stokers were seasonal migrants who filled in the summer as brickmakers, builders' labourers, harvesters, or even as in Southampton, as yacht crews.[58] But we know that a large gasworks would in fact expect to hire most of its last year's staff at the beginning of each new winter season.[59] Where there was, in theory, nothing to link the worker to a particular trade or firm, potential and actual fluidity were easily confused. In the third place, the 'legal' position of the more skilled was often exactly the same as that of the unskilled, from whose ranks they were recruited, and into whose ranks they might at any moment return, either permanently, or for a spell, when business was slack. Technically, the highly specialized docker, or stevedore, who could command a job any time he wanted, might be just as much of a casual as the derelict wharf-rat; and equally looked down on as 'unskilled' by the 'craftsman'.[60]

The fact that workers on both sides of the gap kept to their proper stations as 'artisans' and 'labourers' proved to be of considerable advantage to the general unions in their formative period. They avoided that competition with the 'crafts' which wrecked the Knights of Labor in the more mechanized USA of the late 1880s.[61] For even if it had struck the shipyard labourers or pit-top men that their bargaining strength needed reinforcement by that of boiler-makers or hewers, they were too weak to think, as the Knights did, of forcing union on their terms, and the 'crafts' did not feel themselves in need of it on theirs. In spite of the warnings of their left wing [62] the advance of mechanization and dilution did not, until after 1906, appear to present urgent or unmanageable dangers. The classical policy of restriction still seemed feasible. Either the awkward new grades could be sent to form unions of their own, which would not complicate or weaken the craftsmen's bargains: as the engineers sent the electricians, the hand-bootmakers the machine-bootmakers to form theirs;[63] as the compositors favoured the formation of a separate 'printers' labourers' society, and the iron-moulders made no attempt to organize the machine-moulders.[64] Or the 'craftsman' could attempt to capture the machine for himself, at craftsman's rates, as compositors, engineers and boilermakers attempted to do, and in part succeeded in doing.[65] Only rarely did the craft union feel impelled to extend its jurisdiction over new groups of unskilled or semi-skilled men – the technique which was later to allow the American Federation of Labour to compete with its more modern rival.* Moreover, where 'unskilled' unions had been formed to fight the 'artisans' as much as the masters (e.g., in the shipyards), problems of unity were largely academic.

So long as artisans remained complacent and labourers modest,

* The recruitment of ring-spinners by Cardroom Operatives is a British example.

general unions were free to take root: organizing here a wholly neglected industry (like transport), there the lower grades of an industry
in which craft unions were established higher up (ships, iron and
steel, engineering); or whole areas neglected by the localization of
unionism (Devon and part of the Midlands), or whole groups of
small or scattered skilled crafts (the Welsh Artisans* or the Yorkshire
Wool-combers†) who preferred the resources of a large union, or
needed the support of other grades in their industry.‡ The stagnation of the 'old' unionism after 1875, and the localization of industry
left them with a good selection of strong groups to organize. And the
strong incentive to spread their risks gave them an elasticity which
other unions lacked. Long before a new industry or region had
developed to the point of setting up unions of its own, it would have
been invaded, and, if receptive, organized, by a general union.[66] The
champions of systematic industrial unionism were thus wrong in
believing that general unions would wither away, even if all their
industrial sections went to appropriate unions, and decasualization
reduced their core of 'general' labourers.[67] In the absence of any
overriding authority allocating fields to be organized, they would
retain their residual functions; and would thus tend to benefit abnormally by any major expansion of trade unionism. Thus the Workers
Unions, never more than 5,000 strong between 1898 and 1910,
claimed 150,000 in 1914; almost all were men and women who, while
not 'unattached labourers' simply found no other unions in their
region or industry ready to take them.

Conversely, the incentive to build systematic 'industrial' unions
long remained weak. Until 1914 bargaining was overwhelmingly
local, or at best regional. Until World War I, moreover, the wage-
structure remained, for the 'unskilled' at any rate, overwhelmingly
traditional.[68] To the extent that employers would fix 'unskilled'
wages simply by the 'district rate' for such work, and to the extent
that local variations were substantial,[69] a strong argument for the
'regional closed shop' of the general union ideal remained. The

* Maintenance workers in the tinplate trade (founded 1889). They joined
NUGMW in 1935.
† Also now in NUGMW.
‡ Quarrymen, ore miners, certain knife and small metal trades, coopers in
cement works, threatened by machinery, skilled men in flour-milling, etc.
Unions of flour-millers, paper-makers, chemical workers and other highly
mechanized and new industries came into being in 1889, but had not much
independent success.

various trades which came out in the famous Black Country strike of 1913 quite naturally demanded not only sectional concessions, but a general Black Country minimum of 23 shillings.[70] So long as the worker might feel that his bargain depended just as much on the 'general' labour market in the area as on the situation in his specific industry (locally or nationally), a properly articulated 'general' union might actually prove the most advantageous form of 'industrial unionism'.

No doubt this was a temporary phase. By the time builders and dockers began to negotiate nationally, the traditional structure of engineering wages had been shaken by the war and the railwaymen had adopted a modern policy of demanding such wages as the traffic would bear, the case for systematic 'industrial unionism' was vastly stronger. Moreover, such things as trade boards, minimum wage acts, etc., provided an alternative method of tackling the problem of the 'district rate for unskilled labour'. But in 1911-14, when the decisive expansion of general unions took place, little of all this had happened. General unions were thus the main beneficiaries of the expansion – though in a form not inconsistent with industrial bargaining. This explains, perhaps, their astonishing success after 1911 in absorbing their industrially organized rivals, who had, between 1900 and 1910, been relatively so much more successful. The Tram and Vehicle Workers in merging with the Transport and General Workers, the Municipal Employees in joining to form the General and Municipal Workers, gained a double advantage: that of bargaining with other grades in their industry, and, to some extent, that of co-ordinating their bargains with those of the numerous easily interchangeable jobs (or the numerous jobs whose wage-rates were fixed in relation to each other), of which they organized one lot; quite apart from the fact that, with the giant Transport and General Workers in existence, it was much easier to merge with it than, let us say, to form the nationally organized compound union of road transport workers, of which the carters of 1911-14 still dreamed.[71] The General Unions had come to stay. Their strength and advantages were such that they continued to grow. Certainly, short of a revolutionary transformation of the trade union movement, any hope of eliminating them after 1911 was utopian. Whether their growth, in spite of the flexibility it has given to British trade union expansion, has not raised more problems than it has solved, is another question.

(1949)

NOTES

1 For the traditional definitions of 'craft' and 'industrial' unionism, cf., N. Barou, *British Trade Unions* (1947), pp. 20–6;
W. Milne-Bailey, *Trade Union Documents* (1929), pp. 122–
134; G. D. H. Cole, *Organized Labour* (1924 edn), pp. 28–33,
for a more elaborate classification. The traditional 'industrial
unionism' is here called 'rigorous' or 'systematic' industrial
unionism.

'*Craft unionism*' here means the organization for individual
grades and sections of workers (or groups of closely allied grades)
bargaining independently and separately.

'*Industrial unionism*' here means the type of organization which
seeks to unite and co-ordinate the bargaining of all groups whose
bargains affect each other substantially; 'all-grades' organization.

In view of the changing size of the bargaining area this is to some
extent a distinction of historical periods as well as of function;
but it has nothing to do with 'skill', 'apprenticeship' or 'industries' in the census meaning. Nor are craft unionism and industrial unionism necessarily found in pure form, or mutually
exclusive.

2 All figures are unreliable. Local Trades Council reports, however (e.g., Bristol, Norwich, Bolton, Leicester), indicate the
relative importance of various bodies. For example, in Bristol
1890 'general union strength' made up about half the total 'new
union' strength and 30–40 per cent of total trade union strength
(Bristol T.C. 1891, Ann. Rep.)

3 S. J. Chapman and H. M. Hallsworth, *Unemployment in Lancashire* (Manchester 1909), p. 83.

4 See Webb, *Industrial Democracy*, *passim*, but esp. caps. X and
XI.

5 R.C. on Labour, Group A, Evidence 24, 943.

6 The semi-skilled groups of miners and cotton operatives are in
this as in other respects halfway between 'old' and 'new' unions
(Cole, *Short History of British Working-Class Movement* (1948
edn), pp. 245–6). Cf., also, the debates on the legal 8-hour day in
TUC Report (1889), notably W. Matkin, p. 55.

7 Except the early leaders of NAUL, Birmingham Gas-workers
(who were Chamberlainite) and perhaps the National Amalgamated Labourers' Union – for which see T. J. O'Keeffe, *Rise*

and Progress of the National Amalgamated Labourers' Union (Cardiff 1891).

8 See E. R. Pease (the Fabian), its secretary, on it in *To-day* (June 1887). It collapsed in the early 1890s, its relics joining the Gas-workers. Surviving reports are in Brit. Lib. Pol. Sci., Coll. E.B., CVI.

9 Patrick Kenney's 'General Labourers' Amalgamated Union' (which survived the Great Depression in a shadowy way) was mainly an attempt to apply amalgamated principles to builders' labourers (Postgate, *Builders' History*, pp. 298–9) and not so oecumenically minded. It remained a builders' labourers union. But there were some 'general' unions, e.g., the London and Counties Labour League.

10 Marshall, *Principles*, I, II, 7 (8th ed, p. 26) for an extreme statement. Royal Commission on the Aged Poor (1895), Evidence 16, pp. 545 ff. for the view of a Birmingham working-class city councillor.

11 Palgrave, *Dict. Pol. Econ.*, article: 'Labour, Skilled' (II, p. 527). For less sophisticated versions of this dualism cf., *Oxford English Dictionary*, 'Labourer' (1903); Report of *Industrial Remuneration Conference* (1885), p. 369; Thomas Wright, *Our New Masters* (London 1873), pp. 4–9; and indeed common contemporary parlance.

12 'As his title of "unskilled" implies, he has no handicraft and he has no union' – *Working Men and Women*, by a Working Man (London 1879). 'Instead of being competent to act as an artisan he was often only able to produce one particular article of furniture, and sometimes only a portion of that article was committed to him' – W. G. Bunn in *Industrial Remuneration Conference* (1885), pp. 168–9.

13 See D. E. Schloss, *Methods of Industrial Remuneration* (1892) for methods in vogue.

14 Evidence of R. Knight in R.C. on Labour (Group A, Evidence 20, 801 ff.), and the fantastic chapter on 'The Unskilled Labourer' in *A Working Man*, op. cit.

15 Cf., the complaints about the dominance of coal and cotton in the Notes of the Month of the (conservative) *Trade Unionist* (October 1899).

16 Cf., Webb, *History of Trade Unionism* (1st ed 1894), pp. 388–9, where match-girls and gas-stokers are bracketed as weak and unskilled. They should have known better (cf., H. W. Massingham, their colleague, on 'The Trend of Trade Unionism' in *Fortnightly* (1892), LVIII, p. 450).

17 Thus Cardiff trimmers, Tyne dock and river workers, won immediate and permanent recognition, and a virtual closed shop. (NUGMW Souvenir (1929), p. 13.) The same is true of Gasworkers in various towns.

18 Cf., evidence of Sir B. Browne in Royal Commission on Poor Law Append., vol. VIII, pp. 86,211 ff., 86,286, 86,299, 86,301; Prof. S. Chapman, ibid., p. 84,798; or the Charity Organization Society's Report of Special Committee on Unskilled Labour (1908), p. 6.

19 For the IWW, P. F. Brissenden, *The IWW* (New York 1920) and J. S. Gambs, *The Decline of the IWW* (New York 1932). For the Navvies, John Ward's evidence in R.C. on Poor Law (vol. VIII) and e.g., the report on the Leighton Reservoir strike in Navvies Union Quarterly Report (January 1914), pp. 31–4.

20 Problems of such mixed branches are discussed in J. Commons and associates, *History of Labour in the US* II, pt. 6, cap. 10 (Mixed Assemblies of the Knights of Labor); L. Lorwin, *The American Federation of Labour* (1933), pp. 70–1 (Federal Labour Unions); and H. A. Logan, *Trade Unions in Canada* (1948), pp. 347 ff., 389 ff.

21 Their quarterly Balance Sheets and statements are the most important sources; followed by the Conference Reports and such Executive Minutes as survive. For the Union see the two Jubilee Souvenirs (1929 and 1939), the Jubilee Souvenir of its Northern District (Newcastle 1939), and the memoirs of Will Thorne and J. R. Clynes. There is no real history of it. In 1924 it merged with the NAUL and Municipal Employees to form the General and Municipal Workers. It has absorbed numerous other unions.

22 1890 Conference, p. 7.

23 From Workmen's Compensation statistics 1904–5 Quarterly Reports.

24 Conference Reports (1892), p. 37; (1894), p. 91; (1898), p. 50; (1900), p. 17. For NAUL stewards, see their Delegate Conference Reports, (1890), pp. 7, 20; (February 1892), pp. 48–9.

25 Annual Report (1895), p. 7. This was about half the nominal, two-thirds the paid-up membership.

26 Annual Report (1893), pp. 7 ff. A full and most valuable analysis of branches.

27 'Why the New Union was Founded', Leaflet I of the Workers Union, 1898 (Brit. Lib. Pol. Sci., Coll. E.B., XI).

28 Amalgamated Union of Machine and General Labourers, Annual Report (Bolton 1893) (Brit. Lib. Pol. Sci., Coll. E.B. CVI).

29 Gas-workers, General Executive Minutes: 13 March 1904, 13 November 1904, 19 February 1905 (NUGMW Library).

30 Gas-workers, Fourth Quarterly (1905), p. 15 (Bristol).

31 Gas-workers, Fourth Quarterly (1901), p. 13 (Lancashire).

32 The Tyne shipbuilders recognized the union's scales of help at least as early as 1893 (Tyneside and National LU Executive Minutes; March, p. 7; April, p. 10). NUGMW Library.)

33 1902 Conference (Gas-workers), p. 16; Second Quarterly, (1904), p. 15.

34 J. H. Jones, *The Tinplate Industry* (1914), pp. 229–30. The General Unions were firmly established there, from 1900.

35 Presidential address of W. Beard in Workers Union Record, July 1916, pp. 3, 6.

36 'What we are all so desirous of seeing . . . an Amalgamation of all Labourers', Gas-workers, First Quarterly, 1897, p. 11.

37 Gas-workers, Second Half-yearly Report (1889–90), p. 5; Second Annual Report (1894), p. 9, 1894 Conf. 117–18.

38 Special Conference on Amalgamation (National Transport Workers' Federation and General Labourers' National Council) 1914; p. 47. An important document.

39 Ibid., p. 28.

40 Joint Proposals for Amalgamation 1914 (National Transport Workers' Federation and General Labour National Council) contains a summary of events from 1906. Cole, *World of Labour* (1915 edn), pp. 235–7. 'The Union, Its Work and Problems' (London, TGWU 1945) I, pp. 5–7 discusses the issue, though not quite accurately.

41 For the organization of trade autonomy see 'The Union, Its Work and Problems' I and II. The General and Municipal Workers merely have specialized industrial officers at HQ to look after sectional interests.

42 Report on Trade Unions, 1912–13. No doubt this failure was why the National Federation of Women Workers set up as an independent general union from 1906.

43 Lorwin, op. cit., on the Teamsters (p. 536).

44 Will Thorne, *My Life's Battles* (n.d.), p. 142; Gas-workers, Third Quarterly (1896), p. 9, for official statements to this effect.

45 NUGMW (1929), Souvenir, p. 47, for beginnings.

46 Turn-over was considerable. Thus the Sunderland district of the Gas-workers in 1900–2 recruited 4,072 and lost 4,432 to maintain a total membership of 4,000 odd (1902 Conference, p. 11).

47 For example, Mann and Tillett, *The New Trades Unionism* (1890),

a plea for leadership by trades councils; or J. L. Mahon, *The Labour Programme* (1888). See also Clem Edwards on 'Labour Federation' in *Economic Journal*, 1893.

48 'Why the New Union Was Formed', loc. cit. W. Beard in Workers Union Record, loc. cit.

49 Cole, *Organized Labour* (1924 ed), p. 32: 'in the minds of some of its officials an embryonic Industrial Workers of the World with all labour for its province.'

50 Dockers Record (March 1911), p. 2.

51 TUC Report (1927), pp. 99 ff.

52 Gas-workers, General Executive Minutes (7 August 1904).

53 1894 Conference, pp. 119, 127–8. For similar – less successful – rows in NAUL, see Delegate Assembly (February 1891), pp. 7–8.

54 Dockers Record (March 1911), p. 5; (June 1911), p. 2.

55 For example, Workers Union Record (September 1916), p. 11: 'we were all elated at what we all considered our marvellous success (in 1904) . . . more so as the class of men organized (in BSA, Birmingham) were looked upon as impossible. It was in the days when the class of semi-skilled machinists was not generally known and certainly not recognized.'

56 Gas-workers, Third Quarterly (1896) (Will Thorne): 'Does not Mr Stevenson recognize that there is greater competition be- tween the labourers than there is between the mechanics, through the rapid development and simplification of machinery; that the skilled artisan is more tied to his particular trade than the unskilled labourer?' (pp. 8–9). 'Labour-saving machinery is reducing the previously skilled to the level of unskilled labour' (which was, of course, conceived like the classical 'fetching and carrying') ('A Speech by John Burns on the Liverpool Congress' (1890), p. 6).

57 Cf., from a series of weekly biographies of prominent members of the Workers Union: a 32-year-old Bilston toolmaker was in his time half-timer in boot and shoe factory, butcher's and farmer's boy, 'drifted into factory life' and became in turn hard- ware pot welder, blacksmith's striker, machinist, bench-hand in an engineering shop and toolmaker. (WU Record March (1917), p. 9.) Learning by migration, following up and picking up are well discussed in N. B. Dearle, *Industrial Training* (1914), caps. V–VII.

58 Trans. Gas Institute (1890), p. 80.

59 R.C. on Labour, Group A, Evidence 25, 744 (W. A. Valon).

60 John Burnett of the Board of Trade's Labour Department,

an engineer, classified coal-trimmers, grain-porters and casual dockers as 'unskilled' in Report on Strikes (1889).

61 See J. Commons and associates, op. cit. II, cap. 8–10; S. Perlman, *History of Trade Unionism in the USA*, pp. 114–16.

62 For example, John Burns, op. cit.; J. B. Jefferys shows that the Engineers' admission of certain semi-skilled men in 1892, on left-wing pressure, was nominal. (*Story of the Engineers* (1944), pp. 136–8.)

63 '*50 Years of the ETU*' (Manchester 1939); Webb, *Industrial Democracy* (1902 edn), pp. 418–19.

64 R. B. Suthers, *The Story of Natsopa* (1929), pp. 12–13; Amal. S. Plate and Machine Moulders (Oldham), Annual Report (1894), p. 5 (Brit. Lib. Pol. Sci., Coll. E.D., p. 163).

65 Webbs, *Industrial Democracy*, cap. VIII, 'New Processes and Machinery'; Ellic Howe and H. Waite, *The London Society of Compositors* (1948), pp. 231–3.

66 Cf., the Gas-workers campaign to organize telephone workers in the 1890s (Quarterly Reports (1896–7); e.g., I, 1897, pp. 43–7).

67 Cole and Mellor, *The Greater Unionism* (1913), p. 17; Cole, *World of Labour* (1915 edn), pp. 239–40 is less extreme.

68 J. W. F. Rowe, *Wages in Practice and Theory* (1928), pp. 151–6.

69 Rowe, op. cit., pp. 69–71, 74–5. See also F. W. Lawrence, *Local Variations in Wages* (1898). The sizes of trade union districts are guides to the smallness of the bargaining area. The Wage Census of 1906 (e.g., LXXXIV of 1910 Building and Wood-Working) allows us to observe the remarkable variations of standard labourers' wages in quite small areas – for example, S. Lancs.

70 Askwith, *Industrial Problems and Disputes* (1920), p. 252, cap. XXV.

71 Special Conference on Amalgamation (1914), pp. 22, 25–6.

11

National Unions on the Waterside

I

THE MOST DRAMATIC BATTLES, triumphs and defeats of the so-called 'New Unionism' of the late nineteenth and early twentieth centuries occurred on the British waterside. Its strikes, such as the conflict of 1889 led by John Burns, Tom Mann, and Ben Tillett, are remembered by many to whom few other episodes in labour history are familiar. Its lock-outs and employers' counter-offensives were on an equally vast scale. A dockers' leader, Ernest Bevin, has become the most familiar twentieth-century trade unionist among the lay public. It is therefore natural that the history of waterside agitations has been most commonly written in terms of its dramatic events and personalities, though as it happens not even an adequate narrative history of this kind as yet exists. However, it is not my object to retell or to complete such a narrative, but rather to consider the reasons why trade unionism on the British waterside emerged as it did and when it did.

Broadly speaking, it emerged between 1889 and 1914. Before 1889 waterside labour was not seriously or permanently organized at all. After the great strikes and lockouts of 1911–12, trade unionism never relapsed into insignificance. The first question with which we are concerned is therefore that of the late and difficult start of waterside unionism. This requires explanation, because nowadays it is a platitude that waterside labour is in an extremely strong bargaining position. Dock strikes, like railway strikes, can cause massive financial loss or disruption to a large sector of the economy – especially in areas dependent on overseas trade – by delaying or preventing the transport of goods and raw materials. Dock labour is powerful because its capacity to strike is powerful; and in general waterside unions have a strong tradition of militancy. From Santos to San Francisco, from Sydney to Liverpool, the threat of a dock strike is still taken extremely seriously. Yet in fact – with the exception of certain specialized crafts such as the lightermen – trade union organization on the waterside has generally been slow to develop. In this respect Britain does not differ greatly from most other advanced industrial countries.

The second question concerns the form which waterside organization took, and here British experience is less comparable to that of other countries. The waterside is an industry with fluid frontiers and no very exact shape, since its labour consists of the loading and unloading of cargoes, the transport of goods across water (by lighter or barge), on the quayside (by truck, trolley and other mechanical equipment), and from quay to railways, warehouses and elsewhere (by rail, and at the end of the nineteenth century, horse and cart). It also comprises the maintenance of the permanent dock installations and machines, the complex of 'white collar' and clerical jobs of checking, dispatching and in general disposing the goods, small but key forces for the direction of the flow (pilots, tug-crews, shunters), and a larger force of supervisors, official and unofficial policemen and guards to prevent excessive losses of goods.[1] Hence the waterside has no obvious and pre-destined core for its union, such as the retort-house men in the gasworks, the fitters and turners in old-fashioned engineering works, the hewers in mining or the spinners in cotton. At various times and in various places, almost any group can become the core of a union. In Bristol (which was to become the home base of the modern Transport and General Workers' Union), the quayside men and shiploaders were its heart; in Harwich the railwaymen; in Grimsby the outside general union of the Gas-workers and the seamen (who also started the movement in Glasgow and Liverpool).[2] In yet other ports each section of the work was separately organized on a semi-craft basis. Certain groups, notably the permanent maintenance staffs and machine operators, might be organized by outside craft or non-craft unions such as the Gas-workers, or even – like the Glasgow cranemen – by the Steel Smelters. Every possible pattern of unionism may be found on the waterside: separate and local craft unionism, as among coal-trimmers; compound craft unionism, as among some carters and the seamen; general unionism, as among the members of the various general unions in the ports, and all varieties of local, regional and national industrial unionism.[3]

205

Similarly, the natural geographical base of union strength on the waterside is the port, or even, within the port, the specialized dock or wharf. A strongly organized port, such as Birkenhead, can exist when unionism elsewhere has virtually collapsed. A strongly organized part of a port, such as the south of Liverpool or London, can exist amid the disorganization of the rest. There is little strategic or tactical reason why waterside trade unionism should not therefore grow up as a mosaic of locally based unions of very different structure, perhaps in loose federation, perhaps not. And indeed this is what looked not unlikely at one time. In 1913, for instance, at least seven organizations monopolized waterside unionism in one or more ports, and a coaster visiting the ports of, say, the East coast of Britain, might encounter a different union pattern in each.*

Yet the basic direction of British waterside unionism was not local or sectional, but from the beginning regional or even national, and its final outcome was the Transport and General Workers' Union of 1922, in effect an industrial union of waterside and road transport workers wrapped up in a general union. It has been suggested that this remarkable achievement was due to the skill and personality of Ernest Bevin, but this is to exaggerate the merits of any individual union leader, even so impressive a figure as his. Trade union leaders, unlike army generals, do not learn their strategy and tactics in staff colleges and practise them on exercises, but exclusively on the job itself and in the course of battle. Bevin's school was the waterside unionism of 1889–1914, and his very consciousness of the need for national union, and of the strategic and tactical implications of this need, reflect the experience and the tendencies of waterside work in this period. What were these tendencies?

---

* Thus at Aberdeen it would deal mainly with the National Union of Dock Labourers, in Dundee with the Scottish Union of Dock Labourers, in the Fife ports and Leith once again with the NUDL, in Blyth with the North of England Teemers and Trimmers, in Newcastle with a variety of unions, in Sunderland with the North East Coast Federated Societies, in the Hartlepools once again mainly with the Teemers, in Middlesbrough with the London Dockers, in Hull with practically all unions in the industry, in Goole only with the NUDL, but in Grimsby with the Gas-workers, and in Boston and ports south with the London Dockers.

II

Technically speaking, docking was still amazingly primitive in 1889. It is of course true that the essential irregularity of the arrivals and departures of ships sets limits even today to the rationalization and mechanization of waterside labour,[4] but in the late 1880s there was, with the exception of quays, cranes, winches and dockside railways, virtually no mechanical equipment at all. The technical revolution which was to mechanize the loading and unloading of grain and coal, and to some extent timber, was not seriously initiated until the late 1890s and early 1900s, and its progress was slow. The best description of work in the London docks in 1908[4a] hardly mentions mechanical equipment except in the Victoria Dock (wheat, frozen meat, coal), and as late as 1914 much coal-heaving in Liverpool was done with hand baskets, while grain-discharging by sacks was far from extinct in Bristol even after the mechanization of World War I.[4b] The specialized jobs were done by specialized men, unspecialized jobs by unspecialized men. Technically the Liverpool docks as described by Sexton in the late 1880s, like the Genoa docks of the same period, were nearer central-African porterage than modern industry.[5] It follows that the habitual picture of an industry composed overwhelmingly of casual and unskilled labourers is highly misleading. On the contrary: the specialized meat or grain-porter, the coal-heaver and salt-porter, the stevedore or lumper who stowed export cargo on board ship, had to have at least the qualities of the iron-puddler – strength and dexterity within a limited range, and very frequently the qualities of the all-round craftsman or supervisory worker – initiative, wide experience, the ability to make a variety of decisions to fit the necessities of loading and unloading the hundred and one non-standardized ships, the ability to supervise men. Even if not very highly skilled by conventional standards – the Board of Trade's Labour correspondent, an engineer, described coal-trimmers as 'unskilled'[6] – their bargaining strength was considerable.

But, like the 'process men' in chemicals, the footplate staff on the railways; like, in fact, the key grades in any modern industry as distinct from craft production, the specialists made up only a percentage, though a sizeable one, of the total.[7] In wholly specialized ports, like the coal-ports of the north-east and South Wales they might form a higher percentage, as again they would in wholly specialized docks, such as the grain wharves at Millwall, the salt-wharves at

Liverpool or the timber-wharves on the East Coast. In the export ports, where stowage aboard ship was of greater importance, they might be more important than in import ones. Yet in general – especially in the three great general ports of London, Liverpool and Hull, and in the great import port of Bristol, the 'process men' were merely the spearhead of a vast army of carriers, pushers, carters, general helpers and whatnot, whose skill and strength needed to be small, whose hiring was genuinely casual, and whose trade union organization was heart-breaking.[8]

The whole of this labour structure was wrapped in the fog of 'casual hiring'. The effects of this were, of course, to widen the gap between the 'strong' and the 'weak' dockers even further. The stevedore or grain porter, even when officially unorganized, was virtually immune from casualism. The number of men out of the milling crowd at the dock gates who were strong, balanced and iron-nerved enough to try running up and down vibrating gang-planks with a hundredweight sack on their shoulders – let alone to succeed – was very small. For practical purposes the specialized man was as irreplaceable as a patternmaker.[9] On the other hand, especially at times of rapid expansion of trade, the chance of an odd day's work would attract to the less specialized docks great numbers of residuals, men unable, for whatever reason, to work at anything else, and willing to try the job for which the minimum of strength, experience and regularity would do.[10] The existence of a considerable reserve army of labour, inefficient though it was, naturally depressed the standards of the remainder, and caused the lower ranges of the profession to become more and more residual. There were, therefore, two – or rather three – problems for the trade union organizer on the docks. The first was the normal problem of the craft union: how to establish and maintain restriction of entry into the trade. The 'skilled' and 'supervisory' dockers had much the same methods of solving it as normal craftsmen.[11] Indeed, as the volume of business expanded steadily without any equivalent mechanization, the men at any established dock would always tend to be a little ahead of the game – by just so much as it took time to train new coal-porters or salt-heavers, and to make reasonable bargains. Where entirely new docks were opened, their position might not be so easy, though with a little drive and organization it could soon be stabilized. One fancies that the shock of the 1889 movement provided just the stimulus for such extra effort, for in the coal-ports of the north and South Wales, and a good many

208

other places, organizations of 'craft' dockers established themselves very rapidly and secured all the advantages of restriction, recognition and closed shop which they were never afterwards to lose.[12]

But the problem of the unskilled could not be solved by old-fashioned restrictionism. In theory it might have been, for there were enough economists to point out the staggering inefficiency of the casual labour system, and every serious measure of decasualization involved a relative or absolute decrease in the competing labour force. After all, had it not been demonstrated that the 1912 labour force on the Liverpool docks was almost twice as large as that which could have dealt with the peak demand under conditions of optimum efficiency in hiring?[13] But though some trade union leaders might have appreciated the advantages of decasualization from a bargaining point of view, the men opposed it. It was one thing to stop new men entering the trade; quite another to throw Bill and Jack (and perhaps oneself) out on the streets. It was one thing to secure more or less regular work, because one was quicker and stronger, or because one had bribed the foreman, or knew his mother in some Waterford townland; quite another to condemn Bill and Jack (or quite possibly oneself) to become a permanent 'B preference', doomed to less regular work and less money. The poorer and more casual the docker, the more he would cling to the rough justice of casualism, even if it was only the justice of the lottery, in which anyone could draw the lucky number. Whatever the economist or the organizer said, therefore, self-preservation drove the unskilled docker to a policy of solidarity; of the 'fair' spreading of what work was available. In London, where decasualization was imposed by the employers as a business measure, the preference system was in force. In Liverpool, where the Union was strong, it could not be introduced; and even then, the rank and file struck against the new scheme, and the arrangement which gave the Union a virtual control over the entire labour force of the port, had to be forced on the Birkenhead men by means of blacklegs.[14]

Of course, restrictionism could operate in the long run. As the volume of port business grew, even a labour force stabilized at some 29,000, instead of some 16,000 or 20,000 could begin to use its scarcity value in bargaining – and in due course this has vastly increased the strength of dockers' or longshoremen's organizations in Britain and abroad. In the short run, however, dock unionism was forced to evolve novel tactics of combined bargaining and 'industrial' unionism. From 1910, when we first find the Bristol dockers deliberately recruiting 'strategically vital' groups of port workers,[15] and the National Transport Workers' Federation was founded, the problems of industrial unionism were constantly discussed in the industry; and not merely, as in some other places, by the intellectuals. But this raised the third problem of the dockyard organizer: how to prevent the 'strong' sections from forming their own quasi-crafts unions, leaving the 'weak' to the mercies of the market; or, failing this, how to ensure the most effective co-ordination between the various types of union. The danger of separate unionism was a real one. The port in which all important sections of waterside labour were in a single union was rare. Bristol was perhaps the major example. In London, for instance, stevedores, lightermen, cranemen and coal-porters had their own societies, while the specialized porters on the south side joined in a local federation of independent trade union locals (some in, some not in docking) called the Labour Protection League. The Dockers' Union was left with a mixed lot of specialized men and ordinary quaysiders.

Fortunately there were several reasons which prevented the two levels from drawing too far apart, as seemed likely at one time. In the first place, to the outside world they were all alike 'labourers'. Indeed, to some extent their technical position was the same: that of in theory wholly 'casual' labourers, with no claim to regular employment.[16] Of course, in practice, the 'skilled men' were regular, but, like the wealthy villein in the late middle ages whose servile status binds him to his less fortunate fellows, the comfortable stevedore did not find it easy to get 'accepted' by the outside world. The London union had some trouble with the London Trades Council in 1885 on this account. In the second place, unlike boilermakers or carpenters, skilled dockers did not possess a fairly standard set of qualifications and experiences. Each wharf or dock had its special set of problems and customs, not necessarily duplicated anywhere else, and those who were skilled in them were, as like as not, a purely localized body. Hence they were, in spite of their skill, relatively weak; for in the increasingly integrated structure of the modern great port, the bargaining strength sufficient to terrorize one wharf was not, after all, so very great in the whole of London. Moreover – and this is no doubt the most important factor – hardly had the 'craftsmen' established their position than mechanization began to drive them out of it. The grain-chute killed the specialized grain-porter; mechanical coaling weakened the trimmers. The distinction between stevedores and non-stevedores began to disappear in some ports[17] as 'semi-skilled' men came to do the job. The short-term result of this might well be to make the craft-union close its ranks, and draw the demarcation line between it and the rest of the workers more closely; and this seems indeed to have happened. Or else new 'craft' unions might be formed.[18] But in the longer term it would also impress on them the necessity of common action within the industry as a whole. The stevedore's problems could not be effectively tackled without tackling those of the common dockers. Of the numerous 'craft' unions few survived the amalgamations of the early twenties, except the Cardiff Trimmers, and some 'specialist' stevedores. Whether they went into the TGWU, or, like a few, into the NUGMW,[19] they joined the lesser grades. Of course, long before amalgamation was seriously considered, the needs of bargaining had driven the various societies into fairly close federation.

III

From the business point of view the prospect of strong port unions was – in theory – not unacceptable. The industry was badly in need of rationalization. It is hardly too much to say that it was still in the stage of the Stockton-Darlington railway or the turnpike roads: common capital equipment provided for a miscellaneous assortment of private and unstandardized users. (In some cases – notably London before 1908 – not even the basic equipment was centrally planned and administered.) A tangle of small and large users, great dock companies, municipalities (as in Bristol) large shippers and masses of small wharfingers and master stevedores lined the waterside, each with its reservoir of casual labour from which it supplied its violently fluctuating labour demands, each making its own terms on every wharf and every cargo. The small man, the sub-contractor, dominated the entire picture, for even the large units sub-contracted a great deal of the work, and when they did not, the casual system of hiring put foremen into something very like the position of sub-contractors – though their profits might well be made illicitly, by bribery, money-lending and the like.[20] This group, of course, had the strongest vested interest in the continuance of the system. The small wharfinger or master porter was content with a system which provided him with a permanent reserve of labour against sudden fluctuations, thus safeguarding him against the competition of larger users. The Liverpool foremen imported into Manchester refused point-blank to work any but the absolutely casual hiring system which gave them so favoured (and no doubt so profitable) a position.[21]

Against this system several objections could be made on business grounds. The efficiency of the derelict labour it encouraged was appallingly low, and the total labour force far in excess even of peak requirements. Still, these were points which struck outside economists taking a bird's eye view of the whole situation rather than shippers and wharfingers concerned with loading or unloading a series of disconnected cargoes. More troublesome was the utter lack of standardization, which made the negotiation of the price of each cargo somewhat unpredictable. A strong union might well, so the London coal merchants told the Labour Commission, simplify and standardize matters.[22] That is, provided it was 'sensible' and did not attempt to raise labour costs 'unreasonably', for where even large firms paid anything up to two-thirds of their annual expenditure or up to 50 per cent of total trading receipts on labour,[23] the industry was naturally sensitive. On the other hand where there was no unionism the ordinary unspecialized dockers could take the job or leave it, on the terms offered; and in any case the fluidity of labour – someone would always move from wharf to wharf – tended to even out labour conditions somewhat. Thus there is no evidence in Liverpool that they differed substantially in the unorganized north and in the smaller, but unionized south of the port.[24]

On the other hand, short of systematic reorganization, the business of the expanding great ports had become so clotted as to cause all except the sub-contractors really serious losses. Williams – the champion of the Liverpool scheme – gives any number of instances.[25] A boat is partly discharged, but the cargo cannot be shifted rapidly from the quays, where it is dumped; it holds up others, and costs overtime pay to shift. Goods are deliberately left on the quays, ready to catch an early boat, for the sender prefers to pay extra charges rather than to risk the delay of the ponderous warehousing and handling apparatus; meanwhile they too clog the available space. The merchant's man traditionally comes down to the docks in the morning to take delivery of his goods; but he may have to go to three or four places, and by the time he gets to them, the hiring is over, the dockers are engaged or gone and the goods have to wait another day – using up yet more valuable space. Clearly, mechanization and any arrangement which made for more rational and flexible hiring over the whole port would recommend itself to the business community, provided they could get together to look at the matter from a common point of view rather than from the limited angle of the individual firm. The stimulus of a vast trade union upheaval, and the tactful assistance of government officials helped them to do so.

Before 1914 we have, in fact, a few examples of such deliberate rationalization: in the great London Dock Companies (1891–1912), in Liverpool, and in some smaller ports like Goole and Sunderland – though the 1,000–2,000 men involved in the two latter cannot compare in importance with the 4,000–8,000 in London or the 29,000 in Liverpool.[26] The London scheme was only indirectly the result of the upheaval of 1889, though it was adopted on the recommendation of Charles Booth of the social surveys, himself a great shipowner. It was, of course, limited to one large firm and its associates – the London and India Dock Company, and eventually the various companies associated in the 'Joint Committee' – and was far more a straight measure of internal rationalization, virtually unaffected by the complexities of negotiating with a multitude of separate employers and with a strong union. Its result was far more to increase the intensity of work than to decasualize; for while the percentage of work performed by 'permanent' dockers rose from 30 to 38 per cent between 1894–6 and 1902–4,[27] the percentage of piece-work increased at the Victoria and Albert Dock from just under 19 per cent in 1894 to just under 81 per cent in 1904.[28] Moreover the transference of the more fluctuating types of work to sub-contractors made even the existing decasualization more apparent than real. The Liverpool scheme, though more modest from the technical point of view, was far more ambitious, for it covered some 60 firms and a union over the entire port. On the other hand the real concentration of production, and the regularization of waterside labour, had gone somewhat farther on the Mersey than on the Thames. Eleven of the 63 firms employed some 17,000 of the 28,000 workers, chiefly of course large shippers with their regular liners; two great firms alone – White Star and Leyland Dominion – were allocated no less than 7,000 dockers in the actual scheme.[29] By common consent, moreover, the northern liner docks, which used almost 80 per cent of the labour, and the middle docks[30] which catered for the coasting trade, had exceptionally regular demands. Indeed, as in the gas industry, the gradual regularization of demand did more in time to iron out labour fluctuations than the actual schemes for decasualization. It will be evident that conditions for a reorganization were not unfavourable – especially as the port was wildly prosperous. Moreover, under the oligarchy of the big shippers something like the Detroit symbiosis between employers and trade unions might well come into existence. In fact, it did.

IV

But the rise and recognition of trade unions is not such a simple matter. Quite apart from the considerable local variations, it tended – it always tends – to go through a series of 'figures' like an old-fashioned dance or courtship; or, since the military metaphor is apposite, through a series of lunges and ripostes. The history of unionism before 1889 is still very obscure, but the first general movement seems to have occurred in the boom of 1871–3, and left behind, apart from the first London wage settlement within the memory of later unionists, a permanent organization of stevedores. Developments in Liverpool are even less clear, though there seems to have been a strike in 1879 and a wage settlement in 1885.[30a] At all events, the first national movement occurred in 1889–90, and it established strong unions, amounting to virtual closed shops, in several major ports. For some of the specialized and skilled unions and ports this was the end of the bout – on the Tyne, for instance, or to some extent in South London – for they were immediately and permanently recognized. Elsewhere the counter-attack developed, stimulated by the excessive power which vast closed shops were believed to wield; for it is one thing to recognize the 1,000 or 1,500 Cardiff coal trimmers, whose strategic importance was as great as their share of the total cost of coal production and export was small,[31] and quite another to recognize a wholly unionized port.[32] Sometimes the counter-attack was unco-ordinated, a leading firm or group of firms deciding to make a stand, and the rest awaiting developments. This was the pattern among London coal-merchants, seed-crushers, and for that matter, gas-workers.[33] Sometimes it was a planned and co-ordinated counter-attack along the whole front, led by the newly-founded Shipping Federation, as in Cardiff (1891) and Hull (1893).[34] Sometimes it was halfway between the two. As a result of this counter-offensive serious trade unionism was wiped out, except among 'strong' bargainers like the specialized skills, stevedores, watermen, etc.; in certain specialized ports, notably the coal-exporting ones; and in certain relatively favourable areas like Birkenhead and Bristol. In the former, trade unions had always held on – even the relics of a union of the 1840s survived into the twentieth century – and the special problems of export loading, as well as the absence of concentration among employers, and the isolation from Liverpool, assisted the union.* In the latter port, the union may have been helped by the fact that the city itself was not merely in control of the harbour installations, but was itself a large employer of dock labour, especially in the grain trade; and hence subject to some political pressure.

Comparatively little changed between the collapse after 1889 and the expansion of 1910–14, which once again covered virtually every port. The strong ports registered a few modest advances, the weak ones – the majority – none at all, though probably the case of Liverpool, whose wage-rates remained unchanged from 1885 to 1915, was exceptional. In 1910–14 the pattern of 1889 repeated itself, but under conditions more favourable to the unions. Quite apart from the political and administrative changes of the intervening period, no break in the prosperity of the ports came to encourage employers to cut costs. Moreover, the organizations which now expanded beyond even their former peaks were not raw fighters, but experienced veterans of more than twenty years' campaigning. The expansion was no longer the barely co-ordinated series of independent revolts – on Clyde, Mersey, and Thames – but contained within the loose, but not wholly ineffective framework of a *National Transport Workers' Federation*, set up in 1910.[35] Strategy and tactics were more highly developed than in 1889, for leaders like Mann and Tillett had thought a great deal about them, and the experiences of continental and American revolutionary syndicalists were available and, what is more, discussed by the cadre of militant leaders. As a result no national counter-attack developed, and the most serious of the local counter-attacks, that on the Thames, was only partly successful.

The difference between Thames and Mersey is especially instructive. In both, the upheaval began in much the same way; in Liverpool, indeed, it was far more spontaneous than in London, where the official union stood behind it, though the revolutionary leadership of Tom Mann gave it cohesion. In both, the masters settled, as they had

* On differences between Liverpool and Birkenhead labour conditions – especially the absence of distinction between shipmen and quaymen – see *Shaw Enquiry*, p. 142 (344).

so often done in 1889 and were doing all over the country, because they were caught unawares and frankly lost their nerve.[35a] Yet while in London they soon regretted their concession and counter-attacked, in Liverpool the strike merely strengthened the collaboration of the two parties. Perhaps, all considerations of business differences apart, the existence of the new Port of London Authority, under the uncompromising leadership of Lord Devonport, explains this divergence. Certainly there is no doubt of the deliberation with which London employers, under their commander-in-chief, set out to provoke the union into a second strike, the ruthlessness with which they pressed home their superior strength in a show-down, and the equal ruthlessness with which they set out, after their victory, to reduce the London dockers to a state of disorganized casualism. The Joint Committee's scheme for decasualizing its labour was deliberately jettisoned, the old 'Permanent' and 'A' Preference lists were scrapped, and the blacklegs of the 1912 strike were given preference over all others.[36] The bitterness generated by this strike has not wholly disappeared. Even today (1964) men will refuse to work with the sons of 1912 blacklegs. Yet in spite of the catastrophic decline in the unions' membership, London did not revert to disorganization; and the union was now so strong that even the temporary relapse of one region or another no longer interrupted the general rise. With the First World War, of course, the hope of destroying dockers' unionism vanished for good.

The Mersey strike, on the other hand, led directly to full recognition. A joint committee of owners and men was set up, and the Dock Scheme evolved. The effects of this were immediately seen. When the hard-pressed Londoners appealed for a national sympathy strike in 1912, Liverpool, careful to do nothing that could disturb its now privileged position, refused to come out (though Bristol, the old centre of industrial unionism, did). The Liverpool unions remained on the extreme right wing of the movement, for they had by now established a virtual strangehold on the hiring in their port, and – for practical purposes – their sectional battle was won.[37]

V

Yet this intensification of regional differences – the Scottish dockers even broke away from Liverpool and formed their own union – was only temporary. The general trend was in the opposite direction. The

216

initial impetus towards national union or federation was – on the men's side – almost wholly strategic. Faced by especially concentrated enemies, including the powerful, and nationally organized, Shipping Federation, it was desirable to co-ordinate the various union forces; though in the years of relative union inactivity between 1892 and 1910 the whole issue was somewhat academic. Moreover, the bulk of the transport workers were unstably organized, and unrecognized, and the weaker their unions, the greater their desire to widen the scope of organization. When the London dockers and the seamen failed, in the mid-nineties, they attempted to strengthen themselves by forming a vast international Transport Workers' Federation which should meet the national union of the employers by a yet vaster concentration of workers' forces; a plan which was not very successful.[38] Nor is it surprising that the initiative for the Transport Workers' Federation of 1911 should have come from the struggling London union. But in a period of militancy and general expansion even established unions – while reserving their special rights – could see advantages in a wider link-up. The waterside industry was constantly haunted by the spectre of the blackleg – the unskilled farm labourer flooding the docks, the spare seaman or docker from the pool of casual labour which existed elsewhere, transported by the masters to a striking port to replace the striking unionist. Nobody was really immune. In a real showdown, it was clear that the masters could normally win, provided the fight went to a finish; and even the sheltered 'craft' unions were therefore keen – at a time when major demands impended – to avoid the isolated battle which meant certain defeat. In addition to this, the great wave of radicalism among the rank and file tended to swamp local vested interests, and poohpooh the argument that a local arrangement with employers was the ideal at which the union should aim. Moreover, all the ports were linked by the seamen, whose organization was necessarily national, and whose agitations started off the movements both in 1889 and 1911.[39] Agitations leaped from port to port, as they did not easily spread along land routes. Within a few months of the outbreak in 1889 the Clyde-Liverpool union had established itself from Limerick to the Fife ports.[40] However great the local differences, however self-contained the local bargaining, however irrelevant the demands of, say, Tyne dockers were to those in Plymouth or Sligo, they were easily linked into a general movement. In 1889 they had in fact formed two broad movements – one based on the Thames in the

H   217

south and east, the other based on the Clyde and Mersey, and also covering the rest of Scotland and the Irish Sea.[41] The expansion of 1911 linked these into one, though rather loosely.

On the other hand, a genuinely national union could not come about until the actual demands of the dockers were themselves capable of being reduced to a common denominator. But this was exceptionally difficult, except in the vague sense that all dockers at a given time were likely to feel the need of a wage-rise, and the more precise factor that the movements of the shipping industry produced a certain amount of inter-port standardization, and incidentally made temporary alliances with the seamen not only possible but highly desirable. Thus the 1889 outbreak was not merely British: there had also been dockers' strikes in Hamburg (1888), Bremerhaven (1888), Rotterdam (1889) and doubtless elsewhere. On the other hand there was no generally acceptable standard demand like the Eight-Hour Day which could bind the ports together. In view of the casualism of the work and the wide variations of wage-rates (see Appendix II), even the demand for a minimum wage was not easily standardized.

However, the co-ordination between employers, to which Bevin drew attention at the Shaw Enquiry, already suggested the need for national co-ordination among the men. The ship-owners, the most monolithic in attack as well as in retreat, decided on national wage standardization after the 1911 strikes (which brought the recognition of the seamen's union and its rapid conversion into a virtual company union); 1913 already brought a national seamen's wage-rise, 1917 actual national wage standardization.[42] How far the movement would have advanced on the docks without the war, we can only guess. At all events the war speeded it up, because the rises in the cost of living – and the post-war threat of renewed unemployment – forced dockers everywhere to consider much the same problems at the same time, and the radicalization of the labour movement unified them. Once again the London union took the initiative in a national movement for a minimum daily wage of 16 shillings and a national system of decasualization (which was not achieved, for in 1939 three-quarters of the dockers were still casual). The Shaw Enquiry of 1920 which investigated the claim, is remarkable for two reasons. It formed the basis of a national agreement for the entire industry; and the success of the campaign, ably led by Ernest Bevin, convinced the separate unions of the value of national negotiation. A national union would henceforth rest on firmer foundations than mere class solidarity or the intermittent demands of great strike battles. The Transport and General Workers' Union was formed shortly after.

What light does this survey of waterside unionism before the Transport and General Workers' Union throw on our initial questions? It suggests that they must be answered in terms of the logic of the dockers' position, but also of the historical changes which altered the setting of the waterside collective bargain.

The waterside organized relatively late for three reasons. First – though this was probably of no great moment in the main British ports – because ancient ports may have developed traditional guild-like or corporative forms of entrepreneurial and labour organization which, even in decay, may stand in the way of trade unionism, while rarely capable of being adapted to the functions of trade unionism.[43] Second, because of the nature of the labour force from which most dockers were recruited and the high proportion of the unskilled and organizationally weak on its margins. But third, and chiefly, because the potential strength of the waterside was simply not mobilizable in the conditions and under the assumptions of the mid-nineteenth century.

Craft unionism was applicable only to limited sections of the industry, and these – unlike the hewers in coal or (in Britain) the spinners in cotton – did not automatically affect the rest, let alone carry them along. The employers required far more proof of the capacity for permanent organization of what they and most others regarded as a heterogeneous force of unskilled hands than they would have done with, say, shipwrights or boilermakers. Hence the characteristic waterside history of a series of gigantic battles before the granting of recognition. At the same time the employers had to achieve a degree of concentration which allowed them to see the problem as one of the industry as a whole, and not merely as one of individual entrepreneurs or sections within it; or else sections of large employers, with wider views, had to be effectively counterposed to the multiplicity of small ones with a narrower outlook. On the waterside this impetus probably came from the ship-owners rather than the dockside entrepreneurs, for reasons which belong to the economic history of British shipping. However, while big shippers such as Holts in Liverpool might be keenly aware of the inconvenience of dockside anarchy, which a regularization of industrial relations might mitigate, the hostility of shippers to seamen's organization, which was closely tied to waterside

219

organization, made them initially into a powerful anti-union force, and thus postponed union recognition in the ports.[44]

Lastly, a new economic perspective of government was probably required to smooth the path of recognition. It was the consciousness of the possible dangers to the entire economy of any major strikes, and especially of major disruptions of transport, or of the political risks of immense labour conflicts, which brought about that increasing tendency of government to mediate in labour disputes and eventually to regulate industrial relations, and which first emerges with Rosebery's intervention in the coal war of 1893.

Before the Great Depression of 1873–96 this triple reorientation of labour, employers and government was hardly to be expected. But the Depression produced the feeling that the British economy as a whole was for the first time vulnerable, because 'our position as the chief manufacturing nation of the world is not so undisputed as formerly'.[45] Before this period even middle-class apologists, anxious to discover reasons against strikes, could hardly claim more than that at some unspecified but remote date in the future the economy might be damaged by them.* From 1889 on, however, the argument that such disputes are 'prejudicial . . . to the producing power of the country'[46] is increasingly heard. And so – perhaps due to the experience of large strikes of this sort – are statements about the disruptive force of national transport strikes.[47]

The period of the Great Depression also created that sense of industrial concentration which helped to teach labour that the 'industry' rather than the 'master', singly or in small or local groups was the force which confronted it in industrial warfare; and it was this feeling that capital was extending outside the narrow boundaries of firm and trade which was the chief argument, on the labour side, for such new tactics as those of industrial unionism.§ That concentration

* Leone Levi, *Work and Pay* (London 1877), p. 94: 'I have, indeed, proved in my previous lecture that up to 1873 at least the trade and industry of England had not suffered from the many disturbances which have taken place, – at least not to any material extent – , and that foreign competitition had not till then gained upon British industry. But what has not yet been may still be. The danger remains, though it may not be imminent.' Even L. L. Price, *Industrial Peace* (London 1887), who specifically analyses strikes in terms of warfare, entirely fails to consider among their possible damage that to the economy.

§ T. Mann, *The Industrial Syndicalist* I, 1910. It is highly significant that Ernest Bevin in the *Shaw Enquiry*, p. 21 (223), argues in favour of a single national claim because 'living conditions have become so standardized *by the operation of the great monopolies and trusts* and the distribution of food'. [My italics. E.J.H.]

proceeded much more slowly and indirectly in Britain than in Germany or the U.S.A. is much less important than that, so far as labour could see, it was proceeding much more obviously than before. What is more, the most patent concentrations were those in which employers united to defeat labour, such as the Shipping Federation and the Engineering Employers' Federation of the 1890s. The process, both in industrial relations and politics, was what the nuclear strategists call 'escalation': each blow by one side produced a greater concentration of forces by the other. The 1890s are already the age of the great, *nation-wide* labour disputes such as the port lock-outs (in which a national employers' body deliberately chose key spots for strategic battle), the coal dispute over the entire federated area in 1893, the national engineering lock-out.

Lastly, the period of the Great Depression produced a national and international socialist movement, which inevitably provided many of the most intelligent and dynamic leaders of the new unions. While in fact this movement (except perhaps for groups on its anarchist wing) was not particularly interested in the strategy and tactics of trade union operations as such, which it regarded as a necessary but subordinate aspect of the general movement, it did provide a systematic body of strategic and tactical thinking about labour movements, such as leaders of workers who would not, or could no longer, use the traditionally evolved tactics of older unionism, were badly in need of. Ben Tillett, deriving his first strategic ideas from an East End lecture on Napoleon by a subsequent archbishop of Canterbury, and later, Arthur Horner, reading Clausewitz in jail, reflect this urgent need of trade union leaders for a *theory* of industrial warfare. Socialism, in fact, gave them such a theory, and this is why both bodies of new union leaders and of new thought about union organization and policy, grew out of it or attached themselves readily to it.

This triple reorientation also explains the tendency of the waterside to develop all-embracing industrial and general, but above all *national* unions, in spite of a built-in tendency to local and sectional self-sufficiency. On the employers' side it was almost certainly the Shipping Federation which imposed a national perspective – if only in the fight against nationally organized blacklegging – on unions which otherwise might not have had one. On the labour side, it was almost certainly the socialist leadership of the London dockers, the most dynamic waterside body, and the one which eventually became the nucleus of the Transport and General Workers' Union – which from the first broke through the local sectional, or in the case of the 'Irish' Liverpool union, the national limits of organization. Had permanent dockers' unions been able to emerge twenty years earlier, they would almost certainly have done so as a collection, perhaps eventually a loose federation, of independent ports and maritime zones. But they emerged in the age of socialist revival, and it is characteristic that within a few years of their birth the British unions (on the London left-wingers' initiative) formed an International Federation of Ship, Dock and River Workers in order to unionize actively not only all British, but all foreign ports: a characteristically socialist enterprise.* On the government side, it was clearly the growing consciousness of 'the docks problem' as a national social problem – one of the many for which government now found itself accepting some sort of responsibility – which set the stage for national solutions. It was, as Beveridge pointed out, the 'leading instance' of casual employment, and casual employment was one of the main components of the unemployment problem, which in turn was the chief reason why government, from the 1880s, found itself obliged to undertake the systematic welfare legislation which eventually led to modern social security.

That national union should emerge in the form of a general rather than an industrial body was clearly not inevitable, though, given the structure of British trade unionism and the fluid boundaries of the industry, it was rather likely. In fact, waterside unionism became industrial, though tied to a general body. Only, we must beware of confusing the 'industry' as it actually operated in terms of labour relations with the ideal industries constructed by the strategists of labour and government or the economists. They thought in terms of 'transport', or at least water transport. Life operated in terms of 'ports'. Sea and land transport met at the port, but the bulk of their problems in labour relations lay for the most part elsewhere, and their conditions of functioning were different. This is why such obvious strategic alliances as those between dockers and seamen never lasted long, and the occasional dreams of national or even international transport solidarity were never of more than momentary importance. It is true that the waterside has a closer and more permanent connection with road transport than with either railways or seamen. For historic reasons the British union has grown up as a joint

* Not only the seamen, but also – more significantly – the Liverpool union joined under London's lead.

organization of these two connected groups, plus a miscellaneous collection of others, though it might possibly not have done so. The point is that, to this day, a dock strike is essentially based on the disruptive power of the men on the quayside and those operating between quay and ship or between ship and ship, and not of those who come in and go out through the dock gates.

Appendix I

Types of waterside labour in some ports:

I. HULL 1897

Labourers and others directly employed by shipowners	6,000
Merchants' grain porters	500
Deal carriers	600
Coal heavers and tippers	600
Lightermen, etc.	900
Lumpers (contractors' men)	1,500
Promenade workers, fruit porters, etc.	500

Source: *The position of the dockers and sailors in 1897 and the International Federation of Ship, Dock and River Workers*, by Tom Mann (Clarion 1897), p. 11.

II. SOUTHAMPTON 1890

Corn porters, coal porters, stevedoring, general cargo and ship discharging.

Source: *Dock, Wharf, Riverside and General Labourers' Union, Annual Report 1890*, 92.

III. BRISTOL 1890

Fruit merchants' labour	Cotton and linseed importing
General goods	Grain porters
Deal porters	Lightermen
Stevedoring	

Source: loc. cit., pp. 44 ff.

IV. GLASGOW 1919

General cargo men	7,000
Grain weighers	120
Timber men	300
Coal men	300
Ore men	350

Wharfinger staff	400
Employees of Clyde Trust	1,400

Source: *Shaw Enquiry*, Appendix 77.

V. LIVERPOOL 1919

Shipmen (including winchmen, holders)	9,200
Porters (including cranemen, checkers, counters-off, weight-takers, coopers, etc.)	13,800
Coalmen	2,000
Bargemen	2,000
Tugmen	600
Watchmen	?
Shore gang men	?

Source: loc. cit., Appendix 52.

VI. SWANSEA 1919

Swansea Harbour Trust:

Labourers (casual)	1,000
Cranemen (casual)	51
Tallymen (casual and permanent)	64
Foremen (permanent)	10
Weighers (permanent)	15
Number takers (permanent)	11
Dock gate men (permanent)	61
Tug and ferry boat (permanent)	16
Dredger crews (permanent)	37
Hydraulic and power houses (permanent)	30
Watchmen (permanent)	7
Clerical (permanent)	68
Other (excluding locomotive department)	25

5 other main employers:

Casual men	345
Permanent men	22

Source: loc. cit., Appendix 98, 101.

VII. ARDROSSAN 1919

Labourers (casual)	80
Coal trimmers (casual)	32
Crane and hoist (permanent)	36
Shippers (permanent)	4
Capstanmen (permanent)	4
Roperunners (permanent)	11

Enginemen (permanent)	4
Firemen (permanent)	4
Electricians (permanent)	2

Source: loc. cit., Appendix 117.

VIII. LONDON 1908

(Corn and timber (Surrey Commercial)	about 10 per cent
Grain discharging (Millwall)	4 per cent
Skilled stevedoring	12 per cent
Others (London & India Docks Co.	20 per cent
Shipowners	13 per cent
Wharves	41 per cent
including some specialised labour, e.g., non-union stevedores in Victoria and Albert docks)	74 per cent

Source: *Charity Organization Society Report on Unskilled Labour*, June 1908, pp. 28–30.

Appendix II
Daily wages in British ports, 1914

Source: *Shaw Enquiry*, Appendix 130. These figures come from the employers' side. They are given in order of ports round the coast from London.

London	from 5s. 3d. to 7s. 6d.
Southampton	5s. 5d.
Plymouth	7s. or 4s. 10d.
Bristol	7s.
Avonmouth	5s. 6½d.
Gloucester	7s.
Cardiff	5s. 6d. or 6s. 6d.
Swansea	7s.
Port Talbot	8s.
Liverpool	4s. 6d. and 5s.
Manchester	5s.
Garston	4s.
Preston	4s. 9d.
Barrow in Furness	5s. 7½d.
Glasgow	5s. or 6s. 8d.
Ardrossan	6s. 4d.
Greenock	6s. 8d.
Aberdeen	5s. 10d.

Dundee	6s. 3d.
Grangemouth	6s. 8d.
Leith	5s. 10d.
Tyne (railway)	5s. 1½d.
W. Hartlepool	7s. 11d.
Middlesbrough	5s. and 8s.
Hull	5s. 7½d.
Goole	6s 6d.

NOTES

1 For a useful classification, C. Gillès de Pélichy, *Le Régime du Travail dans les principaux Ports de la Mer de l'Europe* (Louvain-Bruxelles-Paris 1899).

2 National Transport Workers' Federation: *Map of unions in British ports*, 1913 (?) (LSE Coll. EB cv 18) gives an excellent survey of this variety.

3 Information about waterside unions in this period is copious but unsystematic. The printed reports and '*Dockers' Record*' of the London-based Dock, Wharf, Riverside and General Labourers' Union survive, but little unprinted material from before 1914; the Liverpool-based National Union of Dock Labourers has left only scattered traces. After 1910 the National Transport Workers' Federation supplies valuable information. Parliamentary Papers are of great value, notably the *R.C. on Labour*, the *R.C. on the Poor Laws*, the *Report by a Court of Enquiry concerning Transport Workers* (Shaw Enquiry) of 1920 and, to a smaller extent, the *Joint Sel. Ctee. on the Port of London Bill of 1908*. Of the literature on the great disputes, H. Llewellyn Smith and V. Nash, *Story of the Dockers' Strike* (1889), Watney and Little, *Industrial Warfare* (1912) and Lord Askwith, *Industrial Problems and Disputes* (1920) must be supplemented by periodical accounts. The autobiographies of Ben Tillett, Tom Mann, James Sexton, Harry Gosling and J. Havelock Wilson are more useful for atmosphere than for fact; of the biographies, that of Tom Mann (by Dona Torr, cf., also Tom Mann and His Times 1890–2, *Our History*, pp. 26–7, 1962, C. P. Historians' Group) contains little new. *Ernest Bevin* (by Alan Bullock), says relatively little about the earlier period. There is an ample and excellent literature on the economic and social conditions of the docks, and especially on casualism, which is indispensable to the serious student.

4 H. Jerome, *Mechanization in American Industry* (National Bureau of Economic Research 1934).

4a The valuable paper put in by Ben Tillett to the *Joint Select Ctee. on the Port of London Bill* (*Parl. P.* X, 1908, pp. 677–82 (705–10)).

4b *Court of Enquiry concerning Transport Workers' Wages and Conditions of Employment of Dock Labour* (*Parl. P.* XXIV, 1920) henceforth quoted as *Shaw Enquiry*, pp. 136 (338), 153 (355), 212 (414).

5 *The Life of Sir James Sexton, Agitator, by Himself* (London 1936), pp. 109–13. Cf., for comparison, G. Perillo, Socialismo e classe operaia nel Genovesato dallo sciopero del 1900 alla scissione sindacalista I (*Il Movimento Operaio e Socialista in Liguria*, VI, 4, 1960, p. 109).

6 *Report on Strikes*, 1889, Table II (c 6176).

7 In London three organizations of specialized men – Stevedores, Watermen and Labour Protection League – averaged between 6,000–8,000 members in the years between the union expansions. Some 45,000 dockside men may actually have come out in the big 1912 strike (Watney and Little, *Industrial Warfare*, pp. 90–1). See also Appendix I.

8 H. Llewellyn Smith and V. Nash, *The Story of the Dockers' Strike* (London 1889) is the best introduction to London; Sexton, op. cit., to Liverpool docking in the early days. *R.C. on Labour* (Group B) is a mine of information on most aspects of it. Cf., E. Rathbone, *Report on . . . dock labour in Liverpool* (Liverpool Economic and Statistical Soc. Transactions, 1904).

9 W. H. Beveridge, *Unemployment* (1930 edn), p. 83.

10 Booth, *Life and Labour* III, p. 88, discusses 'residual employment'; on this at the Manchester docks, T. Fox in *R.C. on the Poor Laws*, Q. 83,945.

11 For restrictionism see evidence of H. Gosling (lighterman) to *Joint Ctee on Port of London Bill* 1903 (*Parl. P.* VIII 1903, pp. 250–1) and of Amal. Stevedores Labour Protection League to *Joint Ctee on Port of London Bill* 1908 (*Parl P.* X, 1908), Q. 9,426. London stevedores charged £2 entry fines, the Labour Protection League £1, except for sons of members.

12 The closed shop on the Tyne seems to have come in 1889 (*Jubilee History of National Union of General and Municipal Workers*, 1929, p. 13). In 1910–11 conciliation agreements – a fair index of recognition – covered trimmers in the north-east, Cardiff and Newport, and dockers in Greenock and Bristol. *TUC Report* 1911, pp. 106 ff.).

13 R. Williams, *The Liverpool Docks Problem* (Liverpool Econ. and Stat. Soc. 1912), p. 15.

14 J. Maluègue, *Le Travail Casuel dans les Ports Anglais* (Paris 1913), pp. 297–8.

15 *Dockers Record*, March 1911, p. 2.

16 Bristol employed only about 100 men regularly as maintenance workers. The rest were all technically casual. (*R.C. on Poor Laws* XVI, p. 85.) Cf., *Parl. P.* X, 1908, Q. 9,401 for London stevedores: 'we are all casuals'.

17 *National Transport Workers' Federation*: Map of unions in British ports. 1913? (LSE Coll. EB cv 18), p. 3.

18 E.g., cranemen or such bodies as the Amalgamated Protective Union of Engine Drivers, Crane Drivers, Hydraulic and Boiler Attendants—a small London society. Sometimes these men went into outside unions, e.g., in Liverpool into the Gas-workers, or in Swansea into the NALU.

19 The waterside and quay sections of the National Amalgamated Union of Labour and the Tyne Watermen went into the NUGMW.

20 Sexton's evidence to the *R.C. on the Poor Laws* (Q. 84,243) on 'gombeen men' at the Liverpool docks. Cf., also Beveridge, op. cit. (1909 edn), 264 n.

21 Report by Squire and Maitland, *R.C. on Poor Laws* XVI, p. 84.

22 *R.C. on Labour* (Group C), Q. 27,741, 27,772–5.

23 *Relation of Wages to Cost of Production in Certain Industries* (C. 6,535 of 1891), pp. 172 ff.

24 Maluègue, op. cit., p. 48. But extra payments and overtime differed.

25 R. Williams, op. cit., pp. 21–3.

26 On London, Poor Law Commission, Beveridge and the *Labour Gazette*. On Liverpool, R. Williams, *One Year's Working of the Liverpool Dock Scheme* (Liverpool 1914). The T & GWU have also kept some of their contemporary Liverpool agreements (T & GWU Research Dept).

27 Beveridge, op. cit. (1930 edn), p. 90. The combined percentage of Permanent and 'A' Preference men rose from 63 per cent in 1894–6 to 78·5 per cent in 1902–4.

28 Charity Organization Society: *Report on Unskilled Labour* (London 1908), p. 121. Other docks were already largely on piece-work.

29 *T & GWU files*. The other big firms were W. Berrie, Pacific Steam Navigation, Lamport & Holt, Ellerman, Cunard, Alfred Holt, Mannion, T. & J. Harrison, Elder Dempster.

30 Clarence and Princes docks.

30a Bevin's survey in *Shaw Enquiry*, pp. 5 (207) ff.; evidence of M. Reid on 1879 strike, ibid, p. 133 (335).

31 S. and B. Webb, *Industrial Democracy* (1902 edn), pp. 478–9, for some other examples.

32 Such as Cardiff in 1890, with its 16 branches of Dockers and National Amalgamated Labourers' Union waterside men, two of riggers and boatmen, the trimmers, and a closed shop of seamen. (*Cardiff Trades Council*, Report, 1890).

33 *R.C. on Labour*, Group C: evidence of T. Gardner, G. Adams (Q. 31,626–61).

34 Cf., the documents of the Shipping Federation in *R.C. on Labour*, Group B (*Parl. P.* XXXV of 1892, Appendices;) also Clem Edwards on The Hull Lock-out in *Econ. Journ.* 1893, and in general J. Saville, 'Trade unions and Free Labour', in A. Briggs and J. Saville (eds) *Essays in Labour History* (London 1960).

35 For a discussion of it, see G. D. H. Cole, *The World of Labour*, G. D. H. Cole and W. Mellor, *The Greater Unionism* (both 1913).

35a Watney and Little, *Industrial Warfare* (London 1912), pp. 80–5. The atmosphere is vividly sketched in George Dangerfield's *Strange Death of Liberal England*.

36 Maluègue, op. cit., pp. 286–7, quoting H. Orbell of the union.

37 For their opposition to amalgamation with other unions, until assured of safeguards, see the report of the Special Conference on Amalgamation, called by the N. Transport Workers' Fed. and the General Labourers' National Council, 1914 (LSE Coll. EB civ. ii), p. 24.

38 Tom Mann, *Memoirs* (1923), pp. 135 ff.; Tom Mann, *The position of the dockers and sailors in 1897* (Clarion 1897); for international repercussions, C. Gillés de Pélichy, *Le Régime du Travail dans les principaux Ports de la Mer de l'Europe* (Louvain-Bruxelles-Paris 1899).

39 Board of Trade, Labour Dept.: *Report on Strikes in 1889*, pp. 4–5 (C 6,176).

40 National Union of Dock Labourers, *Annual Report* 1890–1; also Sexton, op. cit.

41 The London union after 1889 covered all the South coast, all the East coast up to the Humber, with colonies in Middlesbrough and Dundee, and shared South Wales with a regional union, the National Amalgamated Labourers' Union. The Liverpool union covered the rest of the British isles. The two were divided by Wales (unorganized) and the north-east coast, where, with other

local and craft bodies, the regional National Amalgamated Union of Labour held the ground. Local bodies of special workers also existed. The flux of movement between then and 1911 somewhat complicated the picture.

42 B. Moggridge, 'Militancy and inter-union rivalries in British shipping 1911–29' (*Int. Rev. of Social History* 6, 1961, 375–412).

43 Walter M. Stern, *The Porters of London* (London 1960) for such early organizations; but H. Llewellyn Smith, 'Chapters in the History of London Waterside Labour' (*Econ. Journal* II, p. 605) already pointed out that the inrush of men from other trades had swamped the old organizations on the north bank of the Thames – the most important section of the port. For accounts of such old organizations, see L. B. C. Gillès de Pélichy, *L'organization du travail dans les ports flamands* (Louvain-Bruxelles-Paris 1899).

44 Cf., L. H. Powell, *History of the Shipping Federation* (London 1950) and J. Saville, 'Trade Unions and Free Labour', in A. Briggs and J. Saville (eds) *Essays in Labour History* (London 1960).

45 *Reports of the R.C. on the Depression of Trade and Industry*, 1887, p. 55 c. 4893).

46 Preamble to a conciliation bill of 1890, quoted in E. H. Phelps Brown, *The Growth of British Industrial Relations* (London 1959), p. 188. For a more familiar and extreme formulation thirty years later, Lord Askwith, *Industrial Problems and Disputes* (London 1920), p. 67: 'If such a fight occurred . . . it would ruin the chances of production on which the future depends.'

47 J. Shield Nicholson, *Strikes and Social Problems* (London 1896), p. 135.

12

Hyndman and the SDF

THE SOCIAL DEMOCRATIC FEDERATION has long been the prob-
lem-child of labour historians, especially Marxist ones or those
anxious to 'place' it rather than merely to chronicle its erratic
development. It cannot simply be approved. It cannot be simply
condemned. It certainly cannot be dismissed. The least subtle student
of its affairs is forced into unaccustomed complexities, contradictions
and nuances. What precisely is its contribution to the evolution of the
modern British labour movement?

It cannot be dismissed for it was, after all, the first modern socialist
organization of national importance in Britain; a pioneering achievement not diminished by Dr Tsuzuki's demonstration* that its Marxism
was shaky and slow to develop, nor by the claims to priority of forgotten local men and groups. For the point about the SDF is not only
that it was first in the field, but that it *lasted*. Through splits, crises,
wild fluctuations of membership and activity, there shines the inex-
tinguishable light of continuity, and what is more, of national political
presence. It was the main British representative of Marxism from the
early 1880s until 1920, when it contributed to the infant Communist
Party the largest bloc of its original members and leaders. Marx dis-
liked it; Engels opposed it; William Morris left it, together with most
of its brilliant members. It survived. The dissidents who broke away
from time to time disappeared in a few years, like the Socialist League
of the 1880s, remained wholly unimportant conventicles like the
SPGB (1906) or became at best bodies of regional influence like the
Socialist Labour Party on Clydeside (1903). Even its founder and
paternalist chief, H. M. Hyndman, was jettisoned when he attempted
to impose his imperialism on it during the First World War. (The

* Chushichi Tsuzuki, *H. M. Hyndman and British Socialism* (Oxford 1961).

Hyndmanites, a body of no further importance, withered away until finally ending the formal history of the SDF in the first months of World War II.)

Time and again former dissidents returned to it, like Aveling or Tom Mann, or rebels against the reformism of other groups joined it or merged with it, for want of any other lasting Marxist organization of national scope. Time and again its sheer staying-power allowed it to recover from the consequences of its gigantic political errors, compounded of a mixture of sectarianism and opportunism. What is more, time and again its rivals of the left faded from sight. It is not a negligible record.

Nor should we overlook its achievements. Though it never elected an MP independently, and was much less successful than the Independent Labour Party in winning local councillors, it established itself as the major socialist organization in several areas, notably in London where the provincial nonconformist tradition of the ILP never made much appeal, while the SDF took over the strong local heritage of secularist radicalism which stretched from Tom Paine via the Owenites to Charles Bradlaugh. (Nowhere is it less true that British socialism is descended from Wesley rather than from Marx). It is no accident that the London Trades Council was a stronghold of the SDF, as later of the Communist Party, until dissolved by official Labour, nor that the first labour majority on a local council (in West Ham, 1898) was a coalition of Radicals, the Irish and the SDF. But its greatest achievement was to provide an introduction to the labour movement and a training-school for a succession of the most gifted working-class militants: for John Burns, Tom Mann and Will Thorne, for George Lansbury and even for Ernest Bevin. Consequently also, in spite of its frequent neglect of trade unionism, its members or those formed in its school were at their most effective as trade union leaders.

Its achievements deserve attention if only because they have so often been overlooked by its critics, who comprise practically the entire body of the modern labour movement, including the Communists, whose official attitude towards their lineal ancestor has in the past been in general determined by the hostility of Marx and Engels and the much-merited criticisms of Lenin. (Only an *a priori* bias against the SDF could explain the attempts made to pretend that the Socialist League of William Morris and his colleagues was anything but an abject and almost immediate failure in politics: wrecked within five years by the very internal bickerings and splits to which the SDF proved so resistant.) But of course the errors and failures of the SDF were so titanic that critics can be pardoned for dwelling on them. It showed a lack of political realism unparalleled by any other contemporary group of socialists, except Sidney and Beatrice Webb between the Boer War and the 1906 Election. In the middle of 1880s it made itself not only ridiculous but unpopular by accepting Tory help for parliamentary candidatures which then gained merely a few dozen votes. It was flatly hostile to the trade unions and, but for the sound instinct of its militants, would have taken no part in the great union revival of 1889. Though it had sense enough to join in forming the Labour Representation Committee, it deliberately left the future Labour Party in 1901 to retire into sectarian isolation. It played no important part in the great swing to the left before World War I, even though this took the ideological form of a return to revolutionary socialism, or even formal Marxism. It was, in fact, as Marx, Engels and Lenin were never tired of repeating, a sect rather than a serious political organization.

Hyndman's Influence

How much of this ingrained sectarianism, which did so much to stultify it, was due to its dictatorial leader H. M. Hyndman, whose biography (as Professor Tsuzuki shows) virtually merged with its history from 1881 to 1914? The question has not been asked by those numerous reviewers of this useful work, who have treated it mainly as an excursion into the history of British eccentricity or into the golden age of Pall Mall Clubs and music-hall. Hyndman is indeed a rewarding subject for the sort of half-admiring and half-ridiculing treatment which nowadays produces West End musicals about the Edwardians or the Twenties, though this is not how Professor Tsuzuki has treated him. There is piquancy in the picture of this gentleman, cricketer and stockbroker leading the toiling masses towards revolution in a top-hat and frock-coat, reinforced by that other stalwart of the SDF, the Countess of Warwick (whose personal relations with H.M. Edward VII were of the closest) in the special train which she ordered to take her home from the Federation conference. Moreover, Hyndman's very marked individual peculiarities and his tendency to regard failures of 'the movement' as a father regards the failure of a disappointing child to pass the General Certificate of Education, make it tempting to write the history of the SDF in terms of his personality, and to ascribe its failures to his own.

To some extent they were. Hyndman's personality made it difficult for him to collaborate except with inferiors. Consequently those SDF leaders who did not drift away, or into opposition, were a loyal rather than a very bright group, though clearly rather more gifted than the equivalent group in the ILP. His tactlessness, lack of hypocrisy, sarcasm and obvious self-satisfaction make his memoirs a pleasure to read, but were a distinct political liability. His highly individual version of theory and uncertain wobbling between utopianism, sectarianism and opportunism in practice, complicated the SDF's relations with the international movement. Professor Tsuzuki, echoing Denis Healey, calls him an 'Anglo-Marxist' (to distinguish his tradition from the 'Russian-Marxist' or 'Marxist-Leninist'). This is nonsense, if only because in Hyndman's day (after 1917 he hardly counted any longer) the only Marxist orthodoxy against which to measure national or other deviations was the German, as represented by, say, Kautsky. But the truth is that Hyndman simply did not represent a clear Marxist trend at all. He was quite an orthodox follower of Marx in economic theory, as he understood it, and he certainly believed in the class struggle, though he had his reservations about historical materialism. At the same time he combined this with a naively utopian idea of revolution, based on French memories, and a consistent strain of jingoist, anti-German – indeed racialist – imperialism, which owed nothing to any British left-wing tradition. (Unlike most other men in the British socialist movement, he originally came from Toryism and not from the Radical Liberal or Chartist atmosphere.) On practical issues he had no consistent policy at all, and hence no consistent theory. Neither he nor anyone else in the SDF – with the exception of the cranky Belfort Bax who wrote pioneer Marxist histories – produced anything much superior to good straightforward propagandist writing. Compared to the contemporary level of theoretical writing in such continental social-democratic parties as the German, Austrian, Russian, Italian and French, the theoretical production of the SDF is wholly negligible. The really interesting and original contributions to Marxist theory in these islands came from men like William Morris and James Connolly.

On the other hand it is surprising how little Hyndman's individual quirks affected the SDF, where they happened to conflict with its fundamental orientation. Thus he succeeded in imposing neither his jingoism, nor his imperialism and anti-semitism on the Federation. On the contrary, when it came to the point, it abandoned him on these issues. This was in part because the SDF was in practice much less centralized, and certainly much less under the control of Hyndman, than he would have wished: its branches were highly autonomous. It was also in part because the Federation, insofar as it was genuinely rooted in the working class, spontaneously adopted the attitudes most familiar to the militant workers, e.g., in trade union matters. It would be too much to explain Hyndman's peculiarities by the peculiarities of the SDF, but not too much to claim that it tolerated them because they either fitted in with its own tradition or (like his jingoism and imperialism) seemed for long to be irrelevant to them.

That tradition was first and foremost a proletarian one, like all the native traditions of the British labour movement in this period. The SDF neither attracted nor held home-grown middle-class intellectuals in any quantity, though as the nearest thing to continental Marxism, it attracted Russian emigré ones like Theodore Rothstein. The junction between the intellectuals and the labour movement was not made until the period of, say, 1910–20, for before then even the Fabians, who did attract them, kept aloof from the labour movement. Hence incidentally the abnormal weakness of British socialist theory, including Marxism, in this, the golden age of international Marxist thinking. The British counterpart of Luxemburg and Hilferding was not a socialist but a liberal, J. A. Hobson.

In the second place this tradition, unlike that which conservatives and reformists equally have tried to foist on to the British people, was not purely empirical and anti-theoretical. Like the traditional Dissenters (but unlike the emotionally soggy Methodists), like the Owenites and Secularists who were their ancestors, the men in the SDF tradition wanted to read, study and discuss, and to work out a general theory of the worker's lot and the world in general by systematic thought. The idea that Marxism was foisted on such men 'from outside' is mistaken: to study and reflect upon a great working-class thinker was as natural to Scots tailors like James Macdonald, or the SDF's atheist Northamptonshire shoemakers, as it had been for their fathers and grandfathers to study and reflect upon Robert Owen, Paine and Spence, and for their great-grandfathers to discuss the Lord's design in the light of Calvin's Institutes. The bent for theory (however crudely and woodenly conceived) was not simply a tribute to the workers' perennial passion for education. It was part of the workers' search for *their* theory, which had led the artisan students of the London Mechanics' Institute to resent the attempt of their Benthamite patrons to concentrate teaching on scientific and technical subjects, to the exclusion of Hodgskin, Owen and Thompson. Class knowledge was power to change the world; and even those who could not get on with Marx's *Capital* (which the SDF, with heroic ambition, tried to get its members to study) were comforted by the knowledge that it was there.

In the third place the tradition was not so much revolutionary as intransigent: militant, firmly based on the class struggle, but quite unable to envisage (as an Irishman like Connolly could) the problems of revolt or the taking of power, for which there was no precedent within living memory in Britain. In one way the reactions of men brought up in this tradition were not sharply distinct from those of old-time Chartists or working-class Radicals, from whom they were indeed descended. Hence it is not surprising that on an issue like the Boer War the SDF's reflex of opposition was far more in line with the ILP's and the Liberal-Radicals' than with the semi-imperialism of the Fabians, or Hyndman's own chauvinist hesitations. In another way they were completely distinct from the Liberal-Radicals. For them, as for so many Chartists, the idea of a middle-class *alliance* was intolererable, however much agreement on particular issues might temporarily throw liberals and workers together. The idea that the liberal or humanitarian capitalist and the left-wing worker both belonged to a single 'progressive' movement which strove against 'reaction' to improve the existing society, outraged them. No SDF member would have seriously considered to ask Lloyd George to put himself at the head of such a united progressive movement, as Keir Hardie once did; let alone a liberal more identified with the capitalists.

Lastly, the SDF tradition was one of a working-class élite and vanguard, rather than of a mass movement: of the thinking, reading, militant workers who put in a great deal of time on the cause, rather than of the average man. Everybody ought to belong to the union, just as everybody was once supposed to sign the Charter and perhaps read or listen to the *Northern Star*; but not everybody was supposed to be an Owenite or Secularist or a Primitive Methodist lay preacher in the coalfield.

Both this élite tradition and the fact that reformism had driven its roots so deeply into the British working class, helped to turn these attitudes of the SDF tradition easily into sectarianism. The SDF's native intransigence was probably not much greater than that of the typical continental social-democratic militant (though the tradition that everybody ought to be a member of the mass party was much stronger there, since there were no other mass labour organizations). But on the continent mass movements could develop on the basis of a political attitude which in Britain merely isolated a militant minority, which in turn reacted to its isolation by exalting it. Marxists in the Saxon or North French textile areas operated in a political universe entirely created by themselves: party, union, press were all theirs. They did not face the problem of, say, the SDF trying to elect a candidate for an old-established union stronghold like Burnley. Nor was SDF sectarianism as great as has sometimes been supposed: it was the ILP and not the SDF which, as Professor Tsuzuki shows, wrecked the proposed fusion of the two groups in the 1890s, and SDF members took to trade union militancy with gusto. Nevertheless, the sectarianism of an isolated minority of 'the advanced' belongs to the SDF tradition, as it belonged to that of the Owenites, and it found the leadership of the unparliamentarian and rigid Hyndman not uncongenial for this reason.

To make Hyndman the expression rather than the creator of the SDF is not to underestimate his individual part in it. He gave it much, notably a firm orientation towards Marxism and the international labour movement. It is not unimportant that, whereas in the USA orthodox Marxism never quite sloughed off its dependence on intellectuals and the immigrant communities which brought it with them as their heritage, in Britain it has become wholly assimilated by the native labour vanguard. (A bent for theory does not automatically mean a bent for *Marxist* theory.) The British Communist Party for this reason developed a first-rate group of native *proletarian* leaders much earlier than many much larger parties of its kind (e.g., Horner, Pollitt, Campbell, Gallagher). This was not historically inevitable, and Hyndman's indefatigable pioneer propaganda work for Marxism should be given some of the credit. On the other hand superior leadership could unquestionably have given the SDF far greater success and made it far more influential in the wider labour movement than it ever became. And Hyndman, who monopolized the leadership, cannot escape responsibility for much of this failure.

Especially, he cannot escape blame for the failure of the SDF to exploit its unique position as the pioneer socialist organization in Britain. Engels' bitterness had good reasons. He saw the SDF throw away one opportunity after another in the 1880s when it had the field virtually to itself, he saw Hyndman alienate valuable supporters, and the major advances of the movement left either to Marxists forced to act independently of it, or to theoretically far more confused or undesirable elements. The 'new unionism' of 1889–90 and the triumph of independent working-class candidates in 1892 demonstrate what could have been achieved: but it was not the SDF which achieved it. Rather, it hindered these achievements and in turn never fully recovered from its loss of initiative.

Professor Tsuzuki's book does not discuss many of these issues. It is, rather, a valuable piece of narrative history – the best of its kind – which will for long remain the basis of further and perhaps more analytical work. Without having read the rather larger dissertation on which the book is based it is difficult to judge how much of the excellent English is due to the author and how much to Henry Pelling's editing, or how much the finished book differs in emphasis from the original. Still, it is a reflection on British historians (and especially Marxists) that the first usable history of the pioneer Marxist organization in this country – if we except the chronologically more limited work of Edward Thompson on William Morris, to which unaccountably little reference is made – should be the work of a Japanese scholar.

(1961)

13

Dr. Marx and the Victorian Critics

SINCE THE APPEARANCE of Marxism as an intellectual force hardly
a year – in the Anglo-Saxon world since 1945, hardly a week – has
passed without some attempt to refute it. The resulting literature of
refutation and defence has become increasingly uninteresting, because
increasingly repetitive. Marx's works, though voluminous, are limited
in size; it is technically impossible for more than a certain number of
original criticisms to be made of them, and most of them have been
made long ago. Conversely, the defender of Marx finds himself increasingly saying the same things over and over again, and though he
may try hard to do so in novel terms, even this becomes impossible.
An effect of novelty may be achieved in only two ways: by commenting, not on Marx himself, but on later Marxists, and by checking
Marx's thought against such facts as have come to light since the last
critic wrote. But even here the possibilities are limited.

Why then does the debate continue among scholars – for it is
natural that it does so among propagandists on both sides, who are
not primarily concerned with originality? Ideas do not become forces
until they seize hold of the masses and this, as advertising agents have
recognized, requires much repetition or even incantation. This applies both to those of us who think Marx a great man and his teach-
ings politically desirable, and to those who take the opposite view.
However, another reason is sheer ignorance. It is a melancholy illusion of those who write books and articles that the printed word sur-
vives. Alas, it rarely does. The vast majority of printed works enter a
state of suspended animation within a few weeks or years of publication, from which they are occasionally awakened, for equally short
periods, by research students. Many of them appear in languages
beyond the reach of most English commentators. But even when they
do not, they are often as forgotten as the original bourgeois critics of

Marx in Britain. And yet their work throws light not only on the intellectual history of our country in the late Victorian period, but on the general evolution of Marx-criticism.

They strike us chiefly by their *tone*, which differs very considerably from what has since become usual. Thus, Professor Trevor-Roper, who wrote an essay on *Marxism and the Study of History* (Problems of Communism V, 1956) some years ago, was far from untypical of the tone of anti-Marxism in that discouraging decade. He spent a good deal of space propounding the very implausible proposition that Marx made no original contribution to history except 'to sweep up the ideas already advanced by other thinkers and annex them to a crude philosophical dogma', that his historical interpretation was useless for the past and wholly discredited as the basis of prediction about the future, and that he had been without significant influence on serious historians, while those who claimed to be Marxists either wrote 'what Marx and Lenin would have called "bourgeois" social history' or were 'an army of dim scholiasts busily commenting on each others scholia'. In brief, the argument was widely accepted that Marx' intellectual reputation had been grossly inflated, for, 'disproved by all intellectual tests, the Marxist interpretation of history is sustained and irrationally justified by Soviet power alone'.

The writings of the Victorian Marx-critics are mostly and justly forgotten; a warning to those of us who engage in this discussion. But when we dip into them we find a wholly different tone. Admittedly British writers found it abnormally easy to maintain their calm. No anti-capitalist movement challenged them, few doubts about the permanence of capitalism nagged them, and between 1850 and 1880 it would have been hard to find a British-born citizen who called himself a socialist in our sense, let alone a Marxist. The task of disproving Marx was therefore neither urgent nor of great practical importance. Happily, as the Rev M. Kaufmann, perhaps our earliest non-Marxist 'expert' on Marxism, put it, Marx was a pure theorist who had not tried to put his doctrines into practice. (*Utopias from Sir Thomas More to Karl Marx*, 1879, p. 241.) By revolutionary standards he seemed to be even less dangerous than the anarchists and was therefore sometimes contrasted with those fire-eaters; to his advantage by Broderick (*Nineteenth Century* Apl. 1884, p. 639), to his disadvantage by W. Graham of Queens College, Belfast, who observed that the anarchists had 'a method and logic . . . wanting in the rival revolutionists of the school of Karl Marx and Mr Hyndman' (*The Social*

Problem, 1886, p. 423). Consequently, bourgeois readers approached him in a spirit of tranquillity or – in the case of the Rev Kaufmann – Christian forbearance, which our generation has lost:

'Marx is a Hegelian in philosophy and a rather bitter opponent of ministers of religion. But in forming an opinion of his writings we must not allow ourselves to be prejudiced against the man.' (*Socialism*, 1874, p. 165.)

Marx evidently returned the compliment, for he revised Kaufmann's account of himself in a later book at the instigation of an unidentified 'mutual acquaintance'. (See Kaufmann's chapter in *Subjects of the Day: Socialism, Labour and Capital*, 1890–1, p. 44.)

English literature on Marxism, as Bonar observed, not without smugness, (*Philosophy and Political Economy*, 1893, p. 354) thus showed a calm and judicial spirit already lacking from German discussions of this subject. There were few attacks on Marx's motives, his originality or scientific integrity. The treatment of his life and works was mainly expository, and where one disagrees with it, it is because the authors have not read or understood enough, rather than because they mix prosecution with exposition. Admittedly their expositions were often defective. I doubt whether anything even approximating to a usable non-socialist summary of the main tenets of Marxism, as they would be understood today, exists before Kirkup's *History of Socialism* (1900). But the reader could expect to find, as far as it went, a factual account of who Marx was and what the author thought he was at.

He could expect to find, above all, an almost universal admission of his stature. Milner, in his 1882 Whitechapel lectures (*National Review*, 1931, p. 477) plainly admired him. Balfour in 1885 thought it absurd to compare Henry George's ideas with his 'either in respect of (their) intellectual force, (their) consistency, (their) command of reasoning in general or of (their) economic reasoning in particular'. (*Report of the Industrial Remuneration Conference*, 1885, p. 344.) John Rae, the acutest of our early 'experts' (*Contemporary Socialism*, 1884, reprinting earlier articles) treated him with equal seriousness. Richard Ely, an American professor of vaguely progressive leanings whose *French and German Socialism* was published here in 1883, observed that good judges placed *Capital* 'on a par with Ricardo' and that 'about the ability of Marx there is unanimity of opinion' (p. 174). W. H. Dawson (*German Socialism and Ferdinand Lassalle*,

1888, pp. 96–7) summed up what was almost certainly the opinion of all except, as he notes, the miserable Duehring, whom recent Marx-critics have been vainly trying to rehabilitate: 'However its teaching may be viewed, no one will venture to dispute the masterly ingenuity, the rare acumen, the close argumentation and, let it be added, the incisive polemic which are displayed in . . . the pages (of *Capital*).'*

This chorus of praise is less surprising when we recall that the early commentators were far from wishing to reject Marx *in toto*. Partly because some of them found him a useful ally in their fight against *laissez-faire* theory, partly because they did not appreciate the revolutionary implications of all his theory, partly because, being tranquil, they were genuinely prepared to look at him on his merits; they were even prepared, in principle, to learn from him. With one exception: the labour theory of value, or, to be more precise, Marx's attacks on current justifications of profit and interest. Perhaps the critical fire was concentrated against these because the moral accusation implied in the phrase 'labour is the source of all value' affected confident believers in capitalism more than the prediction of the decline and fall of capitalism. If so, they criticized Marx precisely for one of the less 'Marxist' elements in his thought, and one which, though in a cruder form, the pre-Marxian socialists, not to mention Ricardo, had already propounded. At all events the theory of value was regarded as 'the central pillar of German and all modern Socialism' (Graham, *Socialism*, 1891, p. 139), and once it fell, the main critical job was done.

However, beyond this it seemed clear that Marx had a good deal to contribute, notably a theory of unemployment critical of the crude Malthusianism which was still in vogue. His views on population and the 'reserve army of labour' were not only normally presented without criticism (as in Rae), but were sometimes quoted with approval, or even partly adopted, as by the pioneer economic historian Archdeacon Cunningham (*Politics and Economics*, 1885, p. 102) – he had read *Capital* as early as 1879 ('The Progress of Socialism in England', *Contemp. Rev.*, Jan 1879, p. 247) – and William Smart of Glasgow, another economist whose fame rests on his work in economic history (*Factory Industry and Socialism*, Glasgow 1887). Similarly Marx's views on the division of labour and machinery met with general

* Readers may find a few of these opinions in Dona Torr's Appendix to the 1938 reprint of *Capital*, vol. I; but she had obviously consulted only a small fraction of the available literature.

approval, e.g., from the reviewer of *Capital* in the *Athenaeum*, 1887. J. A. Hobson (*Evolution of Modern Capitalism*, 1894) was clearly very struck with them: all his references to Marx deal with this topic. But even more orthodox and hostile writers, like J. Shield Nicholson of Edinburgh (*Principles of Political Economy* I, 1893, p. 105) observed that his treatment of this and allied topics 'is both learned and exhaustive, and is well worth reading'. Furthermore, his views on wages and economic concentration could not be brushed aside. Indeed, so anxious were some commentators to avoid a total rejection of Marx, that William Smart wrote his 1887 review of *Capital* specifically to encourage readers who might have been put off by the critique of the value theory from studying the book, which contained much 'of very great value both to the historian and the economist' (op. cit., p. 1).

An elementary textbook designed for Indian university students (M. Prothero, *Political Economy*, 1895) sums up reasonably well what non-Marxists saw in Marx; all the better for being slightly ignorant and thus reflecting current views rather than individual study. Three things were singled out: the theory of value, the theory of unemployment, and Marx's achievement as a historian, the first to point out that 'the economic structure of the present capitalist society has grown out of the economic structure of the feudal society' (p. 43). Indeed Marx made his greatest impact as a historian, and among economists with a historical approach to their subject. (As yet, he hardly influenced the professional non-economic historians in England, who were still sunk in the routine of purely constitutional, political, diplomatic and military history.) In spite of recent writers, there was really no dispute among those who read him about his influence. Foxwell, as bitter an academic anti-Marxist as was to be found in the 1880s, mentioned him as a matter of course among the economists who 'have most influenced serious students in this country' and among those who had produced the marked advance in 'historic feeling' at this period ('The Economic Movement in England', *Q. Jnl. Econ.*, 1888, pp. 89, 100). Even those who rejected the 'peculiar, and in my opinion erroneous, theory of value given in *Capital*' felt that the historical chapters must be judged differently (Shield Nicholson, op. cit., p. 370). Few doubted that, thanks to Marx's stimulus 'we are now beginning to see that large sections of history will have to be rewritten in this new light' (Kirkup, op. cit., p. 159), apparently ignoring Professor Trevor-Roper's demonstration that the stimulus was not Marx's, but Adam Smith's, Hume's, Toque-ville's or Fustel de Coulanges'. Bosanquet (*Philosophical Theory of the State*, 1899, p. 28) has no doubt that the 'economic or materialist view of history' is 'primarily connected with the name of Marx', though 'it may also be illustrated by many contentions of Buckle and Le Play'. Bonar (op. cit), though specifically denying that Marx invented historical materialism – he very properly instances the seven-teenth-century thinker, Harrington, as a pioneer (p. 358) – has nevertheless not previously heard of the following Marxist historical contentions, which amaze him: that 'the very Reformation is ascribed to an economical cause, that the length of the Thirty Years' War was due to economic causes, the Crusades to feudal land-hunger, the evolution of the family to economic causes, and that Descartes' view of animals as machines could be brought into relation with the growth of the Manufacturing system' (p. 367).

Naturally his influence was most marked among our economic historians, of whom only Thorold Rogers can be regarded as wholly insular in inspiration. Cunningham in Cambridge, as we have seen, had read him with sympathy since the late 1870s. The Oxford men – perhaps owing to the much stronger Germanic tradition among local Hegelians – knew him before there were English Marxist groups, though Toynbee's only incidental criticism of his history (*The Indus-trial Revolution*) happens to be mistaken.* George Unwin, perhaps the most impressive English economic historian of his generation, took to his subject through Marx, or at any rate to confute Marx. But he had no doubt that 'Marx was trying to get at the right kinds of history. The orthodox historians ignore all the most significant factors in human development' (*Studies in Economic History*, xxiii, lxvi).

Nor was there much disagreement about his achievement as a historian of capitalism. (His views on earlier periods the reviewer in the *Athenaeum* found 'unsatisfactory and quite superficial', but they were normally neglected, and indeed, most of his and Engels' most brilliant *aperçus* were not as yet available to a wide public.) Even the most extended and hostile British critique of his thought – Flint's *Socialism* (1895, written mainly in 1890–1) – admits:

---

* Toynbee disagreed with Marx's view that the yeomanry had disappeared by 1760 (1908 edn, p. 38). However, recent views are with Marx rather than Toyn-bee. I trust that the revelation of this fact will not drive some historians into revising their views.

'Where alone Marx did memorable work as a historical theorist, was in his analysis and interpretation of the capitalist era, and here he must be admitted to have rendered eminent service, even by those who think his analysis more subtle than accurate, and his interpretations more ingenious than true' (p. 138).

Flint was alone neither in his British distrust of 'a tendency to over-refinement in reasoning' (*Athenaeum*, 1887), nor in his admission of Marx's merits as a historian of capitalism; more especially of nineteenth-century capitalism. It is the modern practice to throw doubts on his and Engels' scholarship, integrity and use of sources (cf., *Capitalism and the Historians* and recent critiques of Engels by W. H. Chaloner and W. O. Henderson), but contemporaries hardly explored this avenue of criticism, since it seemed patent to them that the evils which Marx attacked were only too real. Kaufmann spoke for many when he observed that 'though he presents us exclusively with the dismal side of contemporary social life, he cannot be accused of wilful misrepresentation' (*Utopias*, p. 225). Llewellyn-Smith (*Economic Aspects of State Socialism*, 1887, p. 77) felt that 'though Marx has coloured his picture too darkly, he has rendered great service in calling attention to the more gloomy features of modern industry, to which it is useless to shut our eyes'. Shield Nicholson (op. cit., p. 370) thought his treatment in some respects exaggerated, but also that 'some of the evils are so great that exaggeration seems impossible'. And even the most ferocious attack on his *bona fides* as a scholar did not dare maintain that Marx had coloured a white, or even a gray, picture black, but at best that, black as the facts were, they sometimes contained 'silvery streaks' of evidence which Marx had paid no attention to (J. R. Tanner and F. S. Carey, *Comments on the use of the Blue Books made by Karl Marx in Chapter XV of Le Capital*, Cambridge Economic Club, May Term, 1885.)

Was the modern tone of hysterical anxiety completely absent from the early bourgeois criticism of Marx? No. From the moment that a Marxist-inspired socialist movement appeared in Britain, Marx-criticism of the modern stamp, seeking to discredit and refute to the exclusion of understanding, also begins to appear. Some of it was in continental works translated into English: notably from the mid-eighties. Hostile continental work was now translated – Laveleye's *Socialism of Today* (1885), Schaeffle's *Quintessence of Socialism* (1889). But home-grown anti-Marxism also began to sprout, notably in Cambridge, the leading centre of academic economics. The first serious attack on Marx's scholarship, as we have seen, came from two Cambridge dons in 1885 (Tanner and Carey), though Llewellyn-Smith of Oxford – a far less 'anti-Marxist' place in those days – did not take the criticism too tragically, merely observing, a few years later, that Marx's 'quotations from blue books are very important and instructive, though not always trustworthy' (*Two lectures on the books of political economy*, London, Birmingham and Leicester, 1888, p. 146). It is the tone of denigration rather than the content of this work which is interesting: phrases like 'the mongrel algebraical expressions' of *Capital* or 'an almost criminal recklessness in the use of authorities which warrants us in regarding other parts of Marx's work with suspicion' (pp. 4, 12) indicate – at least in economic subjects – something more than scholarly disapproval. In fact, what made Tanner and Carey mad was not simply his treatment of the evidence – they shied away from 'the charge of deliberate falsification . . . especially since falsification seems so unnecessary' (i.e., since the facts were black enough anyway) – but 'the unfairness of his whole attitude towards Capital' (p. 12). Capitalists are kinder than Marx gives them credit for; he is unfair to them; we must be unfair to him. Such, broadly, appears to be the basis of the critics' attitude.

At about the same time Foxwell of Cambridge developed the now familiar line that Marx was a crank with a gift of the gab, who could only appeal to the immature, notably among intellectuals; a man – in spite of Balfour's warning – to be bracketed with Henry George:

> *Capital* was well calculated to appeal to the somewhat dilettante enthusiasm of those who were educated enough to realize, and to be revolted by the painful condition of the poor, but not patient or hard-headed enough to find out the real causes of this misery, nor sufficiently trained to perceive the utter hollowness of the quack remedies so rhetorically and effectively put forward (loc. cit., p. 99).

Dilettante, not patient or hard-headed, utter hollowness, quack, rhetorical: the emotional load on the critic's vocabulary piles up. To Foxwell we also owe (through the Austrian Menger) the popularization of the German parlour-game of attacking Marx's originality and regarding him as a pillager of Thompson, Hodgskin, Proudhon, Rodbertus, or any other early writers who took the critic's fancy. Marshall's *Principles* (1890) took this over in a footnote, though the pointed reference to Menger's demonstration of Marx's lack of originality was dropped after the fourth edition (1898). The view that Rodbertus and Marx – the two were often bracketed together – made 'mainly exaggerations of, or inferences from, doctrines of earlier economists' (Flint, op. cit., p. 136) or that some other earlier thinker – Rodbertus (E. C. K. Gonner, *Rodbertus*, 1899) or Comte (Flint, op. cit.) – had said what Marx wanted to say about history earlier and vastly better, already brings us into a familiar universe. Marshall himself, the greatest of the Cambridge economists, showed his usual combination of marked emotional hostility to Marx and equally marked circuitousness.* But on the whole the root-and-branch anti-Marxists remained in a minority in the nineteenth century, and for a generation thereafter tended to follow the Marshallian line of tangential sneering rather than full-scale attack. For Marxism rapidly lost that influence which provokes discussion.

Oddly enough the calm type of Marx-criticism proved much more effective than the hysterical type. Few critiques of Marx have been more effective than Philip Wicksteed's 'Das Kapital – a criticism' which appeared in the socialist *To-Day* in October 1884. It was written with sympathy and courtesy, and with full appreciation of 'that great work', 'that remarkable section' in which Marx discusses value, 'that great logician' and even of the 'contributions of extreme importance' which Wicksteed believed Marx to have made in the latter part of volume I. But, whatever we may now think of the pure marginalist approach to value-theory, Wicksteed's article did more to create the mistaken feeling among socialists that Marx value theory was somehow irrelevant to the economic justification of socialism than the emotional diatribes of a Foxwell or a Flint ('the greatest failure in the history of economics'). It was in a Hampstead discussion group in which Wicksteed, Edgeworth† – another marginalist who avoided emotionalism – Shaw, Webb, Wallas, Olivier and some others discussed *Capital*, that much of *Fabian Essays* was matured. And if, a few years later, Sidgwick could talk of Marx's 'fundamental muddle . . . which the English reader, I think, need hardly spend time in examining, as the more able and influential among English socialists are now careful to give it a wide berth' (*Econ. Jnl.* V, p. 343), it was

* His views are discussed at greater length in a special *Note* below.

† Edgeworth, who had never troubled to study Marx seriously, seems to have shared the Cambridge economists' total rejection of and dislike for Marx (*Collected Papers*, III, pp. 273 ff., in a review written in 1920). However, there is no evidence that he expressed this view publicly in the old century.

not because of Sidgwickian jeers that they did so, but because of Wicksteedian argument – and perhaps, we might add, because of the inability of British Marxists to defend Marxian political economy against its critics. Workers still insisted on Marxism, and revolted against the early WEA because they did not teach it; but not until events had demonstrated that the confidence of the Marx-critics in their own theories was misplaced, or excessive, did Marxism revive as an academic force. It is unlikely that it will disappear from the academic scene again.

NOTE
Marshall and Marx

Marshall appears to have begun without any marked views about Marx. The only reference in the *Economics of Industry* (1879) is neutral, and even in the first edition of the *Principles* there are signs (p. 138) that at one time the danger to capitalism from Henry George worried him more than that from Marx. The references to Marx in the *Principles* are as follows: (1) a criticism of his 'arbitrary doctrine' that capital is only that which 'give(s) its owners the opportunity of plundering and exploiting others' (p. 138). (From the third edition – 1895 – this is transposed and elaborated.) (2) that economists ought to avoid the term 'abstinence', choosing rather something like 'waiting', because – at least so I interpret the addition of a footnote at this point – 'Karl Marx and his followers have found much amusement in contemplating the accumulations of wealth which result from the abstinence of Baron Rothschild' (p. 290). (This reference is dropped from the Index from the third edition, though not from the text.) (3) That Rodbertus and Marx were not original in their views, which claim that 'the payment of interest is a robbery of labour', and are criticized as a circular argument, though one 'shrouded by the mysterious Hegelian phrases in which Marx delighted' (pp. 619–20). (In the second edition an attempt is made to substitute a summary of Marx's doctrine of exploitation for the earlier caricature of it (1891). (4) A defence of Ricardo against the charge of being a labour theorist of value, as falsely claimed not only by Marx but by ill-informed non-Marxists. (This defence is progressively elaborated in subsequent editions.) It will be remembered that Marshall had too great an admiration for Ricardo to wish to throw him overboard as an ancestor of socialist theorists, as many other economists – Foxwell for instance – were prepared to do. But the task of showing that Ricardo was not a labour theorist is complex, as he seems to have appreciated. Thus we note not only that all Marshall's references to Marx are critical or polemical – the only merit he allows him, since he lived in pre-Freudian days, is a good heart – but also that his critique seems to be based on a much less detailed study of Marx's writings than one might expect, or than was undertaken by reputable contemporary academic economists.

14

The Fabians Reconsidered

THE FABIANS have always been strong on public relations. Essentially a body of intellectuals, they have never required others to blow their own trumpet, for at its peak of early influence (in 1892) something like ten per cent of the male membership of the Society consisted of journalists and writers, and Bernard Shaw was among them. They have attracted editorialists and historians for this very reason. Those who can blow their own trumpet not only sound louder than those who cannot, but automatically provide material for music critics; those whose career consists in drafting and provoking written or printed comment are a gift to persons who must rely on documents in order to draft footnotes. What is more, the sound of the Fabian trumpets is a particularly tempting one. The society has claimed an extraordinary influence on British public life, especially between its foundation and the end of World War I, and plenty of people have accepted these claims. Fabians have claimed to destroy the influence of Marxism in Britain; to have inspired the Labour Party; to have announced and indeed laid the foundations of the welfare state; or more modestly, of municipal reform and the London County Council.

These claims, and the relative facility of research about them, have attracted a very large number of historians, particularly during the period of the 1945 Labour government, whose direct inspiration appeared to be Fabian, and which contained a Fabian prime minister, nine Fabian cabinet ministers, and a clear majority of Fabians among the 394 Labour M.Ps. Dr Alan Macbriar, the most elaborate Fabian historian, lists at least five theses by scholars from three continents all written since 1942 about the Society, and a clutch of articles ranging from the *Journal of the History of Ideas* to the *Journal of Economic History*. His list, being published in 1962, is not exhaustive. All these scholars must sooner or later have discovered in the course of their work (as the present writer, who is one of them, did) that they were wasting their time, except, of course, insofar as they were getting their PhDs. The Fabian claims are largely mythological and researches on the Society have therefore automatically taken the form, in the main, of their systematic explosion.

The Fabians were not inspirers and pioneers of the Labour Party. As against the other socialist and labour groups of the 1880s' vintage they actually at most times opposed the foundation of an independent party of the working class, and insofar as they did not, 'it seems certain that the Independent Labour Party and the Labour Party would have come into existence without their assistance, which was for the most part equivocal and not very helpful' (Macbriar). One can safely go further and claim that their contribution to the formation of the Independent Labour Party was – as Dr Siegfried Bünger has recently shown in his study of Engels and the British Labour Movement* – distinctly less than that of the small Engels group, and their contribution to the Labour Party incomparably less than that of the ILP and notably less than that of the Marxist Social Democratic Federation. There is evidence that before 1914 (when Sidney Webb joined the executive of the Labour Party) the Fabians even took the new organization very seriously; and then only because, all their other political projects having been wrecked, they had no other choice.

Alan Macbriar dismisses the Fabians' chief claim, to have 'broken the spell of Marxism' in Britain, with equal justice: 'The claim is extravagant, for Marxism had cast no spell over England'. One might also add, that there is no evidence that the Fabians' specific criticisms of Marxism were particularly effective, even in the circles to which they had access. Their private alternative to Marxist economics – including neo-classical marginalism, as put forward by Shaw in the *Fabian Essays* – left hardly any imprint on the rest of the British non-Marxist or reformist socialists.

Their claims to have laid the foundations of the welfare state are slightly more plausible, for the Fabians certainly exercised their most direct influence as the drafters of propagandist material for the labour movement and of various concrete propositions of reform. Moreover, the Webbs were from the early nineties on in contact with a number of actual or future policy-makers in the higher circles of

* Friedrich Engels und die britische sozialistische Bewegung 1881–95 (E. Berlin 1962).

government, opposition and civil service. Yet, in fact, the specific Fabian proposals of social reform were rarely adopted and, when they were, 'in no case reproduced Fabian plans in detail, where these had been set forth in their tracts' (Macbriar). There is doubtless room for argument here, but the argument must be marginal. The claims of other men and other groups to have pioneered the specific reforms of the 1906–14 period (which were sometimes, as in the case of National Insurance, implemented in a frankly anti-Fabian form), and the doctrines on which the future welfare state was to be based, are far stronger. The late Lord Beveridge, though in contact with the Webbs, was never a Fabian or even a socialist of any description. The economic theories of the Cambridge Marshallians and of J. A. Hobson, who was closely associated with the very effective group of left-wing Liberals who came into their own in 1906, are far stronger than the Fabians'.

Even their modest claim as municipal reformers, especially in London, can be seriously scaled down. Recent work by P. Thompson of Oxford has tended to reduce it to considerably smaller dimensions even than past historians, including Macbriar and the present writer, have allowed.

The failure of the Fabians in the big things is to some extent mitigated by their indefatigable activity, their gift as drafters of pamphlets and administrative projects, their wide circle of political acquaintances, and above all, by the self-abnegation with which they were prepared to help any and every person or group which they believed capable of advancing their cause. Yet in reality that failure is even greater than a mere dismantling of the Fabian myth would suggest. It is due to their remarkable a-typicality. They were in neither the liberal nor the working-class stream of British politics, insofar as these ran distinct courses. They were certainly not conservatives. They had, in fact, no place in the British political tradition, nor – in spite of priding themselves on their political realism – did they recognize this state of affairs.

Both their ideology and their politics were quite out of *rapport* with the rest of the left. The Marxists, for instance, whether the sectarians of Hyndman's Social Democratic Federation or the small and relatively unimportant Engels group, were much closer to the main stream of British labour than they. The SDF favoured an independent working-class party, its members (in spite of their leader) took an active part in the labour organization of the 1889–92 period, they took some steps towards the foundation of a Labour Party (though they subsequently left it), opposed the South African War, and in spite of their leader's imperialism and support of World War I, remained predominantly anti-imperialist and anti-war. The Fabians, alone among socialist groups, opposed the formation of an independent party of labour, supported imperialism, refused to oppose the Boer war, took no interest in the traditional international and anti-war preoccupations of the left, and their leaders took practically no part in the trade union revivals of 1889 or 1911. At a time when the entire movement united in total opposition to the Taff Vale judgment, the historians of trade unionism favoured a compromise solution and Sidney Webb was formally declared unacceptable as a representative of labour on the compromise Royal Commission of 1903, which the unions boycotted. It is difficult to find a record less in tune with that of the socialist and labour movement in the period from 1889 to 1914.

They were equally out of tune with the Liberals, though 'permeation' of the Liberal Party was the nearest thing to a consistent Fabian policy which can be discovered during this period. It was not merely that they entirely failed to grasp the essentials of party politics, which were (as Engels recognized) that the Liberals would make concessions to labour only under the threat of losing the labour vote, and not because they could somehow be persuaded to become socialists without noticing it. It was not only the striking lack of political sense which led the Webbs to tie their fortunes to the Liberal Imperialists and to neglect or underestimate the men who really were to count in the Liberal revival – Campbell-Bannerman or Lloyd George – as they also underestimated Keir Hardie. It was also that they quite failed to catch the drift of left-wing liberalism which did actually inject an element of social reform and non-*laissez-faire* ideology into the Liberal Party; and they did so because they were not, in fact, in any sense Liberals, even in the broad and generic sense in which virtually all Englishmen of the left were at least the illegitimate offspring of the radical-liberal tradition.

Their lack of contact with the labour movement isolated them from the workers; their lack of contact with, and indeed hostility to, the liberal-radical tradition, isolated them from the bulk of British left-wing intellectuals. Neither isolation was at all inevitable. There was a moment – between 1890 and 1892 – when for want of any other national nucleus, the working-class socialists and labour militants

253

would have rallied round the Fabian banner; but the Society felt unhappy with them, and allowed its provincial societies to drift off into the new Independent Labour Party after 1893. In the same period its combination of socialist ideas and liberal attachments attracted the type of socially critical, left-wing intellectuals who were unprepared to abandon what they regarded as the radical-democratic and Jacobin heritage of liberalism: W. H. Massingham, J. A. Hobson (who was at one time quite close to the Fabians). Their anti-liberalism drove them away, as their failure to grasp the drift of, say, Hobson's economic and historical analysis of industrialism and imperialism and his anticipations of Keynesianism, led them to reject the most powerful intellectual strain of reformist economic analysis. It is characteristic that, when founding the London School of Economics, the Webbs preferred the orthodoxy of Cannan to the left-wing economics of Hobson, to whom they failed to offer a post.

At the same time the Fabians, or rather the handful of leaders who impressed their policy on a society which contained the usual range and variety of left-wing opinions, were unquestionably socialists, though of an unusual kind. They became the patron saints of reformism, and have no one but themselves to blame for it, though they would hardly have predicted that views which in their youth represented the extreme right of the socialist movement would one day be blamed for excessive radicalism. They were not, of course, radicals. It is merely that the right wing of the Labour Party today is so far to the right that even the Fabianism of the 1890s appears dangerously subversive beside it.[1] Nevertheless, it *is* significant that both Shaw and the Webbs ended their careers as enthusiastic supporters of Soviet Communism. 'Their hearts' writes the latest official historian of the Fabian Society of the Webbs after 1933 – 'were in Russia and in Russia alone.'[2] Embarrassed moderates anxious to advertise their Fabian rather than Marxian inspiration, preferred to put this down to senile decay; but no careful student of either Shaw's or the Webbs' earlier thought will find anything inconsistent with it in their later loyalties. They had always believed in a thoroughgoing reconstruction of society. They had never been committed to the British political apparatus of their youth. They were not only non-liberals, but by the definitions of their time, anti-liberals, and had indeed been attacked as such continuously from at least the early twentieth century. It was their reason and not their heart which led them towards the right; and when under the impact of war and crisis it led them towards the left, and convinced Beatrice Webb that Marx had been right and the Fabians wrong,[3] they followed it without regrets. Only their abnormality defeated them once again. What made converts was their view of the 'inevitability of gradualness', not their conviction of the necessity of socialism. Or rather, what succeeded as an advertising slogan were two or three phrases loosely associated with Fabianism, but not Fabian ideas. Few serious writers about society have had their thoughts more consistently neglected than the Webbs. Their works are appreciated as monuments of scholarship; but the conclusions which they derived from their researches (or for the sake of which they undertook them) are still virtually unknown.*

What is the explanation of such eccentricities in Fabian thought and practice? It must be sought, I think, along two lines: by investigating the intellectual situation of Britain in the 1880s and the social composition of the Fabians. Neither have much more than incidental contact with the labour movement.

II

Two points about the social composition of the Fabians are immediately obvious. They were – and this was perhaps the only unifying factor among an otherwise heterogeneous membership – an overwhelmingly non-proletarian body. They were also, as a middle-class socialist organization, extremely anomalous. For in Britain, perhaps because the rise of proletarian socialism was less massive and precipitous than in continental countries, the 1880s and early 1890s produced none of that impressive, if often temporary, flow of young intellectuals towards the ranks of social-democracy. We have no equivalent of the young Croce and his contemporaries, the young Sombart, of

* This is markedly the case with *Industrial Democracy*, which is not only the best single book ever written on the British trade unions and a piece of special pleading for the 'old' union leaders of the time against the 'new', but contains an entire theory of democracy, the state and the transition to socialism. The contents of the book was sufficiently interesting to inspire Lenin, who translated it, to some crucial passages in *What Is To Be Done*. But so little is *Industrial Democracy* read, that Lenin's use of it is either unremarked or ascribed to a reading of the *History of Trade Unionism*, which lacks most of this theoretical interest. Nor is *Industrial Democracy*, or Webb's Six Lectures on Democracy (1896), or his article on the subject in the *Political Science Quarterly* (1896), both of which cover similar ground, widely or at all mentioned in histories of political thought.

Lucien Herr, Jaurès and the phalanx of *normaliens*, of the brilliant Viennese intellectuals who became Austro-Marxists, let alone of the Russian ones who became ideological social democrats or social revolutionaries almost to a man.* The Fabians were the only British socialist body to appeal specifically to intellectuals, and after 1906 the British socialist student movement developed out of the university Fabian societies. But they had no body of members among university students until the middle 1890s, and then only a handful at Oxford whose subsequent development demonstrates their a-typicality. (The most prominent among them, L. S. Amery, ended as a Churchillian imperialist.) The radical, left-wing, or merely social-reforming trend among intellectuals was stimulated by the labour revival, but – until the first war, or at the earliest the 'strange death of Liberal England' after 1906 – it remained overwhelmingly attached to the Liberal Party. Consequently much of the work done by socialist intellectuals on the continent was done by liberal ones in Britain. The basic critique of imperialism and finance capitalism which a Lenin produced in Russia, a Hilferding in Austria, a Luxemburg in Germany, in Britain came from the Liberal Hobson. A Liberal couple, J. L. and Barbara Hammond, produced the classic left-wing histories – and criticisms – of Britain's industrialization. Even after the collapse of the Liberal Party, the men who elaborated the foundations of modern social-democratic theory were, and often remained, Liberals, like Marshall, Keynes and Beveridge.

The Fabians, like most middle-class socialists at the end of the nineteenth century, were therefore anomalies.† Is there anything in their social composition which helps to explain the appearance of such a group?

* This influx of intellectuals into, or into the neighbourhood of, the labour movement is sometimes mistakenly ascribed to their 'alienation'. Whatever may have been the case after 1945, the *normaliens* of the 1890s were the nearest thing to the acknowledged élite of France, which was after all the 'république des professeurs'.

† A partial exception may have to be made for the aesthetes and arts-and-crafts men of the 1880s, who seem – Morris, Walter Crane, Oscar Wilde – to have been fairly commonly drawn towards socialism. How far the middle-class revulsion against Oscar Wilde, which coincides with the counter-attack against labour, also reflected hatred of political dissidence, would be worth investigating. After all, even in the matter of Parnell, the case against the leader of insurrection and that against the breaker of middle-class family taboos, is not always clearly distinguishable.

Except in 1892, when it attracted a number of otherwise homeless working-class socialists, the number of actual practising workers (i.e., non-official trade union members) never exceeded 10 per cent of the identifiable membership, and was probably a smaller proportion of the total membership.* The mass of middle-class members falls into two somewhat different groups: members of the traditional middle classes who had developed a social conscience, a dislike of bourgeois society, or some other form of dissidence, and the much more interesting body of self-made professionals. Among the first, the large bloc of emancipated and presumably middle-class women deserves special mention. They formed more than a quarter of the total membership in 1890, before expansion, and between one-fifth and one-sixth from then until 1906. It is not surprising that the only amendment ever carried to the Fabian 'Basis' was one in favour of women's suffrage. It is to this group of radicals from the traditional middle class, that Sidney Webb's guide to shareholder members of socialist groups[4] – the problem of what to do with such tainted money was not infrequently discussed among Fabians, and is reflected in Shaw's *Widowers' Houses* – was presumably addressed.

The second group included writers and journalists (like Bland and Shaw), self-made higher civil servants (like Webb), teachers, artists, professional men, and also the professional organizers and politicians who may be regarded as white-collar workers risen from the ranks. In 1890 half the identifiable sample consisted of such people, omitting those in the traditional careers of medicine, the law and the clergy. In 1892 the proportion would have been higher, but for the temporary influx of working-class socialists. If we think of the characteristic Fabian of the 1880s and early 1890s, we shall inevitably think of independent women, often earning their livelihood as writers, teachers or even typists; of self-made newspapermen and writers; of self-made civil servants, political functionaries and itinerant lecturers; of clerks and professional men like T. Bolas who edited the *Practical Socialist* (the first organ of socialist reformism) 'at his chemical, electrical and technological laboratory' and J. M. Fells and E. Garcke, whose *Factory Accounts* (1888) is an early landmark in the British history of scientific management. They were the 'new women' about whom Shaw wrote, but also the 'new men', rising through the interstices of the traditional social and economic structure of Victorian Britain, or anticipating a new structure.

* Printed membership lists are available for 1890, 1891, 1892, 1904 and 1906.

Their importance among the Fabian leadership cannot be numerically estimated, because individuals like Webb and Shaw counted for more than one, but a sample may nevertheless be instructive. Of the twenty-one who sat on the Fabian executive in the course of 1892, five were women, two workers, six probably members of the old middle and upper classes (defined, in the absence of other indications, by education at Oxford or Cambridge), and eight probably members of the lower middle and new professional strata (including one who cannot be identified).

Now these members of what Webb and Shaw called the '*nouvelle couche sociale*', the 'intellectual proletariat', the 'literary proletariat', the 'black-coated' or 'professional proletariat',[5] play a key role in Fabian theory. They were not supposed to be particularly impoverished, though Shaw insisted at times on 'my own class, the shabbygenteel'. Their status was merely the then comparatively uncommon one of a salaried middle class. The Webbs' entire structure of socialism pivots on such professionals. They are the trained, impartial and scientific administrators and expert advisers who have created an alternative court of appeal to profit. By origin they sprang chiefly from the capitalist class, but the growth of democracy and education opened up alternative supplies of brainworkers, and they would therefore increasingly be recruited from below. As early as 1888 Olivier had noted the growing separation of ownership and administration in business, and thus the rise of a class of salaried managers, and the Webbs paid particular attention to the growth of new professions, which they rightly saw as, in the main, having salaried status. And in the ethos of such professions, from the civil service onward, they saw a working alternative to a system in which men worked in proportion only to their financial incentive, a sort of anticipation of the ethos of communism.[6]

It would be an interesting and instructive exercise to trace these managerial, professional, careerist or 'intellectually superior' elements through Fabian theory, especially that of Shaw and Webb; for instance, in their debt to the American economist, F. A. Walker, their version of the theory of the 'rent of ability', in Webb's concern for 'efficiency', which even in his earliest years was a crucial pillar of his belief in socialism, and in a variety of other – often stylistic – ways. In most cases it is a good deal more sophisticated than the heart-cry of the young J. R. Macdonald, who called for socialism as a 'revolution directed from the study; to be one, not of brutal need, but of intellectual development; to be, in fact, a revolution of the comparatively well-to-do'.[7] Yet the assumption that middle-class professionals would play a much greater part than the working class in achieving socialism, that they would themselves be among its beneficiaries, and indeed that their way of life anticipated it, belongs very firmly to Fabianism.

It was, of course, evident that the self-interest of a *socialist* middle-class stratum did not provide a sufficiently strong motive force for the progress of socialism. Indeed, clear heads like Shaw's were aware that an appeal to self-interest would be more likely to lead young and socially rising members of the professional classes away from social-ism.[8] Since they did not believe in the working class or the class struggle, they were forced to fall back upon such vague forces as the progress of education and enlightenment in all classes – Webb even reduced class bias to a sort of eternal debating society[9] – and to the growth of a social conscience and unselfishness. Admittedly this was not *quite* as jejune as it sounds. Both the progress of enlightenment – the recognition of the rationality of socialism – and that of the social conscience of the middle class reflected 'our increasing conscious-ness' of the trend of evolution, as stimulated by the need for the middle classes to come to terms with a working-class electorate.[10] Yet the point was that this recognition of the rationality and neces-sity of socialism was not supposed to meet with any fundamental resistance by the middle class. Once stimulated, they would, as it were, realize that this form of social organization really suited them just as well if not better than the capitalist. In any case, the Fabians never rested their middle-class socialism on a proclivity to do the working class favours, or on conscious transfers of class allegiance. Theirs remained a socialism of the 'comparatively well-to-do'.

At first sight it seems strange for bodies of men representing, if anything, a social stratum rising in power, influence and prosperity within capitalism, to raise the banner of socialism on its own behalf; even that of a deliberately gradualist and non-revolutionary social-ism. In fact, however, the peculiar intellectual situation of Britain helps to explain why the Fabians did so.

III

The economic and political – and with it the intellectual – structure of Britain in the mid-nineteenth century rested on three supports, all of which were subsiding more or less rapidly between 1865 and 1890. Economically it rested on our virtual monopoly of world industrial production, and on an exceptionally 'free' economy of fairly small-scale, owner-managed, competitive private firms which grew up beneath it, and a wealth of spontaneously accumulated or exploitable resources which made elaborate organization or planning of investment or production unnecessary. This, in turn, provided the basis of an orthodoxy of *laissez-faire* economic liberalism which had the force of natural law: a world in which, as in Newtonian physics, prices like water found their natural level, wages, like stones, when unnaturally raised, must come down, and pint-pots did not hold quarts. It was an orthodoxy which made virtually no provision (at least in the all-important field of production) for 'state interference', whose effects, when not directed to 'the sole purpose of disestablishing state interference'[11] must be ruinous. Politically it rested on the peculiar compromise of 1832, by which the old political rulers applied the manufacturers' policy (except in certain fields affecting the social status of a landowning aristocracy), on the absence of a working-class electorate and of any labour movement disposed to, or capable of, seriously challenging social stability. On the military and political side it rested on the stability of the 1815 balance of power, which left Britain in control of the seas and with a deciding voice in international affairs. The electoral reforms of the 1860s, the unifications of the U.S.A. and Germany, the emergence of Japan, and the 'Great Depression' after 1873 undermined all these three pillars.

In consequence the set of theoretical beliefs which dominated mid-Victorian Britain, like the Whig-Liberal-Radical alliance which provided its almost unbroken parliamentary majorities from 1846 to 1874, broke down. A shift from 'individualist' to 'collectivist' thought reflects the necessary intellectual adjustment. It must be noted that, to begin with, this was an intellectual problem of liberalism, for no other coherent body of doctrine was available. There were, for practical purposes, no socialists and such conservatives as essayed thinking rather than feeling were, at least in their economic and legal theories, liberals. Hence, not only did the great majority of middle-class (or any other) native socialists of the 1880s' revival begin their intellectual lives as Liberal-Radicals, but – more para-doxically – the systematic borrowing of the 'Prussian' attitude to the state and its Hegelian justification came via T. H. Green, a left-wing radical, the Milners, Llewellyn-Smiths, Morants, Haldanes, and other reformers of the state machine came from within the same intellectual circles in and around Oxford, and systematic imperialist ideologies were in the first instance constructed not only by the ex-radical Disraeli, but by political left-wingers of more recent vintage such as Dilke, Chamberlain and Cecil Rhodes. Their liberal or radical past indicated little more than some intellectual liveliness. It is as illegitimate to suppose that the theory of the mature Sidney Webb was derived from the orthodox radicalism of his youth, as to suppose that the mature Milner or Haldane would have met with the approval of John Stuart Mill.

Since liberal theory appeared to be so fully committed to *laissez-faire* – some marginal modifications and the willingness of sectional interests to claim exemption as special cases, hardly affect the argument – the most obvious course seemed to be to look for alternative justifications of 'collectivist' or 'state interference'. All these would automatically tend to be regarded as 'socialist', a term which, even in 1897, in the words of an intelligent Frenchman close to the Fabians, meant no more than

> any doctrine opposed to *laissez-faire* . . . and which concedes to society, in whatever form, the right to intervene in the production and above all in the distribution of wealth.[12]

It had until the 1880s no connection with any native socialist movement, for there was none, and foreign ones were too remote to appear threatening. It was in fact the mere antonym of *laissez-faire*, and used as such – sometimes in deliberate preference to its present use – by various non-socialist writers and even by some in the early socialist movement.[13] While it normally, but by no means invariably, had the same sort of connection with social welfare and the condition of the poor as the phrase 'social problems', it had no more and might have less. Archdeacon Cunningham, the pioneer of economic history, traced the Progress of Socialism in the *Contemporary Review* of 1879 and concluded that 'capitalists would welcome any commercial reorganization which would give them a calmer life. It is, we believe, not as a remedy for the miseries of the poor, but as an alleviation of the cares of the rich that socialism is coming upon us'. He seems to have regarded the rationalized state capitalism which he recommended as akin to Marxism. The need to find some alternative to *laissez-faire*, the readiness to define any such alternative as 'socialism', and the capacity for Britons in this period to separate 'socialism' from the working-class movement, therefore provided a very apt background for the Fabians' peculiar version of it.*

However, there were, in theory, two ways of evolving a social theory more nearly in line with realities than the *laissez-faire* orthodoxy of the past, and especially one which legitimized the new activities of state and business. It could be done by developing certain strands of liberal radicalism, e.g., the trust-busting line of argument, which (like the entire Jacobin wing of radicalism to which it belonged) allowed for a great deal more in the way of collective action than *laissez-faire*. On the other hand a variety of possible non-liberal traditions – mostly foreign – could be drawn upon to construct an alternative theory to *laissez-faire*: German Hegelianism in philosophy, the historicist economists and *Kathedersozialisten* (also German), the Positivists (French), and actual socialism (both French and German). All these had the advantage of not being historically intertwined with *laissez-faire*. Both approaches had their champions. But two things are to be noted. First, that the *normal* mode of left-wing advance from liberal-radicalism was *via* a development of radical ideas, because the *normal* location of the British left wing in the immediate past had been on the left flank of the Liberal Party. It was natural for the Social Democratic Federation to develop out of an alliance of Radical workers' clubs, for Henry George to provide the bridge between Radicalism and Socialism for so many of the early British socialists, and for the labour movement to refuse – not entirely logically – to play off Conservatives against Liberals in politics. Conversely, the bodies which deliberately broke with liberal theory (other than the class-conscious Marxists), normally represented imperialist, big business, or other tendencies loosely classifiable as 'right-wing'.[14]

Now the Fabians – at any rate the group which determined the society's policy and ideology – belong very firmly to the second group, partly in their theory, partly in their affiliations. In the international *Methodenstreit* of the economists, which in fact divided the liberals from the non-socialist anti-liberals, the Webbs were extreme, if tacit, partisans of the 'historicist' school. Their debt to the Oxford Hegelians is vastly less than Halévy supposed, but there can be no doubt that the home-baked theories which Sidney Webb was evolving (via Spencer and Darwin) before his marriage to Beatrice, ran strik-

* For the calmness with which even Marx was regarded at this period, see Chapter 13, *Dr. Marx and the Victorian Cities* (pp. 239–48).

ingly parallel with theirs. It is interesting that the Webbs should have found their most congenial political associates for so long in the group of liberal imperialists who formed round that Bismarckian collectivist, R. B. Haldane. It is equally interesting that both the Webbs and Shaw should – partly in line with their debt to the economics of F. A. Walker, the American, have shown a marked preference for big, or even monopolist, business over small and medium business, as being both more efficient, more long-sighted, capable of paying higher wages, and less committed to *laissez-faire*.[15]

These affiliations explain both the anomaly of Fabian attitudes within the labour movement up to the First World War, and their ineffectiveness. For in the actual situation of Britain those who cut themselves off from the powerful and deeply-rooted liberal traditions were likely to fail. The paradox of Britain was that even the theories and policies most at variance with the Cobdenite orthodoxies of the past, succeeded only insofar as they were allied with or operated in the framework of historic liberalism. Joseph Chamberlain failed; Campbell-Bannerman and Lloyd George succeeded. Milner and Rhodes were, in terms of British politics, freaks; but the 'liberal imperialists' were not. Yet neither the Fabian failures nor their affiliations make them into mere ideologists of imperialism, corporation capitalism and the state bureaucracy which belongs to it. They were in their own minds socialists. If they had not been, they would probably not have established links with the labour and socialist movement, let alone have gravitated further into its orbit. Their socialism was of a peculiar kind, partly because their rejection of the main and proletarian tradition of socialism forced them to seek another which did not rely on the working class, and their rejection of liberal-radicalism closed some other obvious theoretical avenues; partly because the deeply entrenched and dominant orthodoxy of mid-Victorian *laissez-faire* really made the differences between the theories demanding greater state action against it appear small and relatively unimportant. The phrase 'we are all socialists now' appeared less cynical then than it does today.

IV

No hypothesis which seeks to link ideas with their social background can be proved to everyone's entire satisfaction. We can therefore merely, in conclusion, summarize the main evidence.

First, the Fabian Society's social composition was peculiar not only because it was resolutely non-proletarian, but because it contained a large proportion of a '*nouvelle couche sociale*', whose importance they fully recognized. Quite possibly in both these respects it was unique in the international socialist movement. While there were plenty of socialist groups in fact composed mainly of non-prole-tarians, it is hard to think of any which did not at least lay claim to honorary working-class status or regard themselves in some sense as subordinate to the working class or 'the masses'.

Second, the leading Fabian group was both non-Marxist, non-Jacobin/radical and non-liberal. It regarded not so much capitalism as the *laissez-faire* Cobdenite type of capitalism of mid-Victorian Britain as its immediate and chief enemy.

Third, the socialist theory which came to dominate the Society was both non-Marxist and non-liberal. Its affiliations were with theories which, in other political contexts, belonged to imperialism, big business, government administration and the political right. Fabians who belonged to other traditions either tended to fall silent or to drift away from the society.* The anti-liberalism of the Society was, of course, widely recognized, at all events from the middle 1890s. 'At heart (its) principal leaders are bureaucrats not democrats' was written as early as 1901, though the hysterical opposition to the 'old gang' on these grounds only developed between 1906 and 1914.[16]

Fourth, the actual policies of the Society, up to just before the First World War, were almost always at variance with those of most other sections of the political left, radical or socialist. The Fabians were in fact, insofar as they cut themselves off from the left, rather more sectarian than the Marxists.

It is the contention of this paper that these four peculiarities are closely connected with each other. If this is so, then the revision of Fabian history must go further than the mere quantitative reduction in Fabian influence which has so far been its main achievement. The Fabians cannot be seen, as Eduard Bernstein saw them when he derived his 'revisionism' from English experience and Fabian con-tacts, as merely a particularly empirical, hard-headed and anti-romantic group within the British socialist movement, and for this

---

* This was notably the case with William Clarke, the Fabian essayist who belonged most firmly into the radical-Jacobin tradition, with Graham Wallas, an instinctive liberal and probably also with Ramsay Macdonald.

264

reason the pioneers of the rejection or revision of doctrinaire Marxism.[17] It cannot be seen, as its latest official historian still sees it, as the founder of a 'basic Fabian' tradition 'of the abolition of poverty through legislation and administration; of the communal control of production and social life, and of the conversion of the British public and of the British governing class . . . by a barrage of facts and "informed" propaganda'.[18]

The Fabians were not 'revisionists' in the sense the word acquired round the end of the 1890s, because few of their more vocal members had ever been Marxists (though several had been in the Social Democratic Federation), because what they rejected was not merely some parts of Marxist theory – by no means all* – but the sectarianism and romantic insurrectionary phrase-mongering, which was in fact rejected by a great many other people, including Frederick Engels, and because the British left had quite sufficient established theories of gradual and piecemeal change without having to wait for the Fabians to formulate them. Nor was there anything specifically novel or Fabian about writing factual pamphlets in support of left-wing, indeed even of socialist or semi-socialist objects. Their refusal to hold 'distinctive opinions on the Marriage Question, Religion, Art, abstract Economics, historic Evolution, Currency, or any other subject than its own special business of practical Democracy and Socialism'[19] (including foreign policy and war), would not prove the Society particularly practical, even if it had been true. Their capacity to draft specific measures of reform would be a sign of hard-headedness only if they had also envisaged (as they rarely did in any effective way) how these reforms could be implemented. For want of this their New Reform Bill of 1891 was as utopian a proposal as their proposal to municipalize the milk supply, the Webbs' Constitution of a Socialist Commonwealth, or for that matter the entirely stillborn Minority Report of the Poor Law Commission. And nothing could have been more impractical than the actual political strategy and tactics of the Fabians during the period when they followed political aims wholly or partly outside the Labour Party's. (After that they ceased to have any policy of their own, and the history of the Society is of no interest to any except its members, or a few specialists in the affairs of the Labour Party, mainly in the 1930s.)

The break with past interpretations of Fabianism must be more

* Few Marxists would have seriously disagreed, or did disagree, with William Clarke's essay on the Industrial Basis of Socialism in *Fabian Essays*.

complete than such negative criticism. They must be seen not as an essential part of the socialist and labour movement (however effective or ineffective, reformist or radical), but as an 'accidental' one. Their history must be written not in terms of the socialist revival of the 1880s, but in terms of the middle-class reactions to the breakdown of mid-Victorian certainties, the rise of new strata, new structures, new policies, within British capitalism: as an adaptation of the British middle classes to the era of imperialism. We would then still have to explain why the Society arose within the small socialist movement of the 1880s (and not, like the other social reforming or imperialist trends of the middle and upper classes, outside it or on its fringes); why they remained within its orbit, and indeed gravitated further towards it; and why several leading individuals among them were always, as their subsequent development demonstrated, socialists within the traditional meaning of the term, and not merely people who used the word socialism as a vague or convenient pseudonym for aims which did not, fundamentally, imply the socialization of the economy.

These are lesser questions, especially the last, which may largely be reduced to the biographical problem of a few individuals. Nevertheless they must be answered. Yet if the Fabians are seen, as I have suggested, as the expression of a 'new social stratum', they can be answered without much difficulty. For the position of the new salaried professional, administrative, technological and intellectual cadres of post-*laissez-faire* capitalism is a double-edged one. Largely indispensable in the modern versions of the capitalist economy, often recruited from the established middle classes or assimilated socially (and in the case of industrial managers, financially) to the wealthy class, neither private enterprise nor the profit motive are essential to their functioning.[20] Moreover (as in the case of the Fabians), they are often an élite of intelligence and ability, recruited from below. There may be social and historical reasons why the members of such strata should consider their fortunes linked to those of capitalism, but, as Sidney Webb was never tired of repeating, no *functional* ones. A 'socialism' equally adaptable to operating under post-*laissez-faire* capitalism or socialism expresses this situation perfectly.

Two final questions arise, if the argument so far has been accepted. The first is why the leading Fabians should have expected, in the actual situation of Britain, the 'new social stratum' to have abandoned the lure of the capitalist fleshpots for the less tangible rewards of socialism; the second, why in social terms such an ideology should have arisen at this time in Britain and not elsewhere.

The first of these questions can also be answered fairly easily. The Fabian view of what rewards the professional should expect is clear. In material terms they are, as we have seen, 'a certain conception of what constitutes a becoming livelihood in (a given) class of society . . . (and) an income representing that standard'.[21] In non-material terms they are the rewards of interesting and creative work, 'a life of fascinating interest to the exercise of faculty, and in the consciousness of service rendered, rather than in accumulating riches for themselves and their descendants'.[22] It is interesting that the writer and especially the scientist should serve as the Fabian model here, but even more interesting that the socialist professional of the future should so strikingly resemble the ideal type of the liberal professional middle class of Victorian Britain: sufficiently comfortable not to need to pursue money for material reasons, sufficiently secure in an accepted and respected social rank to be genuinely without envy of the idle rich or the business profiteers, sufficiently interested in their work to pursue it for their own sake, and sufficiently at one with society to feel themselves to be of social use. Among the many failures of the Fabians, the failure to analyse the nature and historical basis of their model of the socialist élite is not the least striking.

Our second question is already partly answered. The rest of the answer, we suggest, is as follows. Fabianism emerged in Britain and not elsewhere, because in Britain the 'nouvelle couche sociale' was indeed new. The educated senior administrator or bureaucrat, the technologically or scientifically trained manager or businessman, even the office-worker, or for that matter a national system of primary, secondary and higher education, were commonplace in Germany and France from the early nineteenth century, but not in Britain. The archaism of Britain's economic, social and political structure, which explains why any departure from Manchester practice in Cobden's day could genuinely appear indistinguishable from socialism to intelligent men, also explains why the sort of people whom the Fabians believed themselves to represent and to whom they appealed, only emerged en masse in the last thirty years before 1914. As late as 1897 a capable observer of the British scene[23] could still marvel at the first results of primary education and selection by examination. The first London Board School boys who entered the higher civil service, the Church or public school teaching, were still worth recording by name.

The transformation of journalism into 'a liberal profession attracting specialists of all kinds to its columns' was a matter of yesterday. Public administration, which had grown modestly to little more than 100,000 occupied males by 1881 was about to rise to almost 300,000 by 1911; the professions (and their subordinate services) which had risen by a third between 1851 and 1881, were about to rise by two-thirds in the next thirty years. A new stratum was coming into existence. It is never easy for such a group, especially in its earlier stages, to fit into a social structure not designed to hold it, and which it is not strong enough to modify. The middle-class socialism of the Fabians reflects the unwillingness, or the inability, of the people for whom they spoke, to find a firm place in the middle- and upper-class structure of late Victorian Britain.

APPENDIX

Social Composition of the Fabian Society 1890–1907

	1890	1892	1904	1906
Total membership	188	626 (*a*)	767	1,060
Size of sample	67	197	194	244
Workers: at trade	7	48	19	15
not at trade	2	6	15	19
Total (*b*)	9	54	34	34
Middle class jobs:				
(1) Journalists, writers (*c*)	12	32	19	31
(2) Universities	4	10	33	44
(3) Teachers	5	17	13	14
(4) Social and Political (*d*)	4	6	9	13
(5) Public Officials (*e*)	6	8	13	13
(6) Law	1	2	3	7
(7) Business, commerce	3	5	8	8
(8) Arts (*f*)	3	5	6	9
(9) 'Lower middle class' (*g*)	–	14	8	9
(10) 'Professional' (*g*)	5	8	4	6
(11) Doctors	4	8	13	17
(12) Clergy	11	28	31	39
Women	49	117	140	253
	116	314	334	497

For this period several printed membership lists are available, from which I have attempted to trace the occupations of as many Fabians as possible. The sources for this analysis are too numerous to mention, but – such was the character of the Fabian Society – biographical indications are available for a good many members. The resulting sample is not, of course, representative. The number of clergymen, doctors and trade unionists, which is likely to be more or less exhaustive, may serve as a check on the remainder.

Groups 1–10 include some women whose professions are known; but the majority were not yet professionally occupied.

Notes:

(a) without provincial members.

(b) Estimate. TU membership has been taken as criterion. 'Not at trade' refers to men like Keir Hardie, by then full-time politicians or functionaries.

(c) Estimate. People believed to earn most of their income or spend most of their time writing have been counted. This group overlaps with (4).

(d) Settlement work, Charity Organization, Parliament, full-time organizing or propaganda. The numbers do *not* include the similar 'workers not at trade'.

(e) Only some of these are Higher Civil Servants.

(f) Painting, crafts, theatre, music. Technical art firms, like Morris' Emery Walker are, however, under (10).

(g) (9) and (10) are very tentative. (9) comprises shopkeepers, billposters, printers, bookmakers, boarding-house keepers, insurance agents, commercial travellers and clerks. (10) includes scientists, technicians, accountants, publishers, librarians, higher salaried and managerial jobs. But the two are best lumped together as 'black-coated'.

NOTES

1 B. C. Roberts, *The Trades Union Congress 1868–1921* (London 1958), pp. 360–4.

2 M. I. Cole, *The Story of Fabian Socialism* (London 1961), p. 252.

3 B. Webb: *Our Partnership* (London 1948), p. 490.

4 'The personal duty of the rich' in *The Christian Socialist* IV, 1888, p. 427.

5 Cf., Shaw's second Fabian essay, Fabian Tract 41, pp. 26–8; S. Webb's *Socialism in England*, p. 37; Shaw's Memorandum on the Fabian Reform Committee of 13 Dec. 1911 in the *Fabian Papers*; the Webbs in the *New Statesman* I, p. 686, and, developing the theory more fully, in *Decay of Capitalist Civilization*, pp. 121–5.

6 Cf., G. B. Shaw, *Socialism and Superior Brains*, 1894 (Fabian Tract

146, 1909) *passim*, but esp. pp. 15–18; *The Case for Equality* (National Liberal Club, Political & Economic Circle, Transactions: 85, 1913), pp. 6–7. Shaw's argument is mainly in favour of equal incomes, though it should be noted that it implies – and indeed glories in – the superiority of talent of the professional *élite*. But it can also be taken, and by the Webbs is so taken, as an argument for the socialist as against the capitalist incentive to labour. This, in a modest formulation is: 'Wherever you turn you find in every class of society a certain conception of what constitutes a becoming livelihood in that class of society; and everybody in it aims at and claims an income representing that standard. Nobody seriously asks to have more than the other persons of his class' (*The Case*, p. 6). In a more ambitious formulation it is 'the very first peculiarity of exceptional ability, namely that, unlike mere brute capacity for the drudgery of routine labour, it is exercised for its own sake, and makes its possessor the most miserable of men if it is condemned to inaction'. (*S. and S.B.*, p. 18.)

7 *To-Day*, N.S.7, Jan.–June 1887, pp. 67–8.

8 'Whereas the presumption must always be that our recruits from the professions and from business would not have joined us, if they had not lacked the exceptional energy and practical turn which still enable men to make fortunes. . . . Speaking for myself as a professional man . . . I may say that the more my ability becomes known, the more do I find myself pressed to shovel guineas into my own pockets instead of writing Fabian papers. . . . Every clever and warm-hearted young gentleman bachelor enjoys from two to ten years of disinterestedness, during which good work can be got from him, but in the long run he gets tired of being disinterested.' F. Tract 41, p. 27.

9 'All through the tale two views are possible, and we shall take the one or the other according to our knowledge and temperament.' F. Tract 69, 1896, p. 17.).

10 Ibid., pp. 4, 6.

11 G. S. Baden Powell, *State Aid and State Interference* (London 1882), p. 29.

12 A. Métin. *Le socialismse en Angleterre* (Paris 1897), p. 20.

13 Cf., Cairnes, *Some Leading Principles*, p. 316, objecting to J. S. Mill's use of the word; Sidgwick, *Principles of Political Economy*, p. 527; Milner's Whitechapel lectures (*Nat. Rev.*, 1931, pp. 37 ff., 642), Morley, *Life of Cobden* (1903 edn), p. 303.

14 Cf., the excellent B. Semmel, *Imperialism and Social Reform* (London 1960).

15 In addition to the well-known passages from Beatrice Webb (*Our Partnership*, p. 205) and from Shaw (Undershaft in *Major Barbara*, the only half-ironic *Socialism for Millionaires*), it is worth referring to Sidney Ball's *Moral Aspects of Socialism* (F. Tract 72, 1896), with its defence of industrial concentration – 'a monopoly, not of privilege but of efficiency', and esp. H. W. Macrosty's *The Trust Movement in British Industry* (London 1907). The author, a senior civil servant and member of the Fabian executive, opposes trust-busting, and justifies British combinations as being dependent 'solely upon their efficiency as instruments of production and distribution' (p. 345).

16 *Labour Leader* 8 June 1901. Cf., also E. Aves in *Economic Journal*, 1898, p. 512; L. T. Hobhouse, *Democracy and Reaction*, 1904, and *The Nation*, 1907, p. 182 ('The career of Fabianism').

17 *Zur Theorie und Geschichte des Socialismus* II (Berlin 1904), p. 38.

18 Margaret Cole, *The story of Fabian Socialism* (London 1961), XIV.

19 Shaw in F. Tract 70, p. 3.

20 'And just as a manager has become necessary for every enterprise of more than inconsiderable size, so we can confidently predict that . . . he will remain for all time an indispensable functionary, whatever may be the form of society.' S. Webb, *The Works Manager To-day* (London 1917), pp. 5–6. The whole of this little book is extremely revealing.

21 Shaw, *The case for equality*, p. 6. Cf., also Webb, *Works Manager*, p. 156.

22 Webb, *Works Manager*, p. 157.

23 T. H. S. Escott, *Social Transformations of the Victorian Age* (London 1897).

15

The Labour Aristocracy in
Nineteenth-century Britain

THE PHRASE 'aristocracy of labour' seems to have been used from the middle of the nineteenth century at least to describe certain distinctive upper strata of the working class, better paid, better treated and generally regarded as more 'respectable' and politically moderate than the mass of the proletariat. This essay is an attempt to survey what we know about the labour aristocrats in the nineteenth century. It falls into three parts: a general introduction, an attempt to estimate the size of the stratum in various periods, and a discussion of some special problems of it.

I. SOME GENERAL POINTS

The sub-divisions of the nineteenth century. The history of the century, and with it of the working class, falls into three fairly well defined periods, each of which consists of a phase of general business prosperity (1780s to the end of the Napoleonic Wars, 1840s to early 1870s, late 1890s to the First World War) succeeded by a phase of general business difficulties (1815–40s, the 'Great Depression' of the 1870s–90s, the crisis between the wars). The first period (1780s–1840s), the classical age of the 'Industrial Revolution' saw the birth of the modern working class. The second (1840s–90s) saw capitalism as erected on the earlier foundations, rule supreme. It may be regarded as the classical period of the nineteenth-century labour aristocracy. With the third (1890s–1939) we enter the age of imperialism and monopoly capitalism, and, technically speaking, of the development of mass production, and the great expansion of secondary and tertiary industries. We also enter the period of the permanent

272

crisis of the British capitalist economy. However, the most striking changes occurred after 1914. The first half of the period has been included in this discussion, chiefly because the mass of statistical enquiries made between 1890 and 1914 cast an invaluable retrospective light on the nineteenth century.

What is a labour aristocracy?

There is no single, simple criterion of membership of a labour aristocracy. At least six different factors should, theoretically, be considered. *First*, the level and regularity of a worker's earnings; *second*, his prospects of social security; *third*, his conditions of work, including the way he was treated by foremen and masters; *fourth*, his relations with the social strata above and below him; *fifth*, his general conditions of living; *lastly* his prospects of future advancement and those of his children. Of these the first is incomparably the most important, and also the only one about which we have anything like comprehensive information, however inadequate. We may therefore use it as our main criterion. Throughout the century the man who earned a good regular wage was also the man who put enough by to avoid the Poor Law, to live outside the worst slum areas, to be treated with some respect and dignity by employers and to have some freedom of choice in his job, to give his children a chance of a better education and so on. The regularity of the earnings is important. Workers who earned good, but irregular or fluctuating wages, were not normally regarded as labour aristocrats in the national sense – for instance gas-stokers, almost two-thirds of whom earned 35s. a week in 1906.[1] They did, however, in certain instances, regard themselves as aristocrats compared with the mass of their fellow-workers; as for instance, London stevedores did, compared with ordinary dock labourers.

The nature of the labour aristocracy

Socially speaking the best-paid stratum of the working class merged with what may be loosely called the 'lower middle class'. Indeed the term 'lower middle class' was sometimes used to include the aristocracy of labour.[2] In the earlier part of the century this would mean mainly small shopkeepers, some independent masters, foremen and managers (who were generally promoted workers). Towards the end of the century it would also mean clerks and the like. Thus in Bolton in the 1890s it included 'the best-paid clerks, book-keepers, managers

273

and the better sort of working folk'[3] (as distinct from the 'employers, clergymen, solicitors, physicians, tradesmen on a large scale'). In Salford, about the same time, it was reckoned to include 'commercial travellers . . . clerks, lithographic printers, joiners, cabinet-makers, grocers' assistants and down to colliers'[4] – skilled labour aristocrats being, if anything, superior in social status to many white-collar workers. The most comprehensive picture of this composite stratum is given by the Departmental Committee on Pupil Teachers, since this occupation seems to have been mainly drawn from its children. In Birmingham they came from among children of workers (40 per cent) and managers of small works, clerks (15 per cent) and trades-people. In Merthyr they came from among colliers (since practically nobody else lived there) 'or a class slightly removed from it – that of overmen at collieries and gaffers as they call them'. In Bradford they came from a 'better-off class', in Manchester from among 'labourers, mechanics or small shopkeepers', in Lambeth from 'artisan class and tradesmen class', in Exeter from 'clerks and a certain proportion of foremen or cashiers in shops'. The entrants to a Chelsea training college were drawn from carpenters and joiners, clerks, gardeners, tailors and drapers, commercial travellers and agents, engineers, blacksmiths and wheelwrights, painters, machine-workers in mills, managers or sub-managers in mills, grocers, boot- and shoemakers, cabinet-makers, farmers, accountants and butlers (as well as orphans and schoolteachers).[5] However, we must remember that many nineteenth-century British communities consisted almost completely of manual workers,[6] so that the aristocracy of labour would be virtually unalloyed.

This shading-over of the aristocracy of labour into other strata is important, for it helps to explain its political attitudes. Thus its persistent liberal-radicalism in the nineteenth century is easily understood,* as also its failure to form an independent working-class party. Only when imperialism began to cut off the aristocracy of labour (a) from the managerial and small-master class with whom it had merged and, (b) from the vastly expanded white-collared classes – a new, and

---

* Before the period of imperialism, conservative groups among the labour aristocracy occur, e.g., among cotton-spinners, but can normally be accounted for by special circumstances such as liberal opposition to the Factory Acts, exceptional local weakness of the nonconformist sects, dependence on an aristocratic clientèle, recent emergence from a conservative environment in country or small town, etc. On the whole they are exceptional.

politically conservative labour aristocracy – did a labour party attract them.

If the boundaries of the labour aristocracy were fluid on one side of its territory, they were precise on another. An 'artisan' or 'craftsman' was not under any circumstances to be confused with a 'labourer'. 'The artisan creed with regard to the labourers is that the latter are an inferior class and that they should be made to know and kept in their place.'[7] The secretary of the Boilermakers' Union was appalled at the thought of a labourer being allowed to do craftsman's work for 'it would not be desirable for a man of one class to go to another class'; the secretary of the Operative Spinners was certain that his men differed from the piecers and the less skilled in general in their superior ability. 'The employers have had a splendid selection and they select the giants . . . in working capacity.'[8] Before the rise of the New Unions of 1889 the boundaries of the aristocracy and of trade unionism were normally – for the great waves of general and un- skilled organization were temporary – believed to coincide, insofar as these were any unions at all. 'As his title of "unskilled" implies,' wrote A Working Man, 'he has no handicraft and he has no union.'[9] In fact it was commonly believed that unions did not make groups of workers strong so much as indicate that they were already strong.[10] There was truth in this identification of the labour aristocracy with the unionists: the trade union register of 1871 London shows how few, and how weak, the union branches were in the East End dis- tricts.[11] The frontier between labour aristocrats and others was often a geographical one.

Between the 'labourers' and the labour aristocracy there lived workers who belonged to neither group, but shaded into each: better- off labourers, ordinary skilled workers and suchlike. No clear line divided the labour aristocracy from these, though the aristocrat would certainly regard himself as superior in kind to these 'men who, while very honest and anxious to do well, yet from deficiency of education, and perhaps some lack of moral strength and courage . . . [are] not . . . equal to the first class of men.'[12] Indeed the superficial observer might sometimes see the working class merely as a complex of sectional groups and grades with their social superiority and inferiority, without observing the major divisions.

II. THE SIZE OF THE LABOUR ARISTOCRACY

Up to the 1840s

It is doubtful whether in this period we can speak of a labour aristoc-racy at all, though its elements already existed. It is even doubtful whether we can speak of a proletariat in the developed sense at all, for this class was still in the process of emerging from the mass of petty producers, small masters, countrymen, etc., of pre-industrial society, though in certain regions and industries it had already taken fairly definite shape.* This makes the process of analysis extremely difficult. In this period it is probably simpler to operate with the concept of the 'working people' or 'labouring poor' which was then much in use[13] – i.e., to include all those who were exploited and oppressed by industrial capitalism in one group: definite proletarians, semi-proletarian outworkers, small producers and traders in revolt against large capitalists, and the peculiar transitional and interme-diate forms between them.[14] Nevertheless it may be useful from the point of view of analysis to isolate that section of the 'labouring poor' which may be regarded as proletarian; i.e., which consisted substantially of wage-workers who possessed no significant means of production.

We have no general estimates of the proportion of the 'labouring poor' which was proletarian, mainly because contemporary statis-ticians automatically classed skilled and specialized workers with masters and independent producers, distinguishing masters only in agriculture, though they habitually isolated 'labourers' – i.e., the unskilled, the miners and similar groups as a separate class.[15] If we take that section of the country which was still pre-industrial, i.e., those employed 'in retail trade and in handicrafts as masters or workers' in 1841, and compare it with the numbers described as (non-agricultural) labourers, we find that in the English agricultural counties the labourers formed between one-sixth and one-half of the number of craft masters and workmen, and normally between one-quarter and one-third. Their proportion in urbanized areas such as

* Of course *in effect* most British workers already depended wholly on their wages for subsistence; but the *form* of these wages was still often – as among domestic outworkers, some types of miners, etc., that of a price for *commodities* sold (e.g., pieces of cloth) rather than *labour power* sold. The point where such payment ceases to be a price for goods and becomes a piece-rate wage is not always easy to determine in a period of transition.

Middlesex, Surrey, Kent, Edinburgh, York City was much the same, though perhaps a little higher.[16] That for the purely agricultural Scottish counties was much lower. Within the 'masters and workmen' the proportion of each, and of independent petty commodity producers varied. In 1851 (the first Census which made – partial – returns distinguishing masters from workmen) about 80 per cent of master-tailors, about 71 per cent of master-shoemakers, almost 90 per cent of master-blacksmiths employed 0–2 men, though about 60 per cent of master-builders, just over 60 per cent of tanners, rather over 50 per cent brewers and rather under half of machine and engine-makers employed between 3 and 19 men. (The first three groups comprised 8 per cent of the non-agricultural male population of ten years and over, the second four somewhat more.)[17] We may therefore assume, as a rough guess, that in the unrevolutionized industries the wage-earners might average between 50 and 80 per cent of the occupied population, the non-labourers forming at least half of them, and probably very much more. (The building industry is exceptional among craft industries in the high proportion of labourers to crafts-men.) Two pieces of evidence bearing on the matter may be given for what they are worth. An investigation in Hull city in 1839, which distinguished employed from non-employed handicraftsmen, shows about 75 per cent of the occupied population to have been workers.[18] A single zealous enumerator in Newcastle did the same in 1851: about 80 per cent of those classified as neither masters nor labourers or watermen were thus enumerated as 'journeymen', i.e., wage-earn-ers.[19] A rather fuller sample of 12 enumeration districts in Newcastle shows the number of labourers to be about equal to the combined number of journeymen and other non-masters. A sample of five enumeration districts in Bristol gives a somewhat lower proportion of labourers to journeymen, though the difference may not be significant.

In the factory industries – textiles, mining, iron and steel – the proportion of full-time wage earners was of course much higher, for the semi-proletarian outworkers—framework knitters, handloom weavers, etc. – must be reckoned among them. The proportion of unskilled was also notably higher, even where women and child labour was not prevalent. However, all but a few supervisory and specialist workers in these occupations were often still regarded as 'labourers', though of a superior kind.

In general, therefore, it is best for this period not to separate the elements of a proletarian 'aristocracy' from the rest of the 'labouring

277

poor'. An enquiry in Bristol in 1838 established that 15·7 per cent of the heads of working-class families were depositors in savings banks, members of benefit societies or of trade clubs. That in Hull in 1839 shows between 10 and 13 per cent of workers to have possessed 'amply furnished' dwellings, as against between 25 and 30 per cent of 'ill-furnished' ones, which is perhaps a more accurate criterion.[20] This may serve as a rough guide to the size of the upper stratum of the 'working population'. Beyond this we can, of course, establish individual categories of workers who can be regarded as labour aristocrats, and who sometimes showed the typical conservatism and sectional exclusiveness of their type; notably among those craftsmen whose position was substantially unaffected, where it was not actually strengthened, by the industrial revolution: printers, metal-workers,[21] craft producers of luxury goods and the like. It is no accident that the Manchester compositors refused to celebrate the Reform Bill[22] while the ironfounders eschewed strikes and believed in peaceful negotiation, and the engineers failed to take part in the movement for General Union and remained neutral in 1842.[23] Indeed it is hard to think of a machine-builder or ironfounder who was prominent in the great movements of 1830–42, though plenty of other craftsmen were. However, the changes affecting even those who between 1780 and 1815 could have been regarded as labour aristocrats were so complex and far-reaching, that it is best not to attempt a general assessment.*

1840–90s

In this period the problem of the intermediate and transitional strata becomes less troublesome. At any rate a proletariat in the strict sense is now easier to discern – though one working in small units of production. Nevertheless, a large though diminishing zone of petty

---

* These calculations throw some light on the much-discussed problem of what happened to the working-class standard of living. The classical view that it declined in the period after 1815 has been queried by Clapham, Ashton and other economic historians. Their argument rests mainly on the contention that indices of real wages rose between 1815 and the 1840s. It has already been undermined by the doubts which have been thrown on the cost-of-living statistics on which it rests. Still, it can be shown that the real wages of *some* workers probably rose. But if, as I have here argued, the favoured strata of the working population were much less numerous than the rest, the optimistic view falls to the ground. However, this is not the place to pursue this important discussion. See above, Chapters 5–7 (pp. 64 seq).

workshop production still surrounded modern industry. If factory bootmaking and tailoring made progress, especially from the 1870s, in 1891 there was still in Scotland one master to every four wage-earning tailors, one to every two shoemakers. If lace, hosiery, wool, jute and the rest of textiles became factory trades, the numerous small metal industries of the Birmingham and Sheffield areas remained complexes of specialized workshop and outwork production. Indeed in the Birmingham area as late as 1931 almost 10 per cent of those employed in foundry and secondary processes and 'other metal industries', and 25 per cent of those employed in the jewellery and plate industry – and these industries comprised 120,000 persons – were employers or independent producers.[24] Nevertheless, though small-scale production renews itself at every stage of capitalist development to some extent, it does and did so on a decreasing scale and in increasing dependence on large-scale enterprise.

Some general estimates for the size of the labour aristocracy during this period may be made. The first is Dudley Baxter's estimate of that section of the working class which earned an average wage-rate of 28s. or more in 1867. This comprised 0·83 million men out of 7·8 million working-class men, women and children (including agricultural workers and domestic servants) or about 11 per cent. If we deduct agricultural labourers and female domestic servants the percentage is something under 15.[25] The second is based on the membership of the trade unions before the 1889 expansion – i.e., of the characteristic 'strong bargainers' of this period. The first reliable estimate of general trade union membership, that of the Webbs in 1892, puts it at about 20 per cent of the working class, which is probably on the high side. If we halve this to allow for organized non-aristocratic (women cotton-workers, many miners, unskilled unions of 1889 vintage, etc.) we shall not go far wrong.* It may be recalled that Mayhew estimated the percentage of society men in the average London craft at about 10.[26] These estimates are really based on more or less plausible guesses, and are here given only because they are not inconsistent with the better ones for the subsequent period.

* Trade union membership statistics before the expansion of 1871–3 are unrepresentative except for isolated crafts or towns. Those of the mid-seventies – after the subsidence of the influx of 1871–3 but before the contraction of the Great Depression – are vitiated by the uneven organization of different 'aristocratic' trades. Hence those of 1890–4, minus the 'non-aristocrats', are the best guide.

An estimate, also based on Baxter, of the size of the lower stratum – those earning less than 20s. – may be given for the sake of completeness. It amounts to 3·3 millions or just over 40 per cent of the working class, exclusive of agricultural labourers, soldiers and pensioners and women domestic servants.[27] This percentage is also curiously like those revealed by subsequent social surveys.

For the actual composition of this aristocracy Baxter is an unreliable guide, since his estimates neglect irregularity of earnings altogether and average the very high and very low earners in each trade in the habitual fashion of Victorian investigators. The composition of the trade union movement in 1875 is a better guide. Somewhat more than half of it was made up of craftsmen in trades little affected (except in their materials and in the power applied to manual tools) by the industrial revolution: builders, engineers, shipbuilders and the like, and various older crafts (printers, cabinet-makers, tailors, glass-

Table I. *Trades in 1865 with weekly wage-rates of 40 shillings and above*

Source: Leone Levi, *Wages and Earnings of the Working Classes* (1867)

Dockyards: some shipwrights
Railways: some engine drivers
Bookbinding: pieceworkers
finishers
forwarders
Scientific instruments: most workers
Cutlery: file-forgers, strikers, grinders (esp. over 12 in.), saw-makers, many saw-grinders
Shipbuilding: some foremen
Cabinet-makers: some
Hatters: many skilled hand-workers
Jewellery: many skilled men
Iron: some slingers; more forge-rollers; many blacksmiths and strikers

Textiles: calico printing; colour mixers, bleachers, dyers, machine printers, die cutters
Leather: London curriers
Glass: many skilled men
Printing: newspaper compositors, readers, some machine minders and engineers
Musical Instrument Makers: some
Lithographers: many
Woodcarvers: many
Watchmakers: many; some clockmakers
Hosiery: some factory overlookers
Bone and Ivory Turners: some
Pottery: clay modellers, many throwers, many biscuit firemen
Steel: most melters, forgemen and tilters, rollers

* Wages paid by skilled men to their labourers to be deducted. In the iron and steel trades allowance for this has been made.

280

bottle makers, bookbinders, coachmakers and the like). The rest was composed mainly of miners, iron and steel workers and skilled textile operatives of whom the last were the smallest, but numerically the most stable group. A list of the trades with the highest weekly wage-rates may supplement this (see Table I, previous page).

This table indicates the composition of the super-aristocracy rather than the run-of-the-mill of prosperous artisans and may be compared with that for the period 1890–1914 (see Table V, p. 288). We may note that a list compiled for the first half of the century would not have read very differently.

Can we track the labour aristocracy down more closely? Not to the point of making reliable numerical estimates.* Nevertheless, a general survey is possible. Three facts stand out: the decline of domestic work and the corresponding rise of the factory system; the relative decline of textiles and the old consumer-goods trades and the rise of the heavy and metal-working industries; the rise of woman labour. All three are connected. Thus the rise of woman labour is statistically masked by its decline in some domestic industries: while the percentage of occupied women did not increase significantly between 1851 and 1891, no less than 122,000 disappeared from such occupations as ribbon, lace, straw hat, shirt and glove manufacture and sewing.[28]

The decline in domestic work may or may not have increased the proportion of labour aristocrats, or improved the position of workers in the affected industries, but it made the aristocracy of labour more prominent and lowered the political temperature of the industries concerned. Domestic workers in the great putting-out industries tended to live in specialized villages or town districts (e.g., Spitalfields and Cradley Heath) and were easily and obviously formed into large agglomerations dependent on one or two masters. Instances of master-nailers controlling 1,800–2,000 workers are known.[29] Thus their decline in effect *decreased* the average size of unit. In the small factory or the labyrinthine complex of interlocking specialized workshops, such as we find in the hosiery industry, the Birmingham gun trade or some Sheffield trades the indispensable craftsman or specialized operative not only was more important but saw himself to be more important. Also cohesion was more difficult. The Cradley Heath

---

* The figures of the Wage Census of 1886 are unreliable. They differ so substantially from the ranking-order of the Wage Census of 1906 – and without obvious cause – that they are best neglected. Probably the difference is due to 1886 recording wage-rates and 1906 recording earnings.

outworkers made their ill-fated attempts at trade unionism while the Birmingham craftsmen barely knew even craft societies. (The terrorism of Sheffield was a defensive reaction against the rise of the machine and the factory and the depression of a special form of subcontracting outworker, and thus does not affect the argument. In any case it was not a sign of radicalism, but an alternative to it.)[30]

The same is true of the increasing proportion of women (an index of the increasing proportion of unskilled labour) in various industries. Though this created the possibility of an organized female proletariat, which was not widely utilized before the 1880s, and then only in cotton, it tended to leave the skilled males more obviously prominent and dominant. Thus the percentage of male spinners in the total cotton factory labour force fell from 15 in 1835 to 5 in 1886,[31] while the proportion of women and adolescent girls rose from 48·1 in 1835 to 60·6 in 1907, averaging about 55 in our decades.[32] In the worsted industry the proportion of adult males (outside weaving) halved between 1853 and 1886.[33] The same is true of that of male woollen weavers in Leeds and the heavy woollen district[34] though the main decline appears to have occurred after the 1870s. In hosiery the proportion of men fell from three- to two-fifths of the total labour force between 1851 and 1891. Only in the lace industry did it rise in a declining labour-force, thanks to the decline of hand-working. Hence in those textile industries in which aristocracies of labour established themselves – cotton, hosiery, lace – they became more prominent, though the textile workers probably formed a diminishing percentage of the labour aristocracy of the whole country. (However, this may be offset by the decline of the prosperous outworkers and specialists – the wool-combers, hecklers, shearmen and the like, who had found something like an aristocracy in earlier periods.)

The same is true of other consumer-goods industries, with the exception of many small-scale workshop-metal trades. Where the factory system developed further, the situation of the labour aristocracy was similar to that in textiles, though its numbers may have been smaller and its position less assured the more 'modern' the factory system was. Factory production, or analogous systems, only gave rise to a sizeable labour aristocracy in the nineteenth century where machinery was imperfect and dependent on some significant manual skill; the British cotton industry is the only one among European industries of this type which made spinners into such an aristocracy, being the earliest and technically the most primitive.

However, in boot factories in the 1860s the aristocracy (30*s*. and over) seem to have amounted to more than 20 per cent.[35] Where expansion took the form of sub-contracting, putting-out and general sweating, labour aristocracies could maintain themselves – for instance by specializing on high-grade work – but in the midst of an increasing mass of outworkers or depressed craftsmen. Table II, below, drawn from the 1906 Census, illustrates the situation of such craft industries undergoing transition, though these are not necessarily the trades affected in 1850–90.

Table II. *Skilled occupations 1906 with abnormally high percentage of low-paid male workers*

Source: Wage Census 1906

Occupation	Percentage 'aristocrats' 40s. and more	Percentage 'plebeians' 25s. and less
Saddlery, Harness, Whips	12·5	35·4
Portmanteau, Bag, Misc. Leather	19·6	31·9
Hatters	39·7	27·8
Coopers	18·9	27·3
Cabinet-making	19	22·7
Bespoke Tailoring	29·4	41·6
Bespoke and Repair, Boot and Shoe	5·1	40·8

On balance the labour aristocracy of such trades may have declined as a proportion of the total group.

(It may be observed that the rise of factories brought about a diminution of the lowest-paid groups and an increase of the less abysmally paid. However, since the concept of the 'semi-skilled' was not yet familiar to either employers or workmen[36] they were regarded by aristocrats and others merely as labourers who worked machines.)

This decline was accentuated by the rise of almost wholly non-aristocratic industries such as transport and coal-mining, though the aristocracy in both probably increased during the period.[37] In 1851 miners, seamen, railwaymen, carters and the like formed about half a million; in 1881 over 1·3 millions. However, this rise is in fact largely a transfer of farm-labourers or other unskilled workers to somewhat better paid occupations, and thus disturbed the general working-class hierarchy less than one might think.

On the other hand the period saw an immense reinforcement of the labour aristocracy in the rise of the metal industries. Thus ironworkers trebled their numbers between 1851 and 1881, shipbuilders, engineers and the like more than trebled theirs. The percentage of skilled men in many of these industries was extremely high, perhaps as high as 70–75 in engineering,[38] and their relative position certainly improved. The rise of iron ship-building lowered the percentage of the aristocrats, which had been overwhelming on wooden ships, though not all equally prosperous,[39] and it probably stood at 50–60 per cent until the rise of automatic machines.[40] The number of printers – another industry with a high skilled percentage – also more than trebled. The case of the iron and steel industry is slightly different. The percentage of skilled men in iron was high – almost 44 in Levi's 1865 sample[41] and wages were high, but earnings were irregular and the actual amount of poverty among them appears to have been high, as was the general squalor and backwardness of their centres. Towns like Middlesbrough, Wolverhampton and Neath come near the top of any list of illiteracy or old-age pauperism.[42] Nevertheless, the abnormally high nominal wages and the universal prevalence of subcontracting made iron and steel a stronghold of the labour aristocracy.

The building trades also grew relatively, and as they retained their old structure, maintained the strength of the labour aristocracy.

The period therefore probably saw a transfer of the centre of gravity within the labour aristocracy from the old pre-industrial crafts to the new metal industries, and the emergence of some elements of a labour aristocracy in trades previously regarded (wrongly) as composed essentially of labourers. Its relative numerical strength may not, however, have increased.

From the 1890s to 1914

In this period genuinely useful statistics begin to appear. We emerge from obscurity into something like daylight. Above all, we possess reliable general estimates of the size of various working-class strata, semi-proletarian elements now being much less important than before.

Since most social surveys were more interested in isolating destitution from the rest than in separating exceptional comfort, we know more about the bottom stratum than about the top. The estimates are consistent with one another. In Booth's London the 'poor', the 'very poor' and the 'lowest class' between them formed 30·7 per cent of the total population of 40 per cent of the working class. In Rowntree's

York (1899) the equivalent classes formed 27·8 per cent of the population and 43 per cent of the working wage earners.[43] A more impressionistic estimate for the Potteries (1900) gives much the same figure: three-eighths.[44] Forty per cent is therefore a good enough rough measure of the 'submerged' section of the workers, of whom two-thirds would, at one time or another of their lives – mainly in old age – become actual paupers; the ultimate degradation.[45] It should be noted that this section is considerably larger than the number of those earning what was technically a 'labourer's wage'. Thus the families whose income was less than 21s. formed only 13·8 per cent of the York wage-earners, and the 'primary poverty line' in Bowley and Burnett-Hurst's Five Towns survey of 1910–12 was drawn above 13 or 13·5 per cent of households or 16 per cent of workers.[46] (Rowntrees' percentage of those living in 'primary poverty' was 12·7.)

Estimates for the top stratum are also fairly consistent with one another. Owen estimates it at one-eighth – say 13 per cent – in the Potteries in 1900. In Booth's sample of 75,000 London workers 17 per cent earned above 40s., but he considered this somewhat too favourable. Class 'F' in his East End investigations contained 14·9 per cent of workers.[47] However, the sample of 356,000 workers from 38 industries covered in the 1886 Wage Census included only 8·1 per cent with wages over 35s.[48] We may assume as a rough guide that the labour aristocracy included not more than 15 per cent of the working class, though it might be enlarged by the inclusion of 'the best-paid clerks, book-keepers, managers', etc. All impressions agree that they formed a smallish minority.[49]

The important point to note about this aristocracy of labour is that it did *not* include all workers who could be technically described as skilled or as craftsmen. While it is safe to say that practically no woman earned more than a labourer's wage, and almost as safe to say that few 'labourers' earned enough to join the top 15 per cent, hardly any skilled occupation lacked a percentage of men who earned a low-grade income, quite apart from the hierarchy of more or less aristocratic crafts in generally 'skilled' trades, carpenters and joiners among builders, paint-brush makers among brushmakers, newspaper comps in the printing trade, etc.[50] In stable crafts like building and engineering those earning 25s. or less in 1906 (not a bad year) formed about 10 per cent. However, other crafts might, as we have seen, carry a much longer 'tail'.

285

The actual size of the aristocracy varied greatly from one industry to another. We may conveniently divide the industries into three groups: those in which the aristocracy formed about 20 per cent of the total males in 1906, those in which it formed about 10 per cent and those in which it formed significantly less than 10 per cent:

Table III. *Industries with high, medium and low proportion of labour aristocrats in 1906*

Source: Wage Census. (N.B. This did not include coal mining)

Male workers earning	40s. and more	45s. and more
High		
Iron and Steel manufacture	26·8	19·6
Engineering, Boilermaking	21·2	11·3
Shipbuilding	22	14·9
'Various metal industries'	20	11·4
Cotton	18·6	10·1
Building	18·2	6·8
Cabinet-making, etc.	19·1	9·0
Printing	31·6	19·2
Hosiery	19·1	10·6
Medium		
Clothing	11·2	6·2
Pottery	11·3	6·1
Miscellaneous Trades*	10·3	5·4
Chemicals	9·3	4·6
Railways	8·7	5·6
Public Utilities	8·5	3·6
Low		
Food, Drink, Tobacco	7·8	3·7
Wool	5·7	3·0
Ready-made Boot and Shoe	5·4	2·1
Brick and Tile manufacture	5·4	2·4
India-rubber	6·8	3·6
Silk	3·4	1·4
Jute	2·2	0·8
Linen	4·9	2·6

However, the level of the labour aristocracy is not measured absolutely but also relatively. Hence it is important to distinguish those

* Tanning, coach-building, brush-making, seed-crushing, harbour, dock and canal service, carting, india-rubber, linoleum, saddlery, etc., portmanteau-making, etc., musical instruments, umbrellas, coopers, coal storing and carting, other miscellaneous.

industries in which the aristocrats had below them an abnormally large amount of low-paid labour, and the others. The following table brings this out:

Table IV. *Percentage of 'plebeians' in certain industries, 1906*

Male workers earning 25 shillings and less

High Group

Iron and Steel	31·4	Cotton	40·6
Shipbuilding	32·2	Building	25·4
Engineering and Boiler-making	29·7	Cabinet-making	22·7
		Printing	16·0
Various Metals	31·1	Hosiery	33·3

Medium Group

Clothing	36·2	Chemicals	40·3
Pottery	40·4	Railways	49·7
Miscellaneous Trades	42·4	Public Utilities	40·5

Low Group

Food, Drink, Tobacco	47·3	India-rubber	54·6
Wool	50	Silk	51·9
Ready-made Boot and Shoe	39	Jute	69·8
		Linen	66·9
Brick and Tile	50·2		

It is clear that with a few exceptions – cotton, boot and shoe, railways, and perhaps clothing – the size of the low-paid section is, roughly, inversely proportionate to that of the aristocrats. We may therefore assume that the extreme conservatism of the cotton aristocrats sprang from the knowledge that they defended positions of privilege in an industry in which, under normal circumstances, they would have stood much lower; and the somewhat less extreme conservatism of the boot and shoe workers from the fact that they had carved out an abnormally large group of 'middle incomes' from what would otherwise have been a much larger proportion of depressed ones. In fact we know that British cotton workers were the only ones of their kind in Western Europe to build permanent craft unions; boot and shoe workers the only group composed in part of mass-production factory workers to build permanent unions before the end of the nineteenth century.

Indeed, the political and economic positions of the labour aristocrats reflect one another with uncanny accuracy. The following table lists some of the best-paid occupations:

Table V. *Occupations in which more than 40 per cent of male workers earned 40 shillings or above in 1906*

Occupation	40s. and more	45s. and more
Platers (shipbuilding)	81·7	73·7
Caulkers (shipbuilding)	78·3	61·4
Cotton Spinners (80 counts and above)	77·6	52·6
Lace Makers (Lever branch)	77·4	67·0
Engine Drivers (railway)	71·7	54·9
Riveters (shipbuilding)	70·5	60·5
Platers (engineering, piece-wage)	68·5	50·3
Cotton Spinners (40–80 counts)	67·9	48·3
Cogging and Rolling (steel, piece-wage)	61·5	52·1
Riveters, Caulkers (engineering, piece)	56·7	38·0
Turners (engineering, piece)	48·8	30·4
Fitters (engineering, piece)	47·6	26·6
Cotton Spinners (below 40 counts)	44·9	20·4
Platers (engineering, time-wage)	44	16·4
Puddlers (iron and steel, piece)	39·7	27·2

Two things will strike the reader: *first*, the decisive shift of the 'super-aristocracy' from the crafts to the metals, and to a lesser extent the cotton industry, since 1867 (compare Table I); *second*, the fact that all these super-aristocrats (with the exception of railway engine drivers and one grade of engineers) belonged to trades in which piece-work was either prevalent or enforced by the unions.[51] The Amalgamated Society of Engineers, however, only tolerated it, though its highest-paid members were in fact on it. Piece-work proved to be the form of wage-payment most suited to capitalism in more ways than Marx foresaw.

With the partial exceptions of the engineers and the loco-men all the men in this list belonged to unions with an unbrokenly conservative record. The cotton-spinners invested their personal and trade union savings in the cotton mills.[52] The skilled shipyard workers in Jarrow and Newcastle did the same in their industry and the boiler-makers sent their officials to become officials in their employers' associations.[53] The lace-makers were ultra-respectable. The steel-smelters were indeed among the earliest unions to support the Labour Representation Committee. This may be because they were, in a sense, a 'new union' (formed in 1886). Steel was a peculiar industry in that it was more extensively recruited from upgraded labourers than any other aristocratic trade, and the union – probably for this reason – had industrial rather than craft tastes and was a strong supporter of the compulsory closed shop. However, its leader John Hodge was and remained a liberal and not a socialist. The older ironworkers' union refused to affiliate to the Labour Party as late as 1912.[54]

During this period, however, certain old-established members of the labour aristocracy began to feel the competition of machinery and the threat of down-grading. Once again this is reflected in their political attitudes. Not many unions affiliated to the Labour Representation Committee before the Taff Vale judgment. They were, with negligible exceptions, the chief 'new' unions of the 1889 vintage and the following 'old' unions: Brass-workers, London Bookbinders, NU Boot and Shoe Operatives, London Compositors, Painters, French Polishers, Ironfounders, Fancy Leather Workers, Shipwrights, Typographical Association. Of these the Bookbinders were in the midst of a fight against mechanization and dilution, the Compositors busy meeting the challenge of linotype and monotype machines, the French Polishers and Fancy Leather Workers typical of the crafts beset by sub-division and sub-contracting, the Ironfounders threatened by the rise of machine-moulding and the Shipwrights fighting to maintain themselves against the rising crafts of metal-shipbuilders.[55] The painters can hardly be reckoned an aristocratic trade, being in majority semi-skilled and casual. The boot and shoemakers had recently been defeated in a major battle with the employers on the issue of mechanization, and were in a phase of retreat.[56] The brass-workers faced the decline of casting and the rise of the 'less skilled' stamping and pressing, far-reaching changes in demands and a heavy defeat in Arbitration in 1900 which greatly weakened the union.[57]

To sum up: in this period the aristocracy of labour remained substantially of the same type and composition as in the third quarter of the nineteenth century, though its centre of gravity shifted further towards the metal industries.

It is not easy to sum up this discussion of the size of the labour aristocracy. Did its relative size increase or decrease? We do not really know enough to say. At a guess, it was probably no larger in the 1860s and 1870s than the favoured strata had been before 1850 (if only because of the great transfer of non-aristocratic labour from agriculture, where it remained outside the 'proletarian hierarchy', to the industrial areas). But its position as an aristocracy was much firmer. For instance, it was no longer true that slumps affected it more severely than non-aristocrats, as had once been argued.[58] From the 1870s to 1900 it probably increased. In a period of falling prices and living-costs and a new range of cheaper consumer-goods it is easier for the upper marginal strata of the intermediate or average workers to enjoy the benefits of an aristocratic standard, though the 'plebeians' probably got little out of it but a slightly less pinched subsistence. However, it is probably unsafe to conclude anything from our survey except that the labour aristocracy averaged between, say, 10 and 20 per cent of the total size of the working class, though in individual regions or industries it might be larger or smaller.

I have deliberately neglected regional variations in wage-levels. They were extremely large, though from the 1870s signs of standardization and a narrowing of the differential multiply. However, within each region the local aristocracy would occupy the same position relative to its 'plebeians', other things being equal, even though its absolute level – as in Scotland – might be more modest than elsewhere.

III. THE PLACE OF THE LABOUR ARISTOCRACY IN THE SOCIAL STRATIFICATION

In this section I shall consider three problems: the 'differential' between labour aristocrats and the rest, the distance between them and the petty-bourgeoisie and employers, and the problem of 'coexploitation'.

The 'differential'

The main reason why there is a large differential between skilled and unskilled, 'aristocratic' and 'plebeian' occupations under capitalism is that the industrial reserve army of unemployed and underemployed, which determines the general movements of wages, affects different categories of workers differently. It operates in the first instance chiefly by keeping the wages of that kind of labour which is most easily expanded, low: that is, the least skilled. A specific reason for it in Britain was that labour aristocrats generally enjoyed the power to make their labour artificially scarce, by restricting entry to the profession, or by other means. If they lost this – for instance by the uncontrollable rise of machines – they ceased, like the wool-combers, to be labour aristocrats. Hence in Victorian Britain there were always some groups of workers who lived virtually always under conditions of full employment, while a much larger mass lived virtually always in what was for employers a wonderful buyers' market. The development of capitalism was to diminish this relative security of the labour aristocrats, and the two World Wars were to remove the old pressure of the industrial reserve army on the un-skilled. Hence there has been a marked narrowing of the differential since 1914. Before then, however, these forces were not yet strong.

However, in fact another force bound together the wages of differ-ent grades by rigid differentials in trades of an old-fashioned pattern: custom.* The wage of the mason's labourer dangled from that of the journeyman mason, though it did so by a moderately elastic thread. In such industries employers who hired workers bore in mind the traditional wage-scales, and workers in turn determined what sort of wage they asked for by traditional considerations: what had always been considered a 'fair' wage or an established differential; what other workers in a similar position (or in a position which seemed to be comparable) got.[59] We must therefore distinguish between two types of industry: the traditional crafts in which fixed differentials held good, and the new industries, in which capitalist considerations had swept away the older traditions, and the lower grades were con-sequently relatively worse off, the aristocrats relatively better off.[60] We should remember, however, that (a) the 'labourer's' wage in all industries was, in origin or essence always a subsistence wage and (b) that traditional elements long remained effective in British capitalism and are not yet dead. The main result of this during the nineteenth century was to allow employers to hire even labour aristocrats at much less then they might have fetched, since they were slow to learn how to charge 'what the traffic would bear' rather than what they thought a 'fair' wage for a skilled man in comparison to other skilled men and to labourers. On the other hand, under this sytem the fron-tier between the labour aristocrat and the labourer was probably much more clear-cut and fixed.

Broadly speaking, in traditional crafts the 'labourer' or 'helper' received about half the wage of the craftsman or somewhat more. Eden's *State of the Poor* estimated the wages of rural artisans in 1795 at 2s. 6d. to 3s., those of farm-labourers at 1s. 6d. a day. In Maccles-

* See Chapter 17 (pp. 344 seq).

field in 1793 artisans earned 3s., labourers 1s. 8d. Portsmouth shipwrights' wages between 1793 and 1823 averaged about double their
labourers'.[61] In most urban occupations later in the nineteenth century (and perhaps even before) the differential seems to have been
less – perhaps nearer 40 per cent – though we may doubt whether it
would be much less if we took, not the *average* earnings of craftsmen
(which include, as we have seen, a majority earning a sub-aristocratic
wage), but only those of the aristocrats. Thus in the building trades
craftsmen appear to have earned more like 30 or 40 per cent above
labourers.[62] As a general rule we may say that the differential would
come closer to 100 per cent, the stronger, more exclusive and 'aristocratic' the craft; or alternatively become greater, the lower the 'district' rate for unskilled labour (as for instance, in purely rural areas).
Thus in Manchester the labourers' rate oscillated round about 50 per
cent of the engineering fitters' rate between 1830 and 1871 while in
Leeds, where the fitters' rate was lower, so also was the differential. In
Londonderry labourers consistently earned less than half shipwrights'
wages between 1821 and 1834.[63] On balance, 100 per cent is a
sufficiently helpful guide to the difference between the highest and
lowest, though not to the intermediate grades.

The situation is rather different in the new industries, except where
the unskilled labourer's subsistence rate was the basis of the whole
wage-structure.[64] There the differential was both larger and more
elastic. Thus between 1823 and 1900 self-acting mule-spinners' wages
were never less than 221 per cent of their big piecers' and only fell
below 200 per cent of weavers' wages in four years. In the iron
industry puddlers' wages ranged between 200 and 240 per cent of
labourers' from 1850 to 1883. In bleaching the differential between
(male) hand crofters and female bleaching machine minders from
1850–83 (the latter = 100), ranged between 230 and 393. Leading
hands in the Nottingham lace trade in the 1860s earned three times
the wage of dressers and menders, or more.[65]

These exceptionally large differentials were either due to exceptionally high wages for certain workers (especially in highly cyclical
industries, in which the labour supply curve might actually slope
backward in very busy times), or to exceptionally low wages for the
unskilled; such as those of women and children, which could be
safely depressed far below the subsistence minimum. This was
specially important in trades with uncertain differentials but effective
restriction of entry; hence the constant complaints in such trades as

printing about the multiplication of apprentices and the introduction of women. However, there may have been a fixed differential even for these. At any rate Dudley Baxter believed that in most trades the average wages of a boy, woman and girl would add up to those of an adult man.[66]

What happened to these differentials during the nineteenth century? Our information about the first half is too defective to allow us to say much, but it is clear that between the 1840s and 1890 the differential widened, and that it did not substantially narrow (if indeed it did not continue to widen) between the 1890s and 1914. This conflicts with Marshall's statement that the wages of unskilled labour had risen faster than those of skilled, but Marshall's observations on the subject of skilled and unskilled labour are exceptionally unreliable (or perhaps wishful).[67]

The peculiarities in the British labour market made this period abnormally favourable to the development of high differentials. Thus Britain had throughout 1851–1911 about 108 women of working age (15 to 49 years) to every 100 men; a very large surplus of the lowest-paid type of labour, not all of which was absorbed by the rising demand for domestic servants in the second half of the century. As we have seen, domestic industries which had part-employed many women declined catastrophically after 1851 – e.g., lace, glove and straw hat-making, and certain forms of female labour in mining and agriculture also disappeared.[68] Again, child labour remained surprisingly important in this country, showing no significant tendency to diminish in important industries until very late in the century. In 1881 it was still almost 5 per cent of the total occupied population, compared to under 3 per cent in Germany.[69] Inevitably this depressed the standards of many non-aristocrats.

There is plenty of evidence that the gap between the aristocrats and the lower strata widened in the middle decades of the century, quite apart from general statements to this effect.[70] This was certainly so in the London building trades, though in this industry the differential is probably more rigid than in many others. Between 1850 and 1870 the skilled rates rose more often, and sooner by an average of three years than unskilled. The different evolution of men's and women's wages – women being *par excellence* the lowest-paid and most easily replaceable category – point the same way. In the worsted industry the men's average wage increase between 1855 and 1866–8 (1850 = 100) was 66 per cent, the women's 6 per cent. In the cotton industry the

293

average weekly earnings of self-actor spinners rose from 1850–71 by
8s. 3d., of (women) weavers by 3s. Between 1856 and 1870 the index
of the standard rate for patternmakers and fitters rose by six points,
of engineering labourers by four; comparisons for the period 1834 to
1884 in Manchester give similar results. Indeed, a Manchester engineering works shows platers' helpers to have earned slightly less in
1874 than the average of 1851 while platers' wages had risen by 25
per cent. In the Lancashire coal mines wages of unskilled dischargers
fell between 1850 and 1880, those of the semi-skilled carters rose,
those of the colliers and engineers rose even more. In the shipyards
the differential between platers and helpers was 85 per cent in 1863–5,
88 per cent in 1871–7 and 91 per cent in 1891–1900.[71] The absence of
comparable series o f earnings, or even wage-rates for skilled and
unskilled workers – due to our ignorance of unskilled wages – makes
such comparisons difficult. However, a general estimate for Lancashire 1839–59 confirms one's impression.[72]

Naturally we must not expect this differential to have widened
smoothly and steadily. There were times when unskilled wages rose
faster than skilled – e.g., in rapidly expanding areas and some booms.
There were times – especially in slumps – when they fell faster. Since
the normal wage of the unskilled was determined by a normal glut of
the labour market, we should expect it to be rather more sensitive
than the skilled wage, and hence to move much more jerkily. Thus,
according to Pollard's index of earnings in the Sheffield heavy trades
1850–1914, the fluctuations of unskilled earnings were between three
and four times as large as those of skilled foundrymen from 1850 to
1896, between two and three times as large as those of skilled
engineers. The average earnings of engineers in the decade 1890–1900
were 39 points above those of 1851–60, those of the foundrymen were
31 points higher while those of the unskilled had only risen 18 points
in spite of their much greater fluctuations (1900 = 100.)[73] It is possible that the belief in the tendency of unskilled wages to rise faster
than those of the skilled is due to a misinterpretation of this greater
tendency to fluctuate, not unaffected by bias. It is easy to observe that
unskilled wages in Sheffield rose 13 points between 1872 and 1873
(engineers rising 8 points, foundrymen's 5 points), or that they rose
24 points between 1880 and 1881 (against 13 and 6 respectively) or 20
points between 1888 and 1889 (against 3 and 4 points). It is easy to
overlook the fact that they fell 14 points in 1874–5 (against a rise of
5 and and fall of 1 point), that they fell 24 points in 1883–4 (against a

loss of 2 and 2 points), and 35 points in 1890–2 (against 14 and 10 points). Taken all in all, the general tendency for skilled wages to rise faster than unskilled over the long period is in little doubt.

Since the middle decades of the century were a period of rising prices, it follows that the aristocrats' standard of living improved relatively even more than their actual earnings. Once again, we know very little about this. There are few inventories of the possessions in a skilled worker's household.[74] Still, we know enough in general of the well-clothed and well-shod 'artisan' with his gold watch, solid furniture and solid food to point the contrast with the miserable masses who borrowed a few shillings from the pawnbroker – 60 per cent of all pledges in August 1855 were 5s. or less in value, 27 per cent 2s. 6d. or less[75] – and who lived on the margin of subsistence.[76]

It is practically certain that this trend continued until the First World War. Thus Rowe's calculations show the average percentage of unskilled workers' rates in building, in the coal mines, the cotton industry, engineering and the railways falling between 1886 and 1913 from 60·2 to 58·6 of the skilled, in spite of a slight narrowing of the differential among builders. In cotton the matter is quite clear.[77] (It is, of course, entirely likely that there were areas and times in which this was not so.) The real problem of the period of early imperialism is, how important the semi-skilled workers were, and what happened to their wages. In the period 1840s–70s they may have done slightly better than the labourers, but almost certainly – if Chadwick is any guide – their position did not improve significantly relative to the labour aristocrats. Between 1886 and 1913 they lost ground to the labour aristocracy, except – but the exception is important – in the metal industries which were undergoing the first stages of the mass-production revolution and in cotton. Their average rates in Rowe's five industries remained stable at about 77 per cent of the skilled.[78]

Aristocracy of labour and higher strata

The relation between the labour aristocracy and the higher strata almost certainly worsened during the later nineteenth century, and this began seriously to affect its status, though not its earnings. Here we are on badly surveyed territory, for little is known about such subjects as the prospects of promotion, of 'rising out of the working class' and about similar subjects.

Though the best study of the subject has been made for a small

Danish town[79] the general situation is clear. The working class has become progressively more separate from other classes and internally recruited, and the chances of its members (or their children) setting up as masters or independent producers have become progressively worse since the early days of industrialism. Nevertheless, it is evident that until the late nineteenth century the possibilities of labour aristocrats setting up independently or joining the employing classes were by no means negligible. We must, of course, neglect a good many social changes which did not take them out of that 'lower middle class' stratum to which, as we have seen, they were reckoned to belong socially.* Most of the 5 per cent of the members of the plumbers' union who set up independently every year in the 1860s† probably did not leave it; nor did the trade union leaders who set up as publicans, or printers and newsagents.[80] (Conversely, a foreman compositor, son of an independent jeweller and watchmaker, grandson of a whitesmith and stovemaker, or an engineer at BSA, son of a small independent Birmingham engineer would not feel themselves to be declassed.)[81] However, there are plenty of examples of better-off workers rising into the middle ranks of the employing class, though few of their becoming very rich. The small scale of many industries and the universal prevalence of sub-contracting made this quite possible, and indeed blurred the line between worker and master.[82] Moreover, even in those industries in which hardly any worker could hope to start a firm successfully the road to high managerial positions in the small plants lay wide open. Most cotton mill managers in the 1890s and early 1900s appear to have come from the ranks of spinners' union; just as the leading glass-bottle maker in Castleford had once been general secretary of the union. It is accepted that many iron and steel-worker managers were promoted foremen.[83]

However, it would be wrong to assume that the views of the labour aristocracy were greatly affected by the prospects – remote, in the best of cases – of leaving their stratum. What did affect them was the knowledge that they occupied a firm and accepted position just below the employers, but very far above the rest. In most Continental countries there were, even in the 1860s, plenty of rivals for this position. There were strong groups of the prosperous petty-bourgeoisie and rich peasantry; large and respected bodies of public officials, lesser priests, schoolmasters, or even office workers. There

* See above pp. 273–5.
† Calculated from its Quarterly Reports.

were systems of public, primary and secondary education which
provided alternative means of rising in the social scale to the strength,
manual dexterity, craft-training and experience of the labour aristocrat: the social difference between physical and mental labour was
much more marked, even at the lowest levels. In England (the case of
Scotland is somewhat different) none of these existed, except the
priesthood or nonconformist ministry; and the former was largely
recruited from the ruling class, while the latter often served as a link
between the labour aristocracy and the lesser ranks of the employing
class. No system of general primary education existed until 1870, of
secondary education until 1902. The white-collar and official strata
were of negligible importance. (Thus in 1841 there were only 114,000
civil servants and 'other educated persons' – which includes bankers,
merchants, brokers and agents as well as clerks, shopmen, literary and
scientific men – in England out of about 6½ million people of employ-
able age.)

The imperialist era changed all this, substituting non-managing
employers or shareholders for owner-managers, driving a wedge of
white-collar workers, and to a lesser extent of technicians and independently recruited managers between the labour aristocrats and the
'masters', reducing their relative social position, and limiting their
chances of promotion, and creating an 'alternative hierarchy' of civil
and local government servants and teachers. By 1914 this process had
certainly gone some way, though it would make itself more felt in the
South and the port towns than in the purely manufacturing or mining
communities of the North and the 'Celtic fringe'. Admittedly most of
the new strata were, in one way or another, the children of the 'lower
middle class' (including sections of the labour aristocracy), but this
did not alter their effect. At any rate it is safe to say that by the end
of the Edwardian era the gap above the labour aristocracy had
widened, though that below it had not yet significantly narrowed.[84]

Co-exploitation'

Capitalism in its early stages expands, and to some extent operates,
not so much by directly subordinating large bodies of workers to
employers, but by subcontracting exploitation and management. The
characteristic structure of an archaic industry such as that of Britain
in the early nineteenth century is one in which all grades except the
lowest labourers contain men or women who have some sort of
'profit-incentive'. Thus the engineering employer might subcontract

the building of a locomotive to a 'piece-master' who would employ
and pay his own craftsmen out of the price; and these in turn would
employ and pay their own labourers. The employer might also hire
and pay foremen, who in turn would hire, and have a financial interest
in paying such labour as did not work on subcontract. Such a laby-
rinth of interlocking subcontracts had certain advantages. It enabled
small-scale enterprise to expand operations without raising unman-
ageably-great masses of circulating capital, it provided 'incentives' to
all groups of workers worth humouring, and it enabled industry to
meet sharp fluctuations in demand without having to carry a permanent burden of overhead expenditure. (For this reason varieties of
subcontracting are still widely used in industries with great fluctuations of demand, such as the clothing trade, and in primitive
industries undertaking rapid expansion, such as the house-building
boom of the 1930s.) On the other hand it has disadvantages, which
have caused developed large-scale capitalism to abandon it for direct
management, direct employment of all grades, and the provision of
'incentives' by various forms of payment by result. Historically it
may be regarded as a transitional stage in the development of capitalist management, just as the buying and selling of civil service posts
and the hiring of armies by subcontract in the sixteenth and seventeenth centuries may be regarded as a transitional stage in the
development of modern bureaucracies and military forces. I propose
to call this phenomenon 'co-exploitation', insofar as it made many
members of the labour aristocracy into co-employers of their mates,
and their unskilled workers.[85]

How widespread was co-exploitation? What effect had it on the
nature of the labour aristocracy? The second point is easier to discuss
than the first.

It is easy to exaggerate the contribution of co-exploitation to the
constitution of an aristocracy of labour. It was almost certainly most
widespread in the first half of the century, when the aristocracy was
not fully developed. Many aristocrats opposed it in the form of subcontract and subcontracting foremanship, or even in the form of
payment by results, since they rightly felt that it was a device for
sweating them. Thus, such unquestioned labour aristocrats as the
engineers were rigidly opposed to piecework (let alone subcontract),
and perhaps succeeded in reducing payment by results, as they certainly succeeded in slowing down its expansion[86] until the period of
imperialism; while shipwrights, though used to group-subcontracts,

were overwhelmingly paid on time.[87] Trade union hostility to such systems of subcontract as 'piece-mastering', 'buttying', 'charter-mastering', etc., was fairly constant. Again, the widespread practice of skilled men paying their unskilled helpers could and did eventually harden into little more than the usual fixed differential. As such it survived in a vestigial form in cotton-spinning until 1949 and in the shipyards even later. Lastly, subcontract as a general system might well favour the emergence not so much of an aristocracy of labour as of a struggling, and often not particularly prosperous, mass of small masters and sweaters some of whom succeeded in rising clear into the employers' stratum while others relapsed from time to time into wage-labour. The typical 'sweated industries' in Britain and on the Continent were not necessarily those with a strong labour aristocracy. Thus we must consider co-exploitation as something which reinforced the position of an existing labour aristocracy rather than as something which in itself enabled it to come into existence. Probably its main result was to stress the feeling of qualitative superiority which its members had over the 'plebeians' and the intermediate workers. The foremen and supervisors who formed 3–4 per cent of the labour force in many industries in the 1860s[88] and all of whom, throughout the nineteenth century, had an element of co-exploitation and sub-contract attached to them[89] have always been so acutely conscious of this – if only in the form of the right to hire and sack – that they have generally been regarded by workers as 'boss's men'. The mere fact of paying a labourer's wage made the craftsman a superior kind of worker, not merely a better-paid one, even if he did not have an interest in actually sweating him. Moreover such relationships made it easier for labour aristocrats to maintain an exclusiveness and a restriction of numbers which might otherwise have been difficult to keep, e.g., in boilermaking and cotton.

How prevalent was co-exploitation? In the form of subcontracting it was widely prevalent in the iron and steel industry, iron ship-building, a part of coal mining (notably the Midlands), all small-scale workshop or 'sweated' trades, many transport trades such as dock-labour, in the period of rapid construction, in public works, railway and mine-construction and the like, and in several other trades. In the building and engineering industries it was certainly fighting a rear-guard action by the 1850–73 period, and in printing, where it was not uncommon, its teeth had been drawn partly by trade unionism, partly by genuinely co-operative group-contracts (though these were declining rapidly).[90] In the more general form of skilled workers hiring or paying their unskilled, or skilled workers being paid by results while their helpers were paid on time, it was also prevalent in cotton, the potteries, the mines, and indeed in one form or another in most industries in which piece-work obtained. Straight subcontract was certainly declining fast from the 1870s (except for the industries and situations mentioned earlier). Comparatively little survived the First World War.[91] The same is true of skilled men co-employing the unskilled. These systems were increasingly replaced by ordinary piece-work, or (from 1900) by more 'scientific' methods of payment by results, which served to raise the earnings of many aristocrats of labour, but also served – as the event showed – to break down the barrier between them and the semi-skilled piece-workers. However, we may assume that co-exploitation coloured the relations of most labour aristocrats to the lesser grades until the last quarter of the nineteenth century; the major exceptions being the building trades, engineering and some old crafts.[92]

IV. THE LABOUR ARISTOCRACY UNDER MONOPOLY CAPITALISM

If this survey merely concluded in 1914 without a few words about the future development of the nineteenth-century labour aristocracy, it would give a misleading impression. For 1914 marks a deceptive 'Indian summer' for this stratum, as it does for British capitalism as a whole. New tendencies, which were to undermine it had already come into being, though only some had yet made themselves felt. The period from 1914 on was to see a collapse of the old labour aristocracy comparable to the collapse of the old skilled handicrafts, and the specialized key workers attached to the domestic industries – wool-combers, shearmen, hecklers and the like – in the decades after the Napoleonic Wars, though probably more serious. We may briefly note the following factors. *First*, the regions of nineteenth-century 'basic industries' (i.e., the strongholds of the then labour aristocracy) declined into the Depressed Areas of the inter-war years. *Second*, the change in systems of wage-payment caused the differential between 'skilled' and 'unskilled' to narrow steadily from 1914 until the 1950s, though in piece-working industries this was not necessarily reflected in an equivalent narrowing of earnings. *Third*, the rise of a large class of semi-skilled machine-operators mainly paid by results, and the relative diminution in numbers of the old unskilled 'fetching and carrying' kind of labourer filled much of the great gap which had once separated the aristocrat from the plebeian; moreover, in some industries mechanization actually declassed labour aristocrats. *Fourth*, the continued growth in the white-collar, managerial and technical strata (the 'office' as against the 'workshop') lowered their social position still further, relatively and perhaps absolutely; for the new technicians and managers could by now be recruited not only from sons of labour aristocrats of the old type, but also from sons and daughters of the first-generation white-collar and technical strata.

This down-grading is to some extent reflected in the change in the policy of the unions of former labour aristocrats. It is no accident that some of the most conservative unions of the later nineteenth century – engineers, boilermakers, ironfounders, and several groups of mine-workers – have today become the unions in which left-wing leadership is most marked. However, one cannot speak of a *wholesale* down-grading of the labour aristocracy. Some sections (in old-fashioned industries) maintained their differentials virtually intact – e.g., cotton, where unions have also remained very conservative. Some were protected by monopoly from the worst results of the slumps, as in iron and steel; some, like building, survived with very little major change from the nineteenth century; some like printing, had adjusted themselves to the new technological changes before 1914. Yet others benefited by the rise of new industries: cars, electrical work, light engineering and the like. Even today there are a great many groups who belong to the best-paid workers as they would have belonged to the labour aristocracy in 1900. Nevertheless, there has been a change. Even the Birmingham area, which voted for Chamberlain, conservatism and imperialism from 1886 to 1945 subsequently switched to Labour.

The analysis of the labour aristocracy under monopoly capitalism must therefore proceed somewhat differently from that of nineteenth-century capitalism. I can merely conclude by suggesting some of the lines on which it might proceed; observing that it may no longer be possible to make it simply an analysis of the best-paid strata of the British working class.[93] *First*, it will have to note the survivals and adaptations of the nineteenth-century aristocracy; including the expansion of what was then a numerically and politically very small group, the permanent full time officialdom of trade unions and the full time politicians among labour leaders. *Second*, it will have to stress the new labour aristocracy of salaried white collar, technical

301

and similar workers which (so far with sectional or temporary exceptions) considers itself so 'different' from the working class as to remain largely conservative in politics and unorganized, except in special associations. *Third*, it will have to deal with the emergence of a relatively contented stratum of 'plebeians' promoted to semi-skilled factory work, to secure jobs in and about the vastly swollen apparatus of government and so on; of those groups largely organized by the two great General Unions which, though beginning as revolutionary and even Marxist organizations have increasingly become the main strongholds of right-wing trade union policy.[94] *Lastly*, it will have seriously to consider the implications of Engels' remark that 'the English proletariat is becoming more and more bourgeois, so that this most bourgeois of all nations is apparently aiming ultimately at the possession of a bourgeois aristocracy and a bourgeois proletariat *as well* as a bourgeoisie. For a nation which exploits the whole world this is of course to a certain extent justifiable.'[95] To what extent, under the conditions of imperialism, monopoly and state-capitalism, do all – or a majority of – workers receive some benefit from the imperialist position of their country? To what extent is the whole of the British working class in the position of those North Italian strikers against whom in 1917 – as Gramsci tells[96] – a brigade of soldiers from backward Sardinia was sent. 'What have you come to Turin for?' the communists asked them. 'We have come to put down the gentlefolk who are on strike.' 'But those aren't the gentlefolk who are striking; they are workers and they are poor.' 'These chaps are all gentlefolk: they all wear a collar and tie and earn 30 lire a day. I know the poor folk and what they are dressed like. In Sassari they are poor; and we earn 1 lire 50 a day.' In the nineteenth century this problem barely arises, for such crumbs from the super profits as were thrown to the workers certainly went to the labour aristocracy and not to very many others. In the modern phase of British capitalism this may no longer be so. However, the analysis of working-class stratification, and of the political results of workers receiving sectional benefits, however small or unreal, may help us to understand the problems of the British working class in the mid-twentieth century, even if the actual divisions within it are no longer always those which were typical of the nineteenth century.

The concept of 'labour aristocracy' plays a great part in the Marxist analysis of the evolution of labour movements. It has also been used by other observers – for instance J. A. Hobson. Anti-

Marxists have tended to throw doubt upon it, as upon so many other parts of Marxist analysis. Thus a recent polemical work observes that 'the theory of the labour aristocracy is as artificial as the theory of class struggle within the peasantry.'[97] I hope that this essay has shown that, so far as the nineteenth century in Britain is concerned, it rests upon solid foundations of economic and political reality.

NOTES

1 All references to 1906 are to the relevant volumes of the *Earnings and Hours Enquiry* (Wage Census) unless otherwise stated.

2 *Dep. Cttee on Pupil Teachers*, 1898, XXVI, *passim* and esp. p. 2,692; cf., also *R. C. on Poor Law*, 1905–9, App. VIII, p. 86,298, Sir B. Browne (shipbuilder).

3 Allen Clarke, *Effects of the Factory System* (1899).

4 *Interdep. Ctee on Physical Deterioration*, 1904, XXXII, pp. 4,422–4.

5 *Pupil Teachers*, pp. 2,287–8, 8,524, 4,397, 5,329, 11,479–80, 3,471.

6 E.g., E. Potter, *Picture of a Manufacturing District* (1856), pp. 22–3. Out of an estimated population of 21,000 the middle class are estimated at 500, the non-wage-earning lower middle class at 1,500, including families.

7 Thomas Wright, *Our New Masters* (1873), pp. 3, 6. Cf., the extraordinary chapter on 'The Unskilled Labourer' in *Working Men and Women* by a Working Man (1879).

8 *R.C. Labour*, 1893–4, XXXII, pp. 2,801–10, 1892, XXXV, pp. 789–801.

9 Loc. cit. Also G. Howell: *Conflicts of Capital and Labour* (1890) p. 175.

10 Mayhew, *London Labour*, III, pp. 231–2. 'The fact of belonging to some such society which invariably distinguishes the better class of workmen from the worse.' W. B. Adams, *English Pleasure Carriages* (1837), p. 187, who for this reason does not believe unions to be dangerous. *Statistical Tables and Returns of Trade Unions* (1887); *R.C. Trade Unions* Applegarth's evidence (1867, XXXII, Q. 168).

11 *Beehive*, 25 March 1871. Thus the combined Engineers, Bricklayers, Carpenters and Masons Unions had 13 branches with 1,001 members in the present East End boroughs, but 29 with 3,204 members south of the Thames.

12 *R.C. on Aged Poor*, 1895, pp. 16,545–9, evidence of H. Allen,

secretary of the Working Jewellers' Trade Society, Birmingham. See also W. B. Adams, op. cit., pp. 188–9 for the social hierarchy among various classes of skilled carriage-makers.

13 G. Briefs, *The Proletariat* (1937), p. 6 for examples.

14 Thus Mayhew, op. cit., III, p. 311 classifies the 'poor' under three headings: artisans, labourers and petty traders.

15 HMSO: Guides to Official Sources 2. *Census Reports of Great Britain 1801–1931* (1951), pp. 27 ff.

16 Counties with a mining population have been omitted from this calculation. The most convenient source for the occupational figures of 1841 is W. F. Spackman, *An Analysis of the Occupations of the People* (1847).

17 J. H. Clapham, *An Economic History of Modern Britain*, II, p. 35 for most convenient summary of the returns. I follow Clapham in assuming – for these occupations – that masters failing to return the number of employees are mainly self-employed petty producers.

18 *J.R. Stat. S.*, IV (1841), p. 164; but the 75 per cent include many transitional types.

19 MS Returns of 1851 Census, PRO, HO 107. The enumerator reported on 552 4JD. enumer. dist. 17, pp. 434 ff.

20 B. Fripp, 'Condition of the Working Class in Bristol', *J.R. Stat. S.*, II, p. 372; 'Condition of the Working Class in Hull', ibid., V, pp. 212 ff. The figures have been calculated by deducting the number of houses belonging to the 'middle and higher ranks' (213). The higher figure is based only on the number of working-class dwellings whose furniture could be ascertained.

21 K. Marx, *Capital*, I, cap. 24 for reasons for their increased strength.

22 *Minutes of Manchester Typographical Society*, Webb. Coll. EA, XXX, p. 51 (LSE Library).

23 Webb, *Hist. TU* (1894), pp. 180–2; J. B. Jefferys, *Story of the Engineers* (1946), pp. 18, 22.

24 West Midland Group, *Conurbation* (1948), pp. 122–3.

25 D. Baxter, *The National Income* (1868) App. IV.

26 Op. cit., III, p. 231.

27 It has been arrived at as follows: Baxter's subdivisions V–VII (men earning less than 20 shillings) and *all* women and child workers; with the stated exceptions. Since prices were higher in the 1860s than at the end of the century, the limits chosen probably over-estimate the size of the labour aristocracy. In 1858 a wage of 27s. (not counting losses for bad weather) was not reckoned to be enough to keep a Liverpool building worker's

family of three children from 'poverty'; cf., *Town Life* by the author of *Liverpool Life*, etc. (1858), pp. 65–6.

28 T. A. Welton, 'On Forty Years Industrial Changes in England and Wales', *Trans. Manchester Stat. Soc.* (1897–8), pp. 153 ff. gives the figures conveniently.

29 G. C. Allen, *The Industrial Development of Birmingham and the Black Country* (1939), p. 126.

30 The best account of their movements: National Association for the Promotion of Social Science, *Report on Trade Societies* (1860), pp. 521 ff., esp. 540–1; *R.C. on Trades Unions* (1876) *passim*. See also the memoirs of Dronfield and Uttley in *Notes and Queries*, 1948, pp. 145–8, 279–80.

31 A. L. Bowley, *Wages in the Nineteenth Century* (1900), p. 117.

32 G. H. Wood, *History of Wages in the Cotton Trade* (1910), p. 136.

33 *J.R. Stat. S.*, LXV (1902), p. 109.

34 Ibid., pp. 116, 125.

35 *Miscell. Statistics*, 1866, LXXIV, p. 743.

36 I have no record of the modern use of the word 'semi-skilled' before 1894 (*Gas-workers and General Labourers' Union* Conference, p. 77) though the NED does not report it before 1926. For an early recognition of them as a group, *Workers' Union Record*, September 1916, p. 11, referring to movements at BSA Birmingham, 1904.

37 P. W. Kingsford, *Railway Labour 1830–70* (PhD Thesis, University of London Library), 1951, p. 6 shows the 'skilled' rising from about 9 to about 12 per cent between 1847–50 and 1884; but managerial and supervisory grades declined from 6·7 per cent in 1850 to 3·7 per cent in 1884.

38 J. and M. Jefferys, 'The Wages, Hours and Trade Customs of the Skilled Engineer in 1861', *Econ. Hist. Rev.*, XVII, I (1947), p. 30; *J.R. Stat. S.*, LXVIII (1905), p. 384.

39 *The Shipwrights' Journal* (Sunderland 1858), pp. 20–1 for complaints.

40 *R.C. on Trade Unions*, 1867, XXXII, p. 17,167 (35 per cent of Thames Iron Works unskilled), pp. 17,363–4 (about 50 per cent of iron shipbuilders are labourers). *R.C. Labour*, 1892, XXXVI, p. iii, Grp. A, Reply to TU Questionnaires (pp. 274–87). (58 per cent in 8 English yards, 66 in 6 Scottish ones are skilled.)

41 Levi (1865), op. cit., p. 122. Half the ' "slingers" with their helpers' have been assigned to each group.

42 See *Registrar-General's Reports* for illiteracy; C. Booth, *The Aged Poor* (1894), Lady Bell, *At The Works* (1900), p. 84, for old age pauperism.

43 B. S. Rowntree, *Poverty* (popular edition), pp. 150–1.

44 H. Owen, *The Staffordshire Potter* (1900), pp. 346–7.

45 Charles Booth in *R.C. on the Aged Poor* (1895), pp. 10,860–2.

46 A. L. Bowley and A. R. Burnett-Hurst, *Livelihood and Poverty* (1915). This survey neglects irregularities of earnings, except in the building trade.

47 Booth, IX, p. 371; I, p. 35.

48 *General Report on the Wages of the Manual Labour Classes in the UK*, pp. 1893–4, LXXXIII.

49 We do not quite know how these estimates would be affected by greater knowledge of family incomes as a whole. The pioneer figures of Bowley and Burnett-Hurst, op. cit., suggest that in some areas family incomes may have been much increased by earnings other than father's. In their sample one worker supported on average himself and 1·3 others. Earlier figures suggest that in some industrial areas the same was true (e.g., W. Nield, 'Income and Expenditure of the Working Classes in Manchester and Dukinfield in 1836 and 1841', *J.R. Stat. S.*, IV, pp. 320 ff.) But in other areas – coalfields (Bowley and Burnett-Hurst), port towns (Conditions of Working Class in Hull, *J.R. Stat. S.*, V, p. 213), etc., this was probably not so. A sample of MS Census returns for Newcastle in 1851 shows less than 5 per cent of wives working, in Bristol about 15 per cent. Booth's investigations into the family income of workers in twenty London trades – I, p. 381–show that among the higher-paid (38*s.* and above) the earnings of all other family members added only about 10 per cent to the standard weekly rate of the father. Indeed we may assume that the main function of extra earners in the family in such areas or industries was to bring the weekly income up to the normal level of the worker's grade, if the father's earnings should be insufficient to achieve this. Father's wage *was* the family income and men who could not maintain their families would rightly regard themselves as belonging to a far poorer class than the labour aristocracy and might well lose self-respect. The passionate rejection of the Means Test by workers between the wars – often declassed labour aristocrats – supports this view. However, extra family earnings may have increased the size of the labour aristocracy in some cases. On the other hand we do not know how far this was offset by the need to assist poor family members (mainly the old). The returns in Booth, *The Aged Poor* (column: Assistance from Relatives) do not provide sufficiently quantitative information, but suggest (a) that there was a lot of it, and (b) that at the very least the old people's rent

was paid, 'an indication of what is feared above all things' (p. 159).

50 Booth, V, p. 74, IX, p. 210, VI, p. 230; *R.C. Labour*, Gp. C, pp. 18,820–6, 18,860–1.

51 Webb, *Industrial Democracy* (1897), pp. i, 286.

52 Chapman and Marquis, 'The recruiting of the employing classes from the wage-earners in the cotton industry', *J.R. Stat. S.*, LXXV (1912); P. de Rousiers, *The Labour Question in Britain* (1896), pp. 261 ff.; D. M. Good, *Economic and Political Origins of the Labour Party* (Thesis, LSE Library, 1936), pp. 221–2.

53 Booth, *The Aged Poor*, p. 113; D. C. Cummings, *History of the United Society of Boilermakers* (1905), pp. 103, 119; S. Pollard, *Economic History of British Shipbuilding* 1870–1914 (PhD Thesis, University of London Library, 1950), p. 159.

54 A. Pugh, *Men of Steel* (1951), p. 81; John Hodge, *From Workman's Cottage to Windsor Castle* (1931), pp. 61, 138–9.

55 Bookbinders: E. Howe and J. Child, *The London Society of Bookbinders* (1952), chap. xxi: 'The Fight for Full Employment'; Printers: E. Howe and H. Waite, *The London Society of Compositors* (1940), pp. 202–6, S. Gillespie, *A Hundred Years of Progress* (1953), pp. 111 ff.; Ironfounders: see Reports for unemployment indices, also *Annual Report of Amal. Society of Plate and Machine Moulders* (Oldham), 1894, p. 5; Shipwrights: Pollard, op. cit., pp. 156–9.

56 A. Fox, *History of the National Union of Boot & Shoe Operatives* (1958), caps 21–2.

57 G. C. Allen, op. cit., pp. 228–31, 251–2; R. D. Best, *Brass Chandelier* (1940), chap. x, pp. 80–1; Cadbury, Matheson, Shann, *Women's Work and Wages* (1906), p. 263 and in general, W. A. Dalley, *The Life of W. J. Davis*.

58 H. Ashworth, 'Statistics of the present Depression of Trade at Bolton', *J.R. Stat. S.*, V (1842), p. 79. Hence the fear, expressed in Chartist times: 'Only pull down the artisan class of this country to the level of the labourer and the Charter will have to be granted.' *R.C. Trade Unions*, 1867, p. 8,753. The radical and Chartist movements of the 1830s and 40s were so widespread largely because the artisans with some exceptions, were in fact being temporarily pulled down.

59 J. W. F. Rowe, *Wages in Theory and Practice* (1929), pp. 156 ff. for a good discussion of this.

60 Mayhew, op. cit., III, makes this distinction very clearly.

61 Eden, *passim*. Bowley, *Wages in the Nineteenth Century*, p. 61;

'A Statistical Account of the Parish of Madron, Cornwall', *J.R. Stat. S.*, II, p. 217.

62 Postgate, *The Builders' History* (1923); A. L. Bowley, 'Statistics of Wages in the UK in the last 100 years', VI–VII, *J.R. Stat. S.*, LXIII (1900), VIII, *J.R. Stat. S.*, LXIV (1901); Bowley, op. cit., p. 90.

63 A. L. Bowley and G. Wood, 'Statistics of Wages in the UK in the last 100 years', X–XI, *J.R. Stat. S.*, LXVIII (1905), pp. 137, 376–7, 380–1.

64 Kingsford, op. cit., p. 145 for railways, *Journal of Gas Lighting* 52 (1888), p. 286 for gas. Statistics of Trevethin (Pontypool), *J.R. Stat. S.*, III, p. 370 for navvies and colliers.

65 Cotton: calculated from Wood, op. cit., p. 131; iron and bleaching: Levi (1885), pp. 143, 126; lace: *Misc. Stats.* (1866), p. 274.

66 Baxter, op. cit., p. 49.

67 *Principles*, 8th edition, p. 716. Also p. 3.

68 How widespread these were in rural areas may be seen from the 1851 Census map reprinted in Clapham, *Econ. Hist. of Modern Britain*, II.

69 K. Oldenberg, 'Statistik der jugendlichen Fabrikarbeiter', *Schmoller's Jahrbuch*, XVIII, p. 969.

70 J. D. Burn, *A glimpse at the Social Conditions of the Working Classes during the early part of the present century* (1860), p. 30.

71 Building: Bowley, *Wages in the Nineteenth Century*, p. 90; G. T. Jones, *Increasing Return* (1933), pp. 258 ff.; *J.R. Stat. S.*, LXIV (1901). Worsted: *J.R. Stat. S.*, LXV, pp. 110–111. Cotton: G. H. Wood, *Wages in the Cotton Trade* (1910), p. 131. Engineering: *J.R. Stat. S.*, LXIX, pp. 158–9; *Tr. Manchester Stat. S.*, 1884–5, pp. 13, 30; Leone Levi, *Wages and Earnings of the Working Classes* (1885), p. 102. Coal: Levi, loc. cit., p. 136. Shipyards: *J.R. Stat. S.*, LXXII, pp. 174 ff.

72 D. Chadwick, 'On the rate of Wages in Manchester and Salford and the manufacturing districts of Lancashire 1839–59', *J.R. Stat. S.*, XXIII (1859).

73 S. Pollard, 'Wages and Earnings in the Sheffield Trades, 1851–1914' in *Yorkshire Bulletin of Economic and Social Research*, VI (1954), p. 62. Dr Pollard gives an index of annual earnings for various trades, but not, unfortunately, much direct information on differentials. I have added up all the annual increases and decreases to get a rough measure of comparative wage fluctuations. It is worth pointing out that this paper is one of the more important additions to our knowledge of nineteenth-century wages since the days of Bowley and Wood.

74 Le Play: *Les Ouvriers des Deux Mondes*, 2 ser., III, p. 69: also P. de Rousiers, op. cit., pp. 14 ff.

75 *Tabular Returns on Pawnbroking* (Liverpool 1860), not paginated. (Goldsmiths' Library, pp. xix, 60 (2)).

76 Jane Walsh, *Not Like This* (1953) for a picture of the margin of subsistence even in the twentieth century; Mrs P. Reeves, *Round About a Pound a Week* (1913).

77 Rowe, op. cit., p. 49. R. Gibson, *Cotton Textile Wages in the United States and Great Britain 1860–1945* (N.Y. 1948), p. 56.

78 The shift of low-paid labour to somewhat higher-paid occupations which took place throughout the period after the 1840s – e.g., from agriculture into mining and railways, from unskilled labouring to semi-skilled work or from domestic to factory work – does not in itself affect the social stratification.

79 T. Geiger, *Soziale Umschichtungen in einer daenischen Mittelstadt* (Acta Jutlandica, 1951).

80 E.g., John Doherty (Webb, *Hist. TU*, p. 104), Martin Jude (Welbourne, *The Miners' Unions of Northumberland and Durham*, 1923, p. 61), William Newton (Webb, p. 188 n.), T. Dunning the shoemaker (Dunning's Reminiscences, *Trans. Lancs. & Chesh. Antiq. Soc.*, LIX, 1947).

81 T. A. Jackson, *Solo Trumpet* (1953), pp. 26–7, *Workers Union Record*, April 1922.

82 Nat. Ass. for Prom. Soc. Sci.: *Report on Trade Societies* (1860), pp. 530, 534.

83 Chapman and Marquis, op. cit., *R.C. Labour*, Gp. C, 30, 069–81; D. L. Burn, *Economic History of Steelmaking 1867–1939* (1939), pp. 3–12.

84 See also Cannan and Bowley, *Amount and Distribution other than Wages below the income tax exemption limit in UK* (British Ass., 1910). No good figures are available for the decline in owner-management or the rise of a separate stratum of 'technicians and managers'.

85 D. F. Schloss, *Methods of Industrial Remuneration* (1892) is the standard work. See also numerous Parliamentary Enquiries on Labour, Trade Unions, Master and Servant Acts, the Sweating System and similar subjects, and monographs of some sweated industries.

86 J. and M. Jefferys, op. cit., p. 43.

87 84·5 per cent of the 1886 sample in wood shipbuilding were paid on time. The carpenters opposed subcontracts in shipyards from 1882, *R.C. Labour, A.*, 22,077.

88 Baxter, op. cit., p. 48.

89 Schloss, op. cit., chap. xii.
90 Ibid., chap. xiii. For the localization of complaints about sub-contract in certain industries and areas, cf., *S.C. on Mines*, 1866, XIV, *S.C. on Master & Servant*, 1866, XIII, *R.C. Labour* (1891–1893), *passim*.
91 G. D. H. Cole, *The Payment of Wages* (1918) summarizes the position.
92 Webb, *Industrial Democracy*, chap. v, for the best discussion of attitudes in time and piece-work.
93 For a fuller discussion, see Chapter 16, *Trends in the British Labour Movement*, pp. 316 *seq*.
94 See Chapter 10, *General Labour Unions in Britain 1889–1913*, pp. 179 *seq*; G. D. H. Cole, *Trade Unionism and Munitions* (1923), p. 205.
95 Marx-Engels, *Selected Correspondence* (1934), pp. 115–16.
96 A. Gramsci, *La Questione Meridionale* (Rome 1951), pp. 18–19.
97 H. Seton-Watson, *The Pattern of Communist Revolution* (1953), p. 341.

APPENDIX

Some possible ways of discovering the composition of the labour aristocracy. Wage-rates and, where available, earnings have been used as the main criterion of membership of the labour aristocracy. In view of the absence of data before the 1890s some supplementary methods of analysis may be suggested. They have the disadvantage that the facts are open to different interpretations, i.e., that one must know *a priori* which interpretation is to be preferred. That is why they have not been used in the text.

The first is based on the proportion of women and children in an industry. The argument is as follows. A high proportion of women and children always argues either a low general level of wages or a large 'tail' of declassed craftsmen. However, it is not possible to determine from it whether the labour aristocracy in the industry is so small as to be negligible (as in jute) or merely distinct from the mass (as in cotton). Moreover, certain occupations are intrinsically unsuitable for women and juveniles (e.g., gas-making). An abnormally high proportion of boys in these might argue either depressed wages for men or, more likely, an abnormal advantage for the men, and hence a greater potential labour aristocracy (as perhaps in some coalfields).

The second is based on the proportion of aged workers. The

argument here is as follows. An abnormally high proportion of men past, say, sixty in an occupation indicates either that the work is very skilled and very light (as in watch-making) or that it is merely very light (as in gate-keeping) *or* that the occupation attracts the old and infirm and is thus likely to contain a high proportion of non-aristocrats. If the work is specially hard a relatively high proportion may be absolutely quite low. We may thus conclude that 'aged' occupations are either very aristocratic or very plebeian. However, we must bear in mind that in many professions it is physically impossible for old men to work at all, e.g., gas-stoking or iron-puddling.

In considering both these arguments we must remember that unskilled occupations must normally expect to contain a small percentage of the very young and very old.

The third is based on statistics of illiteracy. The argument here is a little more complicated. (*a*) It may be held that 'aristocratic' areas will be less illiterate than 'plebeian' ones. But it must be borne in mind that there is a general tendency for old economic occupations, well or badly paid, to be more literate than new ones – e.g., in the earlier nineteenth century (somewhat surprisingly) for some agriculture to be more literate than industry. (*b*) It may be held that an abnormal disparity between the literacy of men and women indicates an abnormally depressed condition of women, and hence of unskilled and low-grade labour in general.

The fourth is based on statistics of pauperism, especially in old age. Here the assumption is that the less aristocratic areas will also contain more pauperism in old age. However, as against this there is (*a*) the fact that old age pauperism will generally be smaller in tight local communities where neighbourhood and family help is common (e.g., in villages and small towns) and (*b*) that certain regions show a notably greater propensity to save for old age than others.

The first two arguments enable us to track down the labour aristocracy sectionally, the second two regionally or locally. The statistics for them are available in the Censuses, the Registrar-Generals and Poor Law Reports.

To illustrate the first point. The following table shows the proportion of boys and females in various occupations in 1865 (Source: Levi).

It would therefore seem that, in the absence of other information, the proportion of boys and females chiefly helps us to discover skilled trades with a large 'tail' of depressed workers which might otherwise be overlooked. It would be a mistake to use the figures too much – e.g., to conclude that printers in 1865 contained a less strong or marked labour aristocracy than tailors.

Proportion of boys and females in occupations, 1865

Crafts with less than 30 per cent boys, few women:

A Light crafts	B Heavier crafts	C Heavy work
*Musical Instruments	*Engineering	Sugar Boiling
*Lithographers	*Sawyers, Coopers	Millers
*Scientific Instruments	*Shipbuilding	Quarrymen
?*Men's Tailoring	?*Building	Saltmakers
*Skinners, Tanners	?*Baking	Brewers
*Watch and Clock-making	Waterworks	Soap Boilers
*Coach-making		Gas-workers
?*Harness-making		Brickmakers
*Comb-making		

D Crafts with less than 30 per cent boys, more than 30 per cent women:

*Bookbinding	*Woodcarving
Boot and Shoe	*Hatters
*Leather Case Makers	*Gold and Silver

Crafts with more than 30 per cent of boys:

E Light crafts	F Heavy or *strenuous* (over 30 per cent boys and women)
*Printing	Coalmining
?*Cabinet-making, Upholstery	?*Iron
?*Cutlery	Chemicals
?*Brushmakers	*Glass
?*Other woodwork	?*Metal, other than Iron

* known to be aristocratic, or to contain a high proportion of aristocrats.

?* containing an aristocracy, but also many depressed workers.

The second point is equally inconclusive. Thus an analysis of the Scottish census of 1861 shows that men of 60 years and over formed more than 10 per cent of the labour force in numerous factory industries, chiefly textiles and the relics of domestic industry; and from 7 to 10 per cent – a very high proportion – in heavy labouring jobs such as coal-heaving, gasworks and quarries. But they also formed over 10 per cent in a number of crafts, such as the building trade, shoemakers, coopers and cutlers which we have no right to regard as specially depressed.

The third criterion gives more interesting results. We can divide the occupationally, specialized areas of England and Wales into two groups, the 'old' and the 'new'. Within the old areas there is a clear distinction between agricultural areas and the old craft towns. In the former – taking 1863 as our vantage-point – male illiteracy was fairly high – 28 to 36 per cent, 29 per cent for soldiers, and female illiteracy consistently lower than the men's. (But this phenomenon had only developed in the 1850s.) In the latter, generally, illiteracy was much lower than the average, but women were worse educated than men – e.g., in Melksham (West Country textiles) the percentages were 23 and 26 respectively, in Stroud (West Country textiles) 21 and 24, in Bristol 19 and 26, in Rotherhithe (shipbuilding and riverside crafts) 16 and 23. Within the new areas three distinctions may be made. First, there are towns in which skilled labour was strong, with a consistently low illiteracy. These are sometimes difficult to distinguish from the old craft towns, but it is significant that not only old ship-building centres, but new shipbuilding and repairing centres like Birkenhead (15 and 25 per cent) had low illiteracy. Second, there are the backward and illiterate centres of the mining and iron trade and the appallingly barbarized semi-domestic, semi-craft areas of the West Midlands. Here both men and women were ignorant, though the women somewhat more so. In 1863 the joint average exceeded 45 per cent – terrible figure – in such places as Merthyr (64), Dudley (59), Neath (52), Wolverhampton (47), Walsall (46), Monmouth (47) and indeed in Staffordshire and South Wales as a whole. Third, there are the textile areas in which the men were moderately, the women shockingly illiterate. Thus in all the main cotton towns twice as many women were illiterate as men, the men's average being between 25 and 30 per cent. The same is true of woollen towns, though average male illiteracy was much lower, perhaps because of the greater age of the industry. Women in hosiery and lace towns were strikingly better situated.

The progress of literacy between the first recording of statistics in 1838–9 and 1874–8 modifies the picture a little. In 1838–9 the farming areas were not yet so well placed. They may be divided into three parts: the far North (Cumberland, Westmorland, Northumberland) which were the most literate counties of all, bar London, perhaps because of the influence of their educated Scots neighbours; the southern and south-western counties where male illiteracy was about as large as in 1864, though female illiteracy was still much higher, and the Eastern and East Midland counties as well as some of the Thames valley ones in which it was appalling (the joint average reaching or exceeding 50 per cent in Hertfordshire, Huntingdonshire, Bedfordshire – 60 per cent! – Essex and Wiltshire). Nevertheless, Lancashire had a higher male illiteracy rate than all but the nine worst agricultural counties). South Wales and the West Midlands were even then at the bottom of the list. Since the great expansion of coal-mining was yet to come, Durham had very low male and not much less than average female illiteracy (24 and 49 per cent). The expansion of mining was to turn it into a relatively very illiterate area, thus illustrating graphically the shocking effects of industrialization on the condition of the people. Between 1841–5 and 1874–8 progress both among men and women was slowest in London, the North-east, Yorkshire and Worcestershire. In the later 1870s the most illiterate of the industrial counties remained those of South Wales, Worcestershire and Staffordshire and the northern mining areas. The differential between men and women remained widest in Lancashire.

Detailed investigation confirms this picture. The highest percentages for men (over 20 per cent) now occurred in unskilled centres like Liverpool, in mining areas like Easington, Bishop Auckland, Barnsley, Houghton-le-Spring, in iron and steel centres like Middlesbrough, Warrington, Hunslet, but also in depressed woollen centres like Dewsbury. Female illiteracy double that of men occurs in towns like Keighley, Halifax, Bradford, Bolton, Bury, Salford, Manchester, Oldham, Preston, Blackburn, Burnley. In the nature of things the specific literacy of aristocratic workers is increasingly hard to discover because centres of their trades (e.g., Swindon and York with their railway workshops) are often like those medium-sized towns surrounded by rural areas in which one would expect to find good education – e.g., Lancaster. Nevertheless, the difference between the railway town of Doncaster and the mining town of Barnsley is striking.

We may conclude that areas with consistently high illiteracy cannot normally be regarded as 'aristocratic' in the nineteenth century sense, though they may contain highly-paid, if insecure workers. We should, other things being equal, expect to find a high degree of secondary poverty there. Areas with a wide differential between men and women, on the other hand, and those with consistently low illiteracy should be the main centres of labour aristocracy.

The analysis of aged poverty confirms this in part, though it shows coal-mining centres to be consistently better off in this respect than iron and steel centres (e.g., in 1894 in Glamorgan, Monmouth and Carmarthen out of eighteen unions 46 per cent or more of all people over sixty-five were paupers in six: Llanelly (36), Neath (37), Pontypool (38), Swansea (39), Bridgend (40), Bedwellty (42). In Northumberland, Durham and the North Riding, Middlesbrough (46) was by far the worst centre of old-age pauperism.) Broadly speaking (aside from the pauperized villages) the worst centres were those of unskilled port-towns and similar centres – London, Liverpool, Bristol –the iron and steel centres, and the usual black spots of small scale Midland semi-domestic industry – Dudley, Kidderminster and the like.

The analysis of illiteracy and old-age pauperism therefore helps to give some depth to, and to some extent to modify, our picture of working-class stratification.

(1954)

16

Trends in the British Labour Movement since 1850

THIS ESSAY is not a history of the British labour movement, but an attempt to discuss, in somewhat greater detail than is usually done, the operation of two standard concepts which Marxists use to explain certain trends in labour movements under capitalism: the concept of an 'aristocracy of labour' enjoying special privileges and therefore inclined to accept the views of its employers; and that of the 'spontaneity' of the movement, which, in a rather more primitive form, leads to similar results. It is probable that both these were originally derived from British experience. Certainly Lenin's *Imperialism*, which discusses the former, owes much to the earlier work of British socialist and even radical-liberal thinkers on the subject. It is less well-known that his *What Is To Be Done*, which contains a full discussion of the latter, reflects a close and extremely critical reading of the Webbs' great defence of the 'spontaneous' British trade union movement, which Lenin had translated in his Siberian exile a short while before.[1] Certainly Britain is the *locus classicus* for both in the nineteenth century. An analysis such as this may throw light on the strength and nature of 'reformism' in the British movement today. At any rate this sketch may serve to stimulate discussion on a subject by no means as yet fully explored.

I

A few words about the general character of the British economy and the development of the labour movement may serve as introduction. British capitalism in its hey-day (circa 1850–75) was, broadly speaking, an affair of small-scale, highly competitive, individual entrepreneurs. (Even the joint-stock form of organization was slow in spreading until towards the end of the century.) Moreover, it was

316

technically a conservative system. The great age of British technical and organizational revolution in industry was, on the whole, over by 1850. The triumphs of the 'workshop of the world' were gained by applying the technical progress of earlier pioneers more generally, rather than by pioneering new and revolutionary devices. Until World War I new industries, based on the more modern types of mechanization, mass production, etc., were overshadowed by the relatively stable old basic industries like coal-mining, textiles, and old-fashioned machine-building. The merger of state apparatus and capitalist business, so characteristic of modern capitalism, had barely begun. Mid-Victorian Britain was an even more logical supporter of 'free enterprise' than American business, for it even rejected tariffs. That its *laissez-faire* policy rested on certain temporary advantages does not affect the situation.

This was, broadly, the state of affairs up to 1875. Thereafter we may distinguish three main stages in the progress – or rather regress – of British capitalism. From the Great Depression of 1873–96 until World War I, the growth of monopoly capitalism in the sense of industrial concentration, the growth of modern mass-production, etc., was abnormally slow, compared with Germany and the United States, while that of imperialist policy, and the imperialist state apparatus was rather fast. Foreign investment, and the revival of the old basic export trade after the depression, obscured the fundamental deterioration of Britain's international position just sufficiently to make business reluctant to undertake those large and costly schemes of re-equipment and re-organization which had been widely discussed during the depression. (The present generation of business thinkers is blaming the past bitterly for this omission.) On the other hand the rise of serious competitors abroad, and of a political labour movement at home, did oblige the ruling class to make important administrative and political changes, and to break, in certain respects, decisively with a policy of *laissez-faire*.

The gravity of its crisis was borne in on British capitalism between two wars, when Britain rapidly acquired all the standard characteristics of imperialism, as defined by Lenin: notably the concentration of production to the point of monopoly or oligopoly, and the 'creation, on the basis of "finance capital" of a financial oligarchy'. The desperate situation revealed by World War II speeded up the merger of the state and big business.

At the risk of some oversimplification, therefore, we may divide our period into three phases: (1) up to 1875, pre-monopolist; (2) 1875–1918, transitional – with, perhaps, the decisive watershed just about where Lenin put it, round 1900; (3) from 1918, fully monopolist. It should be remembered that the progress of monopoly capitalism was also accompanied by major changes in industrial structure, notably the rise of new industries based on mechanization and modern types of factory organization, as well as by an increase in the size of industrial and business units.

The development of the labour movement falls into much the same periods. Our first phase saw a fairly small movement of trade unions of craft or sectional type, friendly societies and the like, politically tending to accept the liberal framework. Our second saw a series of expansions, which changed the scale of the movement: in 1889–90, in 1910–14 and during the First World War, the beginnings of a political movement separate from the traditional parties and demanding policies incompatible with the *laissez-faire* phase of capitalism; and also the rebirth of revolutionary and socialist groups. Our last saw the movement as a whole converted – in theory – to the need to replace capitalism, though at the same time striking firm roots in the soil of monopoly capitalism, the rise of a Communist Party. These were not, of course, gradual adjustments. The general trend of the movement makes itself felt through a series of zig-zag curves; periods of radical advance succeeded by others of relative conservatism or absolute regression. Thus periods of militancy in the early 1850s, the late 1860s and early 70s, the early 1890s, 1910–14, 1917–26, the middle and late 1930s, and 1941–5 were followed by swings in the opposite direction, such as, for example, the marked rightward shift in the Trade Union Congress after the General Strike, and in the Labour government after 1945.

II

The concept of an 'aristocracy of labour' was familiar to all students of the labour movement in nineteenth-century Britain. But in analysing it, we must distinguish fairly sharply between the pre-imperialist era and the others. In the 'golden age' of British capitalism its share of business profits depended, for practical purposes, on the direct bargaining strength (or, what amounts to the same thing, the scarcity value and the ability to hold out) of individual groups of workers; and in the determination of this, labour organizations – unions, co-ops, friendly societies – played a vital part.* The 'labour aristocracy' tended to be a sharply demarcated group. Between 1850 and 1875 real wages rose only for those whose money income could be made to rise faster than prices. Moreover, only workers with substantial resources could – individually, or through bodies like the co-ops – get access to the only consumer goods of good range and quality, which were at middle-class price-levels. For the rest, the rags and adulterated goods which made 'cheap and nasty' synonymous terms, had to suffice; for cheap overseas food did not begin to arrive until the 1870s, and, with some exceptions, production of consumer goods for a cheap mass market (ready-made clothing, for instance) did not get under way until the Great Depression period. Hence the advantages of the 'strong bargainers' were disproportionately great.

But the terms of the bargains (actual or implicit) emerged almost entirely from the higgling of innumerable labour markets, sectional and regional. (One should not at this period overrate, except for very limited purposes, or in a very general analysis, the role of the 'national' labour market.) In general they were not, initially, the result of conscious policy. Employers were hostile to trade unions on principle, except where forced to deal with them. It was not until the 1860s and 70s that formal mechanisms to smooth labour relations were discovered to be desirable from a business point of view, and that bargaining of bodies of workers with bodies of employers received varying degrees of official or unofficial recognition. This was the period of the trade union legislation of 1867–75, of various bodies for conciliation and sliding-scale agreements, of businessmen's championship of unions as means of avoiding dislocation.[2] But this was largely a recognition of established facts, though it was doubtless hastened by fear of the political strength of town artisans, who won the parliamentary vote in 1867. In other words: the transformation of militant Chartist workers into respectable aristocrats of labour, which Thomas Cooper noted and deplored[3] took place 'spontaneously', without any important change in capitalist policy, and with relatively small conscious changes in labour policy.[4]

* This does not mean, as has often been stated, that only apprenticed craftsmen, or those commanding what was then regarded as 'skill' could enjoy it; though the prevalence of old-fashioned, almost pre-industrial forms of craft skill – e.g., in machine-building and constructional work – did colour much of the trade union movement.

319

With the official recognition of trade unionism, and the coming of the Great Depression in the 70s, conscious and deliberate class-collaboration came into the open. Now the Boilermakers could sing (1872):

> Now 'tis true that capital
> All the risk must run,
> Like a ship exposed to all
> Winds beneath the sun;
> Feels the first trade's ebb and flow,
> Must keen competitition know.
> So 'tis just and meet
> Labour should co-operate,
> And to help with all their might
> Masters to compete.[5]

It was now that the great systems of quasi-business unionism were built up in the major export trades – cotton-spinning, ship-building, the north-eastern coalfields – to be held up to general admiration in the Webbs' *Industrial Democracy*: 'The reasonable employer and the reasonable trade unionist worker; the fair capitalist and the fair worker, the big-hearted bourgeois, friend of the workers and the narrow-bourgeois-minded proletarian condition one another, and are both corollaries of one and the same relationship, whose foundation was the economic position of Britain from the middle of the nineteenth century. . . .'[6]

The class collaboration of labour aristocrats in the 1880s and 90s was, of course, on a more limited scale than the later versions. It took the profitable operation of the British economy for granted, providing free trade continued, and limited its efforts to keep its own boss or its own industry in a fit state to grant concessions. There was as yet no general belief that the movement 'is concerned with the prosperity of industry . . . can find more use for an efficient industry than a derelict one, and the unions can use their power to promote and guide the scientific reorganization of industry, as well as to obtain material advantages from this reorganization'.[7] Such organized business unionism on a national scale as the Mond-Turner conferences of 1927–8 implied, emerged from the unions' discovery that British capitalist economy was in a state of grave crisis. Even less was there any tendency to modify the traditional tactics of unions. Not until the later 1940s was it possible for a TUC General Council to accept a wage-freeze at a time of boom profits, in order to ensure the stability of the economy as a whole. Nevertheless, in essence the sectional attitude of cotton-operatives during the Great Depression, who refused to campaign for an eight-hour day because it might harm the competitive prospects of their industry, or of boilermakers who refunded to their employers any financial loss due to bad workmanship or unauthorized strikes of their members,[8] merely needed to be generalized, and put in a setting of institutional bargaining and twentieth century politics, to resemble the policy of the post-1945 General Councils of the TUC.

It is important to remember that the aristocracy of labour, or, insofar as the two were not the same, the labour movement of the period, necessarily excluded many, perhaps most, workers. To begin with, only a limited number was capable of trade union organization of any sort. The immense mass of semi-proletarians, the floating, irregularly employed paupers, outworkers or hands in small workshops, the half-world of misery which emerges from Mayhew's *London Labor and the London Poor* in the 1850s, or from Charles Booth's survey in the 80s and 90s, was, for practical purposes, outside the range of the unions. Moreover, insofar as certain bodies of workers had affinities with this floating substratum – seasonal migrants, like gas-workers, casually hired men, as in the docks, or many of the then lower grades in factories – they suffered from similar disabilities. The strength of Chartism had lain precisely in its ability to mobilize such vast masses of the incompletely proletarianized. The great militant politico-industrial surges of 1889 and 1911 were to do the same. But all of these succeeded because they went beyond the confines of narrow trade unionism, and gave the movement revolutionary or socialist leadership and perspective. In the absence of such political consciousness, these sections of the working population remained, for any length of time, unorganized and unrepresented. It must not be forgotten that, outside a few centres, a fully developed factory system, or any large-scale unit of production did not develop until late in the century.[9]

A similar reflection of the relative archaism of British industrial structure is the size of what we may call the 'docile' population. American railways, for instance, organized strong unions early. British railways, however, staffed (outside the footplate and workshop grades) primarily from the great reservoir of cheap and cowed village labour, failed to do so until much later; and when unionism came, it was to a great extent in the form of an industrial union. It is, how-

ever, true that the slowness of technical change, and the relative
shelter and immobility of certain trades, offset this to some extent.
Where, for historical reasons, a nucleus of 'strong bargainers', willing
to fight, was already in existence, it was not so easy to swamp it in a
flood of cheap labour. Thus the Lancashire mule-spinners retained
and extended control of their industry, and became the backbone of
a whole series of unions of various grades, including women, in the
cotton industry; while in the United States the more headlong changes
left similar bodies in the northeast high and dry as small groups of
craftsmen, while a cheap labour industry with weak unions was built
up elsewhere. Even among the lower groups factors like the national
solidarity of the Irish helped to bring quite good organizations into
being here and there – among stevedores, for instance. By and large,
however, it took two generations of fighting to weaken decisively the
traditional docility of much British cheap labour.

III

The third and most important factor in limiting the size of the labour
aristocracy was the belief, which dominated the hiring policies of
most employers, that workers could be divided into two groups: the
'artisans', in possession of special skills or qualifications, and the
mass of 'common labour', which could be hired, fired, or inter-
changed at will, without making any appreciable difference to efficiency; of which an over-supply was normally available in most
places, except perhaps at the very top of a cyclical or seasonal boom.
Only certain types of workers were in a position to make or keep their
labour scarce enough, or valuable enough, to strike a good bargain.
But the relatively favourable terms they got were, to a large extent,
actually achieved at the expense of their less favoured colleagues; not
merely at the expense of the rest of the world which British business
dominated. We need not stress the prevalence of such relics of early
capitalism as systems of subcontracting, and the like, which made
many skilled or supervising workers into actual co-employers of their
less favoured mates, for unions – like the Engineers' – often fought
against these, or made no effort to perpetuate them.* More important
is the fact that the scarcity of the relatively prosperous workers was a

* A major exception were some forms of child labour in the cotton and coal-
mining industry, which unions fought long and hard to retain; in these cases
members were chiefly sweating their own children.

function of the relative glut in the rest of the labour market. The whole point of the classical craft union was to keep the trade, and the entry to the trade, restricted – quite apart from the actuarial arguments for excluding those less healthy or qualified workers who would merely drain union funds while weakening bargaining strength in other ways. Hence universal trade unionism was out of the question, though most unions honestly favoured it, except where it seemed to threaten their sectional job monopoly.

Nevertheless, sectional unionism of this sort was not without wider value. After all, it had two faces: if it fought against the rest of the working class for its special position, it also fought against the boss (until recognition, at any rate), for the right to a share of his profits – a small and stable share. In the course of this fight it established not merely a series of devices and institutions which have become the common property of the movement since – Trades Councils, the Trades Union Congress, the efficient way of running union business, the strategy and tactics of short-term campaigning – but a whole system of the ethics of militancy.[10] The labour aristocrat might wear a top-hat and think on business matters exactly like his employer, but when the pickets were out against the boss, he knew what to do. Moreover, he developed, if on a narrow basis, a solidarity and class-consciousness, a belief that so long as a man worked for wages his interests were exclusively determined by that fact: a conviction which has become a valuable part of British labour tradition. The secretary of the spinners' or glassblowers' union might become mill manager or entrepreneur; but while he was a union man, he behaved like a union man. And the existence of a strong nucleus of unionism in most basic industries (for British craft unions were, thanks to our industrial structure, much more successful than American ones) made it vastly easier to expand the scope of the movement later on.

IV

The advent of imperialism changed this state of affairs. If we are to speak of an 'aristocracy of labour' of reformist tendencies in this period, we shall be describing something much more complex than the prosperous 'artisan class' of the 1860s. Then there had been masses of British workers, who, for practical purposes, had not benefited from the world monopoly of British capitalism. The further we progress into the imperialist era, the more difficult does it become to put one's finger on groups of workers which did not, in one way or another, draw some advantage from Britain's position; who were not able to live rather better than they would have done in a country whose bourgeoisie possessed fewer accumulated claims to profits and dividends abroad, or power to dictate the terms of trade with backward areas. Or, since there is no simple correlation between the standard of living and political moderation, on workers who could not be made to feel that their interests depended on the continuance of imperialism. It is indeed true that the 'benefits' of imperialism, and its promises, were unevenly distributed among various workers at any given time; and that some of the mechanisms for distributing them did not come into full operation until the inter-war years. It is equally true that the growing crisis of the British economy complicated the pattern. But, on the whole, the change remains.

In the 1860s, then, we seek the 'bourgeois proletariat' of which Marx spoke almost entirely among the favoured 'artisan' stratum. In the imperialist period we find it not only there, and in altogether new groups of privileged workers, but – and this is equally significant – in important bodies of the hitherto unprivileged and underpaid, and in what we may call the professional labour movement of politicians, union officials and others specially susceptible to capitalist persuasion.*

Paradoxically enough, the least 'reliable' of these were some of the old aristocrats of our first period, for the new era undermined their position of special privilege. It is quite probable that, relatively speaking, the position of the skilled British artisan has never been higher than in the 1860s, nor his standard of living and access to education, culture and travel (by contemporary standards) so satisfactory, nor the gap between him and the small local manufacturers who employed him so narrow, nor that between him and the mass of 'labour' so wide.† But the former widened, as production concentrated and the owner-manager gave place to the joint-stock corporation, and as a whole set of novel managerial technical and white-collar grades wedged themselves between the 'skilled man' and his master. The latter gap narrowed, as also intermediate semi-skilled grades – machine-operators and the like – filled the abyss between 'craftsman' and 'labourer', and even pushed the craftsman himself

---

* See above, Chapter 15 (pp. 272 seq).

† He was, in fact, increasingly referred to as 'lower middle class'.

into what he regarded as semi-skilled work. Most members of the Amalgamated Engineering Union today would not have been admitted to its predecessor in the 1880s. Moreover, the spread of cheap food, cheap mass-produced consumer goods, public education and social security decreased the abnormal advantages of higher wages in the earlier period. Lastly, of course, the inter-war crisis was to hit precisely the basic industries of nineteenth-century Britain in which the 'old' labour movement was most firmly entrenched. Step by step the labour aristocrat found himself forced into the ranks of the working class; and, on the whole, he moved to the left. Hence his readiness, after 1900, to ally himself with socialists in the Labour Party; to break with the Liberal Party which he had supported passionately; finally even to support a socialist programme.

Meanwhile, however, new groups of 'labour aristocrats' had arisen in the managerial, technical and white-collar grades, and it is among these that we must seek the real 'bourgeois proletariat of imperialism', flattered by its rulers (the new popular press was chiefly directed at them), refusing even to regard themselves as members of the working class. Their special position was not even dependent on collective bargaining, as that of the 'artisans' had been; their actual earnings at the lower levels were not much higher than that of the artisans: they took most of their differential advantages in terms of a higher social status. Consequently, since their main aim was to raise themselves above the higher-paid grades of the shirt-sleeved workers, their political hostility to labour was gratifyingly intense. Only gradually did the crisis of imperialist economy bring them into the labour movement. White-collar unions appeared, on a small scale, in the 1890s, and again just before World War I. The aftermath of that war brought the beginnings of professional trade unionism among scientists, university teachers and the like, and the firm unionization of at least one group of white-collar employees, the Civil Service clerks. But it was not until the later years of World War II, with their expansion of professional, and supervisory unions, and the political upheaval which made masses of white-collar and managerial men and women vote Labour for the first time, that really important (though probably not, as yet, decisive) shifts in the alllegiance of these groups took place.

Even more important were the changes in the status of the mass of hitherto unprivileged, unrecognized and unorganized labour, illustrated by the narrowing gap between 'skilled' and 'unskilled' wage rates.* Modern developments in production brought the chance of upgrading from unskilled to semi-skilled jobs; from casual under-employment to regular, though not necessarily better-paid engage-ments; from negligible to respectable bargaining strength. Modern social security legislation brought at any rate a slight relief from the awful anxieties of those without any financial reserves at all. Two world wars even brought about the unique contingency of labour scarcity. For the utter pariahs of the mid-nineteenth century slums, even modest improvements seemed absolute gains. The skilled fitter would rightly regard the introduction of a semi-automatic machine, operated at a penny or two above the labourer's rate, as a means of intensifying exploitation. The unskilled labourer might well, all reserves made, regard it as triumphant promotion for a time at least. The archaism of British industrial structure in the earlier period in-creased the effect of such changes.

Moreover, whatever happened to the unprivileged as a whole, sections of them undoubtedly improved their position, if only through the automatic changes in the distribution and structure of industries. While the old centres of skilled labour became derelict areas, popu-lated by long-term unemployed, old centres of casual and low-grade labour became relatively prosperous homes of light mass-production industry, distribution, etc. Between 1929 and 1937 the unemployment rate in London never reached half that of the north-east coast.† In the 1880s the dockers had been regarded – and, though they con-tained stronger groups, rightly regarded – as a typically weak and helpless body; in 1948 they were among the most highly-paid workers. Again, the vast expansion of central and local government provided a great many sheltered and relatively secure jobs for low-qualified workers who, earlier, would inevitably have formed part of the casual reservoir. It would be interesting to trace the growth of these net-works of 'vested interests in stability', for instance in areas like South Wales and London in which the Labour Party has had control of municipal patronage for a long period. One could multiply such examples.

* Thus the building labourer's rate, 50 per cent of the craftsman's before 1914, is today 80 per cent of it. The spread of payment by results has meant, however, that earnings have not been levelled in the same way as rates.

† Compare Schulze-Gaevernitz' judgment early in the century that 'The problem of unemployment is mainly a London problem and that of the lower proletarian stratum.'

What is even more important, the unprivileged for the first time became capable of using the bargaining methods of the labour movement on a large scale. The scale of the collective bargain increased; it took place more and more in a web of public or semi-public institutions; it was backed by the pressure of an independent and threatening political labour movement. For the established trade union (say of Boilermakers or Compositors) this meant little; for it was already recognized, and its bargaining strength was in any case formidable. For the hitherto weak and unprivileged, it brought a profound change, and, as we shall see, major temptations.

It is true that the crisis of the British economy counteracted these tendencies. Possibly, had the country faced a catastrophic crisis whose effects on the standard of all workers had become palpable, it would have overborne them entirely. But the accumulated profits of world monopoly and empire, the strategic position of British capitalism, cushioned both workers and employers against too harsh an impact of reality, until such time as the narrow 'free enterprise' labour movement of the 1870s had had time to broaden into the powerful Fabian-reformist movement of our century. Thus the leftward movement among the old labour aristocrats was slower and more partial than one might have expected, even though it has been unmistakable in such classical craft unions as the Amalgamated Engineers; even though the General Secretary of the Boilermakers today may be heard saying things which would make his predecessor of the 1880s turn in his grave, and the venerable Ironfounders, who date back to 1809, are today a left-wing union of relatively low-paid semi-skilled grades. But if they have changed, so, even more startlingly, have others, notably the two great General Unions of Transport and Municipal Workers, who today form a quarter of the total union membership. The ancestor of the Municipal Workers, Will Thorne's Gas-workers' Union, began life in the year of upheaval, 1889, as the nearest thing to a 'red' body conceivable before the foundation of communist parties. Eleanor Marx was a power on its executive; her husband drafted its rules and aims; virtually all its national and district leaders were Marxian social-democrats. (We may add that it was easily the most successful of the general unions founded in 1889.) Yet within twenty years it had shifted considerably to the right; and the great figures of its second and third generation – the Right Honourable J. R. Clynes, Lord Dukeston, Sir Tom Williamson – are about as far on the right wing of the Labour Party as is possible. The story of the Dockers' Union, another child of 1889, and ancestor of the Transport Workers of today, is slightly more complex. It collapsed pretty badly between 1892 and 1910, and had to be revived by another bout of aggressive expansion, which gave its original rebel leadership a second period of prominence; moreover, certain of its constituent sections, such as the busmen, have faced problems which pushed them, too, towards the left. Yet if we follow the career of the greatest of its second-generation leaders, Mr Ernest Bevin, from its Marxian social-democratic origins in Bristol, through its period of active industrial unionist agitation, to success, a career as the far from radical boss of the largest union in the country, and finally into the Cabinet as Foreign Secretary, the general trend is sufficiently obvious. The two great unions of the outcasts of 1889 became the two main pillars of conservatism in the British movement.*

V

What makes these changes so complex is the remarkable combination of political currents flowing both to the right and the left; local intensification of reformism in a general setting of radicalization, for instance. We have seen that in the golden age of British world monopoly, the ruling class had bought social stability, and what it considered efficient production†, at a grotesquely cheap price, as Joseph Chamberlain was the first to remind his colleagues.[11] In theory the case for deliberate reformism, or a conscious 'high wage economy' as a means for obtaining both under the conditions of the new era, was strong; and numerous groups of intellectuals, from Toynbee and Alfred Marshall to Sidney and Beatrice Webb, pressed it. So did some employers, ironically enough often men whose connections with the colonies were specially close, like the cocoa, chocolate and soap firms. In practice, however, capitalists were conscious of a growing threat, and rarely inclined to grant concessions except under duress. British imperialism, after all, right from the start, marked a step back, from potential world monopoly to actual quarter-world monopoly; even though in absolute figures the latter might be larger than the

* The Transport and General Workers' Union has shifted to the left again, thanks to the somewhat unexpected succession to the throne of F. Cousins who owed his rise in the union to, and represented, this left-wing element.

† By modern standards of labour management it was grossly inefficient. See below, Chapter 17 (pp. 344 seq).

former. But precisely at the time when the limitless horizon was contracting for them, British businessmen seemed to be called upon, through direct concessions, through taxation or otherwise, to pay out more of their profits than before to more of the workers. (I am not here discussing whether, in fact, they were; but that is what it looked like to the individual businessman.) Certainly they were called on to abandon that absolute right to 'do what ones likes with one's own' to which they were accustomed.

Concessions were therefore extorted by force; and followed by increasingly desperate counter-attacks, which forced even moderate labour to the left. The unions' decision to form a Labour Party (1898–1906) as a result of the attack on their legal status is the best-known example. Indeed, both reformism and attack may be seen in action simultaneously. Thus after the General Strike of 1926 the coal-owners and the stupider sections of the Conservative Party hit back in the traditional way by union-smashing and punitive anti-trade union legislation. Meanwhile another group of employers, headed by Sir Alfred Mond of the chemical trust, met the threat in exactly the opposite way, by inviting the Trade Union Congress leadership to the notorious conferences on industrial peace and rationalization which, under the name of the Mond-Turner conferences, became a landmark in the history of class collaboration. Similarly, both tendencies co-existed in the labour movement. Thus the general period of the Great Depression (especially from 1880 to the middle 90s) saw both a radicalization of the movement (the rebirth of socialism, the organization of new and militant unions) and an intensification of the '*embourgeoisement*' of the old unions, the beginnings of which we noted above.

The historian looking back over the whole period is therefore struck as much by the massive set-backs to class collaboration as by its great advances. The unemployment of the Depression of the 1880s did more to shake the belief of British trade unionists in unfettered private enterprise than the official recognition of the craft aristocracy did to reinforce it. The desperate counter-attack of employers against the radical unionism of 1889 and after did indeed destroy much of it; but its main long-term result was to push even the conservative old unions into a symbiosis with the socialists – into an independent Labour Party potentially separate from middle-class Liberalism. That party was for years little more than a weak pressure group on the flank of the Liberals; and one easily conciliated. But while

329

parliamentary labour leaders were tamed (few of them had ever been really wild), the failure of Edwardian imperialism to maintain the conditions of the working class precipitated another outbreak of labour unrest, led by rank-and-file syndicalists and industrial unionists. World War I did still more to alienate the workers from a belief in the capitalist system, broke the allegiance of the Labour Party to the Liberals – whom it replaced within a few years; and even committed the party in theory to a socialist programme. True, from 1921 to 1934 the employers counter-attacked with much effect. By 1934 the unions had barely more members than in 1913, the Labour Party was reduced to a rump of 50-odd members of Parliament, and by dint of unparalleled human misery the unexpectedly high cost of the social services, notably of unemployment benefit, had been restored to an 'actuarially sound' basis. Nor did the moderate leaders of the movement resist strongly, being themselves anxious to retreat from the uncomfortably radical position into which the unrest of 1911–26 had forced them; if not, like Macdonald, Snowden, J. H. Thomas and others, to go over to the duchesses entirely. Yet the main result of the hard-faced inter-war decades was to alienate a solid core of millions of citizens permanently (it is safe to say) from any party which does not promise socialism. The landslide of 1945 was the answer. This does not mean that the reformist leadership of the labour movement has become any less wedded to the status quo; if anything the opposite has been the case. It is quite as easy to justify a moderate policy in socialist as it is in liberal or conservative phrases; the former may be even more effective. But if the socialist consciousness of the British working class is potential rather than real; if indeed it is at every moment transformed into its opposite in the context of a reformist movement and imperialist institutions, we should nevertheless be wrong to underrate the bitter process of political education which has taught it utterly to reject capitalism, even though it may not quite know what such a rejection implies.

VI

Yet what strikes the observer is the survival rather than the weakening of British reformism; the failure of a communist party or of the semi-Marxist left to make decisive headway, rather than the change in the political spirit of the movement as a whole.

It used to be argued that this strength was due to the benefits of

330

imperial exploitation and would therefore last only as long as British workers were still protected against the full rigours of their position by it. This argument, though obviously oversimplified at all times, has not yet entirely lost its force, for the most striking thing about post-1945 Britain is the extraordinary slowness with which *all* sections of British politics have adjusted themselves to the decline and fall of the British empire. One can hardly claim that the process began seriously until the middle 1950s, and even by the early 1960s its progress was very modest. It is arguable, and indeed probable, that a genuine exposure of Britain to the economic and political realities of the post-imperial period must bring about profound changes in British home and foreign politics. Indeed, one of the less advertised arguments of the champions of the European Common Market was that exposure to the European economies would break the force of the immense vested interest in economic and technical conservatism among both businessmen and trade unions, by bankrupting the more inefficient of the first and wrecking the second. The argument that British reformism in its present form depends on a certain protection against economic realities does not depend on the assumption that imperial exploitation continues as before.[12] It can be reformulated to depend on one or more of four assumptions.

The first of these is the immense and growing advantage which *all* advanced economies have over all backward or weakly developed ones. The second is the absence of serious economic depressions, i.e., of mass unemployment, since 1941. The third is the abnormal strength of the labour movement in Britain. The fourth is the survival of old-fashioned or restyled economic-imperialist exploitation, which is not entirely negligible. However, it is by no means certain that the adjustment to Britain's real economic position in the world would transform the British labour movement from a reformist to a revolutionary one, if only because there are plainly important factors making against any drastic attempt to solve economic difficulties at the expense of the workers, notably the political competition between the capitalist and socialist sectors of the world.[13] It is therefore foolish to predict such a transformation, though not more foolish than to argue that western labour has entered an age of permanent economic contentment. For the purposes of this essay prophecy is not in any case necessary. We are here concerned rather with the mechanism by which an increasingly reformist leadership has been maintained.

The problem of such a mechanism arises, because it is evident from the persistent struggle between left and right within the labour movement, that reformism in the sense normally given to it by the labour leadership, is far from an unchallenged dominance. In labour movements such as those of the USA no serious left wing exists at all and socialism plays no significant part. In the social-democratic parties which dominate several European countries, such as the West German, the Austrian and the French, serious challenges to the right-wing policies of their leadership either do not exist, or come from outside the party, e.g., from the communists. In Britain they are persistently strong. Moreover, from time to time their strength is evidently on the increase, as in the period from 1957 to 1962, which saw the end of the long domination of the TUC by an automatic bloc of the right, and the consequent defeat of the Labour Party leadership in open battle.

There are four reasons for this strength of the left. The first is that the aspiration towards a *new* and not merely an improved society is deeply rooted in European labour movements, and probably in all but very anomalous labour movements. This does not mean that it is very effective in practice. The second lies in the massive sense of class solidarity and class unity of the British working class. Even today the chief, indeed the overwhelming, appeal of the Labour Party to its electorate is that it is a class party. The third lies in the often neglected fact that British labour did not undergo the split which separated communists from social-democrats in the aftermath of the 1917 revolution, but rather a split which pushed formerly liberal workers into an independent, and officially socialist, working-class party. This fact was recognized by Lenin and the Communist International and led them to favour the exceptional policy of urging British communists to enter the Labour Party in order to convert and capture it, rather than to compete with it. In spite of occasional swerves to the alternative policy, largely under international pressure – as in 1928–35 and after 1948 – the policy of pushing Labour to the left rather than creating an alternative mass party has remained the normal one for British communists. The progressive doctrinal exclusiveness of the Labour Party, and its tendency to ban from membership or association an increasing range of views and organizations, has of course made the original aim of formal communist affiliation to Labour rather academic.

The fourth reason is, that the left in Britain (as in some ways in Australia) has always had a real if non-revolutionary function within

the movement, namely that of making reformism effectively reformist. It has always acted as the brains-trust of the movement, especially
on the industrial side. Virtually all suggestions for the modernization
of trade-union structure and policy have always come from whatever
was the contemporary left – the Marxists of the 1880s, the syndicalist-
Marxists of the 1910s, the communists of the 1930s and 1940s. The
militants and rank-and-file leaders, or the leaders of new and un-
established or old and threatened unions, have tended to gravitate to
the left. If it had not existed, the movement would have had to invent
it, for as we have seen, the fighting conservative or moderate union
leader of the type of John L. Lewis or James Hoffa in the USA, has
been a very rare bird indeed in Britain. In brief, the left has been and
is a massive and integral part of a labour movement which has
remained in essence united, electorally and in its trade-union
activities. How large remains a matter of debate, but even the fog of
favourable publicity which surrounds every right-wing leader – e.g.,
the late Hugh Gaitskell – has never succeeded in obscuring their
relative lack of electoral appeal, and the far greater popularity of the
left among the party militants.*

Nevertheless, whatever its strength, the working-class left has normally been much more ineffective than the right, except at occasional
moments of extreme social tension. Almost always it has been too
weak to do more than modify a policy controlled by the right. Its
strength has been sufficient to make the most convenient position
from which to lead the Labour Party one slightly to the left of centre.
But its policy has almost invariably been at best somewhat to the
right of centre, and at worst (as in 1923–4, 1929–31 and in the 1950s)
very much to the right of it. Even in 1945–50 the Labour government
was 'left' only by liberal and not by socialist standards, or even by
those of a populist radicalism such as that of F. D. Roosevelt's second
administration. It is this quasi-permanent inferiority of the left to the
right (and within the left, of the revolutionaries to the non-revolu-
tionaries) which has to be explained.

* The lack of electoral division in the labour movement has doomed rival
parties to the Labour Party, the lack of division within the trade union movement has favoured them. Thus the Independent Labour Party disappeared from
sight within a few years after disaffiliating from the Labour Party in 1932, in
spite of its numerous MPs, because its trade union base was negligible. The
Communist Party, which has never achieved or relied on a separate electorate,
has remained little affected by its electoral failures, because of its strength in
the trade unions.

333

VII

At this stage the theory of 'spontaneity' in labour movements, best known in the form of Lenin's distinction between the limited 'trade union consciousness' which movements develop spontaneously and the 'socialist consciousness' which they do not, becomes relevant. Lenin's argument is twofold.[14] On the one hand the spontaneous experience of the workers is limited to the problems of their economic struggle, i.e., the relations between employers and workers. But a wider sense of socialist long-term objectives, strategy and tactics is not to be derived from such experience, but only from 'the sphere of the relations between *all* the various classes and strata and the state and government'[15] which is beyond the 'spontaneous' perspective of the proletariat, at least initially. On the other, in the absence of such a perspective, spontaneous movements are likely to drift into the wake of bourgeois ideology. The details of Lenin's analysis are open to query, but the importance of his distinction is fundamental.

For our purpose it is perhaps useful to elaborate and to rephrase it. The 'spontaneous' experience of the working class leads it to develop two things: on the one hand a set of immediate demands (e.g., for higher wages) and of institutions, modes of behaviour, etc., designed to achieve them; on the other – but in a much vaguer form and not invariably – a general discontent with the existing system, a general aspiration after a more satisfactory one, and a general outline (co-operative against competitive, socialist against individualist) of alternative social arrangements. The first group of ideas is in the nature of things far more precise and specific than the second. Moreover they operate all the time whereas the second are of little practical importance – though of immense moral importance – except at the comparatively rare moments when the complete overthrow of the existing system appears likely or immediately practicable.* Under conditions of stable capitalism 'trade union consciousness' is quite compatible with the *de facto* (or even the formal) acceptance of capitalism, unless that system fails to allow for the *minimum* trade unionist demand of

---

* Lenin failed to observe that a vague – and consequently entirely ineffective – utopianism can be as 'spontaneous' a product of proletarian experience as reformism. British craft unions are in this respect no more spontaneous than Spanish anarchism. The weakness of both is to establish no working connection between the day-by-day small-scale struggles of the workers and the main battle for power.

'a fair day's work for a fair day's pay'. (When it does not, trade union consciousness appears automatically to imply changes of the second order.) Spontaneous labour movements therefore are likely to act as though capitalism were permanent, reducing their socialist aspirations, where they exist, to politically irrelevant appendices to their 'real' activities, or to the support of political pressure groups. This is not simply because bourgeois propaganda is older, more influential, and more omnipresent than socialist ideology, but because even socialist movements must, in their day-by-day activities, act *as though* capitalism were permanent for most of the time. Except in the rare times of revolutionary crisis, a higher degree of political consciousness, a special effort, is needed to prevent the movement from drifting into mere reformism; unless some such obvious fact as sheer hunger or mass unemployment maintain the revolutionary mood of the workers.

A conscious socialist movement, and notably a communist party, provide such a special factor. If a working class attached itself to such a movement at the crucial phase of its development when it forms such attachments, it will have some built-in guarantee against the drift into reformism, for class consciousness and unity (solidarity, loyalty) are two of the most elementary lessons of spontaneous proletarian experience. But if, as in the British case, it attaches itself to a movement largely formed in the pre-Marxist mould, it will not. The loyalty and theoretical inertia which it derives from its spontaneous experience will maintain its traditional attachments, and – unless quite extraordinary catastrophes occur, and even then by no means lightly or rapidly – it will stay with them. So long as Labour is 'our' movement, local and sectional disagreements with this or that aspect of its policy and behaviour will not affect the basic loyalty.*

'Spontaneity' allows the rank-and-file to drift passively towards the right (or to maintain loyalty to a traditional left); but it actively propels the cadres of the movement towards moderation. The handful of simple rules of thumb based on class-consciousness and solidarity, by which the base determines its political conduct, do not offer much guidance at a higher level. So long as the movement is out-

* The conditions for a change of loyalty have not been seriously investigated, though several such changes are on record – normally from social-democratic to communist, or from liberal to socialist, but occasionally (as in West Germany) from communist to the right. One might briefly suggest three: an organizational split, the rise of a new region or generation unaffected by the loyalties of the old, and a really spectacular failure or abdication of the old movement. Or a combination of all three.

lawed, persecuted and unrecognized, not much guidance is needed, and one sometimes detects among the theoretical left a certain nostalgia for this straightforward situation, a wish to prolong by means of *a priori* condemnations of all compromise, coalition or manoeuvre the golden age when nothing disturbs the mind of the simple hard-fighting militant. But unless the capitalist system is overthrown earlier, recognition and its attendant complexities come, in one form or another, to all labour movements when they are too strong to be neglected or destroyed. At this point only the firmest and clearest revolutionary theory or moral commitment can safeguard the labour cadre against mere reformism.

In Britain, where the working class has been for almost a century far too strong to be wished away by the ruling classes, its movement has been enmeshed in the web of conciliation and collaboration more deeply, and far longer, than anywhere else. In most European countries the decision to tolerate the labour movement and to operate with it rather than against it was taken not earlier than the end of the nineteenth century. In France it occurred in the 1880s, after the ending of the post-Commune hysteria, in Germany after Bismarck, with the abrogation of the anti-socialist laws, in Italy after the failure of the Crispi repression. In Britain, however, both the official acceptance of trade unionism and of the mass (and, in this instance, predominantly proletarian) electorate occurred in the middle 1860s. Recent historical work has thrown much light on the soul-searching among the ruling classes which preceded the deliberate decisions to do so.[16] From that moment no systematic attempt to suppress the labour movement has been made in Britain, except by particular sections of business, never entirely backed by even the most conservative of governments. On the contrary, the fundamental posture of government and increasingly of the major industries has been that of the lion-tamer rather than the big-game hunter. The most militant periods of labour-baiting or labour-smashing – notably in the later 1890s – were those in which labour policy escaped from the control of governments into the much more short-sighted one of private consortia of capitalists and ultra-conservative lawyers.* The

* What went 'wrong' with the employers' counter-attack of the 1890s – for which, see J. Saville in A. Briggs and J. Saville (eds) *Studies in Labour History* (London 1960) – was that an offensive aimed at new and weak unions, or particular unions, developed – by a series of legal decisions – into one threatening an entire labour movement, including the most moderate sections.

dream of a country free from unions and a Labour Party (let alone from socialists) still sweetens the lunchtime conversations of such businessmen as have no experience of the realities of industrial life – stockbrokers, bankers and their like – or of the helpless little businessmen, and finds an echo in the speeches of the more stupid politicians and the publications of the more feudal press-lords. But even between 1921 and 1933, when the 'fight-to-a-finishers' temporarily gained control and tried to force labour to its knees, they were, as we have seen, always held in some sort of check by the dominant and moderate wing of the Conservative Party tacitly assisted by the Liberals. At moments of fear and hysteria attempts to attack labour all along the line may still be made; but the rulers of a country 90 per cent of whose citizens live by earning wages and two-thirds of which are manual workers, have been far too wise to indulge in them, even in the 1930s, when European fascism made the defeat of labour look tempting and possible.

There are, in such a situation, two factors which drive a labour movement to the right. On the one hand the mere technicalities of recognized trade union activity in a modern capitalist economy involve leaders, above the shop or works level, in a network of joint activities with employers and the state, and so does the mere existence of a working-class party which is a potential government or partner in government coalitions in parliamentary systems. This is a problem for communist as well as for social-democratic parties, as in France during the Popular Front and the immediate postwar periods. On the other, there are the systematic efforts of government and (normally big) business designed to strengthen labour moderation and weaken the revolutionaries. Communists have so far been largely exempt from these, because government and business have regarded them collectively as irreconcilable, but it is by no means impossible (especially since about 1960) that the same tactics will be applied to them.

VIII

We must consider this process from the somewhat different points of view of the employers, the government (i.e., the ruling groups taking a national as distinct from an individual or sectional view of policy) and labour.

Little need be said about the employers, since their attitude remains one of fundamental reluctance to accept the existence of a labour movement at all, except as a lesser evil. This is reflected in the general press treatment of virtually any strike or trade union demand, and in a strongly surviving middle-class folklore about the evils of 'trade union dictatorship'. Even today the worker who refuses to join a union tends to be regarded as a hero-figure, the shop steward as a tyrant, mitigated only by an inadequate education which film-directors affect to find comic, the trade union as a subspecies of totalitarianism. 'Management' – especially large and intelligent firms – have long accepted trade unionism, both nationally and locally, but with relatively few exceptions, employers have not taken the initiative in taming the labour movement.

However, in politics, non-labour parties and governments have, from 1867 on, deliberately taken such initiatives. The Liberal Party attempted to establish itself as the party of 'the people' (which included the workers), and might well have succeeded in doing so, but for the reluctance of older politicians like Gladstone and of certain groups of businessmen in the party to pay the necessary price in 'government interference'. The deliberate sponsoring of working-men candidates, the promotion of working-class ministers (1906), the first grants of royal honours – such as membership of the Privy Council – to workers (1914) belong to this liberal era.

A special characteristic of British capitalism favoured the absorption of labour organizations into the government apparatus, which also began before 1914: the absence of a professional bureaucracy of social administration. Both it and the first rudimentary state systems of labour management and social security had to be improvised almost simultaneously. In the context of a policy of conciliation it seemed as natural to take trade unionists into the civil service – by the 1890s many of them already looked forward to such posts after retirement[17] – as to use their statistical services. The National Insurance Act of 1912 even made the unions into a part of the administration of health insurance as 'approved societies', thus providing those without much bargaining strength with a sound reason for holding their members while at the same time discouraging excessive militancy. Thence it was only a step to the modern techniques of enmeshing labour in a net of advisory and consultative bodies, which were developed particularly in the course of the two World Wars, and have been of major importance since 1945.[18] The trade unions are today vital intermediaries between the state and the workers.

338

The rise of the Labour Party after 1918 posed the special problem of a possible Labour government. Given the moderation of the party's leaders, there was never any serious doubt about its solution. From 1923 it was clear that a coalition of Liberals and Labour, even under a Labour prime minister, was not only tolerable but actually desirable as a means of heading off 'irresponsibility'.[19]

The effect of this policy of conciliation and recognition on the 'spontaneous' labour militant is complex. At its simplest, the armour of ignorance and remoteness from temptation may flake off, leaving him an easy prey to the hospitality, the pseudo-camaraderie, or even the mere courtesy of the mighty. At a slightly less elementary level, the ex-militant may identify the recognition of his party or union, and his own personal success, with the success of the movement. That a man like himself should have advanced so far is not merely, he may reflect, a reflection of the movement's strength, but actually demonstrates its achievements. More objectively, the discovery that higher politics and negotiation are rather more complicated than a simple agitator, propagandist and organiser might have suspected, may unsettle him. If rebellious, the 'spontaneous' militant may react to this discovery with a blanket hostility to parliament, politics, and all other institutions which put the purity of the movement in jeopardy, and a current of such hostility often runs through the first phases of history when this absorption of labour into official life takes place; e.g., in England from 1911 to 1926.

But inevitably, even the most revolutionary must fight the battles for improvement and reform according to the nature of the terrain, which is that of 'realistic' calculation in a capitalist economy and a capitalist state. That is to say they must compromise, make allies, and in general act as reformists. If he is to be effective in a stable capitalist economy, even the communist union leader must do this, whatever his private reservations and calculations. A communist municipality in a non-communist state must for most of the time behave very much like any other left-wing municipality. It is thus only natural that for many 'spontaneous' labour militants the alternative to mindless militancy is for *practical purposes* an efficient reformism within a capitalist environment which is regarded as *de facto* permanent; or which is regarded, at best, as subject only to gradual and piecemeal change.

The appeal of such empiricism is perhaps best illustrated in the career of the late Ernest Bevin, the most influential trade union leader of the post-1918 period, and perhaps with Arthur Horner of the miners, the ablest (though probably Horner's inferior in intelligence and certainly his inferior in unselfishness). Bevin, as we have seen, began as a man of the extreme left – he deliberately chose the Social Democrats over the ILP as being more revolutionary – and cannot be regarded as moderate by natural inclination or tradition. Yet, in fact, his career is one of increasing political moderation. It would seem clear – though his biography throws only indirect light on the matter[20] – that the most important factor in his evolution was the discovery that capitalism was not breaking down, underlined as it was by the defeat of the General Strike and a visit to the then very flourishing industries of the USA. There is no evidence that Bevin abandoned his socialist convictions immediately, or at all. In the early thirties he was still prepared to co-operate closely with G. D. H. Cole and other left-wingers, and as late as 1936 he declared his belief in socialism in a form which the Labour right of the 1950s would have regarded as extremist. Yet, in fact, the business of trade unionism had to go on, and under the conditions operating after the General Strike, it implied, he thought, increasing collaboration with state and management. The logic of this position led him into the Foreign Secretaryship in 1945.

Bevin's career, however, also illustrates another factor in the British labour movement which made the abandonment of 'spontaneity' even more difficult: its marked anti-intellectualism. This characteristic, often found in spontaneous labour movements, is in one sense an index of the strength of their class-consciousness, membership of the class being defined as 'working with one's hands'. In another sense, it is an index of its limitations. Insofar as socialist intellectuals bring into the movement, as Lenin suggested, just that widening of political perspectives which corrects its 'spontaneity', the suspicion of *all* intellectuals perpetuates the movement's narrowness. Of course this suspicion is sometimes justified. The bulk of Britain's Labour intellectuals (and to be fair to Bevin, he distrusted them also), were relatively late migrants from liberalism, whose net effect on Labour was certainly not to push it towards the left. Nor is the spontaneous '*ouvrièrisme*' of proletarian movements inevitably linked to a reformist ideology. In France (where the Communist Party shows signs of it) it is historically linked with a sort of Robespierrist Jacobinism, in Hispanic countries often with anarchist traditions of direct action. However, in Britain the traditions of

340

working-class anti-intellectualism are mostly reformist, and class exclusiveness perpetuates and, indeed, accentuates them.

IX

To sum up. The roots of British reformism no doubt lie in the history of a century of economic world supremacy, and the creation of a labour aristocracy, or even more generally, of an entire working class which drew advantages from it. Conversely, the maintenance of the belief that British capitalism is a going concern, and not liable to immediate collapse, is a necessary (but probably not a sufficient) condition of its survival. A second, and not negligible reason for its maintenance belongs to the superstructure of history. It is, that the British labour movement was formed and moulded at the time when the dominant tradition was that of a reforming liberal-radicalism, whose stamp it still bears. However, the third and perhaps most important reason for its survival is general rather than specific. It is that, in conditions of stable or flourishing capitalism, and of official recognition of labour movements, a reformist policy is 'natural' because it is the obvious and practical policy, and a revolutionary policy correspondingly difficult. Therefore the spontaneous slope of the political and social landscape will tend to make labour movements slip towards reformism, unless they resist it; and even – often – when they do.

This does not mean that labour movements in such circumstances (which are common to all or most of the non-socialist developed countries today) *must* become reformist. Historical factors such as the impregnation of a movement with a revolutionary ideology at the crucial stage of its development, or the refusal of state and employers to conciliate it, may offset the natural drift towards reformism. Revolutionary movements may devise strategies for the transformation of society which do not require (except in self-defence and after victory) barricades or insurrection, or sudden and cataclysmic political change.* They may indeed have no other choice, if they are

---

* Such a perspective seems to have been in the mind of Frederick Engels in his last years for Germany; but like all Marxists at all times, he considered the peaceful, or even gradual perspectives in some countries in the general context of a world situation in which the 'old-fashioned' revolutionary developments of some regions – Engels thought of Russia – would react back upon the non-revolutionary ones.

not to drift into the casual insurrectionism of minorities, such as tempted the European left in the syndicalist period before World War I, or the massive self-exclusion of a labour movement which merely claims to wait for its historic moment to arrive. The first of these tactics is unlikely to be effective in non-revolutionary situations. The second (as the history of the German Social Democratic Party before 1914 shows) may merely amount to a tacit conversion to reformism.

(1949/63)

NOTES

1 *Industrial Democracy* (London 1898).
2 In view of later imperialist developments, Joseph Chamberlain's defence of them in the early 70s is specially significant. See his *Speeches*, ed C. Boyd, I, p. 27 f.
3 *The Life of Thomas Cooper, Written by Himself* (London 1872), p. 393 f.
4 Before the middle 1860s, that is. One may perhaps except the work of the Christian Socialist school of middle-class philanthropists whose efforts helped to secure the friendly societies legislation of the 1850s. As for labour, the Webbs' *History of Trade Unionism* has exaggerated the prevalence of the 'new model' of amalgamated societies, like the Engineers', and the acceptance of liberal economics by labour leaders before the 1870s. To begin with, the Chartist and Owenite leaders of the new movements – whether Engineers or Rochdale co-operators – in no sense intended to abandon their long-term aims. It was simply that the content of the old slogans changed in a new economic context; until, for lack of clear socialist theory, they became increasingly devoid of meaning.
5 Quoted in J. B. Jefferys, *Labour's Formative Years* (London 1948), p. 48.
6 Rosa Luxemburg, 'British Spectacles', *Leipziger Volkszeitung*, 9 May 1899. She is mistaken in thinking that the *unchallenged* domination of British industry was necessary to the functioning of such class collaboration.
7 Report of TUC General Council on the Mond-Turner conferences (TUC Report, 1928, p. 209).
8 See my *Labour's Turning Point* (London 1948), pp. 10 ff. and 104.
9 Cf., Dobb, *Studies in the Development of Capitalism*, pp. 263–7.
10 Cf., Maxime Leroy, *La Coutume ouvrière* (1913), for a discussion of the 'obligations' of unionism, pp. 190–361.

11 'What insurance will wealth find it to its advantage to provide against the risk to which it is undoubtedly subject?' (i.e., now that labour was ceasing to be docile); *Speeches*, ed. Boyd, I, p. 130.

12 It is possible to argue that it never did. Cf., M. Barratt Brown, *After Imperialism* (1963).

13 T. Prager, *Wirtschaftswunder oder keines?* (Vienna 1963).

14 *What Is to Be Done?* Parts II and III, *Selected Works* II.

15 Loc. cit., p. 98.

16 Cf., esp. Royden Harrison, 'The Tenth April of Spencer Walpole: the problem of revolution in relation to reform, 1865-7' (*International Review of Social History* VII, 1962, p. 352) and Asa Briggs, *The Age of Improvement* (London 1959), Chapter X.

17 Beatrice Webb, *Our Partnership* (London 1948), p. 24.

18 Cf., W. Milne-Bailey, *Trade Unions and the State* (London 1934), D. F. Macdonald, *The State and the Trade Unions* (London 1960), V. L. Allen, *Trade Unions and the Government* (London 1960). For the wartime operations of this policy, cf., W. K. Hancock and M. Gowing, *The British War Economy* (1949), Lord Inman, *Labour in the Munitions Industry* (1957), Parker, *Manpower* (1957), all in the official history of the Second World War.

19 Cf., R. Lyman, *The first Labour government* (London 1959).

20 Alan Bullock, *The Life and Times of Ernest Bevin*, vol. I (London 1959), esp. pp. 390, 446, 505.

17

Custom, Wages and Work-load
in Nineteenth-century Industry

THE BASIC PRINCIPLE of the nineteenth-century private enterprise economy was to buy in the cheapest market and to sell in the dearest. For the employer to buy labour in the cheapest market implied buying it at the lowest rate per unit of output, i.e., to buy the cheapest labour at the highest productivity. Conversely, for the worker to sell his labour in the dearest market meant logically to sell it at the highest price for the minimum unit of output. Obviously it was to the advantage of the bricklayer to get 7d. for an hour which meant the laying of 50 bricks rather than 100. The ideal situation envisaged by classical economics was one in which the wage-rate was fixed exclusively through the market without the intervention of non-economic compulsion on either side. For the employers this implied having a permanent reserve army of labour at all required grades of skill, for the workers permanent full, or rather over-full, employment. It also implied that both sides would be actuated by market motives: the employers by the search for the highest possible profit (which implied the lowest possible labour cost), the workers by the search for the highest possible wage (which implied complete responsiveness to wage-incentives). Gross though these over-simplifications are, they nevertheless represent the relevant parts of that simple theoretical model of a self-regulating market economy to which many economists and businessmen aspired and which they believed to be largely in operation.

The point was, that neither employers nor workers completely recognized the rules of this game or what they implied. This was partly due to the fact that they were unrealistic. Thus even the workers most open to wage-incentives are so only up to a point: social security, comfort at work, leisure, etc., compete with money. But it was also due to a tendency to base economic behaviour not on long-term rational analysis, but on custom, empiricism, or short-term calculation. In this essay I propose to discuss some of the effects of this on nineteenth-century labour productivity.* The conclusions of this discussion may be summarized as follows:

1. There are two main watersheds in the nineteenth-century history of the employment of industrial labour: one, probably, in the decades around the middle of the century, the other towards the end of the Great Depression. Both mark changes, or the beginning of changes, in the attitude of both workers and employers. Both, incidentally, coincide with turning-points in the evolution of other aspects of the economy.

2. The first marks the *partial* learning of the 'rules of the game'. Workers learned to regard labour as a commodity to be sold in the historically peculiar conditions of a free capitalist economy; but, where they had any choice in the matter, still fixed the basic asking price and the quantity and quality of work by non-economic criteria. Employers learned the value of intensive rather than extensive labour utilization and to a lesser extent of incentives, but still measured the degree of labour utilization by custom, or empirically – if at all.

3. The second marks the *complete* learning of the rules of the game. (It does not matter, for our purpose, that by this time the ideal model of a self-regulating market economy was, except perhaps in the international money market, ceasing to be even approximately realistic.) Workers began to demand what the traffic would bear and, where they had any choice, to measure effort by payment. Employers discovered genuinely efficient ways of utilizing their workers' labour time ('scientific management').

I

How did workers in the early industrial economy decide what wages and conditions to accept and what effort to put into their work,

---

* *Labour productivity* is usually a synonym for *output per man-hour* or some similar unit. Such a use normally fails to distinguish between those changes in output due to machinery and those due to other causes, e.g., changes in organization, in staffing, in the efficient utilization of the time, effort, and skill of the workers. In this essay the term applies *exclusively* to the second type of change. In practice, of course, the two kinds of change generally go together and are hard to separate.

assuming that they had any choice? They have rarely told us, so that we are forced into conjecture, based partly on observation, partly on the analysis of the scattered historical data.[1]

No initial problem of wage determination arose for the unskilled or those in abundant supply. They had to take (if men) a subsistence wage, or one fixed so as just to attract them away from (say) farm labour.[2] (Women and children of course got less than subsistence, but since their rate was normally fixed in relation to the male wage, we may neglect them.) The fact that the wages of unskilled labour were fixed at or around subsistence costs is overwhelmingly attested by theorists, industrialists, and historians. We may therefore take the subsistence wage of the unskilled or plentiful labourer or farmhand as the point of reference, in relation to which all other grades fixed their own positions. We must neglect problems arising out of the payment of wages in kind. 'Subsistence' was, of course, not a physiological absolute, but a conventional category varying at different times and in different places.

The characteristic skilled worker in pre-industrial crafts would expect to get ideally about twice as much as the common labourer, a differential of great antiquity and persistence, for we can find it in Diocletian's price- and wage-fixing as in that of the English J.P.s under Henry VI and Charles II, in eighteenth-century Italy, in France, in the Barcelona building trades of the nineteenth century, and doubtless elsewhere. (These are, of course, *rates* not *earnings*.) In fact, the skilled man normally tended to get rather less than this differential, especially when unable to restrict entry from the unskilled grades, and more when entry was effectively restricted, as when the skilled man was white, the unskilled coloured. In practice the relation between the rates of the pre-industrial labourer and craftsman – say the mason and his labourer – was more likely to be two to three or three to five, than one to two.[3]

How would a skilled man fix his wage standard in relation to other skilled men? The calculations here, though tacit and often unconscious, were rather complex. On the one hand each worker would regard himself as belonging to a particular stratum – say of craftsmen as distinct from labourers – and would therefore expect a wage conforming to its social status: masons, tilers, and carpenters would expect to earn wages of the same rough order of magnitude, as would smiths, engineers, skilled tailors, and shoemakers. On the other hand within each stratum or industry there was a well-defined hierarchy, though it is not always clear whether this represented earning capacity or whether earnings reflected it. Thus the coachmakers in 1837

are not an equal body, but one composed of classes taking rank one after the other . . . the body-makers are first on the list; then follow the carriage-makers; then the trimmers; then the smiths; then the spring-makers; then the wheelwrights, painters, platers, brace-makers and so on. The body-makers are the wealthiest of all and compose among themselves a species of aristocracy to which the other workmen look up with feelings half of respect, half of jealousy. They feel their importance and treat the others with various consideration: carriage-makers are entitled to a species of condescending familiarity; trimmers are considered too good to be despised; a foreman of painters they may treat with respect, but working painters can at most be favoured with a nod.[4]

Similar hierarchies are attested for the new industries, in Alsace, Lancashire, the engineering workshops, and elsewhere.[5] No doubt status reflected wage differences, or wage differences hardened into custom; but workers did not clearly distinguish between these and the status they believed to be attached to the job: a compositor who did not get a higher wage than, say, a local tailor would regard himself as ill-served, whatever the relative demand for each on the market.

Traditional differentials were, of course, less important in new industries and in those dominated by piece-work (except in so far as the original bidding price for various grades of labour had been set with reference to the previously existing wage-scale). It is dangerous to exaggerate the role of custom in the wage-structure of a fully industrial economy as some recent students have done, though custom undoubtedly somewhat distorted it. (After all, the standards by which workers judged a wage to be acceptable or not were not the only factor in fixing them.) The point is, that the wage-structure of a developed capitalist economy was not formed in a void. It began as a modification or distortion of the pre-industrial wage-hierarchy and only gradually came to approximate to the new pattern; more quickly in areas of acute labour shortage or glut, in economies dominated by sharp business fluctuations, than in others; and certainly more quickly in those economies which succeeded in destroying or disorganizing the self-defence organizations of small producers or pre-industrial workers. However, the important thing to bear in mind is that the *worker's* wage calculation remained for long, and still to some extent remains, largely a customary and not a market calculation.

One important result of this was that employers almost certainly got their skilled labour in the nineteenth century at less than market cost. This applies not only to countries with a generally low wage-level such as Germany and Belgium, but also to Britain. It seems clear that, even allowing for the sharp cyclical fluctuations to which they were subject, ironfounders and engineers in Britain before, say, 1840, lived in a wonderful seller's market and could have demanded much more than the rate of 30s. or so which engineers in Lancashire got in the 1850s.[6] Obviously competition between small firms and the absence of effective unions played its part, as did the fact that the men demanded some of their extra price in terms of non-economic satisfactions, such as independence of supervision, dignified treatment, and mobility. Nevertheless the essential modesty of their demands was and remains important, as any Australian coming to this country is willing to attest. The more traditional and hierarchical their society, the greater it was.

Since we can only speculate on 'what the traffic would bear' in those days, we cannot of course measure the size of the bonus which employers drew from their workmen's unwillingness to charge it. One would guess that it was at least as great as the bonus they had drawn in the eighteenth century from Professor Hamilton's 'profit-inflation'. It also seems likely that their views on individual productivity were affected by it. The worker's labour effort, or standard of output per unit of time, was also determined by custom rather than market calculation, at any rate until he began to learn the rules of the game. The ideal of 'a fair day's work for a fair day's pay' had, and has, little in common with the ideal of buying in the cheapest and selling in the dearest market. The criteria for a fair day's work are probably too complex for a cursory analysis. They depended partly on physiological considerations (e.g., the working speed and effort which a man might maintain indefinitely, allowing for rests during and between working days or shifts); on technical ones (e.g., the nature of the jobs he could be expected to do in the course of a day or shift); on social ones (e.g., the need for a team to work at the pace which allowed slower members to keep up and in turn earn a fair day's wage); on moral ones (e.g., the natural pride a man has in doing a job as well as he can); on economic ones (e.g., how much work can earn a 'fair wage'); on historic ones and doubtless on others. They were enforced by powerful collective pressure.[7] In fact, as we know, such standards were so well accepted that – where workers had the choice – there was

348

often no major difference between time and piece-rates: each could be translated into the other with little difficulty. The employer of time-workers knew roughly how much piece-output he would get, the employer of piece-workers (as Adam Smith observed)[8] knew that he was not likely to get more than the standard output for the accepted working week from them, though they might get it done in fewer days. What statistics we have tend to show that in non-mechanized industries output tended to fluctuate about a level trend. Productivity in the Ruhr mines (except for the period 1796–1802 and the early 1830s) remained pretty steady from 1790 to 1850 at between 87 and 97 per cent of the 1850 level. In the Halle copper-mines it averaged 12–13 tons per man-shift for each trade cycle period between 1800 and 1850.[9] In French coal-mining it was equally stable between 1834 and 1852.[10] This level was not necessarily the highest obtainable, but it is likely that workers laboured as hard as they could, or were traditionally expected to do, subject to the proviso that they felt themselves to be getting a 'fair' wage and that work did not interfere with their comfort at work and at leisure. Of course raw workers, forced labour, or others set to do uncongenial or untraditional work for which they had no customary standard, being untrained or un-practised, workers feeling themselves to be underpaid, or unable to take any pride in their labour naturally worked only as hard as they had to. But pleasure in work is commoner than one thinks. De Man's inquiries in the 1920s showed that in Germany 67 per cent of skilled workers and even 44 per cent of unskilled ones said they felt more pleasure than distaste for their work.[11] The moral stigma against slacking was and remained very great among such groups. The employer who took over such pre-industrial types of workers, or those who modelled themselves on them, could be fairly sure to get as much work per time-unit out of them initially as was socially ex-pected, unless or until he introduced the criteria of the market economy. Naturally such rigidity of output could be troublesome where he required productivity to increase rapidly, or workers to adjust themselves to rapidly changing work-processes.[12]

It is therefore clear that skilled workers, indeed perhaps all workers who felt some self-respect and were not goaded into revolt, did not apply market criteria to the measurement of their efforts. Unskilled ones were of course habitually overdriven and underpaid, but em-ployers did not expect more than the absolute minimum of voluntary work from them anyway, and relied – perhaps wrongly, before the age of modern mass production – on discipline or 'driving' to get as much effort as could be expected of them.[13]

II

Somewhere about the middle of the century we observe a conscious adjustment of skilled workers to the 'rules of the game', at least in Britain. Thus unions began in the 1840s to recognize the peculiar nature of the trade cycle in their provisions for unemployment, and a little later to develop the characteristic policies of the 'new model' unionism: restriction of entry, maximum labour mobility between areas of slack and full employment, emigration benefit, the systematic use of friendly benefits, and so on.[14] As we know, the economic theory behind these policies aimed at the creation of a permanent scarcity of skilled labour, so as to raise its market price. Again, as we shall see, skilled workers as well as employers in the 1850s and 1860s tended to favour the shortest possible forms of hiring contract so as to enable either side to bargain for better terms with the least possible delay. But, even if allowing for the exceptions to *laissez-faire* which unions naturally clung to (especially legal protection and trade unionism), this was only a partial adaptation to free market bargaining. The criteria of a 'fair wage' remained customary in many industries, those of a 'fair day's work' equally inflexible. Indeed some unions combined *laissez-faire* bargaining with strict penalization of bad work, as did the boilermakers.[15]

The period which followed the Great Depression may have seen a more fundamental change of attitude, as it saw a more fundamental revolution in the economy and in the structure of the labour force. In the first place, as Rowe has shown, certain groups of workers – e.g., the railwaymen – for the first time began to demand what the traffic would bear. In the second place there was, in a number of industries in various countries, a very marked slackening in individual productivity, all the more striking in contrast with the very rapid rise of the third quarter of the century. Thus in French coal-mining, output per man-day (underground workers, 1900 = 100) rose from 62 in the 1840s to 100 in 1887–95, after which it fell slowly to 95 in 1909–1914. In Germany, productivity per worker in hard coal-mining rose from 45 in 1844–52 to 101 in 1887–94 (1900 = 100) after which it remained roughly stable until 1913.[16] Output per head in British and Belgian mining, in the London building trades, and Lancashire cotton-spinning from the 1890s on showed similar tendencies.[17] Even if we allow, where necessary, for the effect of diminishing returns, or the increase of non-productive workers sometimes comprised in these totals, or the shortening of hours, the tendency remains suggestive enough. In one or two cases it has been specifically put down to a certain slackening in the men's individual labour effort.[18] It is at least possible that certain groups of workers now began systematically to allow their output to sink unless held up by incentives, or else that the weakening of older forms of labour discipline or tradition produced the same result.

Although industrial militants like Tom Mann developed the theory of free market bargaining by varying the worker's labour effort in the 1890s,[19] conscious and systematic slacking of this kind was no doubt rare. When proposed it met with a great deal of moral indignation not only – naturally, if illogically – from employers, but from skilled workers themselves and their sympathizers.[20] The tendency to slack undermined the workers' self-respect even if it improved his market position; and self-respect is a much more fundamental thing than the historically evanescent categories of the free market economy.

Between 1880 and 1914, therefore, employers began to lose the advantages which they had hitherto enjoyed owing to the workers' ignorance of the 'rules of the game' or their unwillingness to play it, and from which they had drawn considerable benefits. Sometimes, as in British cotton-spinning, quasi-monopoly cushioned them against the effects of this loss;[21] sometimes not. We must therefore turn to the employers' side of the picture.

III

If the failure to learn or apply the rules of the game caused workers often to work harder and for less money than they need theoretically have done, the employers' failure to learn or apply them caused them to utilize the labour they hired with remarkable inefficiency.

In considering the behaviour of nineteenth-century entrepreneurs we must naturally distinguish between what might be inefficient today, but could be rationally justified under then prevailing conditions, and what could not. (We need not agree with the rational justifications of early employers, but need merely recognize that they were rational.) The early industrial entrepreneur believed, not without

351

some justification, that his labour force was largely impervious to monetary incentives, reluctant to work in the way which suited him, or indeed to enter his employ at all. As Townsend observed in 1780:

> The poor know little of the motives which stimulate the higher ranks to action – pride, honour and ambition. In general it is only hunger which can spur and goad them on to labour.[22]

And, we might add, only discipline which would keep them at it. It was therefore logical for employers to use compulsion, non-economic as well as economic, to recruit the labour force and to keep it at work. Hence the first half of the nineteenth century is anything but *laissez-faire* in its labour relations. In Britain it saw the codification of the Master and Servant Law, which penalized breaches of contract more harshly for men than for masters,[23] the systematic if not always effective outlawing of trade unions and strikes – the repeal of the Combination Acts made relatively little difference to this – a marked taste for long-term and inelastic labour contracts like the miner's annual or monthly bond,[24] and that ruthless piece of legal-economic coercion, the New Poor Law. Elsewhere similar devices were common.

These things were in part rationally justifiable in terms of contemporary theory, though not wholly so; for employers were only too willing to abandon *laissez-faire* when it did not suit them. Thus annual bonds, though understandable as a response to local labour shortages, as in the eighteenth-century mines, were not easily defensible by a disciple of Adam Smith. However, what is not justifiable is the extraordinary neglect of the problem of productivity and efficient labour utilization. Broadly speaking, employers assumed that the lowest wage-bill for the longest hours meant the lowest labour cost per unit of time; that the workers' effort could not be much increased above a given norm, though they were often too lazy to reach this; that the problem of productivity was essentially one of mechanization combined with discipline; and that incentives were mainly useful as an auxiliary to this, if at all. Handbooks for industrialists and managers, though devoting much attention to the economic utilization of raw materials, neglected the problem of labour management almost completely.[25]

This is, of course, to oversimplify the part played by incentives in the early entrepreneur's scheme. They were in fact widely used, partly in the form of piece-wages, partly in that of subcontract. Yet neither was inconsistent with the view summarized above. The subcontractor was a form of entrepreneur, and entrepreneurs were of course responsive to incentives. Moreover, he set the pace for those under him who did *not* enjoy incentives, and indeed the prevalence of subcontracting appeared to make incentives to the workers themselves largely unnecessary, except in the case of genuine collective task-wages fixed by gangs. The piece-master, charter-master, or whatever he was called, the skilled craftsman – spinner, plater, or smelter – who paid his unskilled assistants himself as often as not on straight time-rates, the foreman or ganger who, almost invariably, worked on a commission basis or as subcontractor:[26] these set the pace and the rest had no option but to follow it.

Nor was payment by results itself (as distinct from subcontract) conceived primarily as a means of raising productivity, but as a means of stopping it from falling below the norm. As Dr John's Welsh ironmaster claimed, it was the only way to ensure that workers 'did their duty' when they could not be effectively supervised.[27] Or, to quote M. Ponson of Liège:

> Daywork is the most disadvantageous method in mines, bcause the workers, having no interest to work actively, mostly slacken the sum of their efforts as soon as supervision ceases.[28]

Indeed we have examples of deep pits being sunk on time-wages for the first few hundred feet, while supervision was possible, but on piece-rates thereafter.[29] In general, if an *increase* in effort was required it was got by 'driving', though this might imply giving incentives to a limited number of 'wheel-horses'. Naturally, grades of workers who resisted disciplined supervision – e.g., skilled craftsmen – could not be so treated.[30]

This argument does not apply in the same way to industries which had always been paid by results, for instance the domestic industries in which piece-work was a degenerate form of the price which formerly independent artisans had been paid for the sale of his product, or in occupations directly modelled on such industries.

Though this attitude cannot be justified, it can be understood. The combination of ultra-cheap wage-costs with standard customary labour efforts gave employers a considerable surplus, once workers were trained and experienced; larger perhaps than they might have got by high wages and more intensive efforts. Thus Belgian coalminers were worse paid than those in the Ruhr; their output per manshift between 1886 and 1910 was consistently 30 to 40 per cent below the Germans. But over the same period (1892–1910) the labour cost of Belgian coal, measured as a percentage of its pithead price, was less: 53·9 against 55·9 per cent.[31] Again, small works may be able, perhaps by close supervision and other factors, to have lower labour costs than all but very large and efficient works: at any rate Rostas's figures for British industry in 1937 seem to suggest this.[32] Most early works were small, and where this was so and capital was short entrepreneurs might think it good policy to utilize the abundant factor, labour, rather than the scarce one, even at the cost of some labour inefficiency per worker. Lastly it seems probable that even with few incentives, unskilled or simple work can be utilized much more efficiently than skilled or complex work, simply because its pace can be more effectively supervised and controlled, whether by man or machine. A standard American textbook of 'scientific management' estimates that unskilled labour and routine clerical jobs directly supervised in small groups work at 50 per cent efficiency, semi-skilled machine-operators at 38–40 per cent, skilled all-round mechanics at 30 per cent, and highly skilled all-round men such as tool-makers at 25–28 per cent.[33] But this does not alter the fact that for each wage-unit paid employers got much less than they might have done, and were largely unaware that this was so.

Again, the combination of an unskilled, untrained labour force and mechanization tended to blind them. Raw labour could not be expected to be efficient anyway: one must budget with low *per capita* output. The increase in output due to technical innovation was so vast that it was easy to forget how much greater it might have been with efficient exploitation. 'By the aid of mechanical fingers,' exclaimed Dr Ure,[34] 'one Englishman at his mule can turn off daily more yarn than 200 of the most diligent spinsters of Hindostan.' It seemed not to matter that they might have turned out more, because few entrepreneurs realized the potential economies of really efficient labour exploitation. The *Carding and Spinning Master's Assistant* of 1832 warned employers against rearranging their machinery once installed, even if they found the arrangement to be less than ideal, since the costs of reorganization would probably exceed the savings.[35] Yet this was a patent mistake. It is perhaps impossible, at any rate without long and laborious work, to make an estimate of such inefficiency, but we have at least a guide to it in the Report of the UN Commission on Latin American Textile Industries (1950), some of which are ex-

tremely archaic. This pioneer study attempts to separate the inefficiency due to obsolete or defective machinery from that due to other
factors, chiefly bad organization – e.g., over-staffing, in other words
inefficient labour utilization. It concludes that both are equally important causes of inefficiency. In Brazil and Ecuador, the most technically old-fashioned of the industries studied, reorganization would
improve efficiency more than new investment. 'Contrary to what has
always been supposed,' says the report, 'bad organization and administration affect productivity as much as the traditional shortage
of capital.'[36] No historian of early industrial Europe will be in the
least surprised at this discovery.

The temptations of a cheap labour economy made employers
equally reluctant to recognize their inefficiency when it was pointed
out to them. Admittedly, few were prepared to instruct industrialists
in scientific management except the rare scientist like Charles Babbage.[37] On the other hand, the fact that low wages and long hours
were not necessarily identical with the lowest labour costs was proved
time and again in business, and could indeed be observed. Brassey
gave wide publicity to his proof.[38] As Lujo Brentano pointed out,
even the experience of the great wage rise of 1872 proved it, though he
was regarded as enunciating a paradox and many observers flatly
refused to believe their eyes.[39] Owen's New Lanark had made the
point decades before. The judicious Ponson, who gave statistics for
output per man-day for coal-hewers of 113 pits in four countries
whose shifts ranged from six to fifteen hours, concluded in 1853,
without any detectable philanthropic bias, that eight hours would
seem a reasonable average shift at the coal-face.[40] But as late as 1901,
80 per cent of all Belgian workers still laboured in excess of eleven
hours.[41] When in 1889 unions forced the British gas industry to adopt
three eight-hour shifts instead of two twelve-hour ones, the industry
believed itself to be facing (a) a net loss in efficiency and (b) a completely unprecedented method of working; but several gasworks in
the country had operated on eight-hour shifts for up to fifty years,
their results were available to inspection, and the industry happened
to be one in which technical discussion was particularly lively and
informed.[42]

This resistance to knowledge is also understandable. In practice
great labour efficiency implied higher wages and shorter hours. But
in the first place no businessman likes to raise his costs unless he is
certain to recover them, and entrepreneurs had no cast-iron guaran-

tee. In the second, it was undesirable to encourage workers to demand higher wages and shorter hours, for where would such demands stop? It was safer, if less efficient, to stick to the old ways, unless pressure on profit-margins, increased competition, the demands of labour or other inescapable facts forced a change. But the periods of major economic adjustment after the Napoleonic Wars and the slump of 1873 subjected employers to just this kind of pressure, and hence led to major modifications in the method of labour utilization. In the post-Napoleonic period the effect was delayed, since employers first attempted to exhaust the possibilities of cutting labour costs by extending hours and cutting money wage-rates. During the Great Depression (1873–96) new methods tended to be adopted more quickly. Roughly speaking, the mid-century brought the beginning of the substitution of 'intensive' for 'extensive' labour utilization, the latter part of the Great Depression the beginning of the substitution of rational for empirical 'intensive' utilization, or of 'scientific management'.

IV

Though it is very probable that the efficiency of labour utilization rose after the 1840s, this is not easy to establish statistically. However, it is clear that the system of labour relations in Britain underwent fundamental changes, and analogous ones are observable elsewhere (for instance, in Napoleon III's legalization of strikes). Non-economic compulsion virtually disappeared with the decline of the miners' bond and other long contracts, the abolition of the Master and Servant Laws and the full legalization of trade unionism. We can trace the extension of short-hiring contracts in the 1850s, particularly in Scotland,[43] but also in a variety of local building-trade agreements. Piece-mastering and subcontract, those almost invariable concomitants of rapid capitalist industrialization in its early stages, may well have passed their peak, at any rate in the older industries.[44] Modifications in the Poor Law (e.g., in 1867) also tended to turn it from an instrument of labour coercion into one of relief.[45] As often as not these legal changes ratified a *de facto* situation. Obviously the substitution of a willing for an unwilling bargain was likely to improve the morale of skilled operatives, and hence their productivity. (This was more important in doctrinaire *laissez-faire* countries than where paternalism was widespread, as in German heavy industry, but this is not the place to discuss these interesting differences.) More important, the movement to shorten hours gained ground, partly through legislation, partly through private arrangements and bargains, as in the Saturday half-holiday, which came into fairly wide use from the 1840s among the builders and in some parts of the provinces, and in London from the mid-fifties.[46] Shorter hours virtually obliged employers to raise productivity, and the fact that this could be done was now more widely appreciated.

We know so little about systems of management and wage-payment that it is dangerous to generalize about them, especially in view of the incredible complexity of the industrial scene. Only three facts are at all certain. First, that from the 1830s on the economists, who had previously discussed systems of wage-payment only incidentally – as in Adam Smith, Malthus, Say, and Sismondi – began to pay systematic attention to them. From the end of the 1830s economic treatises normally contained a special section on the form of wage-payments.[47] Where writers had been neutral about, or slightly hostile to, piece-rates, they now became very enthusiastic about them, e.g., McCulloch and Michel Chevalier.[48] Second, employers in several countries showed a marked tendency to extend payment by results – i.e., incentive payments – initially mostly in combination with sub-contracting and piece-mastering. All this led Marx to the familiar view that payment by results was the type of wage system best suited to capitalism.[49] Since we have no reliable statistics, we cannot estimate the success of these efforts. Sometimes they failed, as among British engineers and builders.[50] Sometimes they succeeded, as when Krupps introduced piece-work after 1850 together with mass production,[51] or when new coalfields such as those of South Wales paid most of their workers by results, while in older fields (as in the North-east) only certain grades such as coal-getters had been so paid.[52] But the tendency – observed in the British factory inspectors' reports – is not in doubt[53] It was vastly accelerated by the massive construction of the railways, which was paid almost entirely by results, and helped to spread the principle of piece-work widely, e.g., into German agriculture,[54] and into the building industry. Lastly, it is clear that the reluctance to increase money-wages diminished. Money wage-rates took a marked turn upwards in most West European countries after the mid-century, and the first timid defences of a 'high wage economy' could be heard.[55] However, we are pretty much in the dark about the actual increase in labour efficiency, and it is clear that vast areas of industry remained resolutely old-fashioned.

After 1880 we sail much less uncharted waters. Since this was precisely the period when labour efficiency came to be considered a subject of special study, at least as important as that of the efficient use of equipment and raw material, it attracted the researcher, the engineer, the government department, and other suppliers of historical material.

The main incentive to change came from the well-known tendency of profit-margins to decline in the Great Depression. This is also the period when imperfect competition made itself felt on a large scale, when the 'second industrial revolution' got under way, and when a powerful labour movement emerged in several countries, composed, moreover, of workers who increasingly knew the 'rules of the game'. Whether pressure from competition or from labour was more important in turning employers' thoughts towards labour efficiency is uncertain. A case has been made for both.[56] From our point of view labour pressure is the more interesting, though it must be borne in mind that the increasing scale and complexity of industrial production made firms more vulnerable to it than they had previously been, as well as making old methods of labour management less applicable. As one of F. W. Taylor's disciples put it: 'We used to drive workers, but – especially if they are skilled – . . . they do not have to stand it'.[57] One reason why they did not need to, as a historian of scientific management observes, was that there now had to be 'a substitute for the effective supervision characteristic of the small shop'.[58]

'Scientific management' was the result.[59] In its initial phases, with which we are here concerned, it consisted of three main elements:

(a) a careful analysis of the production process, its break-up into simple segments and the establishment of labour norms for each;
(b) a system of costing which enabled the firm to discover the labour cost of each operation and to keep it under constant observation;
(c) the elaboration of systems of incentives or supervision capable of making workers labour at maximum intensity. For practical purposes this then meant payment by results.

In practice these were generally combined with mechanization, though this is not theoretically essential. It is possible to have mechanization without conscious scientific management as in the early nineteenth century, and scientific management without capital

358

investment in new machines. To begin with, scientific management shared the old view that there was an optimum labour effort, the manager's job being to stop workers from falling below it. But in abandoning custom and tradition scientific management discovered that the optimum effort was so much higher than had been believed possible, and thus in practice became a set of methods for raising rather than for maintaining effort.

All this involved considerable changes in the behaviour of employers. We can follow the evolution of their thought – or rather of that of production engineers – in the debates of the American Society of Mechanical Engineers from about 1886. They began as a search for incentives to replace the effective supervision or 'driving' of earlier days. Hence their first concern was with the elaboration of new forms of payment by results, and the main methods at present in vogue – the premium bonus systems of the Halsey and Rowan types, the Taylor, Gantt, etc. – were invented in the following decade. The engineers were then led into a consideration of costing systems; and indeed in some countries the cost-accountants were the real pioneers of the movement, as in Britain, where Fells and Garcke (two young members of the Fabian Society, interestingly enough) published their *Factory Accounts* in 1887.[60] Thence the discussions naturally turned to organization and management itself, and it was at this point that Frederick Winslow Taylor intervened, henceforth to dominate the whole movement.

Before 1914 and outside the USA we are still hardly concerned with scientific management in the modern sense – rationalization based on time-and-motion study and suchlike. However, in a more empirical way even this was implicit in mass production by specialized machines or processes which now expanded greatly; particularly where labour was the expensive factor. Innocent of Taylorism, the Bristol boot-and-shoe employers, who devised the 'team system' around 1890, applied his principles. They sub-divided the process and made sure that the team was 'waited upon hand and foot and never kept waiting for anything, whereas when they have to "shop" their own work a waste of time is involved'.[61] Any new process automatically involved such labour-costing. Where it was carried out by cheap and docile labour, as in many new consumer-goods factories, this was not important, because wage costs were in any case low. However, the core of the new industrial revolution was an industry which had been hitherto overwhelmingly operated on a semi-handicraft basis by self-reliant and highly paid workers: metals and engineering. Here the transition to the new system had to be thought and fought out much more consciously than elsewhere. Nor is it surprising that in consequence the metal-workers, hitherto rather conservative, became in most countries of the world the characteristic leaders of militant labour movements. The history of such movements since the British lock-out of 1897 can be largely written in terms of the metal-workers, so much so that – for instance – the anti-war movements of 1916–18 followed a pace set almost exclusively by them. (We need merely think of Merrheim's union in France, the Berlin shop stewards, the British shop stewards, the Putilov works in Petrograd, the Manfred Weiss works in Budapest, the Turin and Milan metal-workers.)

However, if rationalization was in its infancy, payment by results and incentive schemes made their way rapidly. In Britain they were imposed on the Amalgamated Society of Engineers by 1903, after bitter conflicts in the 1890s, and increased steadily up to the 1914 war.[62] Armstrong-Whitworth went over to scientific management before 1900; Siemens-Schuckert in Vienna adopted premium bonus in that year.[63] The rapid spread of payment by results is not in doubt. In Britain 5 per cent of all engineering and boilermaking workers were on it in 1886, 27·5 per cent in 1906. (Among turners: 6–7 per cent in 1886, 46 per cent in 1914; among machine-men: 11 per cent in 1886, 47 per cent in 1913.[64]) We can frequently observe the change from time- to piece-wages, as in the Lorraine ironworks (especially the larger ones),[65] British railway workshops,[66] the German railways, and elsewhere.[67] Even where piece-wages had long been the rule, as in cotton, the Great Depression brought significant modifications. At the very least – as in the Bolton spinning list of 1887 – it produced a general systematization of piece-rates; but it could also lead to the frank recognition of 'speed-up' as an element in piece-wages, as in Oldham, where joint-stock companies predominated.[68]

The object of such innovations was, of course, to lower labour cost per unit of output. If this was not achieved, the employer gained nothing by intensification of labour except perhaps some general savings in capital and labour in other sections of production. Backward or docile workers presented no problem. Ideally it might be possible to 'drive' them simply by the speed of the machine or the effectiveness of supervision, paying them flat time-rates and appropriating the entire gain. This, the so-called 'continental system',[69] was sometimes applied, e.g., when the Coventry ribbon trade went over to factory production in the 1850s and in many early boot-and-shoe factories.[70] The widespread practice of bribing 'bell-horses' or 'chasers' as pace-makers for the rest also evaded the problem of incentive payments. Slightly less helpless or stupid workers might be paid a simple bounty or premium for all production in excess of the norm, irrespective how much. Until the weavers' unions stopped it, this system was much used in Lancashire.[71] Yet strong or 'educated' workers had to be given more realistic incentives, otherwise they would merely go 'canny'.

The overwhelming importance of payment by results at this stage therefore reflects largely the fact that employers now had to operate with a working class which knew the 'rules of the game' and would make an effort proportionate to reward, whether or not it was organized in unions. This also discouraged ordinary piece-work; for under such a system labour costs were only lowered by periodic rate-cutting, always an unpopular process. Hence all the new systems of payment by results tended to make payment automatically regressive, i.e., paid for each increment of production at a lower rate than for the preceding increment; a fact generally, and often intentionally, obscured by their immense complexity. But though the lowering of labour costs thus became automatic and tacit in theory, in practice this seldom happened. Firms rarely had enough skilled efficiency experts or rate-fixers to price jobs for good and all. Mass production was rarely so standardized that goods remained the same for long periods. Technical methods and products changed. The new payment-schemes therefore often failed to secure tranquil adjustments. They might even, as in engineering, create those constant conflicts over the pricing of new jobs or machines which have made the fortune of shop stewards. Hence the modern tendency to revert to flat time-wages (based, however, on a much more scientifically calculated and controlled output norm per time-unit), as in the American motor industry. However, before 1914 scientific management and the extension of payment by results still went together, as the writings of Alfred Marshall bear witness.[72]

There is hardly any need to demonstrate the results of the new methods. Jewkes and Gray have calculated the extent of speed-up in cotton-spinning between 1876 and 1906, their estimates tallying with those given at the time by the Royal Commission on the Depression of Trade.[73] However, the actual saving in labour cost – 23 per cent between 1876 and 1886 – was halted thereafter by the resistance of the operatives. The increase of output per head which followed a change from time to result wages – and that of accidents which also frequently ensued – is so obvious as hardly to need documenting. Our American textbook estimates the efficiency of piece or premium work at 78 per cent as against the percentages for time-work quoted earlier.[74] A single example from our period should suffice. In the Belgian glass industry output per man remained stable at 750–800 foot-units during the 1890s; rose by about 25 per cent until 1903 when payment by results was introduced, together with a lengthening of the working day; and thereafter shot up, with fluctuations, to about 300 per cent of the 1890 and 200 per cent of the 1903 level by 1909.[75] Employers were at last aware of the fantastic savings in labour cost which scientific labour utilization could bring. It is at least arguable that the tapping of this reserve by efficient exploitation was as important for the continued progress of the economy as the reduction of other costs.[76]

In this summary discussion I have necessarily and deliberately over-simplified. Thus I have concentrated on one aspect of incentive schemes – regressive piece-work wages – to the exclusion of various other methods of achieving substantially the same results; sometimes, as in the case of Taylor's own system, at the expense of other firms by skimming the cream off the local labour market. Moreover, I have concentrated on one aspect of scientific management, the actual direct saving of labour-time per worker, rather than on other aspects which, though capital- rather than labour-saving, have a very direct bearing on the efficient use of labour-time also; for instance, various shiftwork and continuous work systems which were also greatly reformed and expanded in the period after 1880, partly in response to labour pressure for shorter hours.[77] I have also illustrated the argument mainly from a few Atlantic seaboard countries, in order to avoid complicating the discussion further by considering major differences in the chronology of industrial development. The object of this simplification is to direct attention to the main conclusions, as set out earlier. These are obviously very tentative. Until much further work has been done on nineteenth-century work-loads and output per man, they cannot be satisfactorily verified. Such studies ought to distinguish, so far as possible – as research has often failed to do – between the various cost-reducing effects of mechanization and other forms of reorganization in the division of labour, in the ways attempted by the UN Commission for the Latin American Textile

Industry. This will involve considerable work, and the co-operation of students with good engineering and accounting as well as historical qualifications, for it will involve the analysis of working processes and the cost accounts of many individual works. Perhaps because the available material rarely throws much light on individual work-efforts and because historians are rarely qualified to undertake such analyses, the importance of the changes to which this paper has tried to direct attention, has been somewhat underrated.

NOTES

1 J. W. F. Rowe, *Wages in Practice and Theory* (1928), and Barbara Wootton, *The Social Foundations of Wage Policy* (1955), suggest ways of tackling this problem.
2 E.g., P. W. Kingsford, *Railway Labour 1830–70* (PhD Dissertation, London Univ. Library), p. 145. A useful discussion of the basis of this 'district rate' for labour from the management's point of view is in *Journal of Gas Lighting*, lii (1888), p. 286. It forms part of a series on 'The Management of Workmen'. For some factors tending to raise this 'district rate' above the strictly economic minimum, cf., R. Newman, 'Work and Wages in East London Now and Twenty Years Ago' (*Charity Organization Review* (July 1887), p. 273); Charles Booth, *Life and Labour* . . . 2nd ser. V, pp. 365 ff.
3 E. Young, *Labor in Europe and America* (Washington 1876); L. Dal Pane, *Storia del laboro in Italia – secolo XVIII* (Milan 1944), App. III; H. Sée, *Histoire écon. de la France*, ii, p. 179; Angel Marvaud, *La Question sociale en Espagne* (Paris 1910), p. 426. For differentials in Britain, see Chapter 15 of the present work, *The Labour Aristocracy in Nineteenth-Century Britain*, pp. 272 seq.
4 W. B. Adams, *English Pleasure Carriages* (London 1837), pp. 188–9.
5 E.g., Volz, 'Die Fabriksbevoelkerung des Oberelsass im Jahre 1850' (*Ztschr. f. d. ges. Staatswissenschaft*, vii, p. 136): 'Der Drucker hasst den Stecher, dieser faehrt stolz an jenem vorueber; der Zeichner und der Maler spricht mit Verachtung von Spin-nern . . .' and the various remarks about the refusal of 'mechan-ics' to abandon their status even under great economic pressure in Charity Organization Society, *Special Committee on Unskilled Labour* (1908), e.g., pp. 102, 112.
6 J. B. Jefferys, *The Story of the Engineers* (1945), p. 23; D.

Chadwick, 'On the Rate of Wages in Manchester and Salford
... 1839–59' (*Journ. Stat. Soc.*, xxiii, 1859).

7 E.g., Mr Dent's evidence – a building foreman – on such collective levelling in *Special Ctee. on Unskilled Labour*, op. cit., p. 104.

8 *Wealth of Nations*, cap. viii (Cannan (ed) i, pp. 83–4). Cf., also F. Smith, *Workshop Management* (n.d., ? 1884), p. 1: 'For convenience sake time is computed as the equivalent of work done'.

9 J. Kuczynski, *Geschichte der Lage der Arbeiter in Deutschland* (6th edn, Berlin 1954), i, pp. 112–16.

10 Ministère des Travaux Publics, *Statistiques de l'Industrie minérale* (Paris 1935).

11 H. De Man, *Joy in Work* (1928). However, it must be noted that the pioneer German investigations of A. Levenstein into this question give diametrically opposite results (*Die Arbeiterfrage*, Munich 1912). 60·5 per cent of his sample of miners, 75·1 per cent of his textile workers, and 56·9 per cent of his metalworkers (all working on payment by results) expressed distaste for work; 15·2, 7·1, and 17 per cent respectively, active pleasure.

12 Cf., some of the complaints of American employers against British skilled workers, e.g., R. T. Berthoff, *British Immigrants in Industrial America 1790–1950* (Harvard 1953), p. 66. But possibly also the converse complaints of British employers and foremen about Americans, that they did no work without specific incentives, e.g., *Special Ctee. on Unskilled Labour*, pp. 108–9.

13 Geo. White, *A Treatise on Weaving* (Glasgow 1846), complains that there is too much purely coercive labour management, and ascribes this partly to the poor quality of labour, partly to the fact that 'such a state of society where, as with us, labour generally exceeds the demand for it, has a tendency to beget indifference to its improvement and it becomes treated as a state of things in necessary association together' (pp. 330–1). The syntax is obscure, but the general drift is clear.

14 S. and B. Webb, *Industrial Democracy, passim*; J. B. Jefferys, op. cit.; A. Youngson Brown, 'Trade Union Policy in the Scots Coalfields 1855–85' (*Ec. Hist. Rev.*, 2nd ser., vi, I, 1953) See also Chapter 4 of the present work, *The Tramping Artisan*, pp. 34 seq.

15 *R.C. on Labour*, Group A, 1893–4, xxxii, Qs. 20, 769.

16 J. Kuczynski, *Short History of Labour Conditions in France* (1946), p. 179; *Short History of Labour Conditions in Germany* (1945), p. 151. It may be observed that these calculations command all the more confidence because their results do not fit well into their author's general thesis.

17 M. Saitzew, *Steinkohlenpreise u. Dampfkraftkosten* (Leipzig 1914), p. 141; G. T. Jones, *Increasing Return* (Cambridge 1933), p. 90; Jewkes and Gray, *Wages and Labour in Cotton Spinning* (Manchester 1935), pp. 42 ff.

18 E.g., in the building industry. Early complaints that employers have difficulty in getting 'a day's work for a day's wages' and that workers are lazier than they used to be, are referred to in J. M. Ludlow and Lloyd Jones, *Progress of the Working Class 1832–67* (1867), pp. 267 ff., but the discussion is too vague to allow us to judge what, if any, weight there was in these complaints.

19 Cf., 'If labour and skill are "marketable commodities" then the possessors of such commodities are justified in selling their labour and skill in like manner as a hatter sells a hat or the butcher sells beef. . . . If (the housewife) . . . will only pay two shillings, she will have to be content with an inferior quality of beef or a lesser quantity.' (*What Is Ca' Canny?*, leaflet issued by the International Federation of Ship, Dock, and River Workers, 2 October 1896.) Cf., also E. Pouget, *Le Sabotage* (Paris, n.d.), chapter 2: 'La "Marchandise" travail'. The question is discussed, *à propos* of the alleged fall in productivity in this period, by Saitzew, op. cit., p. 155.

20 E.g., S. and B. Webb, *The Decay of Capitalist Civilization* (1923), p. 162.

21 Jewkes and Gray, op. cit., p. 45.

22 (J. Townsend) *Dissertation on the Poor Laws by a Well-Wisher of Mankind*, J. R. McCulloch (ed), *Scarce and Valuable Economical Tracts* (1859), p. 404.

23 D. Simon, 'Master and Servant', in J. Saville (ed), *Democracy and the Labour Movement* (1954), pp. 160 ff.

24 Its history is told in 'The Miners' Bond in Northumberland and Durham', by Hylton Scott, *Proc. Soc. Antiq. of Newcastle-upon-Tyne*, 4 ser. II (1946–50), pp. 55–78, 87–98.

25 Of the handbooks on cotton-spinning I have consulted, the following confine themselves to workshop calculations, in some instances omitting even wage calculations: W. Etchells, *The Cotton Spinner's Companion* (Manchester 1827); G. Galbraith, *The Cotton Spinner's Companion* (Glasgow 1834); A. Kennedy, *The Practical Cotton Spinner* (Edinburgh 1845); Daniel Snell, *The Manager's Assistant, being a condensed treatise on the cotton manufacture* (Hartford, Conn. 1850). (R. Scott) *Scott's Practical Cotton Spinner and Manufacturer* (3rd edn, London and Manchester 1851) considers the problem of payment for spinners and

advises keeping pay-books in a form suitable for the calculation of productive efficiency – 2 pages out of 395. The only book worthy of its name, J. M. (J. Montgomery), *The Carding and Spinning Master's Assistant or the Theory and Practice of Cotton Spinning* (Glasgow 1832), treats the problem of labour management – in 3 or 4 pages – essentially as one of 'uniform good order and proper authority' (p. 221). Of the weaving handbooks, C. C. Gilroy, *The Art of Weaving* (1845), is purely technical and historical, and Geo. White, op. cit. (Glasgow 1846), considers the management of the hands one of the four non-weaving matters which must be mastered, but devotes only 5 pages to it (pp. 329–34) as against 16 to the selection of yarn, 31 to various calculations connected with the work, and 9 to warping on handlooms.

26 Cf., D. Schloss, *Methods of Industrial Remuneration* (1892), chapter xii.

27 A. H. John, *The Industrial Development of South Wales* (Cardiff 1950), p. 80.

28 A. T. Ponson, *Traité de l'exploitation des mines de houille* (Liège 1854), iv, p. 120.

29 A. T. Ponson, loc. cit., iv. But Ponson also advises incessant supervision, where possible, even when excavations are paid by the cubic metre (i (1832), pp. 320–1).

30 However, the wise employer or foreman would also take account of local custom among workers for, even when this was not based on practical considerations arising out of local experience, 'l'abandon des habitudes invétérées des ouvriers est chose difficile à obtenir', and not to be imposed except when absolutely necessary, in the view of Ponson (op. cit. ii, p. 598).

31 Saitzew, op. cit., pp. 141, 175–6.

32 L. Rostas, *Productivity, Prices and Distribution* (Cambridge 1937), p. 37.

33 L. P. Alford, *Cost and Production Handbook* (New York 1942), p. 1,333.

34 *Dictionary of Arts, Manufactures and Mines* (1863 ed), i, p. 529.

35 Op. cit., p. 218.

36 The report is summarized in *International Labour Review*, August 1952.

37 *On the Economy of Machinery and Manufactures* (1832). Babbage, incidentally, also strongly urged incentive payments in the form of profit-sharing.

38 T. Brassey, *On Work and Wages* (1873), *passim*. The subject seems first to have attracted wide attention during discussions on

the shortening of the working day or week. Cf., 'By exacting seven days' work you get less than six days' labour. This is a truth widely verified.' – The superintendent of machinery of the Eastern and Continental Steam Packet Co., quoted in John T. Baylee, *Statistics and Facts in Reference to the Lord's Day* (1852), p. 68.

39 L. Brentano, *Ueber d. Verhaeltnis v. Arbeitslohn u. Arbeitszeit zur Arbeitsleistung* (2nd edn, Leipzig 1893).

40 Ponson, op. cit., iv, pp. 275–82.

41 *Handwoerterbuch der Stadtswissenschaften*, article 'Arbeitszeit'.

42 *The Journal of Gas Lighting*, liii (1889), p. 894, professed itself to be unaware of any town where the three-times-eight-hour shift system was in vogue, though in fact (loc. cit., pp. 953, 1,000, 1,043) it had been functioning for fifteen years in Burnley, for eighteen in Hull, for twelve in Bristol, and for at least nine in Birkenhead, not to mention Dundee and Liverpool, where the system went back 'forty or fifty years' (loc. cit., 1 (1887), pp. 109–10). Similar ignorance of well-established practices by leading business-houses is combated by (J. Lilwall), *Practical Testimonies to the Benefits Attending the Early Payment of Wages . . .* (Early Closing Association, 1858), which prints an impressive list of London firms paying on Fridays and/or giving a Saturday half-holiday.

43 E.g., W. H. Marwick, *Economic Developments in Victorian Scotland* (1936), pp. 178–8; *Proc. Industrial Remuneration Conference* (1885), p. 106; *Sel. Ctee. on Master and Servant* (1866), xiii, pp. 1,281–1,320, 2,320 ff., 701–15, 469 ff., 562 ff.; National Association for the Promotion of Social Science, *Report on Trade Societies* (1860), pp. 290, 332–3; N.A. Prom. Soc. Sci., *Papers and Discussions on Social Economy* (1863), pp. 24, 37 (hours system among masons and in Scotland); Webb Collection, *Coll EA* 31 (British Library of Political Science), MS. pp. 258–64 (hours system introduced among Birmingham Bricklayers, 1865), p. 311 (unsuccessful Glasgow strike against it, 1849); R. W. Postgate, *The Builders' History* (n.d.), p. 209. F. Smith, *Workshop Management* (n.d., ? 1884), originally addressed to builders and cabinet-makers, observes that payment by the hour 'gradually but certainly' supersedes payment by the day against the opposition of the workers (p. 32).

44 Except, of course, on the Continent where this *was* the period of early industrialization and hence of the expansion of piece-mastering and subcontract. Cf., L. Bernhard, *Die Akkordarbeit in Deutschland* (Leipzig 1903), *passim*.

45 P. Aschrott, *The English Poor Law System* (1888), Pt. I, sect. xii–xiii.

46 On the general literature of sabbatarianism, which multiplied from the middle forties, cf., R. Cox, *The Literature of the Sabbath Question*, ii (Edinburgh 1865). On the activities and successes of the Early Closing movement, J. R. Taylor, *Government, Legal and General Saturday Half Holiday* (4th edn, 1857); John Lilwall *The Half Holiday Question* (1856); (J. Lilwall), *Practical Testimonies . . .* (1858), which deal mostly with London, but contain incidental information about the (earlier) progress of the movement in the provinces. Of the London firms practising early closing and giving dates of its introduction, most claim to have started it within the last three years, practically all in the 1850s.

47 I owe this point to L. Bernhard, op. cit., pp. 3–8.

48 Cf., McCulloch, *Statistical Account*, ii, p. 43, who goes so far as to ascribe the superiority of English industry to the prevalence of piece-work.

49 *Capital*, i (1938 English edn), pp. 561 ff.

50 Jefferys, op. cit., p. 63; Postgate, op. cit., p. 149.

51 R. Ehrenberg, Kruppstudient III (*Thuenen-Archiv*, iii, pp. 53, 89 ff.).

52 G. D. H. Cole, *The Payment of Wages* (1928 edn), p. 10.

53 Cf., Leonard Horner's observation in 1851 on 'the proportion [of piece-work] to fixed weekly wages being daily on the increase'.

54 L. Bernhard, op. cit., pp. 39 ff.

55 Partly as a means of avoiding the political radicalization of the workers, as by Mundella (W. H. Armytage, *Mundella*, 1951, p. 23) and later by Joseph Chamberlain, but also on grounds of productivity, e.g., Brassey and John Ward, *Workmen and Wages at Home and Abroad* (1868), a great believer in the truths of political economy: 'An opinion is entertained, by a considerable number of persons, that high wages tend to generate habits of idleness and dissipation amongst workmen. This opinion rests upon very uncertain and inconclusive data. Wages are the reward and encouragement of industry, which, like every other human quality, increases in proportion to the encouragement it receives. Where wages are high, we generally find the workmen more active, diligent, and persevering than where they are low' (p. 216).

56 C. B. Thomson, *Scientific Management* (Harvard 1914), pp. 684 ff.; N. Brisco, *The Economics of Efficiency* (NY 1914), p. 5. Cf., also F. Smith, op. cit. (1884), p. 2, 'In these days of excessive competition, it is more than ever necessary that the employer should obtain the full equivalent of what he spends in wages'.

57 Thompson, op. cit., p. 685.
58 H. S. Person, *Scientific Management in American Industry* (NY 1929), p. 7.
59 H. B. Drury, *Scientific Management* (Columbia 1915), for a brief outline and history of the American movement in its earliest stages.
60 L. Urwick and E. F. L. Brech, *The Making of Scientific Management*, ii (1946), pp. 22, 90, 148. The value of payment by results as against time-wages for costing is stressed in, e.g., C. Heiss, 'Die Entloehnungsmethoden in der deutschen Metallindustrie' (*Schmollers Jahrb.*, xxxvii, 1913), p. 1,479.
61 *Report of Factory Inspectors for 1894*, p. 213; S. and B. Webb, *Industrial Democracy*, p. 399. Cf. also the advice for F. Smith, op. cit., to the same effect, for 'every minute [the craftsmen] spend away from their proper occupation [is] so much loss to the employer', and the advisability of having specialized semi-skilled labour trained for each machine (pp. 5-6, 13-14).
62 Jefferys, op. cit., pp. 129-30, 154-5; M. L. Yates, *Wages and Labour Conditions in British Engineering* (1937), pp. 86, 88, 98.
63 *S. C. on Govt. Contracts* (2,469); J. Deutsch, *Auslese u. Anpassung in den Siemens-Schuckert Werken, Wien* (Schriften des Vereins f. Sozialpolitik, vol. cxxxiv).
64 Yates, op. cit., p. 98; *Wage Census of 1906*, Cd. 5,814 (1911), p. 15.
65 A. Carbonnel de Canisy, *L'Ouvrier dans les mines de fer . . . de Briey* (Paris 1914), pp. 81-2; L. Bosselmann, *Entloehnungs-methoden in d. suedwestdeutsch-luxemburgischen Eisenindustrie* (Berlin 1906), p. 144.
66 A. Williams, *Life in a Railway Factory* (1916).
67 A. Zimmermann, 'D. Arbeitstarifvertrag im Deutschen Reich' (*Schmollers Jahrb.*, xxxi, 1907, p. 339), Dora Landé, *Arbeits- u. Lohnverhaeltnisse i.d. Berliner Maschinenindustrie* (Schriften des Vereins f. Sozialpolitik, vol. cxxxiv, 1910) and much other German literature.
68 Jewkes and Gray, op. cit., pp. 60 ff., 82 ff.
69 *R.C. on Labour*, Group C, 1893-4, xxiv, Qs. 33,296-9.
70 S. and B. Webb, *Industrial Democracy*, pp. 397 ff., 401 n.
71 Schloss, op. cit., p. 53.
72 *Industry and Trade*, Book 2, cap. xii.
73 Jewkes and Gray, op. cit., pp. 41-2; *Royal Commission on the Depression of Trade*, quoted in Schulze-Gaevernitz, *D. Gross-betrieb* (1895), p. 117.
74 Alford, op. cit., p. 1,333.

75 E. Mahaim, *Untersuchungen ueber Preisbildung: Belgien* (Schriften des Vereins f. Sozialpolitik, vol. cxliv B), p. 269. (The book is in French.)

76 And that the superiority of American industry over British was largely due to it. Cf., the pregnant observation, made in 1872, that in Britain 'labour-saving' meant something which *displaced* labour, while in the USA it meant something which *cut down* time or labour on a given job. (J. Richards, *A Treatise on . . . Woodworking Machines*, London and New York 1872, pp. 55–6.)

77 P. Boulin, *L'Organisation du travail dans les usines à feu continu* (Paris 1912), and J. Rae, *Eight Hours Work* (1894), for developments in our period.

_____

18

Labour Traditions

WHAT PART do custom, tradition and the specific historical experience of a country play in its political movements? So far as the labour movement is concerned, the problem has been more frequently discussed by politicians (Marx versus Wesley) than by historians. I propose in this essay to illustrate it from a comparison of the experience of France and Britain, the countries with the longest history of the labour movement.

The labour movement, whether politically or industrially considered, is, of course, a novel phenomenon in history. Whether or not there is continuity between journeymen's associations and early trade unions, it is mere antiquarianism to think of the movement of the 1870s, or even of the 1830s in terms of, say, the early hatters' and curriers' trade societies. However, historically speaking, the process of building new institutions, new ideas, new theories and tactics rarely starts as a deliberate job of social engineering. Men live surrounded by a vast accumulation of past devices, and it is natural to pick the most suitable of these, and to adapt them for their own (and novel) purposes. The historian, of course, who traces these processes, must not forget the specific function which the new institutions are expected to fulfil; neither must the functional analyst forget that the specific historical setting must colour (and perhaps assist, hamper or divert) them.

Let us take a pair of extreme examples. In 1855 the slate-quarrymen of Trelazé, discontented with their economic conditions, decided to take action: they marched on Angers and proclaimed an insurrectionary Commune,[1] presumably with the memory of the Commune of 1792 in their minds. Nine years later the coal-miners of Ebbw Vale were equally agitated. The lodges from the valley villages marched on to the mountains, headed by bands. Speeches were made, tea provided

371

by the Ebbw Vale lodge at 6*d*. a head and the meeting ended with the singing of the Doxology.[2] Both Welsh miners and Breton quarry-men were engaged on rather similar economic agitations. Clearly they differed, because the histories of their respective countries had differed. The stock of past experience, upon which they drew when learning how to organize, what to organize for, where to pick their cadre of leaders, and the ideology of those leaders embodied, in part at least, specific French and British elements: broadly speaking we may say, in the former case, the revolutionary, in the latter the radical-nonconformist traditions.

Again, concrete illustrations may be useful. The Lyons weavers and subcontractors, wishing to organize a trade union in 1828, naturally organized their society of 'Mutualists' on the revolutionary model. Thus they described their foundation year as 'Year One of Regeneration', an obvious echo of Jacobinism, and organized in small conspiratorial groups, which seem to have owed something to Babouvist devices,[3] though perhaps also to the old Compagnonnages,[4] and to the practical need to circumvent the Chapelier Law. Again, under the Second Empire, the labour programme was patently derived from classical Jacobin-radical doctrine; the left-wingers merely went to Robespierre and St Just, if not to Hébert and Jacques Roux for inspiration, while the liberals sought theirs further on the right. As late as the 1890s Emile Pouget the anarchist and later leader of the CGT modelled his journal *Le Père Peinard* in title and style on Hébert's Père Duchêne. Moreover, it was the revolutionary ideology which automatically commended itself to the advanced workers and intellectuals who formed the core of the movement's leadership. The porcelain workers of Limoges were republicans, and easily switched from trade unionist to political methods; thus when their union was held up, they promptly organized an insurrectionary commune.[5] The Left in the Nièvre department opposed Louis Napolen's *coup d'état*, and was organized in a secret society known as the 'Jeune Montagne'.[6]

In Britain the situation is more complex, because the original radical-democratic tradition had developed two wings, the line between them being (I oversimplify) largely that between the artisans and craftsmen unionists in the older towns, and the new factory and mining centres: radical-secularist on one hand, dissenting-Methodist on the other. In London, for instance, the nonconformist tradition never really took root as a left-wing one; which may explain the

372

relatively greater influence of Marxism here in later times. Even so naturally religious a worker as George Lansbury found himself in the Marxist Social Democratic Federation at the outset of his political career, and was never drawn to the dissenting chapels, but to the Church of England – a most unusual state of affairs. In the provinces the road led much more naturally to ILP or Methodist lay-pulpit. We have, in fact, two lines of intellectual descent. One goes from men like Tom Paine, through men like the atheist radicals of the Owen-Carlile period, to mid-Victorian secularists like Holyoake and Bradlaugh, and, after 1880, the Marxists. From this tradition the British labour movement derives some of its most important organizational devices: the 'Corresponding Society' of the 1790s, the pamphlet, the working-class newspaper, the petition to Parliament, the public meeting and public debate, etc.; also, of course, what little interest it takes in theory.

In a sense this first tradition goes back to that branch of the seventeenth-century dissenters which, in the eighteenth, evolved towards deism and later agnosticism. Part of the other tradition – especially in calvinist Scotland – goes back directly to that seventeenth-century revolution which was still fought out in terms of religious ideology. Even in England the independent sectarian persisted as a pure type – e.g., in Mark Rutherford's Zechariah Coleman.[7] In the main, however, the labour tradition of dissent derives from the Methodist revival; more specifically, from the series of breakaways after 1810 of which the Primitive Methodist is the best-known. It was in this school that the new factory proletarians, rural labourers, miners and others of the sort learned how to run a trade union, modelling themselves on chapel and circuit. One has merely to read the district report of an East-Anglian farm-labourer's union[8] to see how much they owed to it. From Methodists too, as Dr Wearmouth has shown, came important devices of mass agitation and propaganda: the camp meeting, the class meeting and others. Above all, however, dissent provided the ideological rallying-ground for the leadership of the movement, especially in the mining areas. When Lord Londonderry evicted the leaders of the Durham miners' agitation in 1843, two-thirds of the local Primitive Methodist circuit found itself victimized,[9] and when in the 1870s a Lincolnshire farm-labourers' union found itself in difficulties, it considered merging with the Primitive Methodists. Clearly this sect was to the Durham miners of the 1840s or the Lincolnshire labourers of the 1870s, what the Communist Party is to the French workers today, the cadre of leadership.

Such a religious phenomenon is not quite unknown in France. In parts of the South the Huguenot minority has always been, for obvious reasons, inclined to anti-conservatism, and has therefore provided a disproportionate number of left-wing leaders. But on the whole this is not of great importance for the French labour movement. It is easy to explain the different degrees of political radicalism in Britain and France by such difference in tradition. But is the explanation true?

A revolutionary tradition may be politically moderate; a religious one need not be so. When the leading Communards returned from exile in 1880 they found themselves in the main[10] on the extreme right wing of a movement which was rapidly coming under socialist influence. A willingness to raise barricades does not necessarily indicate an extremist programme. For most of the nineteenth century the French revolutionary tradition was merely an aspect of French liberal-radicalism, whose supporters were ideologically quite on a par with respectable British secularist republicans like George Odger. It is significant that the modern form of revolutionism, the Communist Party, in some ways marked as great a break with French traditions as with British ones, though in others it continued both.

The fortunes of what is ostensibly one of the most violent trends in French labour, the anarchist, illustrate the point. In general the small craftsmen and artisans who formed the mainstay of French anarchism were extremely militant. (However, their spiritual father, Proudhon, was markedly pacific.) They fought, often with no holds barred – as did their counterparts in the small Sheffield metal crafts – and they easily attracted radical intellectuals. But just as the Sheffield terrorists were extremely moderate in their politics,[11] so the French anarchists were essentially on the moderate wing of their movement. Their greatest triumph, the CGT, moved from apparent ultra-revolutionism to a careful social-democracy with remarkable speed after the outbreak of World War I. Moreover, that section of French socialism which was later to support the policy of appeasement most passionately, and to collaborate with Pétain – Dumoulin, Belin and others – drew its strength largely from the anarchizing wing of the pre-1914 movement. By and large the French political system had long learned to cope with these older, and often intrinsically moderate, forms of

374

revolutionism. When the French Communist Party was formed in 1920, it was immediately joined by large numbers of respectable middle-class figures, for 'the tradition that the son of the family begins his career on the extreme left, under the indulgent eye of the clan, to end it in the most respectable of postures'[12] was well established. Indeed, a group of revolutionary railwaymen who were to provide several leaders of the new party (Sémard, Monmousseau, Midol) at first refused to join it for this reason. It was not 'bolshevized' until some years later.[13]

A religious tradition, on the other hand, may be very radical. It is true that certain forms of religion serve to drug the pain of intolerable social strains, and provide an alternative to revolt. Some, like Wesleyanism, may do so deliberately. However, insofar as religion is the language and framework of all general action in undeveloped societies – and also, to a great extent, among the common people of pre-industrial Britain – ideologies of revolt will also be religious.

Two factors helped to maintain religion as a potentially radical force in nineteenth-century Britain. First, the decisive political event of our history, the revolution of the seventeenth century, had been fought out at a time when the modern secular language of politics had not as yet been adopted by the common people: it was a Puritan revolution. Unlike France, therefore, religion was not primarily identified with the *status quo*. Moreover, habits die hard. As late as the 1890s we find an almost pure example of the medieval, or puritan approach: the Labour Churches. John Trevor, who founded them, was a misfit springing from one of those small and super-pious sects of working-class or lower-middle-class hellfire puritans which were always splitting away to form more godly communities. Like other mid-Victorian intellectual movements, Dissent was slowly cracking under the impact of political and social change after 1870, and during the Great Depression, Trevor was drawn towards the labour movement after various crises of conscience and a somewhat chequered spiritual career. Incapable of conceiving a new political movement which should not also have its religious expression, he turned labour into a religion. He was *not* a Christian Socialist; he believed the labour movement to be God, and built his apparatus of churches, Sunday schools, hymns, etc., round it. Of course the dour dissenting artisans of Yorkshire and Lancashire did not follow his peculiar theology, which can best be described as a very etherealized unitarianism. However, they had been brought up in an atmosphere in which

375

chapel was the centre of their social and spiritual life. The Great Depression (and such things as the McKinley Tariff of 1891) made them increasingly aware of the cleavage of interests within chapels between employer and worker brethren; and nothing was more natural than to suppose that the political split should take the form of a chapel secession, just as earlier the split between Wesleyan and Primitive Methodists had been one between politically radical and conservative groups. So the Labour Churches, with their familiar paraphernalia of hymns, Sunday schools, chapel brass bands and choirs, dorcas clubs, etc., sprang up in the North. In fact, they were a half-way house between orthodox political liberal-radicalism and the ILP with which the Churches soon merged.[14] This phenomenon, which occurred less than sixty years ago, would clearly have been impossible in a country in which pre-secular traditions of politics had not sunk particularly deep roots.

The second factor was the extraordinary psychological strain of early industrialism in the pioneer industrial country – the rapid transformation of a traditional society, based on custom; the horror; the sudden tearing-up of roots. Inevitably the masses of the uprooted and the new working class sought an emotional expression of their maladjustment, something to replace the old framework of life. Just as today Northern Rhodesian copper-miners flock to Jehovah's Witnesses, and among the Basutos the cataclysm of social change finds expression in a revival of magic and witch-cults, so all over Europe the early nineteenth century was an age of overcharged, intense, often apocalyptic religious atmosphere, which expressed itself in revivalist campaigns in mining areas, giant camp meetings, conversions, etc. Now wherever organized religion was, by and large, a strongly conservative force – as was the Roman Catholic Church – the active labour movement necessarily developed independently of it. In France, moreover, the great emotional experience of the Revolution had generated, out of purely secular fuel, its own emotional fire to heat the cold life of the workers. We remember the old man of the 1840s dying with the words 'Oh sun of 1793, when shall I see thee rise again?' The great image of the Jacobin Republic beckoned, and it was round the personified republic that the emotions of struggling men and women most easily gathered, just as later in Germany and Austria they gathered round the personification of their own struggles, the Marxist parties and their leaders. In Britain there was no such living experience; but there were the dissenting conventicles and sects, independent of the State, comparatively democratic, and alive. Hence that experience which is so typical of the British labour movement, the young worker 'seeing the light', often as a Primitive Methodist, and translating his political aims into the terms of the New Jerusalem.[15]

This did not necessarily make him any less class-conscious or militant. Evidence of the strongly militant nature of the Primitive Methodists in some regions abounds; and on occasion – as in far-off Dorset – even the conservative Wesleyans could find themselves the rallying-point for local labour leaders. Nor did this tradition prevent men from making further political advances. In our own days Arthur Horner (a boy-evangelist) and William Gallacher (whose first political experience was in that by-product of dissent, the teetotal movement) both became communists.

Are we then to regard our two traditions as so many lumps of plasticine, to be moulded to fit the shape of their movements' mood and practical situation? No theory could be less suited to conversion into a doctrine of the 'inevitability of gradualness' than Marx's; yet between the end of the Great Depression and World War I this was done, tacitly or by startling pieces of exegetical acrobatics, in a number of countries. The Roman Catholic Church has insisted on few maxims of social politics more firmly than on the undesirability of organizing masters and workers separately; yet, without significant exceptions, the joint organizations it has sponsored in industrial countries have either drifted out of the labour movement or – after some struggles – turned into ordinary trade unions.[16] Ideas, in truth, are more elastic than facts. Yet a political or ideological tradition, especially if it sums up genuine patterns of practical activity in the past, or is embodied in stable institutions, has independent life and force, and must affect the behaviour of political movements. The plasticine theory is patently an oversimplification.

When, however, we try to estimate the real part which such traditions play, we tackle one of the most difficult tasks of the historian. A few points may, however, be legitimately suggested. Thus, in the first place, the dissenting tradition, being politically rather imprecise, was far more malleable than the revolutionary. Behind it there was no such specific historical experience as the French Revolution, with its programmes, lessons of tactics, and political slogans, however unsuitable. It was extremely difficult to get away from the fact that the revolutionary tradition glorified the armed revolt of 'the people' against 'the rich'; or from the hallowed methods of such a revolt – insurrectionary communes, revolutionary dictatorships, etc. If it was to be turned into its opposite, a theory of gradualism and social collaboration, for example, this could only be done indirectly; for instance, by using its liberal-radical aspects against the communists, as the inter-war CGT and the post-1945 Catholic Church have attempted to do in idealizing its Proudhonian as against its Babouvist and Blanquist traditions; or – as Gambetta did[17] – by stressing the common interest of all classes of 'the people' against some common outside enemy, like 'Reaction' or 'Clericalism'. But the very process of rounding off its edges in practice could only be achieved by glorifying Revolution in theory. The genuine conservative had, sooner or later, to make a clean break with it. But the dissenting tradition, insofar as it was religious, was not tied to any special programme or record, though long associated with particular political demands. The fallacy of the modern claim that 'British Socialism derives from Wesley, not from Marx' lies precisely in this. Insofar as socialism (or for that matter radical liberalism) was a specific critique of a particular economic system, and a set of proposals for change, it derived from the same secular sources as Marxism. Insofar as it was merely a passionate way of stating the facts of poverty, it had no intrinsic connexion with any particular political doctrine. In any case, only a slight shift of theological emphasis was needed to turn the actively revolutionary dissenter into the quietist (both Anabaptists and Quakers had made it in the past), or to allow the militant left-winger to become the moderate. The difference between the elasticity of the two traditions may be illustrated by individual cases: John Burns's change from revolutionary agitator to Liberal Minister inevitably implied a breach with his former Marxist beliefs. On the other hand, Mr Love the mine-owner of Brancepeth, a union man in his youth, who wrecked the Durham Miners' Association in 1863–4, could end his life as he had started it, as an active and pious Primitive Methodist.[18]

A second point follows from the first. A revolutionary tradition is by its very existence a constantly implied call to action, or to sympathy with action. The Newport Rising of 1839 was, numerically speaking, a much more serious, though a much worse-managed affair than the Dublin Easter Rising of 1916; yet its effect on the ten years following was much smaller than that of the Irish venture, and its impact on the British, or even the Welsh popular tradition incomparably less. The one fitted into a picture in which pride of place had long been reserved for 'the rebel'; the other did not.

The one therefore easily became inspiration or myth, the other merely an obscure historical incident. The difference is of considerable importance, for it is not the willingness to use violence, but a certain political way of using or threatening violence which makes movements revolutionary. No other European country has so strong a tradition of rioting as Britain; and one which persisted well past the middle of the nineteenth century. The riot as a normal part of collective bargaining was well-established in the eighteenth century.[19] Coercion and intimidation were vital in the early stages of trade unionism, when the immorality of blacklegging had not yet become part of the ethical code of organized labour. It would be foolish to claim that, had Britain possessed a revolutionary tradition, she would therefore also have had a revolution. It is, however, fair to claim that episodes like the Derbyshire and Newport Risings might well have occurred more frequently, and extremely tense situations, like that in Glasgow in 1919, might not have been so easily settled.[20]

It is, of course, quite true that in the normal day's work of the labour movement, the presence or the absence of a revolutionary tradition is not of immediate importance. From the point of view of getting higher wages and better conditions, the Trelazé quarrymen's willingness to proclaim the social republic at the drop of a hat was no more and no less than a specially militant form of mass demonstration. It might not even be the most effective way of achieving their immediate economic demands. Or else, it might merely be useful, because in organizing weak and unorganized workers against strong opposition, aggressive and flamboyant tactics are always the most effective. (Hence political revolutionaries have always done a disproportionately large share of such organizing, whether in the British 'new unionist' movements of 1889 and 1911, the sardine canners of Douarnenez, the British light engineering of the 1930s, or even the American and Canadian unions of the same decade.) At times of rapid political change and great tension, however, its presence or absence may well be a serious independent factor; for instance in Germany after 1918.

The revolutionary tradition, then, was by its very nature political; the dissenting tradition much less directly so. How much this fact contributed to the much more political character of the French labour movement, it is not easy to say. Weak trade union movements generally tend to draw on political campaigning for additional strength, while strong ones tend not to worry about it; and the French trade unions were throughout the nineteenth and twentieth century vastly weaker than the British. Nevertheless, this does not wholly account for two striking phenomena: the much greater speed with which French working-class opinion turned socialist, and the much greater interchangeability of political and industrial agitation.

Thus in France the labour and socialist movement began to capture municipalities about twenty years before it did so in Britain. The first British borough to have a labour-radical-Irish majority was West Ham in 1898. Yet as early as 1881 the Parti Ouvrier won its first majority in Commentry. By 1892, when socialist councillors (often not even elected as such) were still exceedingly rare in Britain, the revolutionary Marxists alone – not counting the Possibilists, Allemanists and the various other bodies sporting the socialist label – commanded over 12 municipalities, among them places like Marseilles, Toulon, and Roubaix. The disparity is even more marked in parliamentary elections.

Again, the political activities of the British trade unions have always been extremely limited, though this has been obscured by the fact that those who took part in them were often also trade unionists. They finance the Labour Party, though it is far from clear (except in certain rather special cases) how far trade unionists vote for Labour *because* their unions are supporters of the party, or whether they are both unionists and Labour voters because they are 'working-class people'. Certainly *pure* trade-union candidates have rarely been successful. In the London of the 1870s and 1880s the candidates put forward by the London Trades Council polled notably worse than those put forward by political organizations like the National Secular Society,[21] and in the 1950s the elected (communist) convenor of shop-stewards at a great motor-factory might poll a derisory vote in an area full of men who, in their factory, voted for him and – what is even more important – followed him. The sharpness of the distinction is specially clear in the case of a man like Arthur Horner, who was both a political figure and a trade unionist – a combination which is very rare. (Aneurin Bevan, for instance, was a political figure of major importance, but never played a part of any great consequence in the miners' union.) Horner's career falls into two distinct segments: the early period, when he was primarily a political leader, with a powerful local base in Maerdy, and the later, when – after his extrusion from leading positions in the Communist Party – he concentrated on his union work. But the Horner who became the ablest leader the British miners have ever had, though he was an ornament of his party, was not in any significant sense a leader of it.[22]

Similarly, it is hard to think of any successful or even seriously attempted political strikes in Britain, though sympathy and solidarity strikes (which enter into the narrowest terms of reference of trade unionism) are common. The General Strike of 1926 belongs to this class. It is hard to conceive of a British equivalent for the general strikes in favour of electoral reform which the Marxist-led movements on the continent led, often with much success, between 1890 and 1914; as in Belgium and Sweden. Political strikes are not inconceivable in Britain, especially at times of intense and almost revolutionary excitement, as in 1920, when one was threatened against British intervention in the Russo-Polish war. Yet the existence of a political tradition almost certainly favours them more, though of course their scope is always more limited (except during times of revolution) than their advocates have often supposed.

Third, and most important, a revolutionary tradition by definition envisages the transfer of power. It may do so so inefficiently, as among the anarchists, that it need not be taken seriously. But its possibility is always explicit. The historian of Chartism, for instance, can hardly fail to be saddened by the extraordinary feebleness of this greatest of all the mass movements of British labour; and what is more, by the equanimity with which the British ruling class regarded it, when not frightened by *foreign* revolution.[23] This equanimity was justified. The Chartists had no idea whatever of what to do if their campaign of collecting signatures for a petitition were to fail to convert Parliament, as of course it inevitably would. For even the proposal of a general strike ('sacred month') was, as its opponents pointed out, merely another way of expressing an inability to think of anything to do: 'Are we going to let loose hundreds of thousands of desperate and hungry men upon society without having any specific object in view or any plan of action laid down, but trusting to a chapter of accidents as to what the consequences shall be? . . . I shall oppose fixing a day for the holiday until we have better evidence, first as to the practicability of the thing, or the probability of its being carried into effect; and next as to the way in which it is going to be employed.'[24] Moreover, when something like a spontaneous general strike did occur in the summer of 1842, the Chartists were incapable of making

381

any use of it, and it was less effective than the spontaneous rioting of the agricultural labourers in 1830, which did, in fact, largely succeed in its limited object of holding up the progress of mechanization on the farms. And the reason for the ineffectiveness of Chartism was, in part at least, due to the unfamiliarity of Englishmen with the very idea of insurrection, of the organization needed for insurrection, and of the transfer of power.

Conversely, the French Resistance movement during World War II was deliberately *not* an attempt to take power, at all events on the part of the Communists who, as usual, formed by far its most important and active contingent. The argument that it was, put forward as an excuse for propagandist purposes after 1945 and during the 'cold war', is a *canard*, and has been conclusively disproved.[25] It never had any plausibility or evidence to back it, except conceivably the independent activities of a few local groups which either went against central policy or were unaware of it. Yet the point is that in the conditions of the French movement a special effort was needed to *prevent* the Resistance from taking what would have appeared to be the logical (though not necessarily the best-advised) form of a bid for power; that resistance groups, left to their own devices, might well have followed their noses into local attempts to seize power.[26] It is extremely unlikely that any British movement, however militant and radical, would spontaneously do so.

How important such differences of tradition are in practice, must remain a matter of speculation. Clearly they are not decisive. They affect the *style* of a movement's activities rather than their, or its, nature. Yet style may be of more than superficial interest, and there may well be times when it is the man, or rather the movement. Obviously this will rarely be so where – for instance – movements conform to rigidly determined patterns of organization, ideology and behaviour, as among Communist parties. Yet every one with knowledge of communist movements knows that the extreme international uniformity which was imposed on them from the mid-1920s on ('bolshevization') no more prevented striking differences in the national atmosphere and style of communists than the uniformity of the Catholic priesthood makes the Irish church identical with the Italian or Dutch. Where the conscious forces shaping the movement are less strong, the stylistic effects of tradition may be even more obvious.

An instructive example is that of the 'peace movement', which has always been abnormally strong in Britain, and relatively weak in France. (It is not to be confused with the anti-militarist movement, which sometimes runs parallel with it.) An aggressive and sometimes militant patriotism has, since the Jacobins, been deeply engrained on the French extreme left, and indeed had dominated it except at certain historical periods (e.g., from *circa* 1880 to 1934) when the tricolour was seized by other hands. One might go so far as to suggest that the periods of maximum unity and power of French labour have been those when it could stigmatize the ruling classes not merely as exploiters but also as traitors: as during the Paris Commune, during the Popular Front period and especially during the Resistance. (In a sense this is merely another expression of the built-in aspiration to power in a revolutionary tradition: the Jacobins and their heirs have always seen themselves as potentially or actually a state-carrying or governing force.)[27] On the other hand, a moral dislike for aggression and war as such has always been deeply ingrained in the British labour movement, and is plainly one of the most important parts of its liberal-radical – and often, specifically of its dissenting – heritage. It is no accident that in 1914 the ILP was the only non-revolutionary socialist party in a belligerent country – and indeed almost the only socialist party in any country – which as a body refused to support the war; but then, Britain was the only belligerent country in which two ministers – both Liberals – resigned from the cabinet for the same reason. Time and again opposition to aggression or war has been the most effective method of unifying or dynamizing the British left: in the late 1870s, at the time of the Boer War, during the 1930s, and again in the late 1950s.

The contrast between the peace movements of France and Britain after 1945 is particularly illuminating, because it is difficult to find any factors other than those of tradition to explain it. France has had no spontaneous mass peace movement, but only a phase when the Communist Party put its energies behind an anti-nuclear appeal, and therefore collected a great many signatures. The British have had no important political organization willing to mobilize public opinion against nuclear war or capable of doing so. (The close connexion between the 'World Peace Movement' and the Communists probably postponed the emergence of a broadly-based mass peace movement in Britain until after the end of the worst hysteria of the 'cold war'.) On the other hand, an unofficial group of people could improvise the implicitly pacifist Campaign for Nuclear Disarmament, which has

383

not merely become the most massive anti-nuclear movement in the world, with the possible exception of that of the Japanese, and a model for (less successful) foreign imitators, but a major force in British politics outside its narrow terms of reference. For it was largely on the issue of 'peace' that the left wing within the labour movement rallied to overthrow the long domination of a right-wing party leadership.

NOTES

1 G. Duveau, *La vie ouvrière en France sous le second Empire* (Paris 1946), p. 543.

2 Ness Edwards, *The history of the South Wales Miners* (London 1926), p. 39.

3 E. Labrousse, *Le mouvement ouvrier et les idées sociales en France de 1815 à la fin du XIX siècle.* (Les Cours de la Sorbonne: Fasc. III), pp. 83–4.

4 W. Lexis, *Gewerkvereine u. Unternehmerverbaende in Frankreich* (Leipzig 1879), pp. 123–4.

5 W. Lexis, op. cit., pp. 183–4.

6 Duveau, op. cit., pp. 89–91.

7 Mark Rutherford, *The Revolution in Tanner's Lane.*

8 Reprinted in E. J. Hobsbawm (ed), *Labour's Turning Point 1880–1900* (London 1948), p. 89.

9 R. F. Wearmouth, *Some working-class movements of the nineteenth century* (London 1948), p. 305.

10 A. Zévaès, *De l'Introduction du Marxism en France* (Paris 1947), pp. 116 ff.

11 For the combination of direct action and extreme moderation in Sheffield, cf., S. Pollard, *A history of labour in Sheffield* (Liverpool 1959).

12 A. Rossi, *Physiologie du parti communiste français* (1948), p. 317.

13 On this crisis in the French CP, cf., L. Trotsky, *The first five years of the Comintern* II (New York 1953) almost *passim*, but esp. pp. 153–5, 281–2, 321.

14 Cf., K. S. Inglis, 'The Labour Church Movement' (*International Review of Social History* III (1958).

15 For this and the following passages, see the chapter on Labour Sects in my *Primitive Rebels* (Manchester 1959).

16 Cf., R. Goetz-Girey, *La pensée syndicale française* (Paris 1948), pp. 96 ff.

17 Cf., esp. Discours prononcé le 12 août 1881 à la réunion

électorale du XXe arrondissement (*Discours . . . de Léon Gambetta*, ed. J. Reinach, Paris 1895).

18 E. Welbourne, *The miners' unions of Northumberland and Durham* (Cambridge 1923), p. 115.

19 Halévy, op. cit., I, pp. 148 ff. For collective bargaining by riot, see above, Chapter 2 (pp. 5 seq).

20 W. Gallacher, *Revolt on the Clyde* (London 1936), cap. X for a self-critical account by one of the 'strike leaders, nothing more; we had forgotten we were revolutionary leaders'.

21 Thus in the 1882 London School Board elections the trade-unionist candidates (except for one already sitting member) did extremely poorly; while Helen Taylor and Aveling, whose links were primarily political or ideological, were elected.

22 Conversely in France, Pierre Semard, a pure unionist by origin, was for a time general secretary of the Communist Party, and Léon Mauvais (secretary of the CGTU in 1933) became organizing secretary of the CP in 1947. Charles Tillon, also with a mainly trade-unionist background in Britanny – but combined with municipal politics – became chief military organizer of the communist resistance and minister in De Gaulle's government; as did Lucien Midol. The list could be prolonged.

23 Cf., F. C. Mather, *Public order in the age of the Chartists* (Manchester 1960).

24 William Carpenter in *The Charter*, 21 July 1839.

25 A. J. Rieber, *Stalin and the French Communist Party 1941–7* (NY and London 1962) discusses the matter at length, pp. 142–55.

26 Rieber, op. cit., pp. 150–1.

27 The most obvious apparent example to the contrary, the Dreyfus affair, proves the point. Its effect within the labour movement was to divide and not to unite; for against the 'rallying of the Socialist politicians to the cause of the threatened Republic and a *rapprochement* between most of the Socialist groups' there must be set the strengthening of an anti-political syndicalism (G. D. H. Cole, *History of Socialist Thought* III, p. 343), not to mention the split caused by the acceptance of cabinet office by Millerand.

INDEX

blog and newsletter

For literary discussion, author insight,
book news, exclusive content,
recipes and giveaways, visit the
Weidenfeld & Nicolson blog and
sign up for the newsletter at:

www.wnblog.co.uk

For breaking news, reviews and exclusive competitions
Follow us @wnbooks
Find us facebook.com/WNfiction